BRITAIN AND AFRICA SERIES

*THE GOVERNMENT AND ADMINISTRATION
OF AFRICA, 1880–1939*

BRITAIN AND AFRICA SERIES

Series Editor: *David Sunderland*
Advisory Editor: *Godfrey N. Uzoigwe*

TITLES IN THIS SERIES

Economic Development of Africa, 1880–1939
David Sunderland (ed.)

Communications in Africa, 1880–1939
David Sunderland (ed.)

CONTENTS OF THE EDITION

THE GOVERNMENT AND ADMINISTRATION OF AFRICA, 1880–1939

EDITED BY
Casper Andersen and Andrew Cohen

Volume 1
Recruitment and Training

Routledge
Taylor & Francis Group

LONDON AND NEW YORK

First published 2013 by Pickering & Chatto (Publishers) Limited

Published 2016 by Routledge
2 Park Square, Milton Park, Abingdon, Oxfordshire OX14 4RN
711 Third Avenue, New York, NY 10017, USA

First issued in paperback 2015

Routledge is an imprint of the Taylor & Francis Group, an informa business

BRITISH LIBRARY CATALOGUING IN PUBLICATION DATA

The government and administration of Africa, 1880–1939. – (Britain and
Africa)
1. Great Britain – Colonies – Africa – Administration – History– 19th century
– Sources. 2. Great Britain – Colonies – Africa – Administration – History –
20th century – Sources.
I. Series II. Andersen, Casper. III. Cohen, Andrew.
325.3'41'096-dc23

ISBN-13: 978-1-138-66098-4 (pbk)
ISBN-13:978-1-1387-6044-8 (hbk)
ISBN-13: 978-1-84893-318-7 (set)
Typeset by Pickering & Chatto (Publishers) Limited

CONTENTS

ACKNOWLEDGEMENTS

The Editors

A project of this nature would be impossible to complete without the help of others. Countless research hours were saved through the knowledge of librarians and archivists around the United Kingdom. We wish to thank the staff of the Derbyshire County Record Office, the National Archives and the Sudan Archive at Durham University Library. Particular thanks go to Lucy McCann and all the staff at Rhodes House Library, Oxford, whose assistance over the last decade has proved invaluable to both of us. We also owe a debt of gratitude to Robert Fletcher and Vincent Kuitenbrouwer, whose camaraderie and keen minds it has been an honour and a privilege to enjoy. It has also been a pleasure to work with Ruth Ireland and Stephina Clarke at Pickering & Chatto. Finally we would wish to thank David Sunderland for commissioning our help with this instalment of the Britain and Africa series. This collection is dedicated in memory of Alfred.

Casper Andersen

My contribution to this project was made possible with of the generous support of the Carlsberg Foundation (grant number 2009_01_0676). Numerous friends and colleagues have kindly shared their expert knowledge, and offered invaluable advice and support. I would like to express my particular thanks to Jan-Georg Deutsch, Peter C. Kjærgaard, Festo Mkenda, Mathias Hein Jessen, Ellen Feingold, Kathleen Vongsathorn, Anthony Kirk-Greene, Joseph Hodge, Bernard Sebe and Henning Høgh Laursen. A very special thanks to my partner and favourite companion Ulla Hjorth Jørgensen.

Andrew Cohen

I have been lucky to spend the final months working on this project at the University of the Free State where the rector, Jonathan Jansen, is committed to creating a vibrant research culture. In this day and age it is a rare pleasure to work in such enlightened surroundings. I continue to owe a huge debt of gratitude to Ian Phimister. Over the last decade I have been lucky to enjoy his support first as supervisor, then colleague and as a friend. I also wish to express my thanks to Wayne Dooling, Rachel Johnson, Lize Kriel, Miles Larmer, Kate Law, Ilse Le Roux, Alois Mlambo, Neil Roos, Jonathan Saha and Dan Spence. In addition I also wish to thank Dave, Jude and Amy Cohen for never leaving me hanging. Special thanks go to my fiancé Helen, whose love, patience and understanding made this project far easier than it otherwise would have been. Finally, my greatest debt of gratitude goes to my parents, Peter and Eileen Cohen whose unconditional love and support gave me the opportunity to work on this project.

GENERAL INTRODUCTION

During the decades from 1880 to 1940 Britain established and consolidated an extensive colonial empire in Africa. This collection concerns the development and implementation of the administrative structures by which those possessions were governed. It is divided into five overarching themes which reflect the influence, priorities and limitations of Britain's imperial administration in Africa: (i) recruitment and training of personnel, (ii) the administration of law, (iii) taxation policies, (iv) land usage and (v) administration of health, labour and other issues. The individual themes and sources are introduced in each of the volumes. The purpose of the General Introduction is to place these in a wider historical and institutional context.

Metropolitan Structures

The Colonial Office was created in the mid-1850s when the War and Colonial Department was divided in to two departments. It was a comparatively small department in Whitehall; in 1903 it had a staff of 113, by 1935 this had grown to 372 and by 1939 it had reached 450. Colonial Office staff belonged to the United Kingdom Civil Service and, unlike the developing Colonial Service, appointments were based on competitive examinations. In 1907 a separate Dominions Office was created within the department to deal with the affairs of Canada, Australia, New Zealand and the four self-governing South African colonies. These 'white dominions' received their own Secretary of State and Dominions Office in 1925.[1] However, the positions of Secretary of State for the Colonies and Secretary of State for the Dominions were first held by different people in 1930 and in theory all but the most senior staff in the two departments were interchangeable until after the Second World War. This should have led to a close relationship between the two departments; however, this was not the case.[2] As the late Imperial and Commonwealth historian Nicholas Mansergh, who had previously worked in the Dominions Office, reminisced in the 1950s 'between these two departments, divided geographically only by the width of a Whitehall quadrangle, there was surprisingly little contact and a marked difference of outlook'.[3]

Prior to 1925 the work of the Colonial Office was essentially divided along geographical lines and was concerned with supervising colonial governors rather than directly administering territories. Importantly, the day-to-day responsibility for administration was effectively devolved to colonial governments and particularly to the Governor whose powers were officially defined in the form of Letters Patent, Royal Instructions and the *Colonial Regulations*. A specimen of the latter issued in 1911 is included in the first volume and shows the extensive power vested in the Governor. Indeed, colonies in Africa were not ruled from Whitehall during this period. In minutes produced in 1936, a Colonial Office official revealingly complained that a former parliamentary Under-Secretary of State for the Colonies had held the fixed idea that 'colonies are governed from here'.[4] There were many cases where the Colonial Office made demands on colonial governments (as several sources in this collection show) but in most respects the British colonies in Africa were governed internally rather than from the imperial centre.

In some respects this changed over time as the nature and speed of communication improved and political priorities changed. In the 1920s and 1930s the colonial empire began to be viewed as an arena where more interventionist action could be taken thereby revitalizing a proactive agenda for colonial development and administration that had been pursued by Joseph Chamberlain during his period as Colonial Secretary (1895–1903).[5] From the mid-1920s the Colonial Office was restructured to deal with this new situation. As several sources in the first volume show, a number of agendas were negotiated in this protracted process. In 1927 and 1930 there were two Colonial Office Conferences which brought together a mix of governors and senior officials in the colonial civil service with their Colonial Office colleagues in London. It demonstrated an attempt to create a better understanding in Whitehall of the 'man-on-the-spot' and also the desire to review the organization of the Colonial Service which did not constitute a single entity with unified pay-scales and terms of employment.[6]

In the event, a committee presided over by the Permanent Secretary of the British Treasury, Sir Warren Fisher, advocated that the Colonial Office should not be amalgamated with the Colonial Service as its work was 'in its essentials different from the work of Colonial Administrations'.[7] As a result of the committee it was decided, however, that all new entrants to the Colonial Office staff would typically spend two years secondment to a colonial administration early in their career. By the same token, a similar number of colonial civil servants would be sent to London to spend a similar period of time at the Colonial Office.[8] Another result was the creation of several subsections: the Personnel Division was created in 1930 and the General Department was subdivided in 1934 into Economic, International Relations (dealing with mandated territories), Defence, Social Service and Development. It should be noted, though, that the geographical departments continued to retain their importance and it was only with the outbreak of the Second World War that the development of functional departments came to the fore. The introduction of the Colonial Development and Welfare Act in 1940 underscored this move towards a more interventionist stance at the very end of the period covered.[9]

Alongside the subject departments the Colonial Office developed a network of advisors and advisory committees consisting of outside experts, representatives from other departments and Colonial Office officers. The Colonial Office had particularly close relationships with experts working in institutions such as the Imperial Institute, the Royal Botanical Gardens and the London and Liverpool Schools of Tropical Medicine.[10] It had also enjoyed the counsel of a legal advisor since 1866 and from the 1920s the following advisory posts were created: Medicine (1926), Fisheries (1928), Finance (1928), Fisheries (1928), Agriculture (1929), Animal Health (1930), Education (1934) and Labour (1938). A number of informative advisory reports are included in this collection.[11] It should be emphasized that the Secretary of State was not obliged to refer matters to advisory committees or to follow their recommendations. Like today, expert advisory committees were sometimes brought in to sanction political decisions already taken; in other instances their conclusions profoundly shaped future policies.[12]

An important metropolitan component in the administration of the African empire was the Office of the Crown Agents for the Colonies – a quasi-governmental body attached to the Colonial Office. Crown Agents acted as commercial and financial agents for all non-self-governing territories and were financed from the territories they represented. Their offices in Millbank in Westminster contained also permanent engineering staff whose primary concern was the supervision of contracts and the inspection of equipment ordered by the colonies. There were never more than three Crown Agents but the office employed a group of assistants that by 1914 numbered 468.[13]

Although there was a degree of institutional knowledge in the Colonial Office, the idea of an 'official mind' dictating imperial policy needs substantial qualification.[14] There is little evidence of a period in the decades under discussion here when the Colonial Office spoke with a single voice. As Ronald Hyam suggests, 'in all small communities of intelligent people, there were tensions and strongly argued disagreements which could quickly acquire a personal dimension'.[15] Moreover its relations with other Whitehall departments which enjoyed a share in the administration of imperial affairs – the Treasury, the War Office, the India Office and the Foreign Office – were often fraught with distrust and strained by discontinuous communication. The atmosphere in the department was 'clubish and donnish' among officers 'bound together by common ties of church, school and university' and Colonial Office officials were often dismissive of outside opinions.[16] They had a low regard for the directors of chartered companies and were generally impatient with missionary and humanitarian pressure groups. This was usually not because they were unsympathetic to humanitarian aims, but rather that they believed themselves to be far better placed than outside groups to uphold the moral duty of the Empire.[17]

In disputes with government agents on the ground, Colonial Office officials often claimed that any disadvantage of distance and lack of local knowledge was offset by the department's years of accumulated institutional knowledge and impartial, wider views. The Colonial Office believed itself to be acting *in loco parentis* for the Crown colonies and consequently on occasion local legislation could be disallowed and in the last resort Parliament could be called to act.[18] Parliamentary control over the Colonial Office was, however, limited. Unlike the Reichstag in Germany, Parliament had no budgetary oversight over colonies and the House of Commons did not have power over the appointment of a governor or over his legislation.[19] Parliament could, however, raise inconvenient questions and pass motions for select committees to investigate controversial issues of colonial administration. As several sources in this collection show, agitators and politicians sought to raise and influence the attention of Parliament through public speeches, pamphlets and articles strategically placed in highbrow journals.[20]

Colonial Administrative Structures and Connections with London

Britain's African territories were composed of differing types of political units. First, there were Crown colonies that possessed differing degrees of autonomy. Some had representative councils containing one or two chambers, consisting of Crown-appointed and 'unofficial' or locally elected members. Colonies such as Southern Rhodesia and Kenya which operated along these lines possessed the greatest level of autonomy. Others, such as Sierra Leone, had nominated councils which were staffed entirely by Crown appointed members, with some appointed representation for the local population. The remainder were those territories which were ruled directly such as the High Commission Territories of Basutoland, Swaziland and Bechuanaland which fell under the British government through a resident commissioner appointed under the direction of the High Commissioner for South Africa.[21]

Secondly, Britain possessed territories known as protectorates whose absorption into the British Empire was often due more to strategic or humanitarian reasons rather than for economic exploitation. Initially the British protectorates in Africa were the responsibility of the Foreign Office, however they were all transferred to Colonial Office administration before the First World War.[22] Contemporary notions of what a protectorate entailed were hazy and the duties of the protecting state loosely defined. As Bernard Porter has noted,

> In a 'protectorate' the metropolitan country had some responsibilities but not many. The word implied that some indigenousness authority did the actual ruling, but with the privilege of being allowed to call on the metropolitan country's help and protection if they were needed. Protectorates were generally legitimised by treaties between both parties to this effect. In practise the 'protection' afforded by Britain took a number of guises, and in some cases it was a legal fiction covering what was in effect a piece of political puppetry.[23]

Confusion about protectorates persisted also after diplomatic exchanges associated with the Berlin Conference stimulated more structured thinking. This international attempt to define the authority of European occupation in Africa raised questions of sovereignty and particularly what constituted 'effective occupation'. These discussions convinced Britain to take a more robust and even interventionist stance to stake out its claims on the ground and pre-empt its European rivals' designs. In an attempt to rein in the expense and limit its own commitments, Britain pursued two courses: the revival of the chartered company as a quasi-official vehicle of government and the reinvigoration of consular activity which pointed towards the creation of protectorates.[24] In the case of protectorates as well as chartered company territories the supervision by the Colonial Office or other Whitehall bodies was very loose. Indeed, as the *Papers relating to the Southern Rhodesia Native Reserve Commission, 1915* reproduced in Volume 4 of this collection demonstrates, even a supposedly neutral commission could find itself staffed by people with a vested interest in the result.[25]

Another territory with a unique constitutional position in Britain's African empire was Sudan. From 1899 it had been administrated as a joint Anglo-Egyptian Condominium headed by a Governor-General appointed by the Khedive on the recommendation of Britain. Its unique position also derived from the fact that Sudan was the responsibility of the Foreign Office, both before and after independence in 1956. Furthermore, British officers of the higher echelons of the Condominium administration were recruited into a separate body, the Sudan Political Service, which had a reputation similar to the Indian Civil Service and was more competitive to join than the Colonial Service.[26]

After the First World War a third type of political unit joined Britain's African empire: League of Nations Mandates. The post-war period saw Britain take responsibility for the former German colonial possessions of Tanganyika, German South-West Africa, Togo and parts of Cameroon.[27] A new administrative ideology came to the fore in this period: trusteeship. Although this term had a long and chequered history in British imperial thinking its renaissance in the inter-war period was linked to the legitimacy given to the word through the adoption of the term in the Covenant of the League of Nations.[28] This fledgling international organization tasked Britain with fostering the 'well-being and development' of territories which were perceived to be 'inhabited by peoples not yet able to stand by themselves under the strenuous conditions of the modern world'. In doing so, Britain would fulfil 'a sacred trust of civilization'. The mandated territories were judged to have not 'reached a stage where their existence as independent nations can be provisionally recognised' and therefore British administration subject to internationally proscribed conditions would be applied. It was deemed necessary to protect the population of mandates from potential exploitation from slavery, forced labour, traffic in arms and spirits, the obstruction of missionary activity and the utilization of the territories manpower to reinforce the armed strength of the European colonial power. Furthermore, apart from South-West Africa which, at the insistence of the Union of South Africa's government who held the mandate, was administered as an integral part of the mandate power, there was an added obligation to maintain a non-discriminatory trade policy which gave 'equal opportunities for the trade and commerce' of all League of Nations Members.[29]

The imperial dependencies in Africa thus covered a wide range of governmental forms that were often reconfigured during the period. Moreover, from 1880 to 1939 the relations between London and the dependencies were affected by the changes in the nature and speed of the exchange of information. The replacement of clippers with steamships from the mid-nineteenth century and the development of oceanic telegraph cables revolutionized the speed by which messages could reach Britain's African colonies from London. The first telegraph cable was laid down the East African coast to Durban in 1879, in part a response to imperial embarrassment in the Anglo-Zulu War. Overland cables were then constructed linking Cape Town to the system. In West Africa outposts such as Dakar, Freetown, Accra and Lagos had been linked to Europe by 1886, after growing French competition in the area made speedy communications necessary. By 1889 this line had also been extended to Cape Town giving the capital of the Cape Colony a second communication route to London.[30]

It is, however, questionable as to how far the telegraph revolutionized the Colonial Office's control over events in its colonies. They received messages from the Eastern Telegraph Company who were based in the City of London. Every day they were couriered to Whitehall where they were left in a postbox to be retrieved and handled in the exact same way as minutes and dispatches. As late as 1900 the Colonial Secretary Joseph Chamberlain went to the telegraph company in person to complain that a cable he was expecting from South Africa had never arrived.[31] The nebulous communication systems ensured that, despite technological improvements, British governors and proconsuls in Africa held an important mediating position, being able to fashion broader imperial policy in order to suit their local circumstances. As such they played a pivotal role in dictating the strength and course of imperial rule in their territories. Consequently, the latitude afforded to these individuals could give them the opportunity to pursue their own ambitions, often at the expense of broader metropolitan concerns. Lord Cromer in Egypt, Lord Lugard in Nigeria and Sir Alfred Milner in Southern Africa provide clear examples of such individuals. While London did possess the ability to recall governors who wilfully disregarded its policies, exasperated acquiescence was a more common outcome.[32]

The Rise and Fall of Indirect Rule

British administrative policy across these decades was often characterized by a tension between policies of assimilation or diversity. Would the creation of British institutions or the retention of indigenous forms of governance best achieve British interests? It is clear that there was no simple single answer to this question. Administration and governance varied greatly, particularly between those colonies that possessed sizeable settler minorities and those tropical colonies with a small, transient European population. So ideas of assimilation and diversity were profoundly influenced by local conditions, but also shaped by prevailing ideas and cultural fashions in Britain itself.[33] The sources presented in these volumes provide examples of both trends of governance.

The relations between ideas of assimilation and diversity were particularly complex with respect to the policies of indirect rule that after 1900 found favour in both London and the African dependencies. Principally during the 1920s and 1930s indirect rule was the subject of continuous discussions among colonial administrators and experts. One source of inspiration for indirect rule in Africa was India, where the princely states covering one-third of the Indian Empire administrated themselves under British paramountcy.[34] More importantly, indirect rule represented a pragmatic response to the difficulties of controlling vast tracts of territory with little in the way of personnel and revenue. Although it became the orthodox view of how Britain's tropical colonies should be administrated, it was subject to many variants as local conditions dictated the ways in which such policy could be enacted. Some colonies lacked sufficiently strong elites to effectively deploy the system, and in other colonies chiefs and headmen became colonial appointees, directly subordinate to white District Officers. Indirect rule was further complicated in territories with large settler minorities.[35]

In some variants of indirect rule the British brought in people from outside into regions as 'native authorities' or promoted locals with little authority to high positions. This approach caused problems in regions with little or no tradition for chieftainship as in south-eastern Nigeria where longstanding grievances with an imposed system of 'Warrant Chiefs' culminated in risings in November 1929 during which colonial troops killed fifty Igbo women.[36] The most widespread and well-known form of indirect rule consisted in the incorporation of strong 'native authorities' into the British governing structure. These authorities would collect taxes shared between local and colonial governments and thus possess treasuries that allowed them varying degrees of financial autonomy. The other core feature was the juridical system which gave the native authorities a measure of control over prisons, policing and a court system whereby most classes of cases were tried according to what was perceived as traditional law and customs. Variations of this form of indirect rule were employed in Northern Nigeria, parts of the Gold

Coast, Tanganyika, Southern Rhodesia (Matabeleland) Northern Rhodesia (Barotseland) and the High Commission Territories as well as Southern Sudan.[37]

Indirect rule in Africa is invariably associated with Frederick Lugard, the most famous of Britain's governors in Africa. In the traditional accounts – stated by Lugard himself as well as his first biographer and protégé Margery Perham – Lugard developed and practised indirect rule in his tenure as High Commissioner in Northern Nigeria (1900–6) and during his governorship of Nigeria (1912–18).[38] His reputation as the *doyen* of British colonial governance was further established through the publication in 1922 of *The Dual Mandate in British Tropical Africa* where Lugard explicitly linked together ideas around 'development' and 'trusteeship' and put forward his views on how Britain should best administer its colonies. Lugard insisted that in Africa Britain had the 'task as trustee on the one hand, for the advancement of the subject races, and on the other hand, for the development of its material resources for the benefit of mankind'.[39] This was a dual mandate that could be honoured only through indirect rule. Continuity in the machinery of Government run by men of character and a mode of administration that ruled in accordance with 'native traditions' were the key characteristics of sound administration. As his authorities on 'native traditions' Lugard in *The Dual Mandate* cited a mixed group of retired administrators, nineteenth-century social theorists as well as the ancient Chinese philosopher Confucius. Upon his retirement from colonial service Lugard established himself as a leading expert on 'the colonial question' and became involved in a number of institutional initiatives that aimed to harness knowledge on Africa in the service of colonial administration.[40]

If Lugard's reputation rose with the empire in Africa it also declined with it. A revisionist historiography has demonstrated that Lugard was not a great administrator and has argued forcefully that his autocratic approach to governance failed to deliver the results that Lugard as a skilful propagandist had claimed.[41] The assessment of indirect rule has in many respects followed Lugard's trajectory. Indirect rule was generally an inefficient form of governance; however it benefitted in the eyes of many from being relatively inexpensive. It had no place for educated Africans and confined local authorities in positions with little connection to the central administration. In the 'native administrations' – where 'tribes' were designated arbitrarily or 'invented' as the administrative units – the British helped to sanction and inflate the credentials of their native allies as 'traditional' and 'authentic' in ways that openly favoured conservative forces in African communities and undermined the legitimacy of those opposed to colonial rule.[42] The protagonists of the principles of indirect rule, most influentially Margery Perham, argued that indirect rule, particularly if guided by the enlightened influence of functionalist anthropology, represented an alternative to policies of assimilation and of segregation.[43] In reality indirect rule was by no means void of segregation. As such a strong case can be made that the importance of indirect rule was not as a fixed, clearly defined system of administration but rather as a philosophy and a justification of British rule in tropical Africa in a situation where the option to incorporate people in the operation of a large, direct centralized administration did not exist.

Africans in Government Employment

There was little contemporary study of Africans in government employment. Their numbers were, however, comparatively small; perhaps 30,000 to 40,000 by the late 1930s. This provides a stark contrast to British administration in India where, according to the 1931 census, there were as many as one million government workers employed. This discrepancy between India and Africa was in essence the difference between direct and indirect rule.[44] The vast majority of Africans in administrative posts were employed in minor positions as clerks, messengers, nurses, toll collectors and district police. Very few non-Europeans occupied positions in the higher layers of the colonial governments during this period. In East and Central Africa no African was employed above the level of minor clerk before the Second World War. In West Africa the governments had some non-Europeans in specialist departments. In the *Colonial Office Lists* non-Europeans in the West African governments were sometimes labelled as such (e.g. 'African Surveyor') but this was not always the case.[45] There is, however, no question that these numbers remained very low and that it was official policy to exclude educated Africans firmly from the 'political service'.[46] Moreover they had declined since the 1890s – another significant contrast to India where about one-quarter of the Indian Civil Service was Indian by 1939.[47]

In the West African region – with its long standing links with Europe resting on trade in slaves and commodities – Africans and men of mixed black and white ancestry did initially hold important positions in the nascent British colonial governments. In 1883 in the Gold Coast Africans held nine of the 43 highest posts in Government. However, before the turn of the century the doors to higher positions in the administrations were closing to non-Europeans. In 1908 only five of the colony's 274 officers were African.[48] Improved health conditions for Europeans undoubtedly proved a crucial factor in bringing about this change. The expansion of colonial rule from the coastal towns with its well-established Western educated elites into the hinterland also favoured Europeans expatriates over African intermediaries in government employment. Racial theories and economic interests of expatriate administrators played a seminal part as well. Economic and racialist factors for example converged when the West African Medical Service was established in 1902 and officially barred any candidate not of European descent from joining its ranks. It was the first department in the empire to make exclusion based on race official policy.[49] Moreover, the number of Africans in government service in West Africa also declined systematically as policies of indirect rule separated 'native' and 'colonial' administrations more firmly. In Nigeria and elsewhere a division developed in the small 'colonial' administrations before the First World War with the highest ranks in effect reserved for white administrators and African clerical staff re-graded into a lower salary range.[50] Unsurprisingly, the most talented and best educated West Africans sought to satisfy aspirations outside government employment. Even in the Gold Coast, regarded as the most 'progressive' of the West African dependencies, the Africanisation of the Civil Service made little headway prior to the Second World War.

In East Africa and Central Africa colonial rule did not develop from strong pre-existing trade links. Unlike the West African colonies African and Krio intermediaries did not occupy high positions in government employment in the early phases of colonial rule. In addition to men appointed from Britain, Asians, however, played an important role in some colonial administrations and staff were also hired from within settler communities.[51] By 1900 the government services in East Africa were organized on a three tier system with the British administrators at the top, Indian and Goans in the middle and the few African and Arab clerks at the lowest level in the administrative hierarchies.[52] In a report from 1936 on the Kenyan administration (included in this collection) Sir Alan Pim discussed this issue in detail. He noted a more recent trend to replace Asians with Europeans and concluded that the Arab and African share in all branches of the administration until the time of writing had been minimal.[53]

The exclusion of Africans in the colonial governments caused grievances throughout this period. When the *Provincial Council of Chiefs* in the Gold Coast in 1931 petitioned against the proposed introduction of income taxes the Council urged that 'the generally accepted proposal of suitable and competent Africans being appointed to higher posts in the Government Service in the place of Europeans as far as possible, should be adhered to for the purpose of reducing expenditure'.[54] The Hailey report of 1941 would make similar recommendations on financial and other grounds but in effect little happened until the 1950s.[55]

Women and Administration

British policy was often influenced by issues of gender. The higher echelons in the administration of Britain's African colonies were almost exclusively a white, masculine affair.[56] As Kate Law, building on the pioneering work of Joan Scott, has shown in her recent work on white women in Rhodesia, women may not have been directly involved in wielding political power, yet gender issues remained a constant influence in colonial political discourses.[57] There are in this period a few examples of women enlarging the role allotted to them, to play a more proactive role in the distinctly masculine world of colonial governance.[58] For example, during a tour of the Niger Province in January 1939 Lady Bourdillon, wife of Sir Bernard Bourdillon, Governor of Nigeria from 1935 to 1943, carried out a tour of inspection and met with the Emir of Kontagora after her husband was taken ill. She did recall later that overall her official involvement in Nigeria had been 'negligible.'[59] This collection focuses on instances where women can clearly be seen to play a more active role in administration than Lady Bourdillon managed, for instance in nursing and education. The formation of the Colonial Nursing Association in 1896 provided an institution which was dominated by women and sources are included in what follows.[60] A woman whose influence on the development on British administration in Africa in both the pre-and post-Second World War period was Margery Perham, perhaps the leading Africanist of her generation.

Margery Perham won an open scholarship to read history at Oxford University in 1914. After graduating with a first-class degree she became a lecturer in history at the University of Sheffield. The death of her favourite brother in the First World War seriously affected Perham and the fact that her students in Sheffield were former servicemen provided a constant reminder of her loss. Consequently she suffered a nervous breakdown in 1920 which forced her to take a year's leave. Perham's decision to convalesce with her sister's family in Somaliland had a huge bearing on her future career. Her brother-in-law had been appointed as District Commissioner for Hargeisa and during Perham's time there she became deeply committed to Africa and also developed an idealized role for a colonial officer in administering justice and developing his district for the betterment of its inhabitants. Although her opinion would change in the post-Second World War period, it is clear that throughout the 1920s and 1930s Perham fully believed that African communities could be best served by impartial advisors, preferably Oxford and Cambridge graduates or through the implementation of indirect rule. At no point did she advocate the greater inclusion of educated Africans into colonial government.[61]

Upon her return to Sheffield Perham introduced a course on imperial history, however she never really settled at the university and returned to Oxford in 1924 as a tutor of modern history, politics, philosophy and economics at her former college, St Hugh's. In 1926 both Oxford and Cambridge introduced training courses for Colonial Service probationers. Although Perham's knowledge of the role and duties of colonial officers was hardly expansive, her time in Somaliland had given her insights which her colleagues in Oxford could not hope to match and for the next five years she taught a mixture of undergraduates and Colonial Service probationers. During 1928–9 Perham applied for a Rhodes Trust travelling scholarship to study native administration in both the British Empire and the United States. The support of the Rhodes Trustees was crucial in securing the cooperation of the Establishment in both Britain and overseas. Her travels, which began in 1929, took her to the United States, the Pacific Islands, Australia, New Zealand and much of Africa south of the Sahara. During this period she wrote voluminous notes on her experiences and published several articles on colonial administration in *The Times*. The extension of her travel grant in 1930 had resulted in Perham having to resign her fellowship at St Hugh's.[62]

Upon her return to Britain in 1932 Perham cemented her position as a leading authority on colonial administration. In the period under consideration in these volumes she wrote *Native Administration in Nigeria* (1937), edited *Ten Africans* (1936) and also with Lionel Curtis, the former member of Alfred Milner's Kindergarten and fellow of All Souls College, published a collection of their *Times* newspaper articles as *The Protectorates of South Africa* (1935). The patronage of Lord Lugard helped promote Perham's reputation as an academic expert on British colonial rule in Africa and in the 1930s she secured a Rockefeller fellowship to cover an extended research trip to East Africa in order that she could produce a book on administration in the region. In the event, a combination of ill health, the outbreak of war and the demands of her academic and public life meant that the work was never published. Perham returned to Oxford in 1935 and was appointed research lecturer in colonial administration and in 1939 became the first and only female fellow at Nuffield College. She was also appointed to the committee advising Lord Hailey on the compilation of *An African Survey* (1938). Perham enjoyed contact with colonial officials, politicians and opinion makers at all levels. Her extensive travels in Africa had brought her into contact with many officers in the field as had her role educating probationers in Oxford. She also had contact with influential officials in Britain such as Sir Ralph Furse. It was following 1939 that Perham adopted a more direct role in advising government on matters of administration.[63]

Geographical Issues of Administration

Any attempt to periodize British administration of its African colonies will invariably be crude. The sources in the collection are testament to the fact that the administrative systems had markedly different origins and developments. African polities, the presence of white settlers, the extent of economic development, regional ecology and demography, the strength of local, central and metropolitan authorities all influenced how territories were administered. Some broad trends, however, are notable.

The first collection in this Britain and Africa series stressed that 'among the many motivations behind Britain's scramble for Africa the most important were economic'.[64] Prior to the period covered here, it is clear that British politicians and officials had no explicit territorial agenda for the continent as a whole by the 1870s. Africa was seen primarily as a base for fighting the slave trade, a staging post for India and the East and an *entrepôt* for resources and trade. It was a component in a larger imperial system.[65] Before 1880 differences of opinion regarding Africa between Conservatives and Liberals were slight, they often amounted to a different emphasis being placed on methods of access and control and whether at public or private cost. During this period African polices fell to secretaries of state and their officials while prime ministers busied themselves with European affairs. The exception to this rule was Egypt. Both Gladstone and Disraeli were concerned with managing the Ottoman Empire's decline and consequently they became involved in Britain's North African policy, using diplomatic channels to internationalise Egypt's monetary problems. Two further tactics were employed elsewhere on the continent. Carnarvon, in his second period as Colonial Secretary (1874–8), highly influenced by his previous experience in North America and also a plan taken over from his predecessor, Lord Kimberley (1870–4) favoured the creation of a 'federation' of the disparate republics, colonies and African societies south of the Zambezi ruled from a self-governing Cape Colony. The second tactic favoured was continued public and private support for existing British commercial and missionary enterprises in tropical Africa. All three policies proved unsound however they do accurately reflect Britain's priorities in this period: the protection of a world-wide trading system and British subjects overseas.[66]

The first decades covered in this collection were dominated by the scramble for territories by the European powers. In this period formal colonial rule was extended to areas inland and rudimentary governmental structures were established. Generally, the administrations retained strong military elements as constabularies and locally recruited armies – later to become the West African Frontier Force (1900) and the Kings African Rifles (1902)[67] – continued conquest and 'pacification'.[68] Chartered company rule was instigated but with the exception of the British South Africa Company the areas under company administration were transferred to the Colonial Office.

The First World War had a profound impact on British colonial governments in Africa. Armed forces were normally kept small on account of economy but the war saw the recruitment of military and other personnel on an unprecedented scale. European control was intensified in some areas and in others troops withdrew. In both cases revolt and unrest often resulted.[69] The war represented the last stages in the scramble for territory eventually adding more administrative units Britain's African empire. The war effort also stripped the colonial governments of experienced British officers in key administrative areas. As Ralph D. Furse, Assistant Private Secretary at the Colonial Office, explained in a 1927 memorandum included in this collection, it took several years to fill these positions with suitable candidates.[70]

During the 1920s a renewed focus on colonial development influenced the outlook of the colonial governments. With a notable influx of technical personnel this was a significant phase in 'the triumph of the expert' in the administration of colonies.[71] Under the tenure of Leo Amery as Secretary of State for the Colonies (1924–9) conferences and committees endorsed programmes of colonial development through the application of the sciences. In 1926 one-year postgraduate training programmes for probationers were established at Oxford and Cambridge in replacement of the shorter training courses organized at Imperial College since 1909.[72] In the actual rule of territories there was, however, a tendency for the British administration to withdraw as variants of indirect rule gained momentum on account of principles and financial necessity.[73]

The downturn in world economy in the early 1930s hit the fragile economies that supported the colonial administrations in Africa hard and it altered metropolitan priorities as well. One implication was that fewer officers were appointed. In some colonies the number of European government officers dropped – though not always at the pace that some African leaders and politicians wanted.[74] Resistance to colonial rule was spurred by economic problems and was on the increase, becoming better organized particularly in urban areas.

This introduction will now consider how these broad themes played out in different parts of the continent. In order to understand how administrative policies developed it is important to have an appreciation of how British rule was initially established in the regions. The British had initially begun to operate in West Africa and the region was free from large-scale white settlement. As the following sections and sources will demonstrate, a crucial factor in dictating the way the administration developed over this period was whether a territory contained a sizable settler minority whose political and economic aspirations had to be considered, against those of the indigenous population. In East Africa, the tension was magnified by a further large minority in the form of the region's Asian community, who had to be taken into account in any administrative issues. In Southern Africa, the settlers were far more organized and enjoyed racial solidarity with the powerful Afrikaner community in South Africa. In Egypt and Sudan the administrations were challenged by intense international pressure and in this region the British inherited imperial administrative structures from the Ottoman and the Egyptian rulers they replaced.

West Africa

British interests in West Africa prior to the 1880s largely revolved around the issues of anti-slave trade measures, steam communications and open access to markets. These were achieved through a combination of the retention of existing colonial outposts, treaties of friendship with interior chiefdoms and, more hesitantly, the extension of jurisdiction in the vicinity of British settlements to protect and control British subjects.[75]

By the last quarter of the nineteenth century it became increasingly clear that a more organized and professional system of colonial administration would be required in West Africa if Britain was to preserve its interests in the region. There were two principal reasons for the move away from a free market *laissez-faire* approach towards more formal structures of governance in this period. The first concerned the economic situation in the late nineteenth century. Following the abolition of the slave trade in 1807, African and British merchants in West Africa had to develop alternative exports to replace the income they had lost.[76] In West Africa palm oil products became the predominant replacement for slaves. In 1807 Britain imported 2,233 cwt. of palm oil products; by the 1840s this figure had risen to an average of 426,087 cwt. and the trade peaked in 1895 with the export of 1,262,933 cwt.[77] The second factor which pushed Britain towards taking a more formal move towards administration was European political rivalry in the region during the 'scramble for Africa'. By 1879 the British concept of 'free trade' was increasingly threatened as the French actively looked to expand their territory on the continent. This would have had the result of placing important regions for British trade behind French protectionist barriers. Britain countered this threat by diplomacy and the renewal of its own existing treaties on important trade routes.[78]

Between 1885 and 1895 Britain secured through treaty making the frontiers of what became Sierra Leone, the Gold Coast Colony, the Gambia and Nigeria. In 1885 Britain established a Protectorate of the trading zone in the Niger Delta as a temporary measure. Meanwhile, Sir George Goldie, a commercial entrepreneur, who headed the National African Company secured treaties with riverine chiefs which established a commercial monopoly in the hinterland. Goldie's company was granted a Royal Charter and reconfigured as the Royal Niger Company in 1886 which gave the commercial concern extensive political powers to enforce justice, make treaties, and collect customs revenue in the ports of call to offset its administration costs.[79] The Royal Niger Company found itself on trial as it began to extend its control through force of arms in Nupe and Ilorin while also contesting French advances. In 1899 administration of the Niger Delta was transferred by the Foreign Office to the Colonial Office and in 1900 the Royal Niger Company lost its Charter.[80] From that date, the land outside of the Lagos Colony was divided into two protectorates named Northern and Southern Nigeria. With the help of the newly organized West African Frontier Force the Protectorate Government of Northern Nigeria subdued the local emirates and in 1903 defeated the Caliphate of Sokoto.[81] By this time protectorates had also been declared over the hinterland of the Crown colony of Sierra Leone (1896), the Gambia (1894) and the Gold Coast (1898).

The incorporation of vast regions of the interior into new governmental structures and the changes in priorities this entailed shaped British colonial governance in West Africa during the first decades of the twentieth century.[82] One implication of this was that the civil colonial administration maintained a strong element of military influence. Revolts occurred early such as the Hut Tax revolt in Sierra Leone of 1898, the Ashanti wars in the Gold Coast and risings continued during the ensuing decades.[83] Wars were costly, strained regional alliances and also provided ammunition for critics in Britain of the imperial policies pursued in West Africa.[84] Elsewhere the increased pressure resulting from British administrative presence inland produced more protracted tensions with African polities. A case covered in this collection is Abeokuta, a Yoruba State and early missionary centre that emerged successfully from the Yoruba wars of the nineteenth century.[85] Despite its relative proximity to Lagos Abeokuta retained a high degree of autonomy during the first years of the century, including the right to collect tolls. Abeokuta was eventually subdued by force after the Amalgamation of Northern and Southern Nigeria in 1914.[86]

Two connected features characterized the administration in the West African colonies. First, contrary to East and Southern Africa, significant white settlement was precluded primarily on account of the climate which encouraged endemic diseases. Administrators in the colonies and officials in London were therefore broadly in agreement on a policy by which the West African dependencies should be developed on the basis of 'native production'. Secondly, although medical advances eventually made it possible to station more European personnel in the region, financial constraints ruled out the introduction of any more other than a small cadre a white officials. Consequently, in West Africa policy dictated that in the main Africans would be governed by Africans.[87] It was in response to this situation that indirect rule as a set of administrative principles first gained currency and from there became the orthodox view during the interwar period of how Britain's tropical colonies should be administrated. The basic definition of indirect rule was simple – 'systematic use of the customary institutions of the people as agencies of local rule'[88] – but also across the West African colonial administrations there were very little agreement about what this entailed.[89] Indeed, the principles of indirect rule offered few solutions or guidelines on how to develop states that would effectively integrate coast and hinterland. In the event the colonial governments struggled to establish and maintain alliances with its preferred African elites while at the same time restricting the influence of Africans who had been educated on Western lines. During the 1930s the difficulty of this task was further aggravated by the economic depression which hit the commodity exporting economies in West Africa particularly hard and gave momentum to the growing resistance to colonial rule particularly in the urban centres on the coast.

East Africa

In the 1880s Britain became increasingly concerned that French and German advances in the area threated the security of the source of the Nile which in turn threatened the security of Egypt. A diplomatic agreement signed in 1886 divided East Africa into British and German spheres of influence and initially London looked for the Imperial British East Africa Company, which received its Royal Charter in 1888, to uphold its claims. Throughout its short existence the Imperial British East Africa Company failed to economically justify its creation and, after the Anglo-German Agreement of 1890 guaranteed Britain a vital corridor between the Indian Ocean and the Upper Nile, the company was liquidated and Protectorates were declared over Uganda (1894) and the rest of British East Africa (1895). The agreement also recognized Zanzibar as a formal British Protectorate.[90]

One consequence of the Anglo-German Agreement of 1890 was the Imperial British East Africa Company's decision to send Frederick Lugard to secure a treaty from the Kabaka of Buganda and hoist the Company flag in Kampala. As John Lonsdale has suggested, all of Britain's conquests in East Africa had their own distinctive character and Buganda was no different. Where there was perceived to be an existing strong state structure there was a cautious administrative preference that continuity could combine with missionary and commercial demands for reformation.[91] A 'Memorandum on the Constitution of the Native Government of the Buganda Kingdom' reproduced in Volume 2 of this collection clearly underlines this point:

> In the old days the Kabaka of Buganda was the supreme Ruler of his people, assisted by his various chiefs from the Katikiro (or Prime Minister) down to the lowest 'Mutongole' Chief. This chain of Chieftainships helped to build up a very strong constitutional form of Government, although not based on sound or civilized principles, yet not unlike that of one of the European civilized countries, and certainly differed entirely from that of any other surrounding Native tribe in Eastern Africa.[92]

As the above extract suggests, elsewhere in East Africa the British found few chiefs, let alone kings to co-opt into their imperial system. As a result if the Imperial British East Africa Company was to collect enough revenue, it would be required to undertake a number of small 'punitive expeditions', including against Muslims in north-west Buganda. The Company, however, was in effect too weak to wage such a campaign and in the end was reliant on missionary propaganda in Britain. The uneconomic position of the territory led to calls from many Liberals to evacuate the territory, however Lord Rosebery, the Liberal Prime Minister (1894–5) held the view of the strategic importance of the territory and arranged for the British East Africa Colony to take over from the Imperial British East Africa Company in 1893. The territory was brought under British administration when the construction of the railway connecting Mombasa to Kisumu began in 1895.[93] This had been achieved between 1889 and 1896 with only twenty-five British officials to administer an African population numbering three million at any one time.[94]

Following this less than auspicious start the financial position of Kenya and Uganda did improve and by 1912 both colonies were financially self-support-ing.[95] Prior to the First World War London was content to rule Uganda's three million people with forty British officials and Buganda's 'sub-imperialism'.[96] The Bugandan Kingdom's willingness to take a proactive approach in engaging with, and subsequently helping to shape, British colonial penetration and admin-istration meant that European farmers could not attain the same preeminent position in the minds of the colonial government as they managed in Kenya. African agriculture in the territory by 1914 was extremely successful accounting for two-thirds of the colony's export income.[97] Kenya, on the other hand, pro-vides a differing example despite the fact that in the pre-First World War black and white interests were similarly matched to those in Uganda.[98] The difference in Kenya was that the overbearing politics of the local settler population masked their underlying weakness which would later be revealed following the Second World War. An example of the vociferousness of the local settler community can be seen in the 'Correspondence Relating to the Flogging of Natives by certain Europeans in Nairobi' reproduced in volume two of this collection.[99]

By the 1920s there were around 13 million Africans, 50,000 East Afri-can Asians, of which half resided in Kenya, and 14,000 Europeans in East Africa.[100] Consequently a central feature of colonial administration was mediat-ing between the contradictory claims for land and power between these three interest groups. In 1922 Winston Churchill, Colonial Secretary, declared that Kenya would become a 'characteristic and distinctly British colony'. On one level, Churchill's call for Kenya to progress to responsible government could be seen as a victory for the territory's settler minority, however, his insistence on a common electoral roll meant that the Indian community would greatly benefit and as a result it outraged the settler community. The 1923 Devonshire Declara-tion[101] reversed Churchill's statement and starkly proclaimed 'Primarily Kenya is an African country', much to the chagrin of the settler community. The arrival of the arch-imperialist Leo Amery in the Colonial Office appeared to auger well for the settlers, and his 1927 White Paper went back on Devonshire's claim and instead advocated a system of 'dual policy' which seem to give as much weight to European interests as to Africans. Amery also advocated closer association of Britain's East and Central African colonies.[102] This was to prove a somewhat *pyr-rhic* victory for the settlers.

In 1929 Sir Edward Hilton Young whose committee was charged with inves-tigating the possibility of closer association of the East and Central African territories published his report. In the event, the committee's final report had been heavily influenced by Sir George Schuster, Colonial Office Financial Advisor, and

J. H. Oldham, Secretary to the International Missionary Council, so much so that Hilton Young refused to sign the majority report. It unequivocally rejected the idea of self-government along the same lines as Southern Rhodesia and also a wider federation of East and Central Africa under settler control. Instead, it reaffirmed the early Devonshire declaration that African interests should come first in the territory and it should be governed through a policy of trusteeship. This idea was further confirmed by the Labour Secretary of State for the Colonies in 1930 who tried to reconcile the two previous approaches. He suggested that the 'dual-policy' approach should not be inconsistent with the policy of trusteeship providing the emphasis stayed firmly on the primacy of African interests. This was followed by his statement on 'closer union' which, to the disgust of the Kenyan settlers, revisited Churchill's proposal for a common voters roll.[103]

The Depression of the 1930s brought economic matters back to the fore in the administration of East Africa as export revenues fell and the cost of debt repayment soared. As poverty in the territories deepened, colonial officials became increasingly concerned with promoting welfare. This had a dramatic impact as conservation and a more systematic approach to problems within the colonies began to be favoured. Towards the end of the decade steps were slowly underway to create a new group of educated Africans who were anticipated to be able to assist the development of the region. Makarere College in Uganda had started to teach the Cambridge School Certificate by 1938 and post-secondary school courses in medicine, veterinary science and agriculture to c.150 African students from all over the region. It was out of this *milieu* that future African nationalist leaders in the region such as Tom Mboya and Jomo Kenyatta would subsequently emerge.[104]

Egypt and Sudan

Britain's involvement in Egypt and the Sudan was a consequence of the internationalisation of Egypt's economic crisis and the decline of the Ottoman Empire. The financial woes of the country were such that in 1879 Britain and France removed Khedive Ismail, replaced him as khedive with his biddable son, Tawfiq and instituted a system of governance through their financial officers known as 'dual-control'. The French were more heavily exposed to Egyptian debt; however, the vulnerability of the Suez Canal in addition to the interests of British investors loomed large in London's view.[105]

The arrival of controllers-general to more effectively enforce and administer finances interfered with local patronage exercised through the Khedive's Civil List and resulted in much dissatisfaction amongst sections of the Egyptian population. Consequently, a protest movement headed by the Egyptian Colonel Ahamad Urabi was formed which threatened to unite reformers, bureaucracy and the army against the system of dual control. British officials in Egypt continued to warn London of the growing support for Urabi and when riots broke out in Alexandria in 1882, resulting in the deaths of around fifty Europeans and 170 Egyptians it sent tremors through the London Stock Exchange. Britain responded by ordering its fleet to intervene and in July it bombarded the city. The French were reluctant to get involved in an armed intervention and British troops set about securing the territory. This was achieved after the victory at the battle of Tel-el-Kebir. The French reluctance to become involved meant that after this point Egypt became a *de facto* a British protectorate.[106] During the occupation political overrule was firmly in the hands of the British consul-general assisted by British advisers who held the real power behind all government departments. Although intended to be temporary, British rule lasted until 1922 when, in response to political unrest, Egyptian protestors secured a greater level of nominal independence.[107]

After the occupation in 1882 the administrators set out to devise a system of government which would keep control of Egypt's finances while allowing a certain measure of political reform so that the previous anger of the population would not be aroused again. They settled on introducing a form of limited representative system and a Council of State. It would, in effect, be administered in a similar manner to an Indian princely state, however with a much lighter touch given that Britain possessed no executive or judicial powers. In 1892 a new Khedive Abbas, who was better educated and commanded a following within the nationalist movement, assumed power. This in no way challenged British control of the state, whose power lay in the form of Sir Edwin Palmer, as financial advisor, and Lord Cromer's command of the civil service and the Egyptian Frontier Force.[108]

During the years of the occupation substantial British communities resided in Egypt. The military and political British elite in Egypt was composed of the officers in the Army of Occupation, and the civil servants attached in some capacity or other to the various ministries such as Finance, Education, Public Works, Interior and Justice. The year after the occupation there were 272 British officials in Egypt. By 1896 there were 690 European officials in the civil service, a number which by 1906 had risen to 1.252, the large majority of which were British. In addition to the senior British officials acting as advisers to the Egyptian ministries, a growing contingent of young Britons were recruited to Egypt from select public schools and universities in Britain to serve as under-secretaries and inspectors in each ministry.[109] Many other influential administrators were like Cromer himself recruited with experience from India. They brought with them institutions, techniques and programmes that fused with existing French, Ottoman, and Egyptian administrative structures.[110] The 'Indianization' was particularly strong in the financial administration and in the Public Works Department which unlike the other administrative departments were not strained of financial resources. Among those who came from India was Sir Colin Moncrieff, who headed the Public Works Department from 1883 until 1892.[111] Moncrieff is the author of a pamphlet included in Volume 5 of this collection on the use and abolition of the *corvée* – unpaid compulsory labour – one of the most debated administrative issues during the first decades of the occupation.

Despite the system of *de facto* British administration in Egypt the financial problems in the territory, ostensibly the reason for the British control over the territory in the first place, continued in the first twenty years after 1882 with foreign debt increasing to £E116.6m due to increased spending on irrigation projects and infrastructure. During this period the administrators adopted a fiscal policy that reduced taxes, postponed administrative reforms and allowed increases in public expenditure to take place exclusively through investments in 'remunerative' public works.[112] As Peter Cain has demonstrated this fiscal course was adopted on moral as well as financial grounds. The 'Gladstonian' regime of public finances was meant to replace what the administrators regarded as a depraved 'oriental system' devoid of financial and moral moderation. Khedive Ismail, known among the British as 'the amazing spendthrift', had been removed but he was seen as a product rather than a cause of a morally rotten system. The small cadre of British administrators saw themselves as the bulwark against the 'oriental mind' that had brought Egypt to the brink of bankruptcy. To them the Egyptians needed protection from themselves and in their eyes Egyptian self-rule was at the most a very distant possibility.[113]

Many other aspects of Egyptian society were affected by the British occupation. Previously Egyptian rulers had tried to introduce European law in the form of the *Codé Napoléon* to replace Sharia law. Ottoman regulations meant that non-Muslims were judged by their own religious sects under the *millet* system. Ismail had previously tried to engineer a legal system which would enable commercial litigation between Egyptians and foreigners. In effect this produced a hybrid-system known as the Mixed Courts, however the judges were predominantly European and there were few Egyptian lawyers qualified to plead before them as lawyers had to be western-trained and conversant in a non-Egyptian language. Cromer, given his thinly-veiled contempt for Islam, continued the westernisation of the Egyptian court system by encouraging the creation of a school for judges and schools of law which taught mostly in French, given the predominant position of the *Codé Napoléon* in the Egyptian system.[114]

It was from Egypt that British rule was extended to the Sudan after the Anglo-Sudanese War of 1896–8. The strategic threat to Britain's position in Egypt as other European power encroached on Sudan, the vengeance of the death of the lionized General Gordon, the protection of the water resources of Nile so central to the financial restoration of Egypt have been identified among underlying causes for the conquest of Sudan.[115] In 1899 a Condominium was declared over the territory. It established a joint Anglo-Egyptian rule over Sudan and was an arrangement which in part was meant to forestall international objections to openly British rule.[116] After British rule in Egypt had been formally abolished in 1922 the designation Condominium continued – now 'more of a misnomer than ever'[117] – until independence in 1956.[118]

The changed status of Anglo-Egyptian relations after 1922 did, however, have a profound effect on the Condominium government. It stripped Khartoum of financial resources which had primarily come from Egypt. Indeed, until this time the arrangement had been that Britain supplied the rulers of the Condominium while Egypt paid for them.[119] It raised the political stakes as well. Egyptian influence filtered through an administrative system that had been built on the foundations of its Turku-Egyptian and Mahdist predecessors and which employed Egyptians in the junior echelons of the government. Under the Governorship of Sir John Maffey (1926–33) indirect rule was formally instituted in part to protect the territory from the subversive influence of Egypt and reduce the sway of educated Sudanese by building instead on the power of 'tribal sheikhs'. As Maffey made plain in a memorandum on 'Devolution of Native Authority':

> If the encouragement of native authority in the true sense of the Milner formula is our accepted policy, before old traditions die we ought to get on with extension and expansion in every direction, thereby sterilising and localising the political germs which must spread from the lower Nile into Khartoum.[120]

As the point was also to exclude 'Northerners' from governmental positions in the politically more backward southern Sudan the number of British officials increased instead making the Sudan a case were indirect rule turned out to be more expensive than direct rule.[121]

The higher stratum of British officers in Sudan belonged to the Sudan Political Service, a small cadre of officials recruited primarily from Oxford and Cambridge.[122] The Sudan Political Service existed from 1899 until the dissolution of the Condominium in 1956. Its officers filled up the premier positions in the political administration of Sudan – from the Governor-General and Provincial Governors to most positions as District Commissioners and Assistant District Commissioners. Although independent from the Colonial Service the structure of the Sudan Political Service resembled the other bureaucracies in the African dependencies. It consisted of a Governor-General and his central secretariat in the capital. Substantial authority was from there delegated to Provincial Governors who in their turn devolved responsibility to District Commissioners supported by Assistant District Commissioners.[123] In rural areas the District Commissioners had few if any European subordinates. In the larger towns largely office-bound District Commissioners were charged with superintending an increasingly bureaucratic administration.[124]

During the decades covered in this collection the Condominium government was above all concerned with maintaining order and – particularly after subsidies from Egypt diminished from 1922 – generating revenue through taxation. With respect to reforms of juridical systems, the abolition of forced labour and improvements in health and education much less was achieved. Limited resources in finance and staff go a long way in explaining these familiar administrative priorities. Yet, as Martin Daly cogently has observed there was also an understanding among administrators that government *should* not extend beyond the maintenance of order:

> Administration was a profession, the proper work of 'political' officers, while the business of education, health, social welfare, economic development and so forth was secondary, incidental, to be left to others. Illiteracy, disease and poverty were less a constant challenge than a perpetual reminder of the rulers' cultural and racial superiority.[125]

This view was not confined to the Sudan; it was in fact widely held among British administrators elsewhere in Africa.

The Rhodesias and the High Commission Territories

During this period Britain established administrations in Northern and Southern Rhodesia and the High Commission territories of Basutoland, Swaziland and Bechuanaland. The ways in which administration developed in these territories were irrevocably shaped by British policies towards South Africa. The fact that the majority of the settler population in the region were of non-British descent with little love for the British imperial project, particularly after the South African War (1899–1902) had resulted in the two Boer Republics of the Orange Free State losing their independence. Post-war negotiations to bring the British Cape and Natal colonies into closer association with the former Boer republics culminated in the South Africa Act (1909). This created the new British dominion of the Union of South Africa on 31 May 1910. Its dominion status for the majority of the period under consideration places South African administration outside of the remit for this collection.[126]

British expansion outside of the Cape Colony was never pursued with much enthusiasm by Westminster or Whitehall and was often driven by local circumstances. As a result, Crown rule was only resorted to when no other options remained. By the latter half of the nineteenth century this normally took two forms: the subordination and incorporation of territory into an existing colony or a vassal-state relationship under the authority of the Cape High Commissioner. The gradual incorporation of the territories which comprised the Eastern Cape is an example of the former, while Bechuanaland which became a Protectorate in 1884 provides an example of the latter.[127] By the time the dust had settled on the late nineteenth century 'scramble' period and the South African War, the Colonial Office found itself with responsibility for Nyasaland and the Commission territories of Bechuanaland, Basutoland and Swaziland. The administration of the British South Africa Company territories of Southern and Northern Rhodesia also later became the responsibility of London in 1923 and 1924 respectively.

By the late 1880s a series of contests, treaties and amalgamations had lain down the main territorial lines of British influence in the region. Independent African polities had either been absorbed into existing British territories or subsumed into relationships of clientage and administrative control under the authority of the Cape Governor. The desire of other European nations to claim territory in Southern Africa played to the advantage of Cecil John Rhodes, Prime Minister of the Cape Colony (1890–6), who managed to convince London to sanction his claim to land north of the Limpopo – despite the underhand methods by which he had allegedly obtained the chief of the Ndebele, Lobenguela's agreement. Consequently, a Royal Charter was granted to Rhodes' British South Africa Company in 1888 giving it a monopoly on land and mineral rights in a vaguely defined territory from Bechuanaland to the Zambezi River.[128] Further boundaries were delineated with the Anglo-German Agreement of 1890 which formalized the creation of the British Central African Protectorate in the territory that later become Nyasaland.[129]

Rhodes, who made his fortune on the diamond fields of Kimberley, believed that the area which became Southern Rhodesia contained a 'Second Rand', a reference to the vast gold deposits which had been discovered on the Witwatersrand in the Transvaal in 1886. However, as early as 1894–5 it was apparent to the British South Africa Company that the comparative scarceness of mineral resources meant that a 'Second Rand' would fail to materialize.[130] Under Company rule the Rhodesias both struggled to cover the costs of administration, never mind realise a divided for the Company's shareholders. Volume 3 of this collection reproduces a source from 1907 on the territories revenue and expenditure to underscore this fact.[131] This period also saw the introduction of schemes designed to encourage the development of commercial farmers in the territory's growing settler community.[132]

The European population in Southern Rhodesia grew steadily across the first three decades of three twentieth century. In 1901, it numbered 11,032; by 1911 it had doubled to 23,606; by 1921 it had reached 33,620 and by 1931 it was at 49,910.[133]Although the white population never numbered more than five per cent of the total population, they managed to gain significant political power. This was assisted by the relatively marginal importance of large-scale mining capital in Southern Rhodesia.[134] During the first two decades of the twentieth century many settlers became disenchanted with Company rule and successfully lobbied for the removal of British South Africa Company control. To those who wished to create a 'Greater South Africa' such as General Jan Smuts, the prime minister of the Union of South Africa during 1919–24 and again 1939–48, the removal of Company rule could lead the territories incorporation into the Union. This desire, however, was not shared by the majority of Africans to whom direct British colonial control would offer more protection than direct rule by a more reactionary settler minority. By the time the referendum was held in 1922, settlers in Southern Rhodesia also opposed incorporation into the Union, despite the desire of Smuts, the Colonial Office and the Chartered Company to see it happen. The vote was close, with a small majority of the 33,000 predominantly British settlers backing self-government.[135] The documents reproduced in this collection clearly demonstrate the differing concerns of colonial administrations in territories with sizable settler minorities differed greatly from those 'tropical' colonies where a permanent settler presence was negligible.

The entrenchment of settler power effectively saw African aspirations and demands pushed firmly to the back of the administration's priorities in Southern Rhodesia. There was no widespread belief that the High Commission Territories of Bechuanaland, Basutoland and Swaziland should become 'white' countries in Southern Africa and consequently administrators dealt primarily with local African leaders rather than with settler politicians. On occasion, as the excerpt detailing conversations held at the Dominions Office between Tshekedi Khama, Regent of the Bangwato, and Lord Passfield, Secretary of State for the Colonies and also Secretary of State for the Dominions, demonstrate, Khama was a highly engaged individual prepared to question British colonial policy.[136] As Michael Crowder has remarked, however:

> the persistence with which he [Tshekedi] followed his own path rather than that laid down by the Administration, his readiness to join issue with officials of all levels up to and including the Secretary of State for the Dominions, his wiliness in obstructing administrative measures with which he did not agree, especially during the first decade of his regency, can have few if any parallels in the history of British colonial Africa.[137]

Constraints and Priorities of Colonial Governance

The most outstanding feature of the British administrations in Africa during this period was how small they were. The general point of Ronald Robinson's assertion, that the colonial empire was 'a gimcrack effort run by two men and a dog',[138] has since been affirmed by statistical accounts of the number of administrators stationed in colonial governments in Africa. Most recently Helen Tilley has made detailed calculations of colonial service employment in the colonial dependencies in Africa. By 1913 – the height of pre-World War I growth – the *Colonial Office Lists* added up to 4,039 personnel divided between 2,613 in 'administration', 626 in 'technical services' and 794 in 'infrastructure'. By 1931 these figures had risen to 7,447 with 3,090 in 'administration', 1,997 in 'technical services' and 2,360 in 'infrastructure'. The 1931 numbers were not matched again during the period covered in this collection.[139] In the 1930s the comparative ratio of colonial administrators to population was 1 to 19.000 in Kenya and for Nigeria 54.000.[140] The civil administration in Sudan was equally minuscule. Thus in 1939 the Sudan Political Service had 125 senior officials. The service never exceeded 400 in its whole existence, and the average intake was only four to twelve a year.[141] Kirk-Greene rightly asserts 'That the "Thin White Line" was exiguous to the point of disbelief may be held now to have been unequivocally proved'.[142]

Despite their small numbers, the cost of European personnel was a severe drain on the resources of the colonial governments. Salaries were set in London and were exceedingly high relative to local incomes.[143] European officers were consequently expensive to field. According to recent calculations the colonial government in Nyasaland in the 1930s, for example, needed 1,600 African earners paying a head tax of 6 shillings (the average income for eighteen working days) to pay for the appointment of just one senior European clerk.[144] An implication of this was that the costs of administration represented a disproportionately high percentage of total government expenditure. Indeed, the administrative expenditure in 1925 absorbed approximately one-fourth of the total government budgets in unweight average across the British colonies in Africa.[145]

The belief that the maintenance of Britain's colonial possessions caused undue strain on the British Exchequer was a further pressure on the colonial governments.[146] As the boundaries of the empire in Africa expanded British policymakers and bureaucrats in London began to encourage the administrators in the colonies to pay for their local expenses without help from the British Treasury. This reflected the modest motivation to rule in Africa and demonstrates that the metropolitan agenda was more to maintain order than to develop the colonies. The adoption of the policy of colonial self-sufficiency was perhaps the single most important and constant structural factor in the administration of the African dependencies during this period.[147] When Sir Alfred Milner ceased to be Secretary of State for the Colonies in 1921 he made his feelings clear referring to the Colonial Office as 'the Cinderella of the great public Departments. In the annual autumnal battle of the Treasury with all the other Offices over the preparation of the Estimates, Cinderella stands a poor chance. When "economy" is in the saddle, she stands no chance at all'.[148]

What were the priorities of the colonial governments under these tight constraints in finance and personnel? David Killingray has perceptively noted that

> Effective colonial government rested on two basic pillars: firstly, the maintenance of law and order to uphold the authority of the administration; and secondly, the collection of adequate revenue with which to finance the running of the colony. Whichever way colonies were gained, whether in 'a fit of absence of mind' or by calculated conquest, and by whatever principles and methods they were governed (directly or indirectly), these two essential features predominated.[149]

These constraints had a much wider impact on administrative policy than merely stressing the need for the maintenance of law and order and the implementation of effective revenue collecting. As the sources in this collection show, such constraints also structured how objectives were pursued; confrontations and conflicts needed to be avoided or downscaled, administration of law was devolved to 'native authority' and when possible easy-to-collect revenue in the shape of custom duties were preferred over direct taxation which required more administrative resources and was prone to cause disturbances. In light of this it is clear that policies of indirect rule (in their many different varieties) were as Peter Borrough's has phrased it 'essentially an idealization of pragmatism and a rationalization of comparative impotence'.[150] Unsurprisingly, the attention and reach of the government became concentrated in geographical areas that were considered key: urban centres and rural lands rich with minerals or agriculture. This increased the pressure on colonial governments from settler minorities and other powerful groups with sectarian interests. Above all, the constraints impeded the ability and perhaps also the desire to allocate resources for health provisions (at least for Africans), for education and for other social services.

Notes

1. R. B. Pugh, 'The Colonial Office', in E. A. Benians, J. Butler and C. E. Carrington, *The Cambridge History of the British Empire, Vol. 3* (Cambridge: Cambridge University Press, 1959), pp. 711–68.
2. R. Hyam, 'Bureaucracy and "Trusteeship' in the Colonial Empire", in J. M. Brown and W. M. Roger Louis (eds), *The Oxford History of the British Empire, Vol. 4: The Twentieth Century* (Oxford: Oxford University Press, 1999), pp. 255–79, on pp. 255–8 and K. Robinson, *The Dilemmas of Trusteeship: Aspects of British Colonial Policy Between the Wars* (London: Oxford University Press, 1965), p. 15.
3. P. N. S. Mansergh, *Survey of British Commonwealth Affairs: Problems of External Policy 1931–39* (London: Oxford University Press, 1952), p. 271.
4. J. E. W. Flood quoted in M. Banton, *Administrating the Empire, 1801–1968. A Guide to the Records of the Colonial Office in the National Archives of the UK* (London: National Archives, 2008), p. 21.
5. R. V. Kubicek, *The Administration of Imperialism. Joseph Chamberlain and the Colonial Office* (Durham, NC: Duke University Press, 1969).
6. The development of the Colonial Service can be followed in the introduction and sources in the theme 'Recruitment and Training', this volume. See also A. Kirk-Greene, *On Crown Service, a History of HM Colonial and Overseas Civil Services 1837–1997* (London: I. B. Tauris, 1999).
7. *Report of a Committee on the System of Appointment in the Colonial Office and the Colonial Services*, Cmd. 3554 (1930), this volume, pp. 193–231.
8. Robinson, *Dilemmas*, p. 37.
9. Hyam, 'Bureaucracy', pp. 255–8 and Robinson, *Dilemmas*, pp. 34–5.
10. Robinson, *Dilemmas*, pp. 30–1.
11. See among others Alan W. Pims 'Colonial Finance and Native Administration', Volume 3 of this collection, pp. 269–97; Nairobi Sanitary Commission, Report, Volume 4, pp. 119–69; and W. J. Simpson 'Report on Plague in the Gold Coast 1908' Volume 4, pp. 105–19.

12. For a list of advisory reports commissioned by the Colonial Office see Banton, *Administrating the Empire*, pp. 300–2.

13. D. Sunderland, *Managing the British Empire: The Crown Agents, 1833–1914* (Woodbridge: Boydell Press, 2004); D. Sunderland, *Managing British Colonial and Post-Colonial Development. The Crown Agents 1914–74* (Woodbridge: Boydell Press, 2007).

14. J. Darwin, 'Imperialism and the Victorians: The Dynamics of Territorial Expansion.' *English Historical Review*, 112:447 (1997), pp. 614–42.

15. Hyam, 'Bureaucracy', pp. 255–79 on pp. 258–9.

16. L. H. Gann and P. Duignan, *The Rulers of British Africa, 1870–1914* (London: Croom Helm, 1978), pp. 50–3.

17. Hyam, 'Bureaucracy', pp. 258–9.

18. P. Burroughs, 'Imperial Institutions and the Government of Empire', in A. Porter (ed.), *The Oxford History of the British Empire, Vol. 3: The Nineteenth Century* (Oxford: Oxford University Press, 1999), pp. 170–97, on p. 173.

19. Gann and Duignan, *The Rulers*, pp. 64–5, 156.

20. See Ernest Eiloart, *The Land of Death*, this volume, pp. 53–61; Harry L. Stephen, 'Rebellion in Sierra Leone', Volume 3, pp. 33–41; Edmund Dene Morel, The Sierra Leone Hut Tax Disturbances, Volume 3, pp. 41–55; and F. Buxton, 'British Administration in West Africa', Volume 5, pp. 269–79.

21. Banton, *Administrating the Empire*, pp. 11–15. An interpretation of the development of the medical service in the territory can be obtained in N. M. Macfarlane, *A Record of Medical Work and of the Medical Service in Basutoland*, Volume 5, pp. 123–49.

22. Gann and Duignan, *The Rulers,* pp. 61–2.

23. B. Porter, *The Lion's Share: A Short History of British Imperialism 1850–1995*, 3rd edn (London: Harlow, 1996), p. 114.

24. Burroughs, 'Imperial Institutions', pp. 191–3.

25. See *Papers relating to the Southern Rhodesia Native Reserve Commission*, Volume 4, pp. 169–225.

26. See 'Series "A" Minutes, Conference of the Governors of the East African Dependencies', Volume 2, pp. 119–35, and H. B. Arber, Unpublished Memoir, this volume, pp. 105–13.

27. See *British Mandates for the Cameroons, Togoland and East Africa*, Volume 2, pp. 77–83; W. M. R. Louis, 'Great Britain and the African peace settlement of 1919', *American Historical Review* (1966), pp. 875–92.

28. M. Mazower, *Governing the World: The History of an Idea* (London: Penguin, 2012), pp. 118–54.

29. Robinson, *Dilemmas*, pp. 19–20.

30. See P. M. Kennedy, 'Imperial Cable Communication and Strategy, 1870–1914', *English Historical Review*, 86 (1971), pp. 728–52; R. Kubicek, 'British Expansion, Empire, and Technological Change', in Porter (ed.), *The Oxford History of the British Empire, Vol. 3: The Nineteenth Century*, pp. 247–69, on p. 259.

31. Kubicek, 'British Expansion', pp. 260–1.

32. Burroughs, 'Imperial Institutions', pp. 176–7.

33. Ibid., p. 174.

34. M. Fisher, *Indirect Rule in India: Residents and the Residency System 1764–1858* (Delhi: Oxford University Press, 1991).

35. Burroughs, 'Imperial Institutions', p. 196.

36. A. Afigbo, *The Warrant Chief: Indirect Rule in Southeastern Nigeria 1891–1929* (Bristol: Western Printing Service: 1972).

37. J. W. Cell, 'Colonial Rule', in Brown and Roger Louis (eds), *The Oxford History of the British Empire, Vol. 4*, pp. 232–54 on pp. 239–40.

38. Frederick D. Lugard, *Memorandum on Taxation*, Volume 3, pp. 133–57; M. Perham, *Lugard. The Years of Authority 1898–1945. The Second Part of the Life of Frederick Dealtry Lugard, later Lord Lugard of Arbinger, Vol. II* (London: Collins, 1960); Lord Lugard, *Political Memoranda* 3rd *with an Introduction by A. M. H. Kirk-Greene* (London: Frank Cass, 1970).

39. Sir F. D. Lugard, *The Dual Mandate in British Tropical Africa* (London: William Blackwood & Sons, 1922), p. 606.

40. See for example 'Oxford Summer School on Colonial Administration Second Session', this volume, pp. 273–91.

41. J. E. Flint, 'Frederick Lugard: the making of an autocrat, 1858-1943', in L. H. Gann and P. Duignan (eds) *African Proconsuls: European Governors in Africa* (New York: The Free Press, 1978), pp. 290–312.

42. V. Y. Mudimbe, *The Invention of Africa. Gnosis, Philosophy and the Order of Knowledge* (Bloomington, IN: Indiana University Press, 1988).

43. Margery Perham, 'A Re-Statement on Colonial Research', this volume, pp. 261–73.

44. Cell, 'Colonial Rule', on p. 235. The estimated number of Europeans does not include Southern Rhodesia and the Condominium of Sudan whose administrators were not included in the Colonial Office Lists.

45. H. Tilley, *Africa as a Living Laboratory. Empire, Development and the Problem of Scientific Knowledge* (London: Chicago University Press, 2011), pp. 333–4.

46. T. Falolo and A. D. Roberts, 'West Africa'Brown and Roger Louis (eds), *The Oxford History of the British Empire, Vol. 4: The Twentieth Century*, pp. 515-29, on p. 520.

47. D. C. Potter, *India's Political Administrators, 1919–1983* (Oxford: Oxford University Press, 1986).

48. Gann and Duignan, *The Rulers*, pp. 257–64.

49. 'The Medical Services of West African Colonies and Protectorates', this volume, pp. 61–9; and *Report of the Departmental Committee on the West African Medical Staff*, Volume 5, pp. 1–33. See also R. Johnson, '"An All-White Institution": Defending Private Practice and the Formation of the West African Medical Staff', *Medical History*, 54:2 (2010), pp. 237–54. Not until 1925 did the East African Medical Service officially bar non-Europeans from applying to the service.

50. J. E. Flint, 'Nigeria The Colonial Experience from 1880 to 1914', in L. H. Gann and P. Duignan (eds) *Colonialism in Africa, 1870–1960*, 5 vols (Cambridge: Cambridge University Press, 1969–75), vol. 1, pp. 220–60.

51. Tilley, *Living Laboratory*, p. 334.

52. Gann and Duignan, *The Rulers*, pp. 264–6.

53. Pim, 'Colonial Finace and Native Administration'.

54. W. J. A. Jones, *Memorandum on the Introduction of Direct Taxation*, Volume 3, pp. 297–345.

55. Cell, *Colonial Rule*, p. 235.

56. See, for example, *Report of the Commission of Inquiry into the Administration of Justice in Kenya*, Volume 2, pp. 263–77.

57. See K. V. Law, 'Writing White Women: Whiteness, Gender, Politics and Power in Rhodesia, c. 1950s–1980s' (unpublished PhD thesis, University of Sheffield, 2012), p. 7 and J. W. Scott, *Gender and the Politics of History*, rev. edn (New York: Columbia University Press, 1999), pp. 28–50

58. H. Callaway, *Gender, Culture and Empire: European Women in Colonial Nigeria* (Urbana, IL: University of Illinois Press, 1987).

59. R. D. Pearce, 'Violet Bourdillon: Colonial Governor's Wife', *African Affairs*, 82:327 (1983), pp. 267–77, on p. 270.

60. See for example Lord Elgin's *Circular Despatch*, this volume, pp. 89–91 and 'An Ordinance to Amend the Laws relating to Quarantine', Volume 5, pp. 69–81.

61. R. Oliver, 'Prologue: The Two Miss Perhams', *Journal of Imperial and Commonwealth History*, 19:3 (1991), pp. 21–6. on p. 22 and P. M. Pugh, 'Perham, Dame Margery Freda (1895–1982)', *ODNB*.

62. A. Kirk-Greene, 'Forging a Relationship with the Colonial Administrative Service, 1921–1939', *Journal of Imperial and Commonwealth History*, 19:3 (1991), pp. 62–82 and Pugh, 'Perham'.

63. C. Gertzel, 'Margery Perham's Image of Africa', *Journal of Imperial and Commonwealth History*, 19:3 (1991), pp. 27–44, on p. 38; D. Lavin, 'Margery Perham's Initiation into African Affairs', *Journal of Imperial and Commonwealth History*, 19:3 (1991), pp. 45–61 on p. 55; Pugh, 'Perham' and K. Robinson, 'Margery Perham and the Colonial Office', *Journal of Imperial and Commonwealth History*, 19:3 (1991) pp. 185–96 on p. 189.

64. D. Sunderland, *Economic Development of Africa, 1880–1939*, 5 vols (London: Pickering & Chatto, 2011), vol. 1, p. vii.

65. C. Newbury, 'Great Britain and the Partition of Africa, 1870–1914', in Porter (ed.), *The Oxford History of the British Empire, Vol. 3: The Nineteenth Century*, pp. 624–50, on p. 624.

66. Ibid., pp. 624–6.

67. Harry Johnston, Uganda Proectorate, Ordinance No. 8 of 1902 King's African Rifles, Volume 2, pp. 47–77.

68. D. Killingray, 'The Maintenance of Law and Order in British Colonial Africa', *African Affairs*, 85:340 (1986), pp. 411–37, on p 420.

69. C. P. Lucas (ed.), *The Empire at War Vol. 1–5, Vol. IV Africa* (Oxford: H. Milford, Oxford University Press, 1924); H. Strachan, *The First World War in Africa* (Oxford: Oxford University Press, 2004).

70. 'Memorandum Showing the Progress and Development in the Colonial Empire', this volume, pp. 117–39.

71. Colonial Office Conference, Summary of Proceedings, 'Recruitment and Training of Colonial Civil Servants', this volume, pp. 163–9; W. Ormsby-Gore, Speech for a Meeting, this volume, pp. 169–75; J. M. Hodge, *Triumph of the Expert. Agrarian Doctrines of Development and the Legacies of British Colonialism* (Athens, OH: Ohio University Press, 2007).

72. Kirk-Greene, *Crown Service*, pp. 21–2.

73. *Tanganyika Terriortory. Native Administration*, Volume 2, pp. 173–203; E. R. Feingold, 'Decolonising Justice: A History of the High Court of Tanganyika c. 1920–1971' (D. Phil thesis, University of Oxford, 2011)

74. *Minutes of the Meeting of the Joint Conference of the Provincial Councils held at Saltpond in April, 1932*, Volume 3, pp. 345–89.

75. Newbury, 'Partition' pp. 636–8.

76. A. G. Hopkins, *An Economic History of West Africa* (London: Longman, 1973), pp. 164–5.

77. M. Lynn, *Commerce and Economic Change in West Africa: The Palm Oil Trade in the Nineteenth Century* (Cambridge: Cambridge University Press, 1997), p. 3.

78. J. D. Hargreaves, *West Africa Partitioned, Vol. II. The Elephant and Grass* (London: Macmillan, 1985).

79. *Report on the Administration of the Niger Coast Protectorate*, Volume 3, pp. 1–9; J. Flint and G. S. Graham, *Sir George Goldie and the Making of Nigeria* (London: Oxford University Press, 1960).

80. Royal Niger Company (1899), Volume 2, pp. 1–23.

81. T. Falola and M. M. Heaton, *A History of Nigeria* (Cambridge: Cambridge University Press, 2008), pp. 104–5.

82. T. Falola and A. D. Roberts, 'West Africa', in Brown and Roger Louis (eds), *The Oxford History of the British Empire, Vol. 4: The Twentieth Century*, pp. 515–29, on pp. 515–20.

83. Killingray, 'Law and Order', pp. 420–4.

84. Morel, *The Sierra Leone Hut-Tax Disturbances*, Volume 3, pp. 41–55; Confidential Despatch to Colonal Office on Toll Collection in Abeokuta and Ibadan, Volume 3, pp. 55–105; B. Porter, *Critics of Empire. British Radicals and the Imperial Challenge* (London: Macmillan, 1966) pp. 240–66; N. Owen, 'Critics of Empire in Britain', in Brown and Roger Louis (eds), *The Oxford History of the British Empire, Vol. 4*, pp. 188–212, on pp. 188–92.

85. Confidential Despatch to Colonial Office on Toll Collection in Abeokuta and Ibadan, Volume 3, pp. 55–105.

86. J. L. Ausman, 'The Disturbances in Abeokuta', *Canadian Journal of African Studies*, 5:1 (1971), pp. 45–60.

87. Falola and Roberts, 'West Africa', pp. 515–20.

88. W. M Hailey, *The Future of Colonial Peoples* (London: Oxford University Press, 1944), pp. 45–6, quoted in Cell, 'Colonial Rule', p. 237.

89. Lugard, *Administration of Tropical Colonies*, Volume 3, pp. 105–33; Lugard, *Memorandum on Taxation*, Volume 3, pp. 133–57; Girouard, 'Political Memo', Volume 3, pp. 157–69; Cameron, *Tanganyika Territory*, Volume 3, pp. 169–89; and Bourdillon, 'The Appointment of Revenue and Duties as between the Central Government and Native Administration', Volume 3, pp. 189–207.

90. Burroughs, 'Imperial Institutions', p. 194.

91. J. Lonsdale, 'East Africa', in Brown and Roger Louis (eds), *The Oxford History of the British Empire, Vol. 4: The Twentieth Century*, pp. 530–44 on p. 532; and R. M. A. van Zwanenberg, *Colonial Capitalism and Labour in Kenya: 1919–1939* (Nairobi: East African Literature Bureau, 1975).

92. See 'Memorandum on the Constitution of the Native Government of the Buganda Kingdom', Volume 2, pp. 35–47.

93. B. Berman and J. Lonsdale, *Unhappy Valley, Conflict in Kenya and Africa: Book One: State and Class* (London: James Curry, 1991), pp. 13–39; M. Mamdani, *Politics and Class Formation in Uganda* (London: Heinemann, 1977) and Newbury, 'Partition', p. 644.

94. R. Hyam, *Britain's Imperial Century, 1815–1914: A Study of Empire and Expansion* (Basingstoke: Macmillan, 1993), p. 310.

95. J. Lonsdale, 'East Africa', in Brown and Roger Louis (eds), *The Oxford History of the British Empire, Vol. 4: The Twentieth Century*, pp. 530–44, on p. 533.

96. J. Illife, *Africans: The History of a Continent* (Cambridge: Cambridge University Press, 1995), p. 199.

97. Lonsdale, 'East Africa', p. 533.

98. R. J. Reid, *A History of Modern Africa* (Oxford: Wiley-Blackwell, 2009), pp. 180–2.

99. See *East Africa Protectorate. Correspondence*, Volume 2, pp. 273–323.

100. Lonsdale, 'East Africa', p. 534.

101. See Devonshire Declaration, *Indians in Africa*, Volume 2, pp. 135–53.

102. 'Series "A" Minutes: Conference of the Governors of the East African Dependencies', Volume 2, pp. 119–35.

103. Hyam, 'Bureaucracy', pp. 267–9.
104. Lonsdale, 'East Africa', p. 534.
105. P. J. Cain and A. G. Hopkins, *British Imperialism 1688–2000*, 2 edn (1993; Harrow: Pearson Education Limited, 2002), pp. 312–7; A. Lutfi Al-Sayyid-Marsot, 'The British Occupation of Egypt from 1882', in Porter (ed.), *The Oxford History of the British Empire, Vol. 3: The Nineteenth Century*, pp. 651–64.
106. Al-Sayyid-Marsot, 'The British Occupation of Egypt', p. 654.
107. E. Goldberg, 'Peasants in Revolt: Egypt 1919', *International Journal of Middle East Studies*, 24:2 (1992), pp. 265–80; J. D. Hargreaves, *Decolonization in Africa* (Harlow: Longman, 1996), pp. 6–7.
108. Newbury, 'Great Britain and the Partition of Africa', p. 643; R. Owen, *Lord Cromer – Victorian Imperialist, Edwardian Proconsul* (Oxford: Oxford University Press 2004).
109. L. Mak, 'More than Officers and Officials: Britons in Occupied Egypt 1882–1922', *Journal of Imperial and Commonwealth History*, 39:1 (2011), pp. 21–46, on pp. 23–5.
110. R. L. Tignor, 'The "Indianisation" of the Egypt Administration under British Rule', *American Historical Review*, 68:3 (1963), pp. 273–94.
111. M. Hollings, *The Life of Sir Colin Scott-Moncrieff* (London: John Murray, 1917).
112. Earl of Cromer, *Reports by His Majesty's Agent*, Volume 3, pp. 207–25.
113. P. J. Cain 'Character and Imperialism: The British Financial Administration of Egypt, 1878–1914', *Journal of Imperial and Commonwealth History*, 34:2 (2006), pp. 177–200.
114. Al-Sayyid-Marsot, 'The British Occupation of Egypt', p. 661.
115. For a recent interpretation see, T. Tvedt, 'Hydrology and Empire: The Nile, Water Imperialism and the Partition of Africa', *Journal of Imperial and Commonwealth History*, 39:2 (2011), pp. 173–94, on pp. 180–4.
116. 'Agreement between Her Britannic Majesty's Government and the Government of His Highness the Khedive of Egypt', Volume 2, pp. 83–7; M. Daly, *Empire on the Nile. The Anglo-Egyptian Sudan 1898–1934* (Cambridge: Cambridge University Press, 1986), pp. 11–18.
117. Daly, *Empire on the Nile*, p. 313.
118. *Notes on the Legislation of the Anglo-Egyptian Sudan*, Volume 2, pp. 87–91.
119. M. Daly, *Imperial Sudan. The Anglo-Egyptian Condominium, 1934–56* (Cambridge: Cambridge University Press, 1991), p. 3.
120. J. L. Maffey, 'Devolution in Native Administration', Volume 2, pp. 203–7.
121. Cell, 'Colonial Rule', p. 241.
122. A. M. H. Kirk-Greene, *Britain's Imperial Administrators, 1858–1966* (London: Macmillan Press 2000), pp. 164–201; R. Collins, 'The Sudan Political Service. A Portrait of the Imperialists', *African Affairs*, 71:284 (1972), pp. 293–303.
123. Kirk-Greene, 'Britain's Imperial Administrators', pp. 165–6.
124. Daly, *Imperial Sudan*, pp. 4–5. Arber, Unpublished Memoir, this volume, pp. 105–13 provides a personal memoir of the experiences of an Assistant District Commissioner during the latter part of the period.
125. Daly, *Empire on the Nile*, pp. 452–3.
126. British–South African relations during this period are well-covered in R. Hyam and P. Henshaw, *The Lion and the Springbok: Britain and South Africa since the Boer War* (Cambridge: Cambridge University Press, 2003).
127. Newbury, 'Partition', p. 629.
128. See ibid., pp. 628–32 and I. Phimister, *An Economic and Social History of Zimbabwe, 1890–1940* (London: Longman, 1988), pp. 4–29.

129. Burroughs, 'Imperial Institutions', p. 194.
130. I. Phimister, 'Rhodes, Rhodesia and the Rand', *Journal of Southern African Studies*, 1:1 (1974), pp. 74–90 on p. 74.
131. See British South Africa Company, *Administration Revenue and Expenditure*, Volume 3, pp. 23–7.
132. See See *Settling Farmers in the Matapo Valley*, Volume 4, pp. 55–9 and Fox, *The British South Africa Company Memorandum*, Volume 4, pp. 59–105.
133. Figures from P. J. M. McEwan, 'The European Population of Southern Rhodesia', *Civilisations*, 13:4 (1963), pp. 429–44, on p. 429.
134. S. Marks, 'Southern Africa', in Brown and Roger Louis (eds), *The Oxford History of the British Empire, Vol. 4: The Twentieth Century*, pp. 545–73, on p. 552.
135. Ibid., p. 548.
136. 'Customs Tariff', Volume 3, pp. 27–33.
137. M. Crowder, 'Tshekedi Khama and Opposition to the British Administration of the Bechuanaland Protectorate, 1926–1936', *Journal of African History*, 26:2 (1985), pp. 193–214, on p. 194.
138. Quoted in A H. M. Kirk-Greene, 'The Thin White Line: The Size of the British Colonial Service in Africa', *African Affairs*, 79:314 (1980), pp. 25–44, on p. 26.
139. H. Tilley, *Living*, pp. 333–67. Tilley's category of administration includes officers in the executive branch, district and provincial officers, juridical staff, police officers, education and customs.
140. Cell, 'Colonial Rule', p. 232.
141. A H. M. Kirk-Greene, 'The Sudan Political Service: A Profile in the Sociology of Imperialism', *International Journal of African Studies*, 15 (1982), pp. 21–48.
142. Kirk-Greene, 'The Thin White Line', p. 40.
143. L. A. Gardner, *Taxing Colonial Africa. The Political Economy of British Imperialism* (Oxford: Oxford University Press, 2012), pp. 9–11.
144. E. Frankema, 'Colonial Taxation and Government Spending in British Africa 1880–1940. Maximizing Revenue or Minimizing Effort?', *Explorations in Economic History*, 48 (2011), pp. 136–49, on p. 143.
145. Ibid., p. 142.
146. Cain and Hopkins, *British Imperialism*, pp. 583–5.
147. Gardner, *Taxing Colonial Africa*, pp. 3–5.
148. Robinson, *Dilemmas*, p. 32.
149. Killingray, 'Law and Order', p. 411.
150. Burroughs, 'Imperial Institutions', p. 196.

BIBLIOGRAPHY

Afigbo, A., *The Warrant Chief: Indirect Rule in South-Eastern Nigeria 1891–1929* (Bristol: Western Printing Service, 1972).

Al-Sayyid-Marsot, L. L., 'The British Occupation of Egypt from 1882', in A. Porter (ed.), *The Oxford History of the British Empire, Vol. 3: The Nineteenth Century* (Oxford: Oxford University Press, 1999), pp. 651–64.

Ausman, J. L., 'The Disturbances in Abeokuta', *Canadian Journal of African Studies*, 5:1 (1971), pp. 45–60.

Banton, M., *Administrating the Empire, 1801–1968. A Guide to the Records of the Colonial Office in the National Archives of the UK* (London: National Archives, 2008).

Berman, B., and J. Lonsdale, *Unhappy Valley, Conflict in Kenya and Africa: Book One: State and Class* (London: James Curry, 1991).

Burroughs, P., 'Imperial Institutions and the Government of Empire', in A. Porter (ed.), *The Oxford History of the British Empire, Vol. 3: The Nineteenth Century* (Oxford: Oxford University Press, 1999), pp. 170–97.

Cain, P. J., 'Character and Imperialism: The British Financial Administration of Egypt, 1878–1914', *Journal of Imperial and Commonwealth History*, 34:2 (2006), pp. 177–200.

Cain, P. J., and A. G. Hopkins, *British Imperialism 1688–2000*, 2nd edn (Harrow: Pearson Education Limited, 2002).

Callaway, H., *Gender, Culture and Empire: European Women in Colonial Nigeria* (Urbana, IL: University of Illinois Press, 1987).

Cell, J. W., 'Colonial Rule', in J. M. Brown and W. M. Roger Louis (eds), *The Oxford History of the British Empire, Vol. 4: The Twentieth Century* (Oxford: Oxford University Press, 1999) pp. 232–54.

Collins, R., 'The Sudan Political Service. A Portrait of the Imperialists', *African Affairs*, 71:284 (1972), pp. 293–303.

Crowder, M., 'Tshekedi Khama and Opposition to the British Administration of the Bechuanaland Protectorate, 1926–1936', *Journal of African History*, 26:2 (1985), pp. 193–214.

Daly, M., *Empire on the Nile. The Anglo-Egyptian Sudan 1898–1934* (Cambridge: Cambridge University Press, 1986).

—, *Imperial Sudan. The Anglo-Egyptian Condominium, 1934–56* (Cambridge: Cambridge University Press, 1991).

Darwin, J., 'Imperialism and the Victorians: The Dynamics of Territorial Expansion', *English Historical Review*, 112:447 (1997), pp. 614–42.

Frankema, E., 'Colonial Taxation and Government Spending in British Africa 1880–1940. Maximizing Revenue or Minimizing Effort?', *Explorations in Economic History*, 48 (2011), pp. 136–49.

Fisher, M., *Indirect Rule in India: Residents and the Residency System 1764–1858* (Delhi: Oxford University Press, 1991).

Flint, J. E., 'Nigeria The Colonial Experience from 1880 to 1914', in L. H. Gann and P. Duignan (eds), *Colonialism in Africa, 1870–1960*, 5 vols (Cambridge: Cambridge University Press, 1969–75), vol. 1, pp. 220–60.

—, 'Frederick Lugard: The Making of an Autocrat, 1858–1943', in L. H. Gann and P. Duignan (eds,) *African Proconsuls: European Governors in Africa* (New York: Free Press, 1978), pp. 290–312.

Flint J., and G. S. Graham, *Sir George Goldie and the Making of Nigeria* (London: Oxford University Press, 1960).

Falola T., and M. N. Heaton, *A History of Nigeria* (Cambridge: Cambridge University Press, 2008).

Falolo T., and A. D. Roberts, 'West Africa', in J. M. Brown and W. M. Roger Louis (eds), *The Oxford History of the British Empire, Vol. 4: The Twentieth Century* (Oxford: Oxford University Press, 1999), pp. 515–29.

Feingold, E. R., 'Decolonising Justice: A History of the high court of Tanganyika c. 1920–1971' (unpublished D. Phil thesis, Oxford University, 2011).

Gann L. H. and P. Duignan, *The Rulers of British Africa 1870–1914* (London: Croom Helm, 1978).

Gardner, L. A., *Taxing Colonial Africa. The Political Economy of British Imperialism* (Oxford: Oxford University Press, 2012).

Gertzel, C., 'Margery Perham's Image of Africa', *Journal of Imperial and Commonwealth History*, 19:3 (1991), pp. 27–44.

Goldberg, E. 'Peasants in Revolt: Egypt 1919', *International Journal of Middle East Studies*, 24:2 (1992), pp. 265–80.

Hargreaves, J. D., *West Africa Partitioned, Vol. II. The Elephant and Grass* (London: Macmillan, 1985).

—, *Decolonization in Africa* (Harlow: Longman, 1996).

Hodge, J. M., *Triumph of the Expert. Agrarian Doctrines of Development and the Legacies of British Colonialism* (Athens, OH: Ohio University Press, 2007).

Hollings, M., *The Life of Sir Colin Scott-Moncrieff* (London: John Murray, 1917).

Hopkins, A. G., *An Economic History of West Africa* (London: Longman, 1973).

Hyam, R., 'Bureaucracy and "Trusteeship" in the Colonial Empire', in J. M. Brown and W. M. Roger Louis (eds), *The Oxford History of the British Empire, Vol. 4: The Twentieth Century* (Oxford: Oxford University Press, 1999), pp. 255–79.

—, *Britain's Imperial Century, 1815–1914: A Study of Empire and Expansion* (Basingstoke: Macmillan, 1993).

Hyam R., and P. Henshaw, *The Lion and the Springbok: Britain and South Africa since the Boer War* (Cambridge: Cambridge University Press, 2003).

Hodge, J. M., *Triumph of the Expert. Agrarian Doctrines of Development and the Legacies of British Colonialism* (Athens, OH: Ohio University Press, 2007).

Illife, J., *Africans: The History of a Continent* (Cambridge: Cambridge University Press, 1995).

Johnson, R., '"An All-White Institution": Defending Private Practice and the Formation of the West African Medical Staff', *Medical History*, 54:2 (2010), pp. 237–54.

Kennedy, P. M., 'Imperial Cable Communication and Strategy, 1870–1914', *English Historical Review*, 86 (1971), pp. 728–52.

Killingray, D., 'The Maintenance of Law and Order in British Colonial Africa', *African Affairs*, 85:340 (1986), pp. 411–37.

Kirk-Greene, A., 'Forging a Relationship with the Colonial Administrative Service, 1921–1939', *Journal of Imperial and Commonwealth History*, 19:3 (1991), pp. 62–82.

—, *On Crown Service, a history of HM Colonial and Overseas Civil Services 1837–1997* (London: I. B. Tauris 1999).

—, 'The Thin White Line: The Size of the British Colonial Service in Africa', *African Affairs*, 79:314 (1980), pp. 25–44.

—, 'The Sudan Political Service: A Profile in the Sociology of Imperialism', *International Journal of African Studies*, 15, (1982), pp. 21-48.

—, *Britain's Imperial Administrators, 1858–1966* (London: Macmillan Press, 2000).

Kubicek, R., 'British Expansion, Empire, and Technological Change', in A. Porter (ed.), *The Oxford History of the British Empire, Vol. 3: The Nineteenth Century* (Oxford: Oxford University Press, 1999), pp. 247–69.

—, *The Administration of Imperialism. Joseph Chamberlain and the Colonial Office* (Durham NC: Duke University Press, 1969).

Lavin, D., 'Margery Perham's Initiation into African Affairs', *Journal of Imperial and Commonwealth History*, 19:3 (1991), pp. 45–61.

Law, K. V., 'Writing White Women: Whiteness, Gender, Politics and Power in Rhodesia, c. 1950s–1980s' (unpublished PhD thesis, University of Sheffield, 2012).

Lonsdale, J., 'East Africa', in J. M. Brown and W. M. Roger Louis (eds), *The Oxford History of the British Empire, Vol. 4: The Twentieth Century* (Oxford: Oxford University Press, 1999), pp. 530–44.

Louis, W. M. R., 'Great Britain and the African Peace Settlement of 1919', *American Historical Review* (1966), pp. 875–92.

Lucas, C. P. (ed.), *The Empire at War Vol. 1–5, Vol. IV Africa* (Oxford: Oxford University Press, 1924).

Lugard, F. D., *The Dual Mandate in British Tropical Africa* (London: William Blackwood & Sons, 1922).

Lugard, Lord *Political Memoranda* 3rd *with an Introduction by A. M. H. Kirk Greene* (London: Frank Cass, 1970).

Lynn, M., *Commerce and Economic Change in West Africa: The Palm Oil Trade in the Nineteenth Century* (Cambridge: Cambridge University Press, 1997).

Mak, L. 'More than Officers and Officials: Britons in Occupied Egypt 1882–1922', *Journal of Imperial and Commonwealth History*, 39:1 (2011), pp. 21–46.

Mamdani, M., *Politics and Class Formation in Uganda* (London: Heinemann, 1977).

Mansergh, P. N. S., *Survey of British Commonwealth Affairs: Problems of External Policy 1931–39* (London: Oxford University Press, 1952).

Marks, S., 'Southern Africa', in J. M. Brown and W. M. Roger Louis (eds), *The Oxford History of the British Empire, Vol. 4: The Twentieth Century* (Oxford: Oxford University Press, 1999), pp. 545–73.

Mazower, M., *Governing the World. The History of an Idea* (London: Penguin, 2012).

McEwan, P. J. M., 'The European Population of Southern Rhodesia', *Civilisations*, 13:4 (1963), pp. 429–44.

Mudimbe, V. Y., *The Invention of Africa. Gnosis, Philosophy and the Order of Knowledge* (Bloominton, IN: India University Press, 1988).

Newbury, C., 'Great Britain and the Partition of Africa, 1870–1914', in A. Porter (ed.), *The Oxford History of the British Empire, Vol. 3: The Nineteenth Century* (Oxford: Oxford University Press, 1999), pp. 624–50.

Oliver, R., 'Prologue: The Two Miss Perhams', *Journal of Imperial and Commonwealth History*, 19:3 (1991), pp. 21–6.

Owen, N., 'Critics of Empire in Britain', in J. M Brown and W. M. Roger Louis (eds), *The Oxford History of the British Empire, Vol. IV* (Oxford: Oxford University Press, 1999), pp. 188–212.

Owen, R. *Lord Cromer – Victorian Imperialist, Edwardian Proconsul* (Oxford: Oxford University Press, 2004).

Pearce, R. D., 'Violet Bourdillon: Colonial Governor's Wife', *African Affairs*, 82:327 (1983), pp. 267–77.

Perham, M., *Lugard. The Years of Authority 1898–1945. The Second Part of the Life of Frereick Dealtry Lugard, later Lord Lugard of Arbinger, Vol. II* (London: Collins, 1960).

Phimister, I. R., *An Economic and Social History of Zimbabwe, 1890–1940* (London: Longman, 1988).

—, 'Rhodes, Rhodesia and the Rand', *Journal of Southern African Studies*, 1:1 (1974), pp. 74–90.

Potter, D. C., *India's Political Administrators, 1919–1983* (Oxford: Oxford University Press, 1986).

Porter, B., *Critics of Empire. British Radicals and the Imperial Challenge* (London: Macmillan, 1966).

—, *The Lion's Share: A Short History of British Imperialism 1850–1995*, 3rd edn (London: Harlow, 1996).

Pugh, R. B., 'The Colonial Office', in E. A. Benians, J. Butler and C. E. Carrington, *The Cambridge History of the British Empire, Vol. 3* (Cambridge: Cambridge University Press, 1959), pp. 711–68.

Reid, R. J., *A History of Modern Africa* (Oxford: Wiley-Blackwell, 2009).

Robinson, K., *The Dilemmas of Trusteeship: Aspects of British Colonial Policy Between the Wars* (London: Oxford University Press, 1965).

—, 'Margery Perham and the Colonial Office', *Journal of Imperial and Commonwealth History*, 19:3 (1991), pp. 185–96.

Scott, J. W., *Gender and the Politics of History*, rev. edn (New York: Columbia University Press, 1999).

Strachan, H., *The First World War in Africa* (Oxford: Oxford University Press, 2004).

Sunderland, D., *Managing the British Empire: The Crown Agents, 1833–1914* (Woodbridge: Boydell Press, 2004).

—, *Managing British Colonial and Post-colonial Development. The Crown Agents 1914–74* (Woodbridge: Boydell Press, 2007).

—, *Economic Development of Africa, 1880–1939*, 5 vols (London: Pickering & Chatto, 2011), vol. 1: Agriculture: Non-Food and Drink.

Tignor, R. L., 'The "Indianisation" of the Egypt Administration under British Rule', *American Historical Review*, 68:3 (1963), pp. 273–94.

Tilley, H., *Africa as a Living Laboratory. Empire, Development and the Problem of Scientific Knowledge* (London: Chicago University Press, 2011).

Tvedt, T., 'Hydrology and Empire: The Nile, Water Imperialism and the Partition of Africa', *Journal of Imperial and Commonwealth History*, 39:2 (2011), pp. 173–94.

EDITORIAL NOTE

Sources have been chosen to reflect the broad themes of administration in the period under consideration. The remit of the project was to reproduce sources which are not easily available in print or electronically. We have endeavoured to provide examples of unpublished manuscript sources where possible. Key sources regarding Britain's colonial administration in Africa have been reproduced regardless of their availability elsewhere to uphold the coherence of our collection. To reduce source length where necessary, tables of contents, indices, sections not relevant to a topic, repetitions and illustrations have all been deleted. Omissions are marked by an ellipsis in square brackets ([...]) and original page breaks are marked by a forward slash (/). Typographical errors in the original texts are reproduced verbatim in this collection and indicated by a following [*sic*].

RECRUITMENT AND TRAINING

The decades covered in this collection saw the establishment of an extensive British colonial empire in Africa, administered by a relatively small number of officials. Day-to-day administration relied heavily on non-Europeans how-ever the higher echelons of the service were reserved for a small cadre of white officials mainly of British descent. The sources reproduced in the first volume concern the recruitment and training of this personnel for the colonial admin-istrations in Africa.

Potential administrators came from a variety of sources organized under the auspices of a number of individual bodies. The most important was the Colonial Service which was established and consolidated over the course of these dec-ades. In recruitment it remained a separate organization from the Indian Civil Service and from the Colonial Office and, unlike these bodies, the Colonial Service did not rely on written formal examination of candidates but rather on recommendations and personal interviews. This patronage-based system mixed meritocracy with ideals of 'leadership', personal 'fitness' and that most elusive of traits: 'character'. This favoured candidates with public school and Oxbridge backgrounds and the Colonial Service found most of its candidates among the sons of the upper-middle classes.[1]

In addition to the Colonial Service the administration of Britain's African empire relied on other sources. The Sudan Political Service (SPS) remained an autonomous organization from its establishment in 1899 until its eventual closure in 1956. Moreover, specific groups such as nurses and engineers were recruited from outside the Colonial Service. The military constituted another important source of officers for civil administrations in Africa while chartered Companies recruited their own personnel through other channels.[2] As discussed in detail in the General Introduction above, the colonial administrations in Africa were thinly stretched and, despite a notable influx of technical personnel in the inter-war years, this remained the case during the period covered in this collection.[3]

Training and guidance for the colonial administration in Africa came in a variety of forms during this period. The sources on training selected in this vol-ume provide information on training and educational activities for probationers to governmental positions and also shed light on training initiatives emanating from individual colonial administrations. The selection moreover reflects the criticisms levied at recruitment and training policies as well as the influence of the discipline of anthropology on administrative training and ideologies during the final years covered in the collection.

The first three sources in the volume provide information on the system and terms of appointment into the Colonial Service as it developed during the first decades of the twentieth century. In comparison with the Indian Civil Service and the Sudan Political Service, the establishment of the Colonial Service as an institution and as a structured career path was a piecemeal process. An important element in the gradual formation of an identifiable Colonial Service was the publication of the annual *Colonial Office List*. The series appeared from 1862 to 1966 and listed the individual members of the civil establishment of individual colonies as well as a range of details concerning the organization of colonial administrations.[4] From 1900 the lists also contained a section on 'Information as to Colonial Appointments' intended for applicants seeking employment with colonial administrations. This section is reproduced as the first source in the volume. It provides information on the distribution of responsibilities between the Colonial Office and colonial governments, particularly in Africa where most future appointments were anticipated. The 'Information as to Colonial Appointments' section became a permanent feature in the *Colonial Office Lists* and source two reproduces the section published in 1939. The stable format of the section makes it possible to gauge developments, continuity and changes in Colonial Service appointments and training during the first four decades of the twentieth century. The third source is taken from *Regulations for H.M. Colonial Service* published in 1911. Regulations for colonial service were drawn up and published as early as 1837[5] and by 1911 the regulations had developed to provide information on the legislative organization of governments, terms of employment, and the relations between the Colonial Office and individual colonial governments.

Despite the existence of official regulations and information on appointments the introduction of formal examinations for the Colonial Service was slow and partial compared with the Indian Civil Service and the Home Service. Partly due to this the system of recruitment into the Colonial Service was subject to much complaint throughout this period.[6] Ernest Eiloart's *The Land of Death* provides an early example of such criticism. In this pamphlet published in 1884 addressed to Members of Parliament, the solicitor Eiloart delivered a vehement and highly personalized attack on the government of the Gold Coast and particularly the system employed in the appointments of officers. According to Eiloart administrative officers recruited in the colony itself were 'for the most part divided between the Governor's relations and his sycophants' while in the appointments made by the Colonial Office for Gold Coast service the 'old patronage system still flourishes in all its iniquity'. Forms of patronage were, indeed, ingrained at the Colonial Office with all forms and files concerning appointments tellingly marked with the headline 'patronage' until reforms where introduced in the late 1920s.[7]

The nascent Colonial Service was transformed during the last decade of the nineteenth century by the need for personnel for the expanding empire in Africa which came to account for nearly three quarters of the Colonial Service thereafter. This development coincided with Joseph Chamberlain's tenure as Secretary of State for the Colonies from 1895 to 1903. Chamberlain's notion of 'constructive imperialism' emphasized a mission 'to cultivate the undeveloped estates' of the Empire for the prosperity of Britain and to the advantage of the inhabitants of the colonies. In this view private trade and industry were the driving forces of economic development, but for this to flourish grants-in-aid from Britain were required in particular for infrastructural development.[8] In most cases these plans were frustrated by the powerful Treasury but Chamberlain was more successful in reorganizing the Colonial Service which according to a report he commissioned numbered 1,500 officers by 1899.[9] Medical officers accounted for 447 of these appointments and this reflects Chamberlain's desire to reform the recruitment, training and organization of the medical services in the colonial empire.[10] An example can be seen with the formation in 1902 of the *Unified West African Medical Service* (WAMS) which was established to enhance recruitment of European personnel for the service in the West African colonies. Source five is a critical assessment of the formation of the WAMS with a focus on the terms of employment for medical officers. It was published in 1902 in the *British Medical Journal*, which during the ensuing decades became a platform for continuous critical debates concerning the organization of colonial medical services in West Africa and elsewhere.[11] The issue of health and recruitment for the infamous 'white man's grave' of West Africa also features prominently in the source that follows, *The West African Pocket Book. A Guide for Newly-Appointed Government Officers* published in 1906.

During the first decades of the twentieth century administrators occasionally transferred between public and private employment. Notably, a recognizable contribution to the evolving Colonial Service was constituted by a number of officials from chartered company administrations who transferred to government employment when the Crown replaced company rule.[12] Similarly retired government officials often engaged in private businesses in their former administrative territories. Lord Elgin's *Circular Despatch* is a despatch on this matter issued in 1907 to colonial Governors by the Secretary of State for the Colonies. The source is testament to the ambivalent official attitude that was adopted in a situation when boundaries between public and private employment were not clearly established.

Not all administrative personnel were recruited into the Colonial Service. During the period covered in this collection positions as engineers, architects, town planners and other technical personnel were filled through the quasi-governmental Office of the Crown Agents.[13] Nurses constituted another group recruited outside the Colonial Service during this period. Nursing services were procured through the Colonial Nursing Association (CNA) formed in 1896 with the aim of providing nurses to care for British colonial expatriates. It was funded privately through subscriptions and the CNA, which in 1919 became the Overseas Nursing Association, acted as a recruitment agency for the Colonial Office. By 1938 it had supplied 2743 nurses for service overseas.[14] The following source is the tenth annual report of the CNA and includes also the sixth annual report of the Scottish branch of the CNA.

Recruitment for service in Sudan is the subject of the source that follows. It is an unpublished memoir by H. B. Archer on his time in the Sudan Political Service which he joined in 1928. The Sudan Political Service was launched after the Anglo-Egyptian Condominium of Sudan was declared in 1899 and it existed until the dissolution of the Condominium in 1956.[15] In the words of the Civil Secretary of the Sudan from 1926 to 1934 (and influential SPS chronicler) Sir Harold MacMichael, 'The method of recruitment of civilians for the "Political Service" was, from first to last, sensible and informal with no competitive examination and fixed rules.'[16] Instead of formal examination selections were made by a board consisting of Sudan Political Service members on leave and the criterions were based on a 'Cromerian' ethos of marked athleticism, good social class and a fair mind.[17] The officers of Sudan Political Service filled up the highest positions in the political administration of the Condominium – from the Governor-General to most positions as District Commissioners and Assistant District Commissioners – with three quarters of the 400 men recruited into the Sudan Political Service coming from Oxford or Cambridge. Among them was Archer whose memoir provides a personal account of the educational background, selection process for the Sudan Political Service and his work in the different positions he held over the course of his career.

The growing need for imperial officers in Africa in the decades around the turn of the century created the impetus that established the Colonial Service as a distinct institution and career path. At the outbreak of the First World War Colonial Service officers totalled 1,400 serving in Africa.[18] The developments of recruitment and training for administrative service in Africa were, however, in many respects more far reaching during the 1920s. Changes were driven by two connected developments: first, a steep rise in recruitment for service in Africa (which now also included mandated territories) where the administrations had lost many European officers due to the war effort and secondly, the influx of experts in technical and scientific fields such as forestry, surveying and agriculture. This created the drive resulting in the unification of the Colonial Service which was the main organizational development of the Colonial Service during the 1930s.[19] A cluster of sources cover these developments. 'Memorandum Showing the Progress and Development in the Colonial Empire' provides information on the institutional changes in colonial training and recruitment during the transitional period from 1924 to 1928 which among other developments saw the establishment of a Dominions Office separate from the Colonial Office. The preceding source is a manuscript note by Sir Ralph Furse on 'Liaison with Universities in the Self-Governing Dominions'. The manuscript concerns the Dominion Selection Scheme first suggested in 1920 as an attempt to expand the recruitment base for the Colonial Service. Initially established with Canada in 1923 the scheme was extended to Australia and New Zealand in 1928 and eventually also to South Africa.[20] The scheme proved successful in the long term – it continued for more than forty years – however, Furse's note outlines the problems that existed with the scheme which initially failed to deliver the anticipated number and quality of candidates.

Ralph Furse is regarded as the architect of the modern Colonial Service. As Assistant Private Secretary (appointments) from 1910 he was highly influential during the transitional period of 1920s. In 1931 he was appointed director of recruitment in the newly established personnel division of the Colonial Office, a position he held until his retirement in 1948.[21] During these years Furse was the driving force in the establishment and running of an organized system of appointment that based selections of officers on references and interviews rather than written examinations.[22] Furse is the author of source twelve, a note on the system of appointment in the Colonial Service from the armistice to 1927.

Furse's note is the first of three sources relating to the Colonial Office Conference held in London in May 1927. The conference was the first of its kind to encompass the whole of the colonial empire. It followed the Imperial Conference held the previous year which defined the constitutional relations between Great Britain and the Dominions as autonomous communities within the British Empire. The Colonial Office Conference brought together Colonial Office officials, Governors or other representatives from different colonial governments with the expressed aim to foster collaboration between the governments and the Colonial Office and to raise the awareness of the colonial empire as a distinct entity separate from the Dominions and India.[23] The source that follows is a memorandum by the Governor of the Gold Coast, Sir Gordon Guggisberg, presented at the conference on the 'local' system of training for new recruits entering service in Gold Coast colonial government. Guggisberg was widely regarded as an authority on the training and education of African and European personnel,[24] and his memorandum urged that substantial resources should be allocated to train of European personnel in local issues and vernacular languages upon arrival in any colony. By outlining the system of training in the Gold Coast the source supplements Furse's note on the metropolitan selection and training criteria and highlights the tensions implicit between these points of view. Source fourteen is the summary of the conference proceedings on the issue of recruitment and training.

During the 1920s a key concern was the organization of the recruitment and training of scientific and technical personnel for service in colonial Africa. It was a widely held assumption among colonial officials and policy makers that developing the resources of the empire required trained scientific experts, a point also emphasized by the Secretary of State for Colonies, Leo Amery in his opening address for the Colonial Office Conference in the 1927:

> The importance of scientific research and organization is being recognized increasingly every year in this country and I think the general movement of thought is one in which we are certainly not being left behind in this office or, I think in the Colonial Empire ... I am sure that the case for pooling resources sufficiently to create some sort of unified service, at any rate in the higher research grades of scientific and technical work, is one to which we ought to give the fullest and most earnest consideration at this conference.[25]

For Amery and other proponents of 'the science for development' ideology during the 1920s the agricultural service was a particular area of focus since colonial development was viewed primarily in terms of establishing tropical agriculture along scientific lines.[26] Two sources concern recruitment and training for the agricultural service. Source fifteen is a draft of a speech delivered in 1928 by the Parliamentary Under-Secretary of State for the Colonies Sir William Ormsby-Gore at a meeting with Vice-Chancellors and Headmasters at the Board of Education. Ormsby-Gore's speech provides information on recruitment of officers trained in agricultural, veterinary, forestry and other biological sciences and is an articulate expression of the outlook of one of the most influential interwar advocates of the agenda to mobilize the resources of Britain's African Empire through the application of the sciences.

The next source reproduced here is taken from a report on the formation of the Colonial Agricultural Service issued in 1928 by the so-called Lovatt commission – one of several successive committees set up during the 1920s to advise on the development of the agricultural services for the colonial empire. Of particular importance in this context is perhaps the commission's proposal to include in a unified agricultural service a 'specialized' wing of research officers and an 'agricultural' wing of administrators working at the district level – a proposal intended to ease tensions between officers adhering to differing principles of imperial administration and development.

The development during the 1920s culminated in the Warren Fisher report issued in 1930 and regarded by one senior Colonial Office civil servant as the *Magna Carta* of the Colonial Service.[27] The committee was named after its chairman, the Permanent Secretary to the Treasury Sir Warren Fisher, who headed the civil service. The report dealt with the internal organization of the Colonial Office and its relations with the Colonial Service. It focused particularly on the system of recruitment and made the recommendation (which was adopted) that a personnel division should replace the highly personalized system based on officially recognized patronage. Moreover, the report recommended the unification of the colonial service which meant that each territory's public service would be unified into a single Colonial Service thereby making all officers eligible for transfer on promotion to vacancies in other territories. The decision to unify the service was taken at the second Colonial Office Conference held in 1930 but unification of the various branches of the service – administrative, agricultural, education, and police among others – was a gradual process taking place during the next decade.[28] Source seventeen is taken from the Warren Fisher Report while source eighteen is a discussion and assessment of the report published in the scientific journal *Nature* which provides an example of the immediate reception of the report.

As colonial administrations in Africa matured the cost of pensions for retired personnel produced a growing drain on colonial budgets. In the British administrations in Africa pensions were normally paid from the regular budget and in 1925 it constituted an average of 4 per cent of the total government expenditure, a figure that rose to nearly 7 per cent by 1938.[29] An interim report of a Pensions Committee established in 1927 to assess the pension schemes of the Colony and Protectorate of Kenya is next reproduced; it concerns the important issue of pensions, a topic that has been neglected in the existing literature. The report provided detailed information on increasing pension costs and discusses the likely effects that different reforms of pensions schemes will have on future recruitment to the administration of the colony.

The concluding five sources in this volume concern the training of administrative personnel during the final years covered in this collection. A consequential development in this period was an increased drive to equip administrative officers in service in Africa with a basic knowledge of anthropology. Officers recruited for the Sudan Political Service had received anthropological training since 1908 but it took another two decades before the Colonial Office considered this to be relevant as well. Thus when the Tropical African Administrative Services courses were in established in Oxford and Cambridge from 1926 to provide postgraduate training for colonial service probationers the courses included lectures on social anthropology.[30] Among the key proponents of the view that administrators and anthropologists needed to collaborate closer was the Parliamentary Secretary of State for the Colonies William Ormsby-Gore who in a report based on a tour of West Africa in 1926 claimed that:

> If we are to succeed in our duties towards these peoples as rulers...we must study them objectively and base our policy on real understandings acquired not only from personal contact, but from scientific study of their mental and moral characteristics, of native law and customs, of native history language and traditions. Native meth-

ods of agriculture, native arts and crafts, should be examined scientifically before any attempt is made to supersede what we find existing. Herein lies the importance of anthropological work, an importance which it is difficult to over-estimate. The wider the knowledge of the elements of anthropology amongst the administrative staff the better, and it is also essential that the trained anthropologist should work in the closest possible touch with them.[31]

During the interwar period Bronislaw Malinowski, foundation professor of social anthropology at the London School of Economics from 1927 to 1941, was the most influential anthropologist with direct links to colonial administrators and policy makers.[32] Source twenty is a memorandum 'On Colonial Research' written by Malinowski for the missionary and colonial educationalist Joseph Oldham in 1927. The memorandum makes the case that the modern functionalist anthropology – with its emphasis on detailed field-based studies of cultural contact and change – constituted a pivotal component in the development of an effective colonial administration. Malinowski's memorandum dealt with an issue that continued to be of great concern among British as well as African anthropologists in the ensuing decades.[33]

Discussions of the relations between anthropology and the needs of colonial administrations in Africa is also central to the two sources that follow both of which are testament to the influence of Margery Perham on British colonial administrative thinking and training during this period.[34] Perham's 1934 article 'A Re-Statement of Indirect Rule' published in *Africa*, the quarterly journal of the *International Institute of African Languages and Cultures* is reproduced as source twenty-one. The article – arguably Perham's most original contribution to interwar theories of colonial administration – seeks to re-state and clarify the administrative principles of indirect rule in the face of wide-spread contemporary criticisms in Britain as well as Africa.

Perham's influence on the training of colonial administrators had several platforms. She had close connections with the Colonial Office, was part of the advisor committee for Hailey's *African Survey* and (like Malinowski) she had affiliation with the *International Institute of African Languages and Cultures*, founded in London in 1926 with the support of the Rockefeller foundation. Moreover, she taught at the Tropical African Administrative Services courses in Oxford and Cambridge during the late 1920s and from 1935 in Oxford as a research lecturer in Colonial Administration.[35] With Beit Professor of Colonial History, Reginald Coupland she also helped to inaugurate the *Oxford Summer School for Colonial Administrators* in 1937, a fortnightly course intended for officers already in the colonial administrative service. Source twenty-two is taken from the second session of the Oxford Summer School held in 1938 during which twenty-five selected experts lectured before an audience that included more than hundred colonial administrators most of whom were employed in

Africa. In addition to two lectures by Perham the source contains the opening speech by Malcolm Macdonald, Secretary of State for the Colonies, an inaugural lecture by Frederick Lugard and a lecture by Reginald Coupland. The selected lectures provide information of the agenda of the people who instigated the summer school and offer insights to the outlook among the highest echelons of colonial experts and policy makers in the final years covered in this collection.

The concluding two sources in the volume shift the focus away from the grandiose debates of the Oxford Summer School. Source twenty-three is a draft pamphlet from 1933 intended to attract new recruits to the colonial service in Nigeria. In addition to information on touring duties, language examinations, cost of living, recreation and daily life the pamphlets reveals how the principles of indirect rule were presented to those changed with administrative powers on the ground.

Source twenty-four is an address delivered by the archaeologist and paleoanthropologist Louis Leakey on 'Colonial Administration in East Africa from the Native point of view'. Leakey spoke at the *Royal Institute of International Affairs* (also known as Chatham House) in London. The institute had been founded by the group of men known as Milner's Kindergarten and had since 1924 contained a special 'African Group' for the study of African issues.[36] Leakey was the son of missionaries with the Church Missionary Society working in the Kenyan highlands. He spoke Kikuyu and had spent his early years in Kenya before his studies in Cambridge which earned a PhD degree in 1930, the same year the twenty-seven year old spoke at Chatham House.[37] Addressing the audience on colonial administration from what he called 'the native point view' Leakey delivered a vigorous and pointed critique of the system of recruitment and training of colonial administrators. According to Leakey training programmes equipped officers with language skills of no use. This left newly recruited officers in ignorance of local customs, a problem that was further accentuated by unwarranted rotations of experienced officers to different districts. The effect was to render the administration of justice and land issues impossible and moreover, to prevent the administration from contributing in any positive way to the development of agriculture, health and education in the colonies.

Notes

1. N. T. Gardiner, 'Sentinels of Empire: The British Colonial Administrative, 1919–54' (PhD dissertation, Yale University 1998); A. Kirk-Greene, *On Crown Service, a History of HM Colonial and Overseas Civil Services 1837–1997* (London: I. B. Tauris 1999); A. M. H. Kirk-Greene, *Britain's Imperial Administrators, 1858–1966* (London: Macmillan Press 2000), pp. 125–63. This more recent research has stressed that the Colonial Service was a diverse body in terms of its social background and persuasively challenged Heussler's finding of a predominantly landed gentry provenance among its members. R. Heussler, *Yesterday's Rulers: The Making of the British Colonial Service* (New York: Syracuse, 1963).
2. L. H. Gann and P. Duignan, *The Rulers of British Africa, 1870–1914* (London: Croom Helm, 1978), pp. 37–44, 320–7.

3. A H. M. Kirk-Greene, 'The Thin White Line: The Size of the British Colonial Service in Africa', *African Affairs*, 79:314 (1980), pp. 25–44.

4. M. Banton, *Administrating the Empire, 1801–1968. A Guide to the Records of the Colonial Office in the National Archives of the UK* (London: National Archives, 2008), pp. 329–32. In 1926 the name of the publication was changed to *Dominions Office and Colonial Office List*.

5. *Rules and Regulations for the Information and Guidance of the Principal Officers and Others in His Majesty's Colonial Possessions* (London: Colonial Office, 1837).

6. The most well-known example of such criticisms during this period was probably that raised by the Professor of Political Science at the London School of Economics Harold J. Laski. See H. J. Laski, 'The Colonial Civil Service', *Political Quarterly*, 9 (1938), pp. 541–51.

7. Kirk-Greene, *Crown Service*, p. 32.

8. R. V. Kubicek, *The Administration of Imperialism. Joseph Chamberlain and the Colonial Office* (Durham, NC: Duke University Press, 1969).

9. CO Misc. 123 (selbourne), 1900, CO 885/7/13843.

10. Kirk-Greene, *Crown Service*, p. 16.

11. R. Johnson, 'The West African Medical Staff and the Administration of Imperial Tropical Medicine 1902–1914', *Journal of Imperial and Commonwealth History*, 38:3 (2010), pp. 419–39. See also Volume 5 of this collection.

12. Kirk-Greene, *Crown Service*, p. 17.

13. D. Sunderland, *Managing the British Empire: The Crown Agents, 1833–1914* (Woodbridge: Boydell Press, 2004); D. Sunderland, *Managing British Colonial and Post-Colonial Development. The Crown Agents 1914–74* (Woodbridge: Boydell Press, 2007); C. Andersen, *British Engineers and Africa 1875–1914* (London: Pickering & Chatto, 2011).

14. A. M. Rafferty, 'The Seductions of History and the Nursing Diaspora', *Health and History*, 7:2 (2005), pp. 2–16. See also Volume 5 of this collection.

15. Kirk-Greene, *Britain's Imperial Administrators*, pp. 164–201; R. Collins, 'The Sudan Political Service. A Portrait of the Imperialists', *African Affairs*, 71:284 (1972), pp. 293–303.

16. H. MacMichael, *The Sudan Political Service, 1899–1956* (Oxford: Oxonian Press, n. d.), p. 2.

17. J. A. Mangan, 'The Education of an Elite Imperial Administration. The Sudan Political Service and the British Public School System', *International Journal of African Studies*, 15:4 (1982), pp. 671–99.

18. Kirk-Greene, *Crown Service*, p. 18.

19. Kirk-Greene, *Britain's Imperial Administrators*, pp. 143–4. For the illustrative example of foresters see R. Rajan, *Modernizing Nature. Forestry and Imperial Eco-Development 1800–1950* (Oxford: Oxford University Press, 2006).

20. A. M. H. Kirk-Greene, 'Taking Canada into Partnership in "the White Man's Burden": The British Colonial Service and the Dominion Selection Scheme of 1923', *Canadian Journal of African Studies*, 15:1 (1981), pp. 33–46.

21. R. D. Furse, *Aucuparius: Recollections of a Recruiting Officer* (London: John Murray, 1962).

22. A. H. M. Kirk-Greene, 'Furse, Sir Ralph Dolignon (1887–1973)', *ODNB*.

23. R. L. Schuylor, 'Colonial Office Conference, 1927. Summary of Proceedings', *Political Science Quarterly*, 43:1 (1928), pp. 107–13.

24. T. D. Williams, 'Sir Gordon Guggisberg and Educational Reforms in the Gold Coast 1919 1927', *Comparative Education Review*, 8:3 (1964), pp. 290–306.

25. *Colonial Office Conference, 1927. Appendices to the Summary of proceedings. Cmd. 2884* (London: H.M's Stationary Office, 1927), p. 824.
26. J. M. Hodge, *Triumph of the Expert. Agrarian Doctrines of Development and the Legacies of British Colonialism* (Athens, OH: Ohio University Press, 2007).
27. C. Jeffries, *The Colonial Empire and its Civil Service* (London: Cambridge University Press, 1938), p. 55.
28. Kirk-Greene, *Crown Service*, pp. 33–4.
29. E. Frankema, 'Colonial Taxation and Government Apending in British Africa 1880–1940. Maximizing Revenue or Minimizing Effort?', *Explorations in Economic History*, 48 (2011), pp. 136–49, on p. 141.
30. This one year training course replaced a pre-posting training course of two to three months instigated in 1908 at the Imperial Institute in London. Kirk-Greene, *Britain's Imperial Administrators*, pp. 132–3.
31. H. Tilley, *Africa as a Living Laboratory, Empire, Development and the Problem of Scientific Knowledge* (London: Chicago University Press, 2011), p. 266.
32. G. Stocking, *After Tyler. British Social Anthropology, 1888–1951* (Madison, WI: University of Wisconsin Press, 1995), ch. 6.
33. J. W. Cell, 'Colonial Rule', in Brown and Roger Louis (eds), *The Oxford History of the British Empire, Vol. 4*, pp. 232–54.
34. M. Smith and A. Bull (eds), 'Special Issue: Margery Perham and British Rule in Africa', *Journal of Imperial and Commonwealth History*, 19:3 (1991); C. Brad Faught, *Into Africa: The imperial Life of Margery Perham* (London: I. B. Taurus, 2012).
35. A. H. M. Kirk-Greene, 'Forging a Relationship with the Colonial Administrative Service 1921–39', *Journal of Imperial and Commonwealth History*, 19:3 (1991), pp. 62–82.
36. Tilley, *Africa as a Living Laboratory*, pp. 70–1.
37. M. Bowman-Kruhm, *The Leakeys: A Biography* (Westport, CT: Greenwood Press, 2005).

W. H. Mercer and A. E. Collins, *The Colonial Office List for 1900* (London: Harrison & Sons, 1900), pp. 326–30.

(4) INFORMATION AS TO COLONIAL APPOINTMENTS.

I. GENERAL.

1. The patronage of the Secretary of State for the Colonies is confined to those colonies and countries which are administered under his directions.[1] He has no patronage in colonies possessing responsible government (viz., Canada, the Australian Colonies and New Zealand, the Cape Colony, Natal (including Zululand), and Newfoundland). With regard to appointments in Egypt, British East Africa (including Zanzibar and Uganda), and British Central Africa, as well as all appointments of a Consular nature, application should be made to the Foreign Office. Aden and adjacent territories are subject to the Government of Bombay. Ascension Island is under the supervision of the Admiralty, and Wei-hai-wei[2] is at present administered under the directions of the same department. All civil officers in Rhodesia are either nominated or appointed by the British South Africa Company, 15, St. Swithin's Lane, E.C. For appointments in British North Borneo application should be made to the British North Borneo Company. 15, Leadenhall Street, E.C. Appointments in Sarawak are in the hands of His Highness the Rajah.[3] The following information applies only to the colonies in which the Secretary of State controls the administration.

2. Each colony has its own public service distinct from that of every other colony; and, as a general rule, it is only the higher officers who are transferred by the Secretary of State from one colony to another.

3. Offices of which the emoluments do not exceed 100*l.* a year are invariably filled by the appointment of local candidates selected by the Governor, who has the absolute disposal of all such appointments.

4. When a vacancy occurs in an office of which the emoluments exceed 100*l.*, and do not exceed 200*l.*, a year, the Governor reports it to the Secretary of State,

together with the name and qualifications of the person whom he has appointed to fill it provisionally, and this recommendation is almost uniformly followed.

5. When a vacancy occurs in an office of which the emoluments exceed 200*l.* a year, the Governor follows the same course as to reporting the vacancy and provisional appointment, and he is at liberty to recommend a candidate for the final appointment; but it is distinctly understood that the Secretary of State has the power of nominating another instead.

6. This power is, however, seldom exercised in favour of persons not already in the public service. Vacancies are usually filled by promotion; and, as a general rule, it is only in the case of the highest offices, and those requiring professional or other special qualifications not to be found in the colonies themselves, that appointments are made by the Secretary of State from this country.

7. In Ceylon, Hong Kong, and the Straits Settlements, including the Federated Malay States, cadetships have been established with a view to training up officers to fill eventually the more important posts in the civil services of those colonies, all the subordinate offices being filled (as in other colonies) by the appointment of local candidates. The cadets, who must be natural born British subjects, and between the ages of 21 and 24, are selected by open competitive examination held by the Civil Service Commissioners, to whom all inquiries on the subject should be addressed. The examination is usually held once a year, and is the same as that at which candidates for the Home and Indian Civil Services compete.

There are a few cadetships in the Gold Coast Colony, which the Secretary of State fills up by selection from his list of candidates. These posts have a salary of 250*l.* a year, rising by annual increments of 10*l.* to 300*l.* a year. Cadets will be employed in the Colonial Secretary's office in the first instance, and will be on probation for three years, during which time they will be required to obtain a satisfactory knowledge of the native languages. If confirmed in their appointment they will be regarded as available for any post in the administrative branch of the services of the West African Colonies which they may prove themselves qualified to fill. Candidates must be between the ages of 23 and 26, and those who have received a University education will be preferred.

There are also a few cadetships in Fiji filled by selection. The salary is 200*l.* Candidates must be between the ages of 20 and 24. They will, in the first instance, be employed on clerical duties in the Secretariat, and will be on probation for three years, during which time they must acquire a satisfactory knowledge of Fijian. The nature of their subsequent employment, if their appointment is confirmed, will depend on the vacancies that may occur and on the capacity they may have shewn themselves to possess.

There are no other junior clerical appointments usually open to candidates in this country; but occasionally the Secretary of State has a clerkship or a supervisorship of Customs to fill up on the West Coast of Africa.

Assistant District Commissioners are appointed from time to time in Southern Nigeria. The salary is at the rate of 300*l.* a year, rising by increments of 50*l.* every 18 months to 400*l.*, with free quarters, or an allowance in lieu. Their duties are mainly administrative, and they are not required to possess legal qualifications. Candidates should not be less than 23 years of age, and preference is given to unmarried men between 25 and 30.

8. Civil engineers, surveyors, and foremen of works, when required from this country, are usually obtained through the Crown Agents for the Colonies. The Crown Agents have in their hands the selection of such officers for public works (railways, etc.) carried out through them, and they also select for clerical and medical appointments in connection with the works.

9. The Secretary of State has occasionally to fill up an educational appointment. In the case of elementary or technical educational posts candidates are obtained when required by advertising in the newspapers, and no permanent list of candidates is kept. When higher education is in question recourse is usually had to some well known agency, but a list of candidates is also kept at the Colonial Office. The better-paid posts, and the headships of colleges and education departments, are almost always filled by promotion from within the Colonial Services.

10. There is very little ecclesiastical patronage now remaining in the hands of the Secretary of State. If a post falls vacant which the Secretary of State has to fill, a candidate is selected in some special manner, with particular reference to the requirements and circumstances of the office. No list of candidates is kept. /

11. Persons possessing a competent knowledge of one or more Indian languages may have their names noted for consideration when vacancies occur in the Immigration Department of any of the colonies to which coolies are imported from India. But these appointments are few in number, and vacancies consequently do not often occur.

12. Offices for which solicitors are required are almost always filled by the appointment of local candidates. But there are a few appointments for which solicitors as well as barristers are regarded as eligible, viz., minor Registrarships and District Commissionerships on the West Coast of Africa, which are described in par. 14.

13. Barristers are required as registrars, law officers and judges, and in some instances as magistrates. The salary of a Queen's Advocate or Attorney-General (who in some Colonies, though not as a rule, is allowed to take private practice)

varies from 400*l.* in the Bahamas to 1.500*l.* in British Guiana; that of a Puisne Judge from 750*l.* in the Leeward Islands to $8,400 in the Straits Settlements; and that of a Chief Justice from 650*l.* in St. Vincent to 2,000*l.* in Jamaica. In some few colonies there is a Solicitor-General as well as an Attorney-General. The better paid appointments, and those in the more healthy colonies, are usually filled by transfer or promotion. Candidates for first appointments should, therefore, be prepared as a general rule to accept a small salary or to go to one of the less healthy colonies. Magistrates are in many cases selected from the Civil Service; but in British Guiana and Trinidad there are magistracies, with salaries varying from 600*l.* to 750*l.* a year, to which barristers are usually appointed. Barristers are also required for the Resident Magistracies in Jamaica, with salaries varying from 500*l.* to 800*l.*, and for the District Courts in Cyprus, where the salaries range from 450*l.* to 525*l.* a year. A Magistrate or a District Court Judge is not ineligible for promotion to one of the higher offices, but has no claim to such an appointment in the ordinary course of promotion. Candidates must be under the age of 40.

14. District Commissioners are required from time to time for the Gold Coast Colony and Lagos, the commencing salary being 400*l.* Candidates must possess legal qualifications, but the duties are administrative as well as legal. They should be unmarried, and not over 40 years of age.

15. Naval officers, or officers of the Royal Naval Reserve, are occasionally selected for appointment as port officers or harbour masters. But there are very few of these posts, and there is already a long list of applicants.

16. For military officers there are appointments of two classes, Civil Police (including prison appointments) and Military Police. Of the former posts there are few, and no precise qualifications have been laid down, but a knowledge of Civil Police work is in all cases essential. Military Police appointments are described in a separate memorandum. All candidates must be between 22 and 30, and unmarried, must hold commissions in the Army or Militia, must hold an officer's certificate from the School of Musketry at Hythe,[4] and (if militia officers) must have served three trainings with their battalion, and be in possession of a *P.S.* certificate or a certificate for promotion to the rank of Captain. Most of the appointments are in the Constabularies of West Africa. Higher military posts are filled by promotion.

17. The salaries attached to appointments in West Africa, whether in the police or in other departments of the public service, are much higher than those attached to similar appointments elsewhere, and West African service also carries with it special privileges in respect of leave of absence and pension. These advantages are granted on account of the unhealthiness of the climate, and any officer desiring to be transferred must be prepared to take less pay in another colony. It should

also be clearly understood that it is impossible for more than a small proportion of all the officers serving in West Africa to be transferred.

18. Medical officers in this country are from time to time selected by the Secretary of State for service in the colonies. The vacancies filled by candidates from home have numbered fifteen a year on the average of the last ten years. A large proportion of these appointments are on the West Coast of Africa, and the proportion has greatly increased during the past two years owing to considerable extensions of the staff in West Africa and to the general reduction in West Indian establishments. Applicants must be between the ages of 23 and 30 (25 and 32 in the case of West African appointments), and doubly qualified: preference will be given to unmarried candidates, and to those who have held hospital appointments as house physicians and house surgeons. A new School of Tropical Medicine has been established in London at Connaught Road, Albert Dock, E., and all candidates are required to undergo a course of training there after selection, and prior to taking up appointments. They will be provided with residence, or an allowance in lieu thereof, at the expense of the colonial government for whose service they have been selected. Their tuition fees will also be paid. The higher posts are filled by promotion or transfer, but the headships of medical departments in the larger colonies, which are posts requiring administrative as well as professional qualifications, are sometimes filled from outside the service, and there are occasional, though very rare, vacancies for which specialists are required, *e.g.*, the charge of a lunatic asylum. Surgeons-Superintendent of vessels carrying coolie emigrants from India are selected by the Crown Agents for the Colonies, who are also entrusted with the selection of medical officers required in connection with public works carried out through them.

19. A considerable number of nurses are required for service under the Colonial Governments. In selecting candidates the Secretary of State is guided by the recommendations of the committee of the Colonial Nursing Association, which has been formed with the express object of providing the colonies with trained nurses, for private as well as Government employment. All applications should be addressed to the Honorary Secretary, Colonial Nursing Association, Imperial Institute, S.W. There are no other appointments in the Secretary of State's gift which are open to ladies.

20. From the foregoing information it will be seen – (1) that the higher offices in the colonies are filled by promotion; (2) that the lower offices, not requiring professional qualifications, are filled either by the appointment of local candidates or by means of open competitive examination at home; and (3) that there are consequently scarcely any openings for candidates from this country, except for those possessing the professional and other qualifications above specified. /

21. All applications for appointments described above as being filled by selection of the Secretary of State, must be addressed to the Secretary of State for the Colonies, Downing Street, S.W. Forms are supplied by the Private Secretary, which the candidate must fill with full particulars regarding his career and qualifications, and the employment he desires; he must name on the form two referees who will answer from personal knowledge for his character and capacity, and he must return it to the Private Secretary with originals and copies of testimonials (not more than six), which must be sent in altogether. The originals will be inspected and returned to the candidate, and the copies retained for record in the Colonial Office. If the candidate is considered suitable his name will be noted in the list, and will be considered with those of other candidates as vacancies from time to time occur; but no promise can in any case be made, and no definite prospect whatever can be held out, that the Secretary of State will be in a position to offer employment to any particular candidate. If a candidate is offered an appointment, he can usually be allowed sufficient time to make preparations and to terminate the employment in which he may be engaged.

22. It is impossible to foresee the occurrence of vacancies, and the Secretary of State cannot undertake to give any information as to the likelihood of a vacancy or vacancies occurring. Nor can he undertake to keep candidates or others informed of the actual occurrence of vacancies. When candidates have been noted on the list of applicants for a class of employment, their names come up for consideration whenever a vacancy in that class occurs; a communication will then be addressed to the candidate or candidates whom the Secretary of State is prepared to place on his select list for the particular vacancy.

23. Information as to the staff of the different colonies, the climate, and local conditions, can be obtained from the "Colonial Office List," published by Messrs. Harrison and Sons, 59, Pall Mall, S.W. That publication also contains the Colonial regulations governing the Colonial services generally, and showing the rules as to leave of absence, free passages, &c.

24. Fuller particulars as to legal, military, and medical appointments are published in separate memoranda, which can be obtained from the Private Secretary. Extracts from the first two of these memoranda are published below.

II. COLONIAL POLICE APPOINTMENTS.

The following information applies only to colonies which are not self-governing. The police forces in the self-governing colonies are entirely under the control of the local governments, and information with regard to them should be obtained from the Agents-General of the respective colonies, a list of whom, with their addresses, will be found on page 16.[5]

Uganda, British Central Africa, and the East African Protectorates are under the administration of the Foreign Office, and applications for appointments in those Territories should be addressed to the Secretary of State for Foreign Affairs.

The West African Frontier Force, the headquarters of which are in the Niger Territories, does not come under the head of Colonial Police Forces. It is a military force on a temporary and provisional basis, and the appointment of officers and non-commissioned officers are made upon the recommendation of the Secretary of State for War. Applications for service with this force must be addressed to the War Office.

The Secretary of State for the Colonies only has control over the police forces of the Crown Colonies and the British South Africa Police. In the case of the former the rank and file consist of natives* recruited locally, in the latter the rank and file are of European descent ordinarily recruited in South Africa.†

The Secretary of State has therefore in his hands only the appointment of officers of the police forces of the Crown Colonies and the British South Africa Police.

APPOINTMENT OF OFFICERS.

Qualifications required. – The conditions of service in the police forces of the colonies and the qualifications required of candidates vary in almost every colony according to local laws and regulations, but as a large proportion of the junior appointments are filled up from the United Kingdom by the Secretary of State, and as it is from time to time expedient to transfer police officers from the service of one Colony to that of another, the following rules have been laid down to cover so far as possible the different requirements of the separate colonies, to which all candidates for appointments from this country must conform.

A candidate –

(1) Must be an officer of the regular army or the militia.

(2) He must at the time of application have completed two years' actual regimental duty at home or abroad, or, if a militia officer, three trainings with his battalion.

(3) He must at the date of appointment be over 22 years of age, and not exceed 30 years of age.

(4) He must be unmarried on first taking up an appointment.

(5) He must hold an officer's certificate in musketry, including machine guns, from the School of Musketry at Hythe, or its equivalent.

---

* In the West Indies the forces are largely composed of Barbadians and many N.C.O.'s are white.

† If recruits are required from this country they are obtained by advertisement in the daily papers. At present there is a good supply of local recruits.

(6) If a militia officer, he must hold a certificate on Army Form E. 516 (promotion to the rank of Captain) or a P.S. certificate (Army Form E. 527).

(7) It is also desirable, though not indispensable, that a candidate should hold an artillery certificate stating that he is "qualified to instruct in the service of 7-pounder and 2-5 inch R.M.L. guns and of war rockets." /

Mode of Application. – All applications should be made direct to the Secretary of State for the Colonies in the first instance, on a form which may be obtained from the Private Secretary, Colonial Office, Downing Street, S.W.; but a candidate on receiving the offer of an appointment (though not before) will be obliged to submit an application to be seconded from his regiment in the manner prescribed by the Queen's Regulations, *i.e.*, through his Commanding Officer (and, in the case of a militia officer, also through the Officer Commanding the Regimental District) and the General Officer Commanding the District, to the Military Secretary, Horse Guards.

Vacancies. – The majority of vacancies for junior officers occur in the West African Police Forces, and it may be roughly stated that there are on an average twelve a year.

In the West Indies vacancies occur only very occasionally, and as there is often a suitable local candidate there are seldom more than three openings a year for candidates from this country.

In the Eastern Colonies the position is much the same as in the West Indies, and vacancies are in most cases filled up by the selection or promotion of some suitable local candidate by the Secretary of State on the recommendation of the Governor.

In the Federated States of the Malay Peninsula any police appointments are made by the High Commissioner of the Federated Malay States.[6]

In the British South Africa Police appointments to the commissioned grades are made by the Secretary of State usually on the recommendation of the High Commissioner, who acts on the advice of the Colonel Commandant of the corps.[7] Many of these appointments are filled up by promotion from the ranks, and for the rest there are generally local candidates available. It rarely happens that an officer is sent out from this country.

MILITARY POLICE.

The police forces which are armed and are available for military duties may be classified as follows:–

West African   {Gold Coast Hausa Constabulary. Lagos Hausa Constabulary. Niger Coast Protectorate Force. Sierra Leone Frontier Police. Gambia Police.

Wes Indian	{British Guiana Constabulary. Jamaica Constabulary. British Honduras Constabulary. Trinidad Police. Barbados Police.* Leeward Islands Police. Windward Islands Police.
Eastern	Malay States Guides.
South African	{British South Africa Police (Bechuanaland, Mashonaland, and Matabeleland Divisions).

It is to be clearly understood that the Service of each colony is separate and distinct, and that, although the Secretary of State is occasionally in a position to transfer police officers from one colony to another, and although this principle is carried out so far as is possible and expedient, the holding of an appointment in one colony does not carry with it the right to look to the Service of another colony for transfer or promotion. An exception to the above is to be found in the police forces of the West African Colonies, which are usually considered together for the purposes of promotion.

Senior appointments. – The senior appointments of the police forces of the Crown Colonies are usually filled by the promotion of officers who have rendered good service, either in the same or in another colony, and it is only very occasionally that a military officer is required from the United Kingdom to undertake these higher posts.

CIVIL POLICE.

Besides the military constabularies there are civil police forces in nearly all the Crown Colonies. The senior appointments in these forces are usually filled locally, but it occasionally happens that officers of the army, the militia, or the Royal Irish Constabulary are required for them. No precise qualifications have been laid down, but a knowledge of civil police work is in all cases essential.

* The preceding conditions are not all applicable.

Sir John Harding and G. E. R. Gent, *The Dominions Office and Colonial Office List for 1939*[1] (London & Dunstable: Waterlow & Sons, 1939), pp. 623–32.

INFORMATION AS TO COLONIAL APPOINTMENTS.
THE COLONIAL SERVICE.

Arising out of the discussions of a special Committee appointed in 1930, to consider the question of the unification of the various Colonial Governments' Services, recognition was given to a single Colonial Service. Within this Service the following unified branches have been established, and it is proposed to proceed with the unification of other branches of the Service:–

Colonial Administrative Service.
Colonial Agricultural Service.
Colonial Audit Service.
Colonial Chemical Service.
Colonial Customs Service.
Colonial Education Service.
Colonial Forest Service.
Colonial Geological Survey Service.
Colonial Legal Service.
Colonial Medical Service.
Colonial Mines Service.
Colonial Police Service.
Colonial Postal Service.
Colonial Survey Service.
Colonial Veterinary Service.

Below will be found a summary of the principal classes of appointment in the Colonial Service which are dealt with respectively:–

(I) By the Director of Recruitment (Colonial Service).[2]
(II) By the Crown Agents for the Colonies.[3]

(I) APPOINTMENTS WITH WHICH THE DIRECTOR OF RECRUITMENT (COLONIAL SERVICE) DEALS.[*]

Applications for the following appointments should be addressed in writing to *the Director of Recruitment (Colonial Service)*, 8, *Buckingham Gate, S.W.1.*, from whom memoranda giving full details of these appointments may be obtained on written request. Intending applicants and others who desire to obtain general information about the history and structure of the Colonial Service are recommended to read the book entitled "The Colonial Empire and its Civil Service," by C.J.Jeffries,[5] published in 1938 by the Cambridge University Press (price 10/6d.).

VACANCIES.

Where information is given in the following paragraphs as to the number of vacancies available annually it is based, unless otherwise stated, upon the average requirements of the four or five years prior to 1931, during which, in the case of certain classes of appointment, a considerable amount of expansion of staff took place. In consequence of the financial depression the number of vacancies available between 1931 and 1934 was very considerably reduced. During the last four years the rate of recruitment has definitely increased in certain directions: but it is not possible to say whether, when conditions have become yet more stable, it will eventually approximate to that of the years immediately preceding 1931.

COLONIAL ADMINISTRATIVE SERVICE.

The Colonial Administrative Service was constituted as a "unified" Service with effect from the 1st of July, 1932.

The following paragraphs contain information regarding Administrative Appointments in East and West Africa (where most vacancies occur), Basutoland, the Bechuanaland Protectorate and Swaziland, Malaya, Hong Kong, Ceylon, Fiji and Western Pacific.

(*a*) QUALIFICATIONS.

A high standard of general education is essential for these appointments. Whilst a University Degree is not an absolutely indispensable qualification, the candidates selected for Administrative appointments in the last few years have nearly all been in possession of a University Degree, usually with Honours. The few

---

[*]   The Secretary of State for the Colonies set up a Colonial Service Appointments Board in 1931[4] to make selections on his behalf for all the first appointments to the Colonial Service which are at his disposal. Selections so made are submitted to the Secretary of State for his final approval and ensuing appointments are made on his authority.

exceptions have been in cases where a candidate has had some special qualifications (*e.g.* legal qualifications), or has acquired some special experience likely to prove of value (*e.g.* such experience as that of an officer of H.M's. Forces, especially one who has commanded native troops with success, and has been recommended for civil employment). There is no reason to anticipate that at future selections the standard in this respect will be any less high. /

(*b*) AGE LIMITS.

Candidates must have attained the age of 20 1/2 and must not have attained the age of 30 on the 1st of August in the year of application. There is a definite preference for candidates who are under 26, and candidates selected for the Colonial Administrative Service who are over 25 are very unlikely to be allocated for duty in Ceylon, Malaya or Hong Kong.

(*c*) APPLICATION AND SELECTION.

One annual selection takes place in the summer, usually in August. Completed applications must reach the Director of Recruitment between the 1st of January and the 30th of April in the year of the selection.

(*d*) TRAINING.

Candidates provisionally selected for appointment to the Colonial Administrative Service are normally required to undergo a course of instruction in this country before embarkation on first appointment. The course commences in October and extends over the autumn, spring, and summer terms at either Oxford or Cambridge University, during which allowances are paid at the rate of £75 at the beginning of the first term, £50 at the beginning of the second and third terms, and £50 on completion of the course.

(*e*) EAST AND WEST AFRICA.

The average number of Administrative Officers recruited for Tropical Africa from the end of the war until 1930 was 95 per annum.

During this period very considerable enlargements of staff contributed to maintain the average recruitment at this high rate despite the small number of 18 vacancies filled in 1922 as a result of the financial depression prevailing at that time, and a continuation of recruitment at so high a rate was not to be expected. In recent years, however, an average of between 50 and 60 cadets would have been required to replace annual wastage through retirement, etc., without allowing for any increase of staff. In 1930 the actual number of vacancies filled was 74, but in 1931 and 1932 it fell to 20 as a result of the financial depression. In 1933, the number of vacancies rose to 23, in 1934 to 33, and in 1935 to 58. 53 vacancies were filled in 1936, 59 in 1937, and 78 in 1938.

An Administrative Officer may be employed either in the Secretariat of a Colony or in a District. His duties may be very varied. If employed in a district his functions are of a magisterial and political nature, and he is the immediate agent of the Government in his District, and his responsibilities extend to all departments of the Administration which have no local representative. His duties may involve a considerable amount of travelling.

In West Africa, salaries start at £400 per annum and rise on a long scale to £1,000 per annum; in East Africa salaries start at £350 per annum and rise on a long scale to £1,000 per annum. There are higher posts above these scales.

(f) Basutoland, the Bechuanaland Protectorate and Swaziland.

It was decided early in 1937 that the recruitment for administrative posts in these territories should, in future, be merged into the annual selection for the Colonial Administrative Service, and that officers selected to fill Administrative vacancies in these territories should normally be appointed as members of that Service. 12 candidates were selected in 1937 and 2 in 1938.

The initial salary is £340 per annum.

(g) Ceylon.

Until 1935, administrative officers for Ceylon were recruited on the results of the open competitive examination held annually by the Civil Service Commissioners for appointments in the Home, Northern Ireland and Indian Civil Services and for Eastern Cadetships (including Cadetships in Malaya and Hong Kong prior to 1932), but the method of recruitment of European candidates is now merged into that already in force for appointments in the Colonial Administrative Service generally. The average number of European Cadets appointed during the years 1919 to 1931 inclusive was between two and three per annum. Three vacancies were filled in 1936, and two in 1937. No vacancies occurred in 1938.

At the present time Cadets receive a salary of £400 a year until they pass the prescribed examinations, and then £450 a year until they complete two years' service when they are eligible for promotion as Second Class Civil Servants with a salary of £500-£40-£700; £760-£40-£1,000; £1,050-£50-£1,300. The salaries of First Class Civil Servants are, for Grade II, £1,400-£50-£1,550 a year, and for Grade I, £1,600-£50-£1,750 a year; above that there are special appointments (not necessarily reserved for Cadets) with salaries ranging between £1,800 and £3,000 a year.

(*h*) MALAYA AND HONG KONG.

The average number of Cadets appointed to Malaya and Hong Kong during the period 1919-1931 inclusive was between 9 and 10 annually. Since 1931, the average has been between 5 and 6 annually. In 1937, 7 candidates were appointed, and nine in 1938.

Prior to 1932 these appointments were filled through the competitive examination for Eastern Cadetships, but the method of appointment is now merged into that already in force for appointments in the Colonial Administrative Service generally.

The Cadet Services provide the higher Administrative staff for all the various Government activities including the Secretariats, the Courts, the Treasuries, District and Land Offices, and in Malaya the Residencies in the Malay States.

In Malaya the Cadet starts at $350 per mensem (£490 per annum) and has the prospect of rising eventually to appointments in Class I, with salaries between $1,050 per mensem (£1,470 per annum) and $1,400 per mensem (£1,960 per annum). /

In Hong Kong the initial salary is £400 per annum and the appointments in Class I are on a scale of from £1,450 to £1,600 per annum. It should be noted, however, that the scales of salary and the rates of certain allowances in Hong Kong are at present under revision.

In both Malaya and Hong Kong there are special appointments (not necessarily reserved for Cadets) above these scales.

(*i*) FIJI AND WESTERN PACIFIC.

Normally not more than two vacancies are likely to occur annually for Cadets in Fiji and the Western Pacific. Five vacancies occurred in 1933, but only one in 1934, and one in 1935. In 1936, owing to exceptional circumstances, seven vacancies occurred, and in 1937, eight. Three vacancies were filled in 1938.

The duties correspond to those of an Administrative Officer in Tropical Africa.

The initial salary is £350 per annum (local currency without exchange compensation) for Cadets serving in Fiji, and £375 per annum for Cadets serving in the Gilbert and Ellice Islands Colony and the British Solomon Islands Protectorate. In the British Solomon Islands Protectorate a local allowance of £50 a year is also paid.

(*j*) OTHER ADMINISTRATIVE APPOINTMENTS.

In many Dependencies, including those in the West Indies, vacancies for junior officers in the Administration and Secretariat are usually filled by the selection of local candidates or by promotion or transfer within the Service.

Vacancies may, however, occasionally occur in Cyprus and Palestine. One vacancy in Cyprus was filled in 1937 and two in 1938. One vacancy in Aden was filled in 1938. In Cyprus the initial salary is £360, rising on a long scale to £840 per annum. In Palestine the initial salary is £P.300, rising by annual increments of £P.25 to £P.800 per annum, with an expatriation allowance of £P.50 up to £P.525 and £P.100 after £P.525.

EDUCATIONAL APPOINTMENTS.*

A number of vacancies for junior Educational officers may be expected to occur in any year of normal prosperity.† The great majority of these occur in either East and West Africa, or Malaya and Hong Kong.

For all the ordinary junior Educational appointments which are dealt with by the Director of Recruitment candidates must have a Degree, usually a Degree with Honours, of a British University.

In the case of vacancies which it is required to fill immediately or during the current year (*referred to, for convenience, as "immediate" vacancies*) candidates must, normally, have also a recognised Diploma in Education, or equivalent professional qualification. Failing such qualification candidates who have had sufficient proved experience of school teaching may sometimes be considered. They must have attained the age of 21 1/2 and must not have attained the age of 35 on taking up their duties overseas if selected; there is a definite preference for candidates of under 30. It should be noted that, with few exceptions, "immediate" vacancies are filled during the summer. Candidates for "immediate" appointments are, therefore, advised to apply as early in the year as possible.

Vacancies may also be expected to occur each summer for which candidates having no professional qualification, and little or no teaching experience, are considered (*referred to, for convenience, as "course" vacancies*) on the understanding that, if selected, they will be required before proceeding overseas to undergo a special course of training in Educational method and practice at the University of London Institute of Education. Fees for this course are paid from public funds, and probationers attending it receive an allowance of £20 a month. Candidates for "course" vacancies, who will often be men expecting to graduate at a University in the current summer, must have attained the age of 20 ½ and must not have attained the age of 30 on the 1st of August in the year of application; there is a definite preference for candidates of under 26. One selection is held annually, usually in August, and completed forms of application must reach the Director of Recruitment between the 1st of January and the 30th of April in the year in which the selection takes place.

---

*   It is proposed, during the year 1938, to constitute a unified "Colonial Education Service."

†   It should be noted, however, that in consequence of the general financial depression comparatively few Educational vacancies have been available since 1931, and it is considered unlikely that there will be any marked increase in the rate of recruitment for the present.

In Tropical Africa, while there is one common Educational policy which aims at providing a sufficient and wisely adapted system of education for the Native populations, there are naturally variations of organisation and method in the different Dependencies, and the duties of a junior Educational officer will vary accordingly. In general it may be said that his work demands both skill as a teacher and ability, born of enthusiasm, to participate in and supervise all forms of school activities, *e.g.* organised games, Boy Scout work, etc., which experience has shown to be of particular value in creating *esprit de corps* and a sense of service and leadership amongst African native boys. Sooner or later an officer may be called upon to undertake the duties of an Inspector of Schools, though the work of administration is generally confined to the higher appointments in the Education Department.

The scale of salary in East Africa is £350 (for 2 years on probation) rising by annual increments to £840 per annum. In West Africa the present scale is £400-£450 (for 3 years on probation) rising to £840 per annum.

In Malaya and Hong Kong a junior officer is usually appointed as a "European Master" for duty on the staff of a secondary school organised on lines somewhat similar to those of a Public School in this country. He will be required to teach either English subjects, or Mathematics or Science up to London Matriculation or equivalent standard. The "English" schools in Malaya are attended by Malay, Chinese and Indian boys. In Hong Kong there are both English and Chinese schools, and also some "Anglo-Chinese" schools, where the study of English and Chinese is carried on side by side. In all cases games, Boy Scout work or Cadet Corps. etc., play an important part. Above the time scale there are a number of senior administrative offices, promotion to which is by merit; and opportunities may occur for appointment to an Assistant Inspectorship, or other post connected with vernacular education, at an earlier stage in an officer's career. /

The scale of salary for European Masters in Malaya is $400 per mensem rising by annual increments to $800 per mensem (£560–£1,120 per annum). In Hong Kong European Masters receive £460 per annum rising to £950. In both cases appointments are in the first instance on three years' probation. It should be noted that the scales of salary and the rates of certain allowances in Hong Kong are at present under revision.

COLONIAL POLICE SERVICE (COMMISSIONED OR EQUIVALENT RANK).

The Colonial Police Service was instituted as a "unified" service with effect from the 1st of October, 1936.

These appointments comprise Police Probationerships in Ceylon, Malaya, Hong Kong and Palestine; Sub-Inspectorships of Constabulary in British Guiana and Jamaica, and appointments in the Police Forces of East and West Africa, Trinidad and Cyprus.

17 appointments were filled during the years 1932-34 inclusive. 14 appointments were made in 1935, 9 in 1936, 19 in 1937, and 21 in 1938.

The selection takes place in the summer and completed applications must be submitted between the 1st of January and the 15th of March.

Candidates for all appointments must be over twenty years of age on the 1st of January in the year in which selection takes place.

For appointments in Malaya, Hong Kong, and Palestine, candidates must be under 22 years of age on the 1st of January in the year in which selection takes place: for all other Colonies, etc., they must be under 26 years of age (22 in the case of Ceylon) on the 1st of August in the year in which selection takes place.

In the case of Police appointments in Tropical Africa, the Secretary of State would, in certain circumstances be prepared to consider an application from a candidate up to 30 years of age who had had such experience as that of a commissioned officer of His Majesty's Regular Forces, especially one who had commanded native troops with success, and had been recommended for civil employment.

Candidates must be in possession of the School Certificate, or of equivalent or higher educational qualifications. In the case of Ceylon, an Honours Degree of a British University is essential.

Police Cadets selected for Malaya are normally required to take a three months' course in the Malay language at the School of Oriental and African Studies in London, during which they receive an allowance of £20 a month.

Candidates selected for Police appointments in Tropical Africa, Ceylon, Hong Kong, Trinidad and Cyprus will normally be required to undergo a year's course of training at the Metropolitan Police College during which they receive an allowance of £175 a year.

Commencing salaries are as follows: – Tropical Africa, between £350 and £400; Hong Kong, £400 (under revision); Ceylon, £380; Malaya, £420; Palestine £300, with pensionable expatriation allowance of £50; Trinidad, £400; British Guiana, £200; Jamaica, £200 (under revision); with other allowances which vary. Salaries in the Far Eastern Services are on a long scale. To take the Malayan Police as an instance. A Cadet who is appointed at £420 receives £490 on becoming a Passed Cadet. On confirmation in his appointment he receives £560 rising by annual increments of £35 to £1,120 a year. Above this scale there are a number of appointments on the scale £1,120 to £1,330. The Inspector-General, Straits Settlements Police, and the Inspector-General, Federated Malay States Police, receive £1,680 each.

The duties of a Police Officer in a Tropical Dependency are extremely varied and should appeal particularly to the young man with a taste for an out of door life who would appreciate doing far more responsible work than would normally fall to a man of similar age in this country.

COLONIAL CUSTOMS SERVICE.

The Colonial Customs Service was constituted as a "unified" service with effect from the 1st of January, 1938.

One selection of candidates to fill vacancies is held annually, usually during July and August, and completed applications must reach the Director of Recruitment between the 1st of January and the 15th of March. An average of six vacancies in Malaya has been filled annually since 1933. One vacancy in Tropical Africa was filled in 1938.

Candidates for appointments in Malaya must be over 20 and under 22 years of age on the 1st of January in the year in which selection takes place. Candidates for appointments in Tropical Africa and elsewhere must be over 21 1/2 and under 26 years of age on the 1st of August in the year in which selection takes place.

The minimum educational qualification entitling a candidate to be considered will be the possession of a School Certificate at the date of application or the production of evidence that he has passed some other examination of equivalent or higher standard. It should be noted, however, that a number of candidates selected in recent years have been University graduates, usually with Honours.

Commencing salaries are £350 in East Africa, £400 in West Africa, and Malaya, £420 per annum.

COLONIAL AUDIT SERVICE.

Normally, four or five vacancies may be expected annually and they are filled as they occur.

Candidates must be over 21 ½ years of age and under 26.

The essential qualifications for these appointments are: a good general education, preferably at a University; a natural inclination for figures and accounts; character and ability such as would qualify a candidate in due course for the higher branches of the Service. /

Selected candidates undergo a short period of training in the Home Establishment of the Colonial Audit Department, during which an allowance at the rate of £20 a month is paid.

Usual commencing salaries are £350 per annum in East Africa and £400 in West Africa, rising to £780 and £810 respectively, with higher posts above these scales.

OTHER APPOINTMENTS OF A FINANCIAL NATURE.

General questions of financial policy and control in the Colonies are dealt with in the central Secretariats, in many of which there is now a separate financial branch staffed by Administrative Officers selected for such work from the general administrative cadre. It is thus possible that when filling vacancies in the Colonial Administrative Service at the annual selection in August, the Secretary of State may occasionally be asked to select a candidate possessing special qualifications and aptitude for dealing with financial and economic questions.

On the other hand, the task of accounting for Government revenue and expenditure is entrusted to a separate department known as the Treasury or the Accountant-General's Department. Officers appointed to Treasury or Accountancy posts are not members of the Colonial Administrative Service, and vacancies in such posts are normally filled by the Crown Agents for the Colonies, 4, Millbank, London, S.W.l, to whom applications should be addressed.

COLONIAL LEGAL SERVICE.

The Colonial Legal Service was constituted as a "unified" service with effect from the 1st July, 1933.

Before 1931, the average number of vacancies filled annually was between 11 and 12, but, on account of the financial depression, considerably fewer appointments were made between 1931 and 1934. 72 vacancies were filled during the period 1935–37 inclusive, and 26 appointments were made in 1938. Vacancies are filled as and when they occur.

The majority of appointments which are filled from outside the Service are for Crown Counsel and Magistrates, for which barristers only are eligible. Occasionally, however, a vacancy occurs for which a solicitor can be considered.

Candidates should be under 40 years of age and should normally have had at least four years' practical experience in their profession.

Initial salaries are seldom less than £600 p.a. and in many cases are substantially higher.

COLONIAL MEDICAL SERVICE.

The Colonial Medical Service was constituted as a "unified" service with effect from the 1st of January, 1934. Officers are appointed to the Service by the Secretary of State and are liable to be posted at his discretion. The wishes of individual officers are, however, consulted as far as possible, both as regards posting on first appointment and as regards subsequent transfer.

The average annual number of appointments for Medical Officers made during the period 1926-1930 was 97. In 1931, as a result of the general financial depression, the actual number of appointments made was 35 and this figure fell to 12 and 22 in the years 1932 and 1933 respectively. 31 appointments were made in 1934; 48 in 1935; 53 in 1936; 47 in 1937; and 54 in 1938. It is not possible to forecast actual requirements in the immediate future.

Vacancies may occur at any time of the year and are dealt with as circumstances require. Candidates should be under 35 years of age, must be fully qualified and must be on the Medical Register. Preference is given to candidates who have held hospital or public health appointments or who have special knowledge of anæsthetics, radiology, surgery, medicine, ophthalmology, gynecology and midwifery, diseases of the ear, nose and throat, venereal diseases, etc. In the case of Lady Medical Officers, for whom there are occasional vacancies, experience in child welfare work is almost invariably essential.

Selected candidates are normally required to undergo a course of instruction in Tropical Medicine and Hygiene before proceeding overseas.

The majority of vacancies for Medical Officers occur in West Africa, East Africa and Malaya. The vacancies for Lady Medical Officers are usually confined to West Africa and Malaya.

Commencing salaries in West Africa, East Africa and Malaya are normally £660, £600, and £700 per annum respectively, but it should be noted that the salary scales in East and West Africa are at present under revision.

Vacancies occasionally occur for Medical Entomologists.

DENTAL SURGEONS.

It is very rarely that a vacancy for a Dental Surgeon occurs. The conditions of these posts vary too much for general information to be given.

COLONIAL AGRICULTURAL SERVICE.

The Colonial Agricultural Service was constituted as a "unified" service with effect from the 1st of October. 1935. It includes appointments for officers for general investigational, advisory and similar duties, as well as for agricultural specialists, such as botanists, mycologists, entomologists and agricultural chemists. In future, almost all vacancies for agricultural officers and agricultural specialists are likely to be filled by the selection of Colonial Agricultural Scholars on completion of their training (see below). For any further vacancies candidates with University degrees in agriculture or natural science who have continued post-graduate study or research for periods similar to those of Colonial Agricultural Scholars would be most likely to be selected. A few vacancies may also be available, in addition to the above, in connection with the inspection of crops and of produce for export. For these appointments candidates are usually required to be in possession / of a degree or diploma in agriculture or horticulture. The Secretary of State is also occasionally asked to fill vacancies of a definitely horticultural nature in connection with the care of botanic gardens or fruit cultivation. For these a horticultural qualification such as that obtainable at the Royal Botanic Gardens, Kew, or the horticultural diploma of an Agricultural College, is required.

The majority of appointments are filled in July and August, but vacancies may be filled at other times. Candidates should usually be over 21 ½ and under 30 years of age. Commencing salaries usually vary from £400 to £500.

The Secretary of State offers annually in the summer a certain number of Colonial Agricultural Scholarships, These are post-graduate scholarships, tenable in most cases for two years, one of which is spent in this country and the other at the Imperial College of Tropical Agriculture in Trinidad or some other institution abroad. The scholarships are intended to provide a pool of men trained in agriculture and agricultural science from which vacancies in the Colonial Agricultural Service can be filled. Candidates should possess, or be about to qualify for, a degree in agriculture or natural science. The value of a scholarship is: –

(i) Whilst a scholar is in this country; £200 per annum with payment of fees for tuition and, if necessary, of matriculation and examination fees;

(ii) Whilst a scholar is abroad: £225 per annum with payment of passages and of cost of travelling, if required, among the West Indian Islands or elsewhere; and also of tuition fees up to a maximum of £75;

(iii) Each scholar will also receive an allowance not exceeding £5 for the purchase of approved books.

COLONIAL VETERINARY SERVICE.

The Colonial Veterinary Service was constituted as a "unified" service with effect from the 1st of October, 1935.

Several vacancies for veterinary officers or veterinary research officers may normally be expected to occur annually in the Colonial Veterinary Service. The majority of these vacancies are normally filled by the selection of Colonial Veterinary Scholars on completion of their training (see below), though urgent vacancies may be filled, as and when they occur, by the appointment of candidates possessing the Diploma of Membership of the Royal College of Veterinary Surgeons or a veterinary qualification obtained in one of the self-governing Dominions. Candidates should be over 21 1/2 and under 30 years of age on assuming their duties overseas. Commencing salaries in the larger Veterinary Departments vary between £560 and £630 per annum.

The Secretary of State offers annually, in the summer, a limited number of Colonial Veterinary Scholarships and Studentships. These are of a post-graduate nature and are intended to provide a pool of qualified candidates from which vacancies in the Colonial Veterinary Service can be filled. It is intended to make not less than four awards annually until further notice. Candidates for Scholarships should possess, or be about to qualify for, a science degree of a British University or some equivalent qualification. A Scholarship will ordinarily be tenable for four years, to enable the holder to qualify for the Diploma of M.R.C.V.S.,[6] and will be of the value of £200 a year, with provision for training fees and an allowance for the purchase of approved books in addition. Candidates for Studentships should possess or be about to qualify for the Diploma of Membership of the Royal Veterinary College or a veterinary qualification obtained in one of the self-governing Dominions. A Studentship will usually be tenable for one year and will be of the value of £300 a year, including provision for training fees; but an allowance not exceeding £5 for the purchase of approved books is payable in addition.

COLONIAL FORESTRY SERVICE.

The Colonial Forest Service was constituted as a "unified" service with effect from the 1st of January, 1935.

A limited number of vacancies for Assistant Conservators of Forests may be expected to occur each year. The average number of vacancies during the past four years has been nine.

For the present, such vacancies will be filled by the selection of graduates in Forestry who will undergo a course of one year's duration at the Imperial Forestry Institute[7] after a period of practical experience in the Colonial Forest Department for which they have been selected. Candidates should usually be over 21 1/2 and under 30 years of age. The commencing salaries of Assistant Conservators of Forests vary between £400 and £500 a year.

It is hoped to bring into operation in 1940 a scheme designed to widen the field of recruitment by offering scholarships in Forestry (on the analogy of the Colonial Agricultural and Veterinary Scholarships) for which candidates who have already taken honours in less specialized subjects will be eligible.

ZOOLOGICAL APPOINTMENTS.

Vacancies occasionally arise in connection with mosquito, tsetse-fly, and similar investigations, which are open to graduates in zoology or natural science who have specialised in medical Entomology. Vacancies for entomologists occur, however, rather more frequently in the Colonial Agricultural Service (see above). There are also occasional openings for trained Zoologists in Colonial Fisheries, Game Preservation and Museum Departments.

THE COLONIAL CHEMICAL SERVICE.

The Colonial Chemical Service was constituted as a "unified" service with effect from the 1st of January, 1939. Some three or four vacancies are usually available in each year for officers for general analytical work (*i.e.*, as Government Chemists or Analysts). A candidate should usually be over 21 1/2 and under 35 years of age, be an associate of the Institute of Chemistry,[8] and should possess a good University Degree in Chemistry. The certificate of the Institute of Chemistry in Branch E. (Foods, Drugs, etc.) is a valuable additional qualification and is sometimes essential. The duties usually include any analytical work required by Government, which falls outside the scope of the Agricultural Chemist (*e.g.*, the examination of stores, foods, drugs, water, ores, etc., and bacteriological and medico-legal work). There are also occasional vacancies for specialists in bio-chemistry for Medical and other Departments. Initial salaries vary between £400 and £600. /

COLONIAL GEOLOGICAL SURVEY SERVICE.

The Colonial Geological Survey Service was constituted as a "unified" service with effect from the 1st of January, 1938.

Vacancies for Geologists are not of very frequent occurrence, and are filled as and when they occur.

Candidates should be between the ages of 21 1/2 and 35. They should possess a University Degree, preferably with Honours, ensuring a good general knowledge of geology, and also have carried out independent field investigations.

Commencing salaries vary from £400 to £600.

COLONIAL MINES SERVICE.

The Colonial Mines Service was constituted as a "unified" service with effect from the 1st of January, 1938. A few vacancies are usually available each year, and are filled as and when they occur.

The age limits are 21 ½ to 35.

Candidates should hold a Degree or Diploma in metalliferous mining of a British University or School of Mines. Practical experience of metalliferous mining is usually required.

Commencing salaries vary from £475 to £560.

COLONIAL SURVEY SERVICE.

The Colonial Survey Service was constituted as a "unified" service with effect from the 1st of January, 1938.

The annual number of vacancies for Survey Probationers before 1931 varied considerably, but about 12 were expected annually. In 1931 only three were filled, and during the succeeding four years recruitment was suspended. Four vacancies were filled in 1936, five in 1937, and seven in 1938.

Selections are usually made during June.

Candidates should be not less than 21 and under 28 on the 1st of July in the year in which the selection takes place. They should either be in possession of an Honours Degree in mathematics, physical sciences, or engineering, or certain other equivalent qualifications.

Completed application forms must be submitted before the 30th of April.

Selected candidates usually undergo a 6 to 8 months' course of training under the Ordnance Survey Office, Southampton[9], followed in some cases by a year's training at Cambridge. During these courses allowances are paid at the rate of £50 a quarter at Southampton and £75 a term at Cambridge. Commencing salaries vary from £400 to £490.

METEOROLOGICAL APPOINTMENTS.

A limited number of vacancies may be expected to arise in Colonial Meteorological Services and Observatories each year. Candidates should usually be between the ages of 21 ½ and 35 and hold a good Honours degree in Mathematics or Physics. Before taking up their duties selected candidates may be required to undergo a course of training in meteorological work of from three to six months' duration in this country during which an allowance is paid to them.

ARCHÆOLOGICAL AND ETHNOGRAPHICAL APPOINTMENTS.

Vacancies of this nature are rare, but the Secretary of State may occasionally be asked to select a trained Archæologist or Anthropologist for a Museum appointment.

ECCLESIASTICAL APPOINTMENTS.

The Secretary of State is rarely called upon to fill an Ecclesiastical appointment. If a post falls vacant a candidate is selected in some special manner with particular reference to the requirements and circumstances of the Office.

No list of candidates is kept at the Colonial Office.

HARBOURMASTER APPOINTMENTS.

Vacancies occur very infrequently for Port Officers or Harbourmasters.

Candidates for such appointments must either – (1) have held a commission in the Royal Navy, or (2) have held a Master's or extra Master's certificate, and be an officer of the Royal Naval Reserve.

The conditions of these posts vary too much for general information to be given. The better paid posts are, however, usually filled by promotion from within the Colonial Service.

IMMIGRATION APPOINTMENTS.

On very rare occasions vacancies have occurred in the Immigration Department of a Colony which provides facilities for the immigration of natives of India.

For such a vacancy a competent knowledge of one or more Indian languages would be essential.

AVIATION APPOINTMENTS.

The openings in connection with aviation in the Colonial Service are at present limited. When a vacancy occurs the Air Ministry is asked to advise as to the selection of a suitable candidate.

PERSONAL STAFF APPOINTMENTS.

Appointments, such as those of Private Secretary and Aide-de-Camp, on the personal staff of the Governor of a Colony are made by the Governor concerned. It occasionally happens, however, that a Governor asks the Secretary of State to recommend a suitable officer to act in such a capacity. A candidate who wishes / his name to be noted for consideration, in the event of such a request being made, should apply in writing to the Director of Recruitment (Colonial Service). As a rule only unmarried candidates are selected for such appointments. Previous experience in a similar position is valuable, but not as a rule essential. For appointment as Aide-de-Camp an officer, or ex-officer, of H.M. Forces is usually selected.

OTHER APPOINTMENTS.

Vacancies in Departments, other than those already mentioned, may occasionally occur. Owing to their diversity, however, it is not possible to give any general account of the qualifications which might be required.

(II) APPOINTMENTS IN THE COLONIAL SERVICE WHICH ARE FILLED BY THE CROWN AGENTS FOR THE COLONIES.

The appointments mentioned in the paragraphs which follow are filled, as and when vacancies occur, by the *Crown Agents for the Colonies, 4, Millbank, S.W.1.,* from whom further details may be obtained on request.

CIVIL, MECHANICAL AND ELECTRICAL ENGINEERING.

The majority of vacancies occur in West Africa, East Africa and Malaya.

The commencing salaries vary from approximately £480 to £600 per annum.

The age limits vary between 23 and 35 years of age.

The qualifications required are as follows:–

CIVIL ENGINEERS.

Assistant Engineers on Government Railways must be Corporate Members of the Institution of Civil Engineers[10] or hold an Engineering degree or diploma recognised as granting exemption from Sections A and B of the A.M.I.C.E. examination[11], and possess experience on Railway Survey, Construction or Maintenance.

Assistant Engineers in Public Works Departments must be Corporate Members of the Institution of Civil Engineers or hold an Engineering degree or diploma recognised as granting exemption from Sections A and B of the A.M.I.C.E. examination, and possess experience on Public Works. It is preferred that all candidates should have had at least 2 years practical experience of good Engineering work after taking their degree or completing their Articles, but consideration will be given to the applications of candidates with less than two years practical experience provided they are in possession of one of the qualifications above mentioned.

MECHANICAL ENGINEERS.

Assistant Locomotive Superintendents and Assistant Works Managers (Railways). – Engineering degree or A.M.I.M.E.[12] and apprenticeship in locomotive works, including running shed and footplate work, and subsequent experience in a railway running department, or in railway works management.

Assistant Mechanical Engineers (Public Works Department). – Engineering degree or A.M.I.M.E. and apprenticeship with subsequent experience of steam, oil and gas engines, motor cars, etc.

ELECTRICAL ENGINEERS.

Electrical engineering degree or A.M.I.E.E.[13] and apprenticeship, with subsequent power station and mains experience.

Shift Engineers. – Apprenticeship to mechanical engineering and subsequent experience in power station running. In addition marine and electrical experience is desirable.

TELEGRAPH ENGINEERS.

Thorough training in telegraph and telephone engineering and experience in a Home or Colonial Post Office Engineering Department or a British Railway. In addition, an electrical engineering degree or A.M.I.E.E. is usually required. A knowledge of wireless engineering is desirable.

DRAUGHTSMEN.

Candidates should be between 23 and 35 years of age.

Engineering. – Experience in Civil Engineer's Office, Plotting Surveys, Levels, etc. Quantities Estimating and Design of buildings, bridges, etc.

Locomotive. – Apprenticeship in Locomotive works and subsequent experience in a Locomotive drawing office.

The commencing salaries vary from approximately £400 to £480 per annum.

ARTISANS.

Vacancies for artisans, etc., in the following trades occur from time to time:
Foremen of Works (Buildings)
Saw Mill Foremen
Plumbers
Loco Foremen
Loco Fitters
Loco Erectors
Loco Turners
Loco Boilermakers
Carriage & Wagon Examiners
Carriage & Wagon Builders
Moulders
Millwrights
Platelayers
Electricians
Cable Jointers
Telegraph Foremen

Telegraph Mechanicians
General Fitters
Well Drillers /

Candidates are required to possess previous experience and to be between 25 and 35 years of age. The commencing salaries vary from £370 to £400 a year, except in the case of Well Drillers, who are usually engaged at fixed salaries varying from £480 to £600 per annum.

ARCHITECTURAL.

Architects and Architectural Draughtsmen.
Candidates should be between 23 and 35 years of age.
The qualification of A.R.I.B.A.[14] is generally required, with experience in design, supervision of building operations, specifications, and the general work of an architect's office. A knowledge of quantity surveying is desirable.
The commencing salaries vary from approximately £450 to £700 per annum.

MARINE.

The majority of vacancies occur in Nigeria, Tanganyika and Kenya (Lake Steamer Service).[15]

Sub-lieutenants of the R.N.R.[16] who are not qualified for promotion to the rank of Lieutenant are not required to resign their commissions as a condition of appointment to the Nigerian and Lake Steamer Services, but they must definitely understand that they are liable to removal from the active list for failure to qualify for promotion to rank of Lieutenant and that, if so removed, they cannot be placed on the retired list.

The qualifications for appointment to the Nigerian Marine Department are as follows:–

Executive Officers. – Officers on the Active List of the Royal Naval Reserve are given preference, though this qualification may be waived in the case of otherwise suitable candidates possessing an Extra Master's or Master's Certificate.[17] Age should be between 25 and 30 years. Preference will be given to ex-cadets from the "Conway," "Worcester" or The Nautical College, Pangbourne.[18]

Engineer Officers. – Officers on the Active List of the Royal Naval Reserve or Special Reserve of or above the rank of Lieutenant, and Mercantile Marine Engineers, possessing First Class Extra or First Class Engineers' Certificates will be given preference. Age should be between 24 and 30 years.

The commencing salary in the case of officers possessing Master's or First Class Engineer's certificate of Competency is £450 per annum rising to £720 per annum. There are higher posts above this scale.

For vacancies in the Tanganyika Territory the following qualifications are required:–

Marine Officers. – Master's Certificate and preferably a commission in the Royal Naval Reserve. Age 22-35. Salary £426 to £660 a year.

Second Engineers. – At least a Second Class Engineer's Certificate. Age, not under 22 years. Salary £372, rising to £480 a year.

For vacancies in the Lake Steamer Service of the Kenya and Uganda Railway and Harbours Department the following qualifications are required: –

Second Officers. – Master's Certificate. *Engineers.* – Chief Engineer's Certificate. Age 25-30. Salary £390 rising to £600 per annum.

ARTISANS.

Vacancies for Artisans in the following trades occur from time to time in Nigeria:–

Shipwrights
Boilermakers
Fitters.
Platers.
Turners.
Coppersmiths.

Candidates are required to possess previous experience and be between 25 and 35 years of age. Salary £400 to £500 a year.

ACCOUNTING AND STOREKEEPING.

Accountants and Storekeepers. – The majority of vacancies occur in West Africa and East Africa. The commencing salaries vary from £300 to £480 per annum.

Candidates should be between 23-35 years of age.

The following is required of candidates:–

Accountants (Assistant).

In Accountant-General Departments usually in West Africa. – Good general education, accounting experience and preferably a recognised accountancy qualification.

On Government Railways in East and West Africa. – Experience of accounting in the Chief Accountant's Office of a British Railway, and some knowledge of mechanical accounting desirable.

In Public Works Departments in East and West Africa. – Experience in keeping cost accounts with a firm of Public Works Contractors.

In Marine Departments in West Africa. – A thorough knowledge of commercial accounts, and of time-keeping and costing for constructional and repair engineering work, ability to supervise the accounting for large quantities of marine and engineering stores and a knowledge of office management generally. /

STOREKEEPERS (ASSISTANT).

On Government Railways in East and West Africa. – Experience of Storekeeping and preferably of Store Accounting on a British Railway.

In Public Works Departments in East and West Africa. – Experience of Storekeeping, including Store Accounting, on Public Works of importance or with a large firm of Building Contractors.

LABORATORY ASSISTANTS, STOCK INSPECTORS, AND FORESTERS.

Vacancies occur from time to time in East and West Africa for Laboratory Assistants, Stock Inspectors and Foresters. Candidates should be between 23 and 35 years of age.

Candidates for appointment as Laboratory Assistants should possess a sound practical knowledge of technical work as applied to Pathology and Bacteriology.

Candidates for appointment as Stock Inspectors should have a good practical knowledge of stock, more particularly cattle, and possess a diploma in dairying or agriculture.

Candidates for appointment as Foresters should have the diploma of the Forest of Dean or Benmore Schools,[19] or have had similar training on large private estates. A practical knowledge of surveying (with prismatie) compass and plane table) is desirable.

The commencing salaries vary from £300 to £400 per annum.

SANITARY INSPECTORS.

Candidates should be under 35 years of age and must possess the Sanitary Inspector's Certificate of the Royal Sanitary Institute[20] or other recognised examining body, or the first class Sanitary Assistant's certificate of the Army School of Hygiene.[21] Experience as Sanitary Inspector is desirable and preference given to candidates possessing also the certificate for Inspector of Meat and other Foods.

The majority of vacancies occur in West Africa and East Africa.

Commencing salary in West Africa is £400 per annum, and in East Africa £372.

POLICE (EUROPEAN NON-COMMISSIONED OFFICERS AND CONSTABLES).

Vacancies occur from time to time in the Police Forces of Palestine, Hong Kong, Tanganyika and Ceylon.

Palestine. – Constables, age 20-25, height 5' 9", single. Candidates must have served in one of the following branches of the British Army: – Horsed Cavalry, Royal Artillery, Foot Guards or Infantry. Section "A" reservists are not eligible. Salary £132 per annum. Free rations, quarters and uniform.

Hong Kong. – Constables, age 21-25, height 5' 8", single. Previous Police experience unnecessary. Commencing salary £190 per annum. Bounty of £25 on first appointment. Free quarters and uniform.

Tanganyika Territory. – Assistant Inspectors, age 22-30, height 5' 9", single. Previous Police experience desirable. Commencing salary £300 per annum. Uniform allowance of £10 on first appointment and thereafter annually at the end of each year's service. Free quarters.

Ceylon. – Sub-Inspectors, age 21-29 (in the case of ex-Navy men the maximum age limit is 32 years), height 5' 9", single. Previous Police experience unnecessary. Commencing salary £200 per annum. Free quarters and uniform.

Chest measurement must be in proportion to height, with good expansion.

Candidates for all the above police appointments must be of good education.

Regulations for His Majesty's Colonial Service
(London: Darly & Sons, 1911), pp. 3–33.

CHAPTER I. – CONSTITUTIONS.

§ 1. *Colonies and Protectorates.*

1. THE British Colonies and Protectorates may be classified as follows:–

I. Colonies possessing responsible government, *now known as the self-governing Dominions,* in which the Crown has only reserved the power of disallowing legislation and the Secretary of State for the Colonies[1] has no control over any public officer except the Governor. In all matters affecting the internal affairs of such a Colony the Governor acts on the advice of Ministers who are responsible to the Legislature. These Colonies fall constitutionally into two groups:–

   (i) Dominion of Canada,
       Dominion of New Zealand,
       Union of South Africa,
       Newfoundland.
   (ii) The Australian Commonwealth and its six component States:– New South Wales, Victoria, Queensland, South Australia, Western Australia, Tasmania. (The Northern Territory and Papua are administered by the Commonwealth.)

II. Colonies not possessing responsible government, in which the administration is carried on by public officers under the control of the Secretary of State for the Colonies (commonly known as Crown Colonies), and Protectorates similarly controlled.

   (i) Colonies possessing an Elected House of Assembly and a nominated Legislative Council:–
       Bahamas,   Bermuda.
       Barbados,
   (ii) Colonies possessing a partly elected Legislative Council, the constitution of which does not provide for an official majority:– British Guiana,
   The island of Cyprus has a similar constitution. /

(iii) Colonies possessing a partly elected Legislative Council, the constitution of which provides for an official majority:–

Fiji,   Malta,
Jamaica,   Mauritius.
Leeward Islands,

(iv) Colonies and Protectorates possessing a Legislative Council nominated by the Crown:–

British Honduras,   Nyasaland Protectorate,
Ceylon,   St. Lucia,
East Africa Protectorate,   St. Vincent,
Falkland Islands,   Seychelles,
Gambia,   Sierra Leone,
Gold Coast,   Southern Nigeria,
Grenada,   Straits Settlements,
Hong Kong,   Trinidad.

In all the above Councils, except British Honduras, the constitution provides for an official majority.

The Legislative Councils of Gambia, Sierra Leone, and Southern Nigeria have power to legislate for the following Protectorates respectively:–

Gambia Protectorate,
Sierra Leone Protectorate,
Southern Nigeria Protectorate.

(v) Colonies and Protectorates without a Legislative Council:–

Ashanti,   St. Helena,
Basutoland,   Somaliland,
Bechuanaland Protectorate,   Swaziland,
Gibraltar,   Uganda,
Northern Nigeria,   Weihaiwei,
Northern Territories of the   Islands included under the Western
    Gold Coast,   Pacific High Commission.

In all Crown Colonies and Protectorates, except Bahamas, Barbados, Bermuda, British Honduras, and the Leeward Islands, the Crown has the power of legislating by Order in Council.

The territories in South Africa which are under the control of the British South Africa Company are not included in the above classification. /

2. In the case of Colonies, the officer appointed by the Crown to administer the Government is styled either:–

Governor-General and Commander-in-Chief,
Governor and Commander-in-Chief, or
Captain General and Governor-in-Chief.

In the case of Protectorates the officer appointed by the Crown to administer the Government is styled either:–

Governor and Commander-in-Chief,
High Commissioner and Commander-in-Chief,
High Commissioner,
Commissioner and Commander-in-Chief, or
Commissioner.

In these regulations the term "the Governor" includes all officers appointed to administer Governments, however styled.

3. The officer so appointed receives a Commission under the Royal Sign Manual and Signet, and, if through death or absence or otherwise he should become incapable of acting, the government devolves on such officer or person as may have been designated for that purpose in the Letters Patent constituting the office.

4. The Governor is the single and supreme authority responsible to, and representative of, His Majesty. He is, by virtue of his Commission and the Letters Patent constituting his office, entitled to the obedience, aid and assistance of all military and civil officers; but although bearing the title of captain-general or commander-in-chief and although he may be a military officer, senior in rank to the officer commanding the troops, he is not, except on special appointment from His Majesty, invested with the command of His Majesty's regular forces in the Colony. He is therefore not entitled to receive the allowances annexed to that command or to take the immediate direction of any military operations, or, except in cases of urgent necessity, to communicate officially with subordinate military officers without the concurrence of the officer in command of the forces, to whom any such exceptional communication must be immediately notified.

5. The Governor, as the King's representative, will give the "word" (parole) in all places within his government.

6. The officer commanding the troops will render to the Governor such returns as he may require relating to the strength and condition of the troops, or to the military defences of the Colony. /

7. On the receipt of the Army (Annual) Act, the officer commanding the troops will communicate to the Governor the "General Orders" in which it may be promulgated.

8. Where several Colonies are comprised in one military command, the officer in command of the whole may transfer troops from one Colony to another on the application of the Governor of the Colony to which the troops are to be sent. This application should when practicable contain the written expression of opinion of the military officer, if any, there in command; but the officer in

command must in all cases consult with the Governor of the Colony from which the troops are sent, and will incur a special responsibility if he sends them away without the Governor's consent, except under special instructions from home.

9. For the purposes of Regulations 4 to 8 Colonies comprised under one government-in-chief are to be regarded as a single Colony.

10. The Governor has no authority over the movements of His Majesty's ships, and is not entitled to issue orders to officers of the Royal Navy. But, it being a general obligation on all His Majesty's civil and military officers to afford mutual assistance to each other in cases affecting the King's service, the Commander-in-chief of a station or the senior officer present at a port is instructed in the King's Regulations for the Navy to pay due regard to such requisitions as he may receive from the Governor, having for their object the protection of his Majesty's possessions, the benefit of the trade of his subjects or the general good of his service.

11. In urgent cases, when the requisitions may conflict with the instructions from the superior naval authority under which he is acting and when reference by telegraph or otherwise to such superior authority is impracticable, a naval officer is instructed to consider the relative importance and urgency of the required service as compared with his instructions, whether general or special; and he is to decide as in his judgment may seem best for His Majesty's service. In so doing he is instructed to bear in mind the grave responsibility that would rest on him if the circumstances were not such as to fully warrant the postponement of the instructions from his naval superior to the more pressing requisition from the Governor.

12. In cases where high political considerations demand the decision of His Majesty's Government in respect of the action to be taken, the Governor should communicate / his opinion that the presence of one of His Majesty's ships is necessary direct to the Secretary of State, instead of direct to the commanding officer of His Majesty's ship, unless the lives and property of British subjects are in such imminent peril as to demand immediate action.

13. The powers of every officer appointed to administer the government of a Colony or Protectorate are conferred, and his duties are defined, by His Majesty's Commission and the Instructions with which he is furnished. The following is a general outline of the nature of his powers and duties, subject to the special laws of each Colony:–

He is empowered to grant a pardon or respite to any criminal convicted in the colonial Courts of Justice and to remit any fines penalties or forfeitures which may accrue to the King. It is his duty to transmit to the Secretary of State by the earliest opportunity a report on each case in which, after sentence *of death*, a pardon is granted or the capital sentence is remitted.

The moneys to be expended for the public service are issued under his warrant.

He has the power, in the King's name, of issuing writs for the election of Representative Assemblies and Councils, and of convoking, proroguing, and dissolving legislative bodies.

He appoints, suspends, and dismisses public servants in the Colony.

He is empowered to administer the appointed oaths to all persons, in office or not, whenever he may think fit, and particularly the oath of allegiance provided by 31 & 32 Vict. c. 72, s. 2.[2]

He has the power of granting or withholding his assent to any Bills which may be passed by legislative bodies, but he is required, in the case of certain Bills, to reserve them for the signification of His Majesty's pleasure or to assent to them only if they contain a clause suspending their operation until they are confirmed by the Crown.

He is on no account to absent himself from the Colony without His Majesty's permission.

§ 3. *Councils and Assemblies.*

14. Legislative Councils nominated by the Crown generally consist in part of the principal executive officers / of the Colony and in part of private persons appointed by name; the former being termed Official, and the latter Unofficial Members.

15. Legislative Councils which are partly elected, generally consist of Official and Nominated Members, appointed as in the preceding regulation, and of members elected by the inhabitants of the Colony.

16. The numbers respectively of Official, Unofficial or Nominated, and Elected Members, are prescribed by the Letters Patent and Instructions to Governors.

17. When a vacancy occurs by the death, resignation, or otherwise, of a Legislative Councillor appointed by name, the Governor may in general appoint provisionally to such vacancy until His Majesty's pleasure be known.

18. Every law, vote or resolution the object or effect of which may be to dispose of or charge public revenue must be proposed by the Governor or with his consent.

19. A law comes into operation immediately on receiving the Governor's assent, unless some other date is prescribe by the law itself. The Crown, however, retains power to disallow it, and if this power be exercised the law ceases to have operation from the date at which notification of such disallowance is published in the Colony.

20. His Majesty's pleasure with regard to a law is signified through a Secretary of State, or by Order in Council where the constitution of a Colony so prescribes.

21. A law passed in a particular year by a Colonial Legislature should, unless reserved for the signification of His Majesty's pleasure, receive the Governor's assent in that year. In the absence of any legal provision to the contrary, it should be dated as of the day on which assent is given and numbered as of the year in which it is passed, whether it comes into operation immediately upon enactment or contains a provision postponing its operation to some future date. A law not assented to by the Governor but reserved by him for the signification of His Majesty's pleasure should be dated as of the day, and numbered as of the year, in which it is brought into force by public notification in the Colony.

22. In Colonies possessing responsible government the Governor is empowered to appoint and remove members of the Executive Council, it being understood that Councillors who have lost the confidence of the local legislature will tender their resignation to the Governor or discontinue the practical exercise of their functions in analogy with the usage prevailing in the United Kingdom. /

23. In Crown Colonies the Executive Council consists of certain principal officers of the Government with or without the addition of unofficial members. These Executive Councillors are either the holders of offices specified in the Governor's instructions or persons appointed in pursuance either of a Royal Warrant or of instructions from the Crown signified through a Secretary of State. The Governor may in cases of vacancies make provisional appointments, subject to the confirmation of the Crown. Members of the Executive Council can be dismissed by the Crown alone, but in case of urgency may be suspended by the Governor, who must however at once report fully to the Secretary of State the grounds of his action.

24. In Crown Colonies the Executive Council has the duty of assisting the Governor with its advice, and the Governor is required by his instructions to consult the Council in all matters of importance, except in cases of urgency (when it is his duty at the earliest practicable period to communicate to the Council the measures which he may have adopted with the reasons therefore), and in cases of such a nature that in his judgment the King's service would sustain material prejudice by consulting the Council thereon. Unless otherwise provided in any particular case by law or by his instructions, the Governor may act in opposition to the advice of the Council, but he is then required to report the reasons for his action to the Secretary of State by the first convenient opportunity.

CHAPTER II. – OFFICERS.

25. The regulations in chapter II. do not apply to any officer in a Colony under responsible government except to the Governor in his relation to the Crown.

§ 4. *Appointments.*

26. The regulations as to appointment to public offices are directions given by the Crown to the Governors of Crown Colonies for general guidance and do not constitute a contract between the Crown and its servants.

27. Appointments to public offices are made by authority of His Majesty, and such offices as a rule are held during His Majesty's pleasure but in some few cases are held during good behaviour.

28. The general rule is that appointments to public offices are made by letter signed by the Governor or written by his direction, except in the case of Judges of / the Supreme Court who are appointed in His Majesty's name by an instrument under the Public Seal of the Colony. This rule applies equally whether the appointments be provisional or definitive.

29. Public offices are divided into three classes:–

Class I. Those of which the initial emoluments do not exceed one hundred pounds per annum.

Class II. Those of which the initial emoluments exceed one hundred and do not exceed three hundred pounds per annum.

Class III. Those of which the initial emoluments exceed three hundred pounds per annum.

30. When a vacancy occurs in Class I the Governor makes the appointment and reports it to the Secretary of State in the next quarterly return as prescribed by regulation 397.

31. When a vacancy occurs in Class II the Governor reports it immediately to the Secretary of State together with the name and qualifications of the person, if any, whom he recommends for appointment. The Governor's recommendation is usually followed.

32. The powers of the Governor under the two preceding regulations do not extend to the appointment or provisional appointment of a person not resident in the Colony.

33. When a vacancy occurs in Class III the Governor follows the same course as to reporting it, but he is distinctly to inform any person whom he may provisionally appoint that he holds the office only until his appointment is confirmed or superseded under directions from the Secretary of State. The Governor may rec-

ommend a candidate for the final appointment but it must be clearly understood that the Secretary of State may select another candidate.

34. In reporting a vacancy in Class III or in reporting the creation of any office in that class, the Governor will furnish in duplicate, in the form given in Appendix 1,[3] full particulars respecting the nature and incidents of the office.

35. In the selection of candidates for vacancies in Classes II and III, the claims of meritorious public officers, whether in the service of the same Colony or of some other Colony, will generally take precedence of those of persons new to the public service. In the case of the chief judicial and chief fiscal offices local connection with the Colony by birth, family ties or otherwise will usually be considered to render a candidate ineligible. /

36. The Governor will make annually a confidential report on the qualifications of persons in the public service who apply or are fitted for promotion otherwise than in their own department whether in the Colony or elsewhere; and on all officers on the active list of the Army seconded for employment in the Colony, *on whom reports are not made to the War Department direct.*

The Governor will make a similar report in the case of persons resident in the Colony when such persons apply through him to the Secretary of State for employment in the public service.

37. The claims of candidates for promotion will be considered in order of their seniority, but the selection will be mainly decided by regard to official qualifications. Seniority in any Department is determined by the date of an officer's appointment to the particular grade or class in which he is serving. Seniority as between officers appointed on probation and subsequently confirmed in their appointments is determined by the date of the probationary appointment. Except where otherwise provided at the time of appointment, seniority as between persons selected for appointment from outside the Colony is determined by the date at which they begin to draw any salary of their new office or, where two or more begin to draw such salary on the same date, by the date of the letter from the Colonial Office confirming the selection.

38. Appointments, provisional or permanent, of gentlemen who have been connected with the Governor as private secretaries, Aides-de-Camp or otherwise are open to objection and must not be made without previous reference to the Secretary of State.

39. Whenever an officer of His Majesty's Imperial Forces who is on the half pay or retired list is appointed to a civil situation in any Colony, a report of the appointment specifying the amount of salary and the commencing date for payment thereof is to be made immediately to the Secretary of State for the Col-

onies, which will be transmitted by him to the proper authorities in this country. Promotions in the Civil Service of such officers are also to be notified forthwith to the Secretary of State for the Colonies for the information of the respective authorities.

§ 5. *Discipline.*

40. Salaried public officers whose remuneration is fixed on the assumption that their whole time is at the disposal / of the Government are prohibited from engaging in trade, or employing themselves in any commercial or agricultural undertaking.

41. All salaried public officers, whether or not their whole time is at the disposal of the Government, are prohibited from directly or indirectly making or holding any local investment, *speculating in the shares of,* or being connected with any *company*, occupation or undertaking, which might bring their private interests into real or apparent conflict with their public duties, or in any way influence them in the discharge of their duties. In all cases of doubt as to the application of this regulation a public officer is required to submit the case for the Governor's decision.

42. No public officer on leave of absence is permitted to accept any paid employment without previously obtaining the express sanction of the Secretary of State or, if his leave is spent in the Colony, of the Governor.

43. No public officer is to undertake any private agency in any matter connected with the exercise of his public duties.

44. No public officer can be permitted to be the editor of a newspaper or directly or indirectly to take part in the management of it. He may not contribute anonymously to any newspaper in the Colony or elsewhere; nor may he write on questions which can properly be called political or administrative, though he may furnish signed articles upon subjects of general interest.

45. No public officer whether on duty or on leave of absence is to allow himself to be interviewed on questions of public policy or on matters affecting the defense and military resources of any British possession.

46. Governors, Lieutenant – Governors, and all other servants of the Crown in the Colony are prohibited during the continuance of their service in the Colony from receiving valuable presents (other than the ordinary gifts of personal friends), whether in the shape of money, goods, free passages or other personal benefits, and from giving such presents.

This regulation applies not only to the officers themselves, but also to their families, and officers will be held responsible for its observance by their families.

It is not intended to apply to cases of remuneration for special services rendered and paid for with the consent of the Government. /

Money which has been subscribed with a view of marking public approbation of an officer's conduct may be dedicated to objects of general utility and connected with the name of the person who has merited such a proof of the general esteem.

47. Presents from kings, chiefs or other members of the native population in or neighbouring to the Colony, which cannot be refused without giving offense, will be handed over to the Government.

When presents are exchanged between Governors or other officers acting on behalf of the Colonial Government in ceremonial intercourse with native kings, chiefs, or others, the presents received will be handed over to the Government, and any return presents will be given at the Government expense.

48. Governors will not without special permission accept or forward any articles for presentation to His Majesty.

49. Holders of patent offices may be removed from such offices by the Governor and Council under the second section of the Act 22 Geo. 3, c. 75, but care must be taken that the officer is heard after being apprised of the charge against him, and it is convenient that the course prescribed in case of suspension should be pursued in any proceedings for removal. Against any such removal an appeal lies to His Majesty in Council, which should be prosecuted like any other appeal.

50. Every other public officer holds office subject to the pleasure of the Crown, and the pleasure of the Crown that he should no longer hold it may be signified through the Secretary of State, in which case no special formalities are required.

51. An officer who has not been appointed by virtue of a Warrant from the Crown, and whose pensionable emoluments do not exceed £100 a year, may be dismissed by the Governor, provided that in every such case *where the officer has not been convicted on a criminal charge* the grounds of intended dismissal are definitely stated in writing, and communicated to the officer in order that he may have full opportunity of exculpating himself, and that the matter is investigated by the Governor with the aid of the head of the department.

If such an officer is convicted on a criminal charge, the Governor may call for the records of the trial and form his / decision thereon, with the assistance if necessary of the officer who tried the case.

In lieu of dismissal the Governor may remove the officer to an office of lower rank in the service, or may require him to serve in his original office at a reduced salary, either permanently or for a stated period, or may deduct a portion of salary due, or about to become due, to the officer. Such dismissal or other punishment will not require the confirmation of the Secretary of State, but any memorial from the dismissed officer must be forwarded to the Secretary of State without delay with a short statement of the grounds of dismissal or other punishment.

52. Notwithstanding the above provisions, if the Governor considers that any such officer should be removed on grounds of general inefficiency, he must call for a full report from the heads of the departments in which the officer has served; and, if satisfied after considering that report that it is necessary in the interests of the public service, he may remove the officer. In every such case the question of pension will be dealt with under the laws or regulations of the Colony.

53. In the case of any officer whose pensionable emoluments exceed £100 a year, the Governor may suspend him from the exercise of his office and from the enjoyment of his salary, in which case the following regulations (54 to 71) must be strictly observed, unless the mode of suspension is otherwise provided for by local law. ...

§ 6. *Salaries.*

74. On appointment to an office of a person not within the Colony, half salary, if available, will be allowed as a general rule from the date of embarkation, and full salary, if available, from the date of arrival in the Colony, provided that the officer proceeds direct to the Colony to which he is appointed; otherwise he will be allowed to draw half salary for such time only as is ordinarily required to perform the journey between the point of embarkation and that of arrival in the Colony.

75. No advance of salary is allowed to officers either on first appointment or on leave of absence, except in special cases to be determined by the Secretary of State, / Collateral security will be required when the advance exceeds a month's salary. The security of another officer serving in the same Colony as the applicant will not be accepted.

76. If an office be vacated in a Colony by the death, removal or absence on half-pay leave of the holder, the person appointed by the Governor to act in his stead will receive half the initial salary of the office. Should that person be the holder of another office, but not performing the duties of it while so acting, he may receive in addition half the initial salary of his own office and all the increments which he has earned in that office.

77. Should the person so appointed by the Governor to a vacant office be required at the same time to perform the duties of his own office, he may be allowed half the initial salary of the temporary office together with the whole salary of his own office; but no person should be appointed to discharge at the

same time the duties of two distinct offices whenever any other arrangement may be practicable; and unless the offices are distinct and separate offices in different departments of the service, or offices not standing to one another in any intimate relation of superiority and subordination, such as two Magistracies, only half salary of each office can be allowed or the officer's own salary if that be greater.

78. The fees of the vacant office (in the absence of any regulation to the contrary) will be paid into the Colonial Treasury, and the Treasury will pay the acting officer one moiety with such further amount as the Governor shall consider advisable in case the services performed are of a special character or involve outlay.

79. Should the officer whom the Governor has appointed temporarily to a vacant office be confirmed therein, he will be entitled to draw the full salary of that office, if available, from the date at which he entered on the duties, but from the date from which he draws such full salary he will not be entitled to salary on account of any other office which he may have held at the same time.

79A. *An Officer who is promoted in ordinary course in the Colony in which he is serving should, in the absence of any statutory provision to the contrary, receive the salary of his new scale, grade, or appointment, if it be available, as from the date when the vacancy occurred in the superior post, / whether he be in the Colony or on leave of absence at the date in question.*

80. When the salary of an officer is on an incremental scale, the holder is not entitled to draw any increment as of right but only by sanction of the Governor. In the case of a subordinate officer a certificate is required from the head of his department that he has discharged his duties with diligence and fidelity.

81. Service for increments is to be reckoned from the day on which an officer first begins to draw any salary of his office. In the case where the salary drawn by the officer at the time of promotion is not less than the minimum salary of his new office he will continue to draw his former rate of salary in his new office; and the period qualifying for the first increment is to be reckoned from the date at which he began to draw that rate of salary. His first increment will be of such amount as will bring his salary to the next incremental step in the scale of the salary of the new office.

When a duty allowance is attached to the new office, it is included with the salary for the purpose of this regulation.

82. The grant of pensions and retiring allowances is governed by the laws or regulations of the Colony concerned. The rates of pension vary in different Colonies, but the general principle is that the pension is based on the length of service and on the average salary drawn during the last three years of service, the maximum

being two-thirds of final salary. In the case of officers who have served in more than one Colony a separate pension is awarded from each Colony based in most cases on the length of service in that Colony and the final salary drawn in that Colony; but in certain groups of Colonies the officer receives a total pension of the same amount as if the whole of his service had been in the Colony from which he finally retires. Commutation of pensions is not allowed. [...]

§ 8. *Salaries and leave of Governors.*

103. A Governor is appointed during His Majesty's pleasure, but his tenure of office is as a rule confined to a period of six years from his assumption of the administration.

104. When the office of Governor becomes vacant or when the Governor is on leave, other than full-pay leave, / the person succeeding to the administration of the Government will (if previously resident in the Colony) receive half of the salary of the Governor. If he be an officer in the service of the Colony, he will receive in addition half the salary of his own office.

105. Should the person called to the temporary administration have been trans-ferred from the public service elsewhere, he will receive the whole salary of the Governor, if available, but in that case he will not be entitled to any portion of the salary of the office from which he has been transferred. During the absence on leave, other than full-pay leave, of a Governor and after the embarkation of a newly appointed Governor, such person is only entitled to the half salary available. Whether he can draw also half the salary of the office from which he has been temporarily transferred will depend on the arrangements made for payment of his substitute, and will be decided in each instance by the Secretary of State.

106. The leave of Governors is regulated by special rules of local application; but in most of the Crown Colonies the Governor may be granted leave with full salary, exclusive of entertainment or duty allowance, for a period not exceeding six weeks in any one year. The officer administering the government is entitled in the absence of the Governor from the Colony to draw in full any allowance provided for entertainment and also any duty allowance.

107. If the period of a vacancy or of the absence of the Governor should exceed nine months, and there should be any salary available, the Secretary of State will approve such arrangements as may appear reasonable for the increase of the sal-ary of the temporary holder for the period of excess.

108. On appointment to a Government, half salary when available and when permitted by law will be allowed as a general rule from the date of embarkation from England or a colony. An officer succeeding to the administration or the

provisional administration of a Colonial Government will be entitled to draw full or half salary, as the case may be, in respect of the day on which he assumes the administration. The officer whom he succeeds will not be entitled to any payment for that day, except the half salary granted in cases of absence on leave.

109. If a Governor is transferred from one colony to another and comes to England on his way thereto, he will, if the Secretary of State is satisfied that such return is / unavoidable or in furtherance of the public interest, usually receive the half salary of the Government which he relinquishes, until the date of his embarkation from England for the Government to which he is appointed; but if such half salary is not available he will usually receive the half salary of the new Government. If no half salary is available from either Government he can receive no salary. ...

§ 10. *Leave and Passage Rules in West Africa.*

122. – (a) Subject to the necessities of the Service, European officers, that is to say, officers who were not themselves born in West Africa and neither of whose parents was born there, may, after every tour of 12 consecutive months of residential service, be granted vacation leave with full pay for two calendar months *plus* the time necessarily taken on the journey to England; and, if specially detained by the Governor on public grounds after the completion of a *such* tour of service, they may be granted vacation leave for ten days more with full pay in respect of each calendar month that they may have been detained, but no additional leave will be granted in respect of any fraction of a month.

(b) In the case of officers who are returning to West Africa, there may be added to their vacation leave a further period of leave with full pay, known as "return leave," for two calendar months *plus* the time necessarily taken on the journey from England. Officers to whom return leave is granted will be required to sign an agreement to the effect that, in the event of their failing to return to the Colony or Protectorate they will, if called upon to do so, refund the amount of any pay drawn in respect of such leave.

122 *bis. Leave may also be granted, in exceptional circumstances, after a tour of less than twelve months' service, where the Governor considers that the arrangement would be in the public interest; and in that case the vacation and return leave will both be on the scale of five days for each completed calendar month of service.*

123. – *(a)* Officers invalided before completing a *full* tour of *residential* service may be granted sick leave with full pay for the time necessarily taken on the journey to England *plus* five days in respect of each completed calendar month of residential service.

(b) In addition to the sick leave which may be granted under the foregoing rule, officers returning to West Africa may be granted "return sick leave" with full pay for five / days more (making ten days in all), in respect of each completed calendar month of residential service *plus* the time necessarily taken on the journey from England, subject to the same conditions with regard to repayment and date of embarkation as return leave.

124. No extension of vacation leave or sick leave will be granted with full pay, but in exceptional circumstances, such as continued ill-health, officers who are not returning may be granted an extension of leave with half pay for any period not exceeding four calendar months, at the discretion of the Secretary of State.

125. Return leave or return sick leave may be extended with half pay on the ground of ill-health for any period not exceeding four calendar months; or with full pay if the officer is detained in England by the Secretary of State on public grounds.

126. Any extension of leave, however short, which may be granted on any other grounds than those mentioned in the two foregoing regulations must be without pay.

127. An officer returning to West Africa will be required to embark by the first steamer leaving England after the date on which his leave of absence expires, and will be allowed pay at the rate which he is then drawing for any days which may elapse between the expiration of his leave and the departure of the steamer; provided that, if there is a later steamer which is timed to arrive at his destination before the first one, he will be required to proceed by the later one. Extensions of leave will date from the expiration of the original leave, and not from the day on which the officer would have had to embark if his leave had not been extended.

128. If invalided out of the Colony, but not to Europe, an officer may either draw full pay and pay all his own expenses or draw half pay and have the cost of his passages paid by the Government, as the Governor may decide; and in such cases (that is to say, if the officer does not visit Europe) he will not be required to begin a new tour of service on his return, but the two periods of service will be regarded as consecutive residential service. Leave granted under this rule should not exceed three months, and must be reported to the Secretary of State.

129. Officers desiring leave, on the ground of "urgent private affairs," before completing a tour of residential service, may, if specially recommended by the Governor, be allowed leave without pay, or if they have completed six months of residential service, leave with half pay, at / the discretion of the Secretary of State; but such leave must in no case exceed four months, inclusive of the time taken on the journeys. Officers to whom leave is granted under this regulation commence a fresh tour of service on their return to duty.

130. – (*a*) Every officer before applying for permission to proceed on leave of absence will obtain from the medical officer of his station a certificate as to his

state of health, and, in case he is not in good health, the certificate must contain a recommendation as to the course he should pursue on his arrival in the United Kingdom, and must be accompanied by the notes of the case. He will forward these papers to the Governor through the proper channel when applying for leave of absence, and they will be enclosed in the dispatch notifying to the Secretary of State the leave of absence which has been granted.

(b) When the officer arrives in the United Kingdom he will receive instructions to present himself to one of the medical advisers of the Colonial Office if that course is recommended by the local medical officer, and in any case he will be required to show that the recommendations of the local medical officer are being carried out.

(c) If an officer falls ill so as to require medical attendance during the voyage home or during his leave of absence and remains ill for a week, he will report the fact to the Colonial Office and will send a fortnightly report form his medical attendant as long as he remains under his care.

(d) Unless these rules are observed, an officer will not be entitled to pay during any extension of leave which it may be necessary to grant him on the ground of ill-health.

131. Officers to whom the foregoing regulations of this section apply are required to discharge any duties upon which the Governor may think it desirable to employ them; and they are not entitled to receive any available half salary under Regulations 76, 77, 104, 105 and 108, in addition to the salary of their own office, for performing the duties of an office vacated by the death or removal or temporary absence of the holder, but they will draw the duty allowance when acting in any office to which such an allowance is attached.

They may also be required by the Secretary of State to discharge any duty or to go through any course of instruction which he may think necessary during their leave of / absence, and will not be entitled to any additional remuneration or leave of absence in consideration of such employment. Allowances granted to cover necessary out-of-pocket expenses are not regarded as remuneration.

132. Free passages to England and out again will be allowed to all officers under the rank of Governor who may be granted leave of absence under Regulations 122 and 123; and a free passage out will be allowed on their first appointment to all such officers on their executing the usual agreement under which they will be bound to refund the cost of the passage in the event of their relinquishing their appointment within three years from the date of their arrival in the Colony or Protectorate for any other reason than bodily or mental infirmity. Passages will not be granted to wives or children under Regulation 121.

133. If an officer is transferred while in West Africa from one West African Colony or Protectorate to another, he will be regarded as having completed a tour of service in the Colony or Protectorate to which he is transferred when the sum of his service in the two Colonies or Protectorates amounts to twelve months, and the whole of his salary during leave of absence will be paid from the funds of the last Colony or Protectorate.

134. Persons engaged under agreements in the West Indies or Asia for certain subordinate posts in West Africa are employed on special terms as to leave of absence, under which, after three consecutive years of residential service, they may be granted vacation leave with full pay for two calendar months *plus* the time necessarily taken on the journey to England, and (if they are returning to West Africa) return leave with full pay for two calendar months *plus* the time necessarily taken on the journey from England, with free passages to and from their homes. Such persons may also be granted the same vacation for the purpose of relaxation from business as is allowed to native officials of similar grade, but this annual vacation must not be continuous with the vacation leave or return leave provided for in their agreements.

135. The foregoing regulations (122 to 134) do not apply to native officers, that is to say, officers who were themselves born in West Africa or whose parents were either of them born there. All such officers are subject to the general regulations as to leave of absence and passages, with the exception that they are not entitled to any pay under regulations 76 and 77, when acting in the place of an European officer. They will, however, in lieu of such pay, / draw the duty allowance when acting in any office to which a duty allowance is attached; and when they are acting for an European officer and not receiving any duty allowance, the Governor may, if he thinks fit, award a gratuity in respect of such acting service, subject to the approval of the Secretary of State. On the other hand, the regulations numbered 84 to 87, 90, 91, 92, 95 to 98, 101, and 102 do not apply to European officers.

CHAPTER III. – CEREMONIES.

136. The regulations in Chapter III. apply to all Colonies and Protectorates except when otherwise stated.

§ 11. *Precedence.*

137. The precedence of officers in Colonies is determined by local enactments, by Royal Charters, by Instructions either under the Royal Sign Manual and Signet or through the Secretary of State, or by authoritative local usage.

138. In the absence of any special authority Governors will guide themselves by the following general table of Colonial precedence:–

The Governor or officer administering the Government.

The Lieutenant-Governor.

The Senior Officer in command of the troops, if of the rank of a General, and the officer in command of His Majesty's Naval Forces on the Station, if of the rank of an Admiral, their own relative rank being determined by the King's Regulations on that subject.

The Bishop.

The Chief Justice.

The Senior Officer in command of the troops, if of the rank of Colonel or Lieutenant-Colonel, and the officer in command of His Majesty's Naval Forces on the Station, if of equivalent rank, their own relative rank being determined by the King's Regulations on that subject.

The Members of the Privy or Executive Councils.

The Puisne Judges (in Crown Colonies).

The President of the Legislative Council.

The Speaker of the House of Assembly.

The Members of the House of Assembly.

The Colonial Secretary (not being in the Executive Council). /

The Chief Commissioners, Government Agents or Residents of Provinces.

The Attorney-General (not being in the Executive Council).

The Solicitor-General.

The Senior Officer in command of the troops, if below the rank of Colonel or Lieutenant-Colonel, and the Senior Naval Officer of corresponding rank.

The Auditor-General or Inspector-General of accounts.

The Treasurer, or other principal financial officer.

The Principal Medical Officer.

The chief officer of customs.

The Director of Public Works or Surveyor-General.} Not being members of Executive or Legislative Councils.

The Clerk of the Executive Council.

The Clerk of the Legislative Council.

The Clerk of the House of Assembly.

In the Colonies possessing responsible government, and having no special table of precedence, the Puisne Judges take precedence next after the Speaker of the House of Assembly.

139. When two or more Colonies are comprised within one military or naval command, the military and naval officers holding the commands in any one of

such Colonies in the absence of the superior commanding officers will take the precedence assigned to them in the Colonial Regulations, and will retain that precedence notwithstanding the presence of the chief superior officers of the whole military and naval commands. No other military or naval officers have any place at all in the general table of Colonial precedence, and the places accorded therein to the Senior Military Officer and the Senior Naval Officer have no connection, except as between those two officers, with the regulations governing military and naval precedence.

140. When a naval officer is a member of a Court of Enquiry into the circumstances attending the loss of a merchant ship but does not preside over the Court he should sit at the right hand of, and so next in seniority to, the President.

141. The precedence of Members of Councils in Crown Colonies between themselves is regulated by the Royal Instructions.

Ernest Eiloart,[1] *The Land of Death: A Pamphlet Addressed to the Members of Both Houses of Parliament; With Some Observations on the Present Mode of Making Selections for Colonial Appointment* (London: Hatchards, Piccadilly, 1887).

Any Communications intended for the Author on the subjects dealt with in this Pamphlet, may be addressed to CLARENCE EILOART, 30 Essex Street, Strand. /

THE LAND OF DEATH.

WHAT is the Land of Death? and why is a pamphlet upon such a subject addressed to Members of Parliament in particular?

The Land of Death is a British Colony; it is a Colony in which many lives of Englishmen are wasted yearly; a Colony in which Englishmen and natives sicken, and live, if they do live, in a state of death-in-life. It is a Colony in which Sickness, Superstition, Barbarism, and Death are the only things that flourish. And of all these things that flourish, the most flourishing is Death.

Why do I address Members of Parliament upon this subject? It is because the evils that I have mentioned are not, as they exist, inevitable, but could, with a modest effort, be reduced to an insignificant minimum. That these things flourish is a fact for which the / Governors of the Colony, then the Colonial Office, and, lastly, Parliament are responsible. But the Governors keep the Colonial Office as much as possible in the dark, and what little light comes to the Colonial Office never finds its way to Parliament.

The Gold Coast Colony is not a place that much is known about in England, even since the Colonial Exhibition and the Imperial Federation League have aroused the minds of the English people to the fact that our Colonial Empire is a reality.[2] The Gold Coast is not a place in which large fortunes are made, or in which fame and promotion are achieved in frequent wars; and the public know very little about it. Only here and there in England is a woman whom the Gold Coast has made a widow, a child whom the Gold Coast has made an orphan, or a father from whom the Gold Coast has taken an only son. Here and there, too, are families who know that every mail may bring them the news that one they love will never return again from the Gold Coast; his last letter may have told them that he was in good health, yet they know well that the fingers that penned that letter may have been / cold and stiff weeks before the letter reached the English home. The proportion of an army killed in a given time in one of our 'little wars' is not greater than the proportion of white men on the Gold Coast who die in an equal time. And those who suffer from sickness that brings them under the shadow of death are far more numerous in proportion than the wounded in a campaign. And men may recover from their wounds, but a man who has undergone the Coast fever will never through all his life be the same man again. In the Ashantee War[3] about a hundred and twenty marines were kept ashore in this place for a few weeks. The fever killed twenty-seven of them, prostrated nearly all the rest, and only two arrived in England in a state of efficiency. Yet English officers for two companies of West Indian troops have to be kept here. Promotion is rapid on the Gold Coast.

Nearly all the people of the country are heathen, who are sometimes stirred up by their priests to fight in order that the fetish may be appeased by human sacrifices. Afterwards the Government demand *their* human sacrifices, and the people who have been allowed to grow / up in barbarism and superstition beneath the British flag, and who have also been allowed absolute liberty to keep and carry firearms, are hanged for indulging in the propensities which are the inevitable result of their surroundings. At these hangings the ropes sometimes break, for the Government of the Colony is nothing if not economical, and the ropes are not always replaced when rotten. The result is, that the victim has to be hanged again: on one occasion the ceremony was performed three times. That was in the time of a Governor who won a great reputation for economy, and was made a K.C.M.G.

The country is 300 miles long, with a maximum breadth of eighty miles; it comprises over 12,000 square miles, and contains half a million inhabitants. The Government feel it their duty to provide education for this country. Accordingly they have provided two schools, with native teachers. This gives occasion to provide a gentleman with an income for performing the duty of inspecting the schools. He runs down once a-year from Sierra Leone, where he earns another salary, inspects the two schools, and earns 400*l.* a year. /

But if there are only two schools, there are a great many prisons. These are very comfortable places, where the prisoners pass the night together in one large room, and shout, sing, and tell stories. They obtain as much rum and tobacco as they can pay for. When the pleasure palls upon them they go away.

As the prisons are not terrible, and as there are no lights in any town, and scarcely any police, burglaries by armed men are frequent, and each merchant keeps an armed force in his store at night.

Now it is apparent that the Government is responsible for the ignorance and crime of the place, but it may be supposed that they are not responsible for the sickliness. Let us see if this is so. What are the causes of the sickliness? They are: – First, Malaria; second, Filth. Malaria is caused by the decay of the vegetation, which grows in inconceivable abundance in the hot, damp climate of West Africa. The Government know this, and have accordingly removed their own quarters from the bush-grown locality of Cape Coast to the grass-surrounded town of Christiansborg. Nearly all the other towns are closely hemmed in with / dense vegetation, which grows, rots, and kills. If the owners were compelled to keep their land clear of useless bush for about three miles round each town, the land would be placed in a cultivable condition, and there would be no more poison and no more malaria. Because this is not done, English homes are made desolate.

As for filth, the people smell it, breathe it, drink it. There is no public water supply in any town. The well-to-do classes dig tanks to store the rain-water from their roofs. The poor people travel a mile or more to fetch on their heads a pot full of discoloured fluid to serve for the day's needs of their families. This stuff is drawn from surface-wells, filled – or *not* filled – with water saturated with the impurities of decaying vegetation. This gives rise to skin diseases and enteric disorders.

There are no sewers. House - slops are emptied into the public streets; some of the more scrupulous natives carry their filth to the sea, and decorum, and the nose, and the health are offended by the sight of women walking down the streets bearing on their heads utensils filled with the day's filth of a family. / The beach, the bush all round the towns, and even the streets, are polluted with ordure. This is because there are scarcely any necessary conveniences attached to the houses; the people are too savage to make them, and the Government leave them to their wallowing in the mire. Then they die. Kitchen refuse is collected in heaps just outside the town, where it rots under the windows of the inhabitants. It might be burnt, but then it would not kill anybody. So the Government prefer to let it rot.

Half the householders keep fowls, sheep, and goats on their premises. These creatures run in and out of the houses familiarly, and prowl about the streets. The Public Health Ordinance says that they are to be allowed to wander about the streets. It would be all the same if the Ordinance forbade them to do so. It forbids pigs; but that does not interfere with the supply of pigs in the streets. Laws are generally made to be enforced, but this is not the case with the Public Health Ordinance. That was made for the purpose of throwing dust in the eyes of the Colonial Office. This is clear from the fact that it discourses of cesspools, ashpits, reservoirs, and aqueducts, while the / officials who drew, discussed, passed, and sent the Ordinance to England, knew that not one of these things exists from one end of the country to the other.

So, also, it is against the Ordinance to keep animals in such a way as to be injurious to health, and it is also illegal to throw filth into the street. Yet the facts on these subjects are what have been stated. The Ordinance empowers the Governor to make rules for the prevention of the keeping of animals on any premises, and for compelling the clearing of bush around towns, and for providing places for the *temporary* deposit of refuse. Seeing that the Governors have never availed themselves of these powers, it is evident that the Ordinance was made to mislead the Colonial Office. But this is not the only instance of misleading statements being sent home by the authorities here. It is stated in the Colonial Office List that there is a road to Coomassie. There are not twelve continuous miles of road in any part of the Colony.

Then, it may be asked, if the Government do not educate, do not repress crime, do not suppress disease, and do not make roads, / What *do* they do? The answer to this is very simple – They draw their pay.

Also, they take holidays.

For watching the people die, and for conferring appointments upon his family, the Governor draws 3000*l.* a year. He also has 500*l.* a year for maintaining official hospitality. He does not maintain it. He pockets the money.

Thus, in effect, the Governor has 3500*l.* a year for doing nothing. In this task he is ably assisted by a Queen's Advocate – at the time of writing, his own son.[4] The usual emoluments of the office (not, however, drawn by the present temporary holder) are a thousand a year, a house, medical attendance, a free passage to and from England for leave, and a holiday of six months on full pay at the end of each twelve months' work. The work is not exhausting. The official conducts prosecutions in the central province. For exactly similar work in another province a local barrister is paid by fees amounting to about 180*l.* a year. The Queen's Advocate has also the labour of attending Councils, and of drawing an Ordinance occasionally. There are other officials with good salaries, houses, medical attendance, and / holidays on full pay at the end of each year's work.

Four per cent of all the imports, without counting specific duties on liquor and tobacco, is taken by the Government. The benefit the Colony receives in return may be inferred from what has been stated.

Lagos, and Sierra Leone, like the Gold Coast, are dirty and deadly. Sierra Leone is, or was recently, insolvent. This is important; the reader will now begin to see that the question is widening. It is not now simply a question of the misgovernment of a single colony; but it is seen that the *only three colonies* of which the writer knows anything are *all* managed in a way that is a disgrace to the British Empire.

The question is then forced upon the mind of every thoughtful person, What is the condition of other Crown Colonies? May it not be that, if we knew, we should find something very wrong in them also? Governors are not specially selected for incompetency for the West African Colonies.

It may be said that in other Crown Colonies there is a larger white population, / and that, therefore, there is a stronger Public Opinion.

Public opinion is only powerful when it dares to express itself.

In this Gold Coast Colony there is a widely held belief that to criticise the Government publicly is to become a marked man. Even the members of the so-called Legislative Council dare not oppose the Governor. They believe that the consequence of such opposition would be that he would punish them by sending them on some unpleasant duty into what would be practically exile – exactly the method of the Czar, in fact. In making such a statement as this a writer is in the unpleasant position of being unable to offer to the public the proofs which have satisfied his own mind. To say, "I had it from one of the oldest members of the Council," would be considered insufficient unless the name of the person alluded to were given. But it is obvious that while the official is still alive it would be improper to give his name, and so surrender him to the tender mercies of a wrathful Governor.

One such communication, however, was made by a gentleman who has passed beyond the reach / of Governors, and whose name can therefore be stated. No less a person than the late Chief Justice of the Gold Coast Colony, in the time of Governor Rowe⁵ gave a friendly warning to the present writer, saying, "If you want a Government appointment, you mustn't write against the Governor. You'll lose any chance that you might have if you do that." The newspaper articles referred to, however, continued to appear, and the event justified the Judge's prophecy. A vacancy occurred, and was filled by a young barrister of a year's standing; another vacancy was bestowed upon a gentleman who, though a member of the lower branch of the profession, had the negative merit of having kept his opinion of the Governor to himself and his friends. At the death of the Chief Justice, it being no longer necessary to consider his words as confidential, they were reported to Governor Griffith with the plain question, 'Is it, or is it not, the fact, that to have criticised the policy of the Government adversely in the public press is considered as disqualifying the critic for office? The late Chief Justice said that it is, and the question is one of public importance.' To this plain challenge / the Governor replied, that he would not answer the question. The question was then repeated to the Secretary for the Colonies, who also replied with a refusal to answer. Sooner or later he will be *made* to answer; what he was ashamed to confess privately he will be compelled to avow in his place in Parliament. Surely there is *some* Member of Parliament who cares to know on what principles the officials of our Colonial Empire are chosen?

English merchants cannot afford to offend the Governor; they may tender for Government contracts, or they may be guilty of some technical violation of the Customs' regulations, and have to beg for the remission of a penalty. They look on with approval while some more reckless man expresses his and their mind in the press. They may bring their grievances to him to be ventilated, but they carefully abstain from all overt acts of opposition to the powers that be.

Now all these checks upon the expression of public opinion are as likely to exist in the West Indies as in West Africa. Therefore we come again to the question, 'What is the probable state of all our Crown Colonies if these we have been discussing are in such an awful / plight?' For, as has been said before, there is no reason to believe that all the incompetent Governors are sent to West Africa. And this suggests the question, – In what way are officials selected for the Crown Colonies?

In two ways: some are residents in the Colonies, temporarily appointed by the Governor, and confirmed at his recommendation by the Colonial Office; others are selected in England by the Colonial Office and sent out.

Let us say a few words upon each of these modes of appointment. And, firstly, concerning appointments made by Governors. We have seen already that one of the principles acted upon is, that any man who has evinced a great desire to improve a Colony is then and there disqualified to have anything to do with it. Experience teaches us, also, that, in the eye of a Governor, the fact that a man is the son of a person who has misgoverned a Colony is held to be the best possible reason for giving that person a chance to do likewise. To test the truth of this assertion, will some honourable Member turn to the index of the Colonial Office List, note the number of times the name of Griffith appears, ask the Secretary for the / Colonies how many more gentlemen of that name, not mentioned in the index, are in the Colonial service, and then inquire if they are related to Governor Griffith, and what their other qualifications are? The answer in one case will be amusing. In an official interview with Mr. Antrobus,[6] of the Colonial Office, attention was called to the appointment of a member of the Griffith family. The official reply was, 'He got on very well at school!'

The next highest qualification is flattery. Comical as the statement must sound to the ears of those who know not colonial life, it is really the fact that a colonial Governor thinks himself an important personage. It pleases him to be encouraged in this delusion. Accordingly, when a merchant or agent, or even a clerk, finds that business is not thriving, he becomes assiduous in his attendance at the Governor's receptions, and before long he is invited to enter the Colonial service.

Thus we see, that the first class of appointments are, for the most part, divided between the Governor's relations and his sycophants, some of the latter being men who have failed in other walks in life. /

Now let us see how the Secretary of State for the Colonies selects men for the purpose of administering a large portion of the British Empire.

There was a time when every appointment in the public service was a job. Private and parliamentary influence was supreme. No one could enter the Indian Civil Service unless he could secure the goodwill of a Director. In the same way, to enter the Home Civil Service, or the Army, or the Navy, it was necessary to know some one who knew the Head of a Department, or else to know a Member of Parliament who could demand an appointment for his *protégé* as the reward for straight voting.

This is abolished now. The old system savoured too strongly of class privilege; it was prejudicial to the interests of the public service, and it might be used as a means of influencing votes. Appointments are now given to those who pass best in competitive examinations. These afford a test of fitness which is not infallible, but is, at all events, better than none at all, and it is free from class privilege, and from all tendency to influence votes, either at elections or in the House. /

And so we are accustomed to say that the days of class privilege are gone by, that the public service is open to all, and that the best man wins. We compare ourselves favourably with the corrupt Americans, who expect a place in return for every vote.

And yet the public forget that, as regards the Colonial Service, the old patronage system still flourishes in all its iniquity.

Go to the Colonial Office and ask on what principle Colonial appointments are conferred. You will be told that the Secretary of State is guided by the recommendation of Members of Parliament. Why, in the name of common sense, Members of Parliament? Are they more competent than the rest of the world to form an opinion as to the fitness of a man to be – say Chief Justice of Trinidad, or Harbourmaster of Hong Kong? Of course the real meaning of the thing is, that the word 'recommendation' is a farce. The word 'request' should be used. And instead of the broad phrase, 'Members of Parliament,' they should say, 'Members of the Government side of the House who have always voted straight.'

The whole system is an anachronism. It is / a relic of the old times of Walpole. It enables parliamentary candidates to influence votes. It enables Ministers to influence divisions. And if neither candidates nor Ministers avail themselves of this ability, it is no thanks to the system. Yet it is scarcely possible to believe that an elector is not influenced sometimes by the thought that if A., and not B., is returned to Parliament, then A. will be in a position to ask for an appointment for the elector's son; whereas B., he thinks, on the wrong side of the House, would know better than to ask for anything. The system is tainted with class privilege, seeing that, even in these days, Secretaries of State for the most part belong to the higher ranks of society, and therefore are only approachable by persons belonging to those ranks.

And above all, the system has no regard whatever for the interests of the public service. It may be safely said that no man sent out from England was ever yet appointed because he was fit for his work. He may or may not be fit, but his fitness is in no case the reason for his appointment. That reason is, that he has a friend who knows a friend of the Private Secretary, who has the ear of the Chief Secretary; / or the reason may be that his father was one of a caucus who returned a member who has voted straight.

The results of this system are what have been shown in this pamphlet. When the Colonial Service shall have been purified, then and not till then it will be no longer possible to describe the Gold Coast as 'The Land of Death.'

CAPE COAST, *November* 1886.

LONDON:
Printed by STRANGEWAYS AND SONS,
Tower Street, Upper St. Martin's Lane

'The Medical Services of West African Colonies and Protectorates', *British Medical Journal* (February 1902), pp. 343–4.

FORMATION OF A "WEST AFRICAN MEDICAL STAFF."

WE are informed by Mr. Chamberlain,[1] Secretary of State for the Colonies, that it has been decided to amalgamate the medical services of the British West African Colonies and Protectorates into a single service, to be known as the West African Medical Staff. The salaries and other conditions of service of the medical officers have been revised in connexion with the scheme of amalgamation. Particulars of the appointments are contained in a Colonial Office paper entitled *Information for the use of Candidates for Appointments in the West African Medical Staff: Colonial Office, African (West), No. 678*. The main provisions are as follows:

The services amalgamated are those of the Gambia, Sierra Leone, the Gold Coast, Lagos, Southern Nigeria, and Northern Nigeria. All the medical officers for the service will be selected by the Secretary of State for the Colonies, and will be on one list for employment and promotion.

Salary and Allowances.

The grades and salaries for medical officers are shown in the following table:

Grades.	Gold Coast, Southern Nigeria, Northern Nigeria.			Sierra Leone, Lagos.		
	Minimum Salary.	Annual Increment.	Maximum Salary.	Minimum Salary.	Annual Increment	Maximum Salary.
	£	£	£	£	£	£
Principal Medical Officer	1,000	50	1,200	800	50	1,000
Deputy Principal Medical Officer	700	25	800	–	–	–
Senior Medical Officers	600	20	700	600	20	700
Medical Officers	400	20	500	400	20	500

The grades and salaries of the establishment on the Gambia are at present under consideration.

The allowances are as follows:

(a) *Duty Pay.*–A deputy principal medical officer or senior medical officer will receive duty pay at the rate of £100 a year while acting for the principal medical officer. Duty pay at the rate of £60 a year will also be paid (I) to each deputy principal medical officer or senior medical officer while employed in Ashanti or the northern territories of the Gold Coast: and (2) to not more than two officers of either of those ranks in Northern Nigeria, when similarly employed in outlying districts, at the discretion of the High Commissioner.

(b) *Horse or Hammock Allowance.*–An allowance of 2s. 6d. a day will be paid to every medical officer for personal conveyance while on duty at his station for any period during which he was required by Government to keep, and has actually kept, a horse, carries, etc., for the purpose.

(c) *Transport of Stores.*–The Government will carry free of cost a reasonable amount of stores for every medical officer, the amount in each case being fixed by the local government.

(d) *Travelling.*–Medical and other officers traveling on duty in a Colony or Protectorate are entitled to repayment of any actual out-of-pocket expenses which they may necessarily have incurred. In some cases in lieu of the repayment of expenses, a traveling allowance is given, which is estimated to cover the average cost of traveling.

(e) *Field or Bush Allowance.*–An allowance of 5s. a day will be paid to all medical officers, whatever their rank, while employed in the field or bush, away from recognised stations. Officers, while in receipt of this allowance, will not be entitled to any repayment or allowance under (d) above.

(f) *Allowances on a Military Expedition.*–All Medical officers, whatever their rank, while employed with a military expedition will be paid an allowance of 10s. a day, and will be given free rations, or an allowance of 3s. a day in lieu of rations. While in receipt of these allowances, medical officers will not be entitled to any repayment or allowance under (d) and (e) above.

(g) *Outfit Allowance.*–An allowance of £12 will be paid to every medical officer on first appointment for the purchase of camp outfit (see under "Outfit.")

Leave of Absence, Passages, Etc.

Medical officers will be in general subject to the Colonial Regulations, Chapter XVIII, the main rules in which are:

1. The ordinary tour of residential service is one year, followed by leave with full pay during the voyages to and from England, and for four or to two months in England, according as the officer is returning or not.
2. An officer detained beyond the year receives additional leave with / full pay for ten or five days, according as he is returning or not in respect to each completed month beyond twelve.
3. If invalided before the end of the first year the leave with full pay is for the voyages and for ten or five days in respect of each completed month according as he is returning or not.
4. "Return leave" is leave granted on the understanding that the officer will return, and any pay drawn in respect of such leave is liable to be refunded if he does not return.
5. Leave may be extended for a limited period with half or no pay on the ground of ill-health.
6. Free passages are given to all officers granted leave as above, and also on first appointment, and half pay is given during the voyage out on first appointment.

A copy of Chapter XVIII of the Colonial Regulations can be obtained free on application to the Colonial Office. It is also contained in the annual *Colonial Office List* (Messrs. Harrison and Sons, 59, Pall Mall; 10s. 6d.).

General Conditions of Engagement.

Every medical officer, unless exempted on account of previous colonial service or other reason, is engaged on probation for one year from the date of his arrival in West Africa, but if found not qualified for efficient service in West Africa the Governor or High Commissioner, subject to the confirmation of the Secretary of State, will have power to cancel his appointment at any time within the year, and a free passage back will be granted at the discretion of the Governor or High Commissioner. At the end of the year of probation the officer may be confirmed in his appointment, but unless so confirmed the appointment will cease at the end of the year.

Private Practice.

"All medical officers, except the principal medical officer in each Colony or Protectorate, will be allowed to take private practice provided that it does not interfere with the faithful and efficient performance of their official duties, and that it will be within the power of the Governor or High Commissioner to withdraw or suspend the privilege in such places and for such periods as he may consider desirable."

Outfit.

Instruments and drugs and all medical appliances are supplied by the Government.

Camp outfit must be taken by every medical officer, who will receive an allowance of £12. It is added as a general rule it is desirable to take out as little as possible, but as circumstances vary the newly-appointed officer should, if possible, consult some one who has recently been on the Coast, and the Colonial Office will be ready to place him in communication with some officer at home on leave of absence who will be able to advise him.

Uniform.

The question of uniform for officers of the West African Medical Staff is under consideration, but a uniform is prescribed for medical officers in common with other civil officers in Northern and Southern Nigeria, and particulars can be obtained from the Colonial Office.

Pensions and Gratuities.

Intending candidates can obtain full particulars from the Colonial Office, but the following is a summary:

Age.–On attaining the age of 50 years, or after eighteen years service, of which at least twelve must have been residential, an officer is qualified for a pension calculated at one-fortieth of the last annual salary for each year of service.

Invalids.–If invalided after a minimum of seven years service he is qualified for a pension at the same rate, if before completing seven years he is qualified for a gratuity not exceeding three-fourths of a month's salary for each six months of service, provided that he has been confirmed in his appointment and is recommended by the Governor or High Commissioner for a gratuity.

Gratuities.–At the end of nine years service, of which not less than six must have been residential, an officer of the West African Medical Staff will be permitted to retire with a gratuity of £1,000; at the end of twelve years, of which not less than eight must have been residential, with a gratuity of £1,250; but all claims to pension are forfeited on the receipt of such gratuity.

In calculating the amount of these pensions and gratuities, leave of absence without salary is not counted, but leave with one-half salary is counted as one-half.

Applications for Appointments.

Applicants must be of European parentage, and between 25 and 35 years of age. Preference will be given to unmarried candidates. Passages for wives and children are not provided by the Government; houses for them are rarely available, and except in the case of an officer dying on active service, no provision is made by the Government for a widow or orphans. The higher grades of the service will usually be filled by promotion from the lower. Candidates may express a preference for a particular Colony or Protectorate, but are liable to be posted in the first instance, or transferred afterwards, to any other Colony or Protectorate. All applications, which must be accompanied by a general statement of qualifications and a certificate of birth, must in the first place be addressed, in writing, to the Assistant Private Secretary to the Secretary of State, Colonial office, Downing Street, London, S.W., to whom intending candidates should apply for a copy of the pamphlet here quoted.

Instruction in Tropical Medicine.

Every candidate selected for appointment will unless the Secretary of State decides otherwise, be required to undergo a course of instruction of eight weeks, either at the London School of Tropical Medicine,[2] Royal Victoria and Albert Docks, E., or at the Liverpool School of Tropical Medicine,[3] University College, Liverpool. The cost of the tuition fees, board, and residence, amounting to £30,178. 4d., will be borne by the Government, and a daily allowance of 5s. (but no pay) will be paid to each candidate during the course, and subsequently up to the date of embarkation. Half-pay begins form the date of embarkation.

'The Organization of the Colonial Medical Service', *British Medical Journal* (February 1902), pp. 347–8.

THE Colonial Secretary[1] is to be congratulated upon the step which he has just taken towards organizing the Colonial Medical Services. It is true that it touches only one part of a larger question, for the new regulations organizing a West African Medical Staff, which are printed at page 343, apply only to one section of the Colonial Medical Service, but we hope that it is only a prelude to further developments.

For some time past the medical profession has been urging the Colonial Office to deal with this matter. The first serious attempt in this direction was made by Surgeon-General Evatt,[2] who in a paper published in the BRITISH MEDICAL JOURNAL of September 26th, 1896, presented a complete scheme for "the organization of the Colonial Medical Service of the Empire." The first public meeting in connection with the subject was held at the Imperial Institute on March 12th, 1898, on which occasion Sir Joseph Fayrer,[3] Bart., presided. At this meeting Mr. James Cantlie[4] read a paper on the Organization of the Colonial Medical Service, and several resolutions were drawn up and forwarded to the Colonial Secretary. The British Medical Association has on several occasions appointed Committees to deal with the whole or part of the question, and from time to time the Council of the Association submitted expressions of opinion to the Government. Mr. Chamberlain has on every occasion welcomed the suggestions made, and the action which he has now taken has no doubt been largely influenced and determined by the representations which he has received.

The West African Medical Staff is formed by the amalgamation of the medical services of the British West African Colonies and Protectorates into a single service. In addition to dealing with the principles of organization, the Colonial Office has revised and improved the salaries and other conditions of service of the medical officers engaging in this branch of Colonial work. The grading of officers is accompanied, we are glad to see, by the grant of definite titles, a most important point in any organization. There will be henceforward four recognized grades: (1) Principal Medical Officer, (2) Deputy Principal Medical Officer, (3) Senior Medical Officer, and (4) medical officer. It will be noticed that there is a difference in pay according to the Colony in which the medical officer is stationed, the officers in Sierra Leone and Lagos receiving a lower rate of pay than in the other districts. The grounds for this regulation have no doubt been carefully examined by the Colonial Office authorities, but the regulation as it stands is open to criticism. In the other public services pay is given according to the number of years' service, and "allowances" are made to cover the special circumstances of this or that locality. We shall hope to see this principle adopted at an early date for the West African / Medical Staff, the actual pay being fixed on a uniform scale in accordance with the rank and length of service, officers employed or engaged in certain regions being compensated by increased allowances. There can be no uniformity of prospects in any service where this is not the case. It is, however, satisfactory to have the rates of pay and allowance, the regulations as to leave of absence, and the terms of engagement clearly and definitely stated, since the medical officer on joining will now know exactly what his prospects are.

The matter of private practice is, and ever will be wherever and whenever an official receives reasonably good pay, a vexed question. Under the new regulations medical officers will be "allowed to take private practice provided that it does not interfere with the faithful and efficient performance of their official duties," but "it will be within the power of the Governor or High Commissioner to withdraw or suspend the privilege in such places and for such periods as he may consider desirable." Under a wise Governor this rule may work smoothly enough; but Governor are changed frequently, and what one Governor may deem "faithful and efficient performance of their official duties" may not be so regarded by his successor. Moreover, according to this regulation a community may suddenly find itself, by an arbitrary decision of the Governor, or by a mere disagreement between an individual medical officer and the Governor, without the services of a medical man. In the West African Colonies medical men are not readily obtainable, and unless the regulation here laid down is always judiciously interpreted on the spot with due consideration for the public benefit, a serious state of affairs might arise.

The question of uniform is as yet only under consideration. It is, we believe, advisable that a uniform should be assigned to the Colonial Medical Service, among other reasons, because it would mean the wearing of an indication of "grade," a most essential factor if discipline is to be maintained in the service.

The scale of pensions, although not too liberal, is fair; and the gratuities which are bestowed upon those retiring at the end of nine and twelve years are on a scale which will, we believe, meet with approval.

The plan of obtaining appointments by nomination is probably the best which could be adopted under the special circumstances, but it would probably be well to establish a competitive examination amongst the nominees. The most successful candidates at this examination might then on entering the service be given the privilege of selecting the Colony or Protectorate in which they wished to commence their service.

This is the more important, because we are strongly of opinion that the Colonial Office will only obtain the best class of men if every opportunity is afforded for individual talent to show itself.

The West African Pocket Book. A Guide for Newly-Appointed Government Officers, 2nd edn (London: Warlow & Sons, 1906), pp. 4–38.

Corrections and suggestions for the improvement of this book will be welcome at any time, and may be sent direct to the Colonial Office. It is hoped that Officers of local experience will fully avail themselves of this opportunity of being of service to new and inexperienced brother officers. /

GENERAL NOTES ON WEST AFRICA.

The British possessions in West Africa are the Gambia, Sierra Leone, the Gold Coast (including Ashanti and the Northern Territories), Southern Nigeria (including Lagos), and Northern Nigeria.

The Gambia is a strip of territory the on the banks of the river of that name, as large as Devonshire and Cornwall together, with a population of about 150,000, of whom only about 115 are Europeans. Sierra Leone is as large as Scotland, with a population of about a million. The Gold Coast, with Ashanti and the Northern Territories, is nearly equal in area to England and Scotland, and has a population roughly estimated at two millions. Southern Nigeria is nearly the same in area as the Gold Coast, and has a population of about six millions. Northern Nigeria is as large as France and Italy together; its population can only be guessed, but is possibly about ten millions.

The number of European officials in each is at present (1906) approximately as follows:–

```
Gambia. . . . . . . . . . . . . . . . . . . . .  .35
Sierra Leone  . . . . . . . . . . . . . . . . . . 120
Gold Coast . . . . . . . . . . . . . . . . . . . . 400
Southern Nigeria (including Lagos). . . . . . . . 500
Northern Nigeria . . . . . . . . . . . . . . . . . 500
```

All these possessions lie within the tropics. Owing to their extent much variation of climate is met with, but considerably heat is general, as there are no very elevated tracts, and on the coast and near it the climate is also very moist. The climate should be regarded with at least as much respect as would be given to that of the less developed parts of India, and officers should study how life may be made comfortable and / healthy under the conditions they are likely to meet with. The general standard of comfort attained by Europeans in West Africa is not equal to that reached in India, but individuals can do much to raise it if they will take the necessary trouble.

The seasons of the year are divided into the wet and the dry, and there is no cold season, except in Northern Nigeria. In the Gambia and Sierra Leone the dry seasons lasts from November to April or May. In the Gold Coast the dry seasons lasts from December to March, and is followed by tornadoes in April and May. The rainy seasons lasts from June to November, usually with a break in August and September. In Southern Nigeria the seasons are similar to those on the Gold Coast. In Northern Nigeria they are similar, but the dry season is cooler and at times cold.

The Harmattan, a dry dusty wind, blows from the Sahara during the dry season. /

OUTFIT AND PREPARATIONS IN ENGLAND.

The health and comfort of an officer largely depend on his taking out from England a satisfactory kit, which need not however be a large one. Details of the various articles required will be found in Appendix A,[1] but it may be repeated here that no one should fail to take out an efficient mosquito net, a tropical sun hat, a white umbrella (or a black one with a white cover), and some quinine. All officers in Southern and Northern Nigeria and all others who are at all likely to have to travel by land will require to take camp outfit, except tents, which will be supplied by the Government when required. Such officers should remember that 50 lbs. or at most 60 lbs. is the heaviest load that can be borne by one carrier, and that everything must be bought and packed subject to this consideration. Accordingly they will do well to limit their baggage to the smallest possible compass and to the lightest possible weight. Those to whom economy is an object should beware of buying everything which the outfitter suggests as necessary, but, on the other hand, nothing is saved by omitting essential articles which will have to be bought later in West Africa, probably at higher prices.

Table crockery and cutlery, table linen, pots and pans and kitchens clothes, are required, except in Southern Nigeria, and bed-clothes must always be taken out.

It is generally economical and often necessary to take out some provisions.

When making his preparations in England an officer should get all his packages together and take them with him as personal luggage. This will cost a little more than sending them by goods train to the Shipping Agents, but it is much more satisfactory. Before now it has happened that an officer's baggage, having been sent in good time, went deep into the hold / of the ship and had cargo piled upon it, with the result that when the officer came to go ashore he could not get his bed or any of the other things he wanted. Another risk is that some mistake may occur on the part of the Railway Company or the Shippers, and that when the passenger gets to the ship an hour or so before she sails he may find that his packages are not on board, and that no one knows anything about them. It is not a serious inconvenience at Liverpool to have a number of packages; there are registered out-door porters who take passengers' luggage from the railway station to the landing stage for a charge of 6d. per package.

If goods must be sent on by goods train before the officer, it is best to address them to the cloak-room at the railway station and to send a covering letter to the stationmaster. The officer can then get them on arrival and proceed with them to the ship.

An officer should provide himself with a list of his packages on a card or strong piece of paper. /

VOYAGE OUT AND ARRIVAL IN WEST AFRICA
Never be parted from your Mosquito Net.

The systematic use of quinine should be commenced the day before touching the West Africa coast, and kept up during residence in West Africa and for at least six months after return to Europe, unless an officer is medically advised to do otherwise. Inability to take quinine should be regarded as an absolute bar to residence in tropical Africa.

The systematic use of quinine may be followed in whichever of the three following ways may best suit the individual:–
1. Five grains every day (recommended).
2. Ten grains on Sundays and Wednesdays.
3. Fifteen grains on the 10th and 11th, 20th and 21st, and 30th and 31st (or last two) days in each month.

The best time to take the five-grain doses is just before the "big" breakfast. When the larger doses are adopted it is best to take them after dinner, so that the buzzing in the ears and deafness which are likely to follow may occur during sleep and rest, and not during the day, when they might prove troublesome. Anyone who finds that the quinine disagrees with him should consult a Medical Officer.

By consulting the rainfall tables in Appendix F, the kind of weather to be expected on landing can be gauged with fair accuracy. If the rains are on, it is necessary to have accessible a mackintosh, an umbrella, and strong boots. /

The landing is made in boats. In the cases of the Gambia and Sierra Leone there is no difficulty. At the Gold Coast there are usually large rollers which break on the shore, making considerable surf. There is generally some water in the bottom of the surf boats: you should watch to see that the box best able to withstand the wet goes into the boat first. Always see all your luggage put in one surf boat and go to the shore in the same boat yourself. When the surf boat arrives at the beach two of the native paddlers will quickly lift the passenger out and place him beyond the reach of the next incoming wave; the other paddlers do their best to carry out all the packages without allowing them to get wet, but it is necessary for going through the surf to have tightly closing boxes, otherwise water may enter. Nothing should be loose. A mackintosh should be worn for landing as a protection against spray, even if it is not raining. If the sun happens to be shining the umbrella will be found useful, as the distance from the ship to the shore is frequently half-a-mile or more.

At Lagos, and sometimes at Forcados, a transfer has to be made to a smaller steamer – a "branch boat" – which is capable of crossing the large sandbanks or bars which are found at the mouths of the rivers and harbours. It is wise to see that on these boats all baggage and the like is placed under cover of an awning or similar shelter, and so protected from the sun or rain.

Officers going to Northern Nigeria are recommended to engage a native servant at Forcados,[2] or at one of the ports which they will touch at before reaching Forcados. / ...

MALARIA.
"Form the Anti-Mosquito Habit."

Only precautionary measures are dealt with under this head. Directions for the treatment of malarial fever, when no doctor is available, will be found in Appendix E.

Malarial fever is a disease caused by the bite of a particular kind of mosquito (*Anopheles*), when the individual mosquito that bites is itself infected by the disease. The bite of a non-infected *Anopheles* cannot cause malaria. Only the females bite.

This disease has been subjected to a great amount of scientific investigation during the last few years, and has become associated particularly with the names of Sir Patrick Manson[3] K.C.M.G., M.D., and Professor Ronald Ross,[4] C.B.

The former had shown that certain mosquitoes carried the germ of another disease.* From this and from what was already known concerning malaria he was led to suspect that malaria might be transmitted by mosquitoes. Professor Ross, after examining various mosquitoes in order to test this supposition, was able to show that there was great probability of its being correct. / Sir Patrick Manson then clinched the matter by two experiments described by him as follows:–

"Finally, on behalf of the Colonial Office and the London School of Tropical Medicine, with the assistance of Dr. Sambon and Dr. Low, I instituted two

---

*   Filariasis (minute worms in the blood.) /

experiments which dispose for good and all of any objections that otherwise might have been advanced against the theory. Dr. Sambon and Dr. Low, Signor Terzi, their servants and visitors lived for the there most malarial months of 1900 in one of the most malarial localities of the Roman Campagna. Ostia, in a hut from which mosquitoes were excluded by a simple arrangement of wire gauze on the doors and windows. They moved freely about in the neighbourhood during the day, exposed themselves in all weathers, drank the water of the place, often did hard manual work, and beyond retiring from sunset to sunrise to their mosquito protected hut, took no precautions whatever against malaria. They took no quinine. Although their neighbours, the Italian peasants, were each and all of them attacked with malaria, the dwellers in the mosquito-proof hut enjoyed an absolute immunity from the disease. Whilst the experiment was in progress mosquitoes, *fed in Rome on patients suffering from malaria,* were forwarded in suitable cages to the London School of Tropical Medicine, and on their arrival were set to bite my son, Dr. P. Thurburn Manson, and Mr. George Warren. Shortly afterwards both of these gentlemen, neither of whom had been abroad or otherwise exposed to malarial influences, developed characteristic malarial fever, and malarial parasites were found in abundance in their blood both at that time and on the occurrence of several relapses of malarial fever from which they subsequently suffered. / ...

The Mosquito-Malaria theory has now therefore, passed from the region of conjecture to that of fact."

These two experiments satisfied the medical world, and, since they were performed, a mass of information has been acquired which confirms them again and again.

It is a simple expedient to have mosquito-proof houses, and to remain in them as much as possible during the period from sunset to sunrise, and it might be thought that West Africa would be a place where mosquito-proof houses were to be found in abundance. But this, chiefly owing to the influence of the "Old Coaster," is not yet the case. The "Old Coaster," is a man who, through the accidents of a constitution exceptionally suitable to West Africa, and a certain amount of good luck, has succeeded in remaining many years on the Coast, and has come, and rightly so, by virtue of the work which he has done, into a senior position. Having passed through the ordeal of living on the coast under the adverse circumstances of ten or twelve years ago, he is often, and not unnaturally, unable fully to appreciate the necessity of precautions against malaria for the great majority of Europeans in West Africa.

A new-comer to West Africa must, therefore, be prepared to meet men who have no belief in the new discoveries and experiments above mentioned, but he is warned not to allow their influence to dissuade him from taking essential precautions.

The chief of these are:–

1. **Always carefully to use a good large mosquito net kept in thorough repair.** /
2. **To take quinine systematically.**
3. **To destroy mosquitoes and clear away their breeding places round the house** as far as possible.

Further details as to these precautions will be found under other heads of this pamphlet.

A mosquito has the same kind of life history as a silk-worm or butterfly. A female mosquito will lay about 250 eggs or more at a time on or close to water. In a day or two, there comes out of each egg a small creature (the larva) which swims about in the water eating minute plants, &c., and comes to the surface of the water to breathe. This stage corresponds to the silkworm or caterpillar. In about a fortnight the larva turns into a shrimp-like creature, which moves with great rapidity through the water by means of its curved thin tail-portion, and which breathes by coming to the surface of the water as the larva did. This shrimp-like creature is the pupa, and corresponds to the chrysalis stage of the silk-worm or butterfly. From the pupa, in the course of a few days, the imago or mature insect – the mosquito – emerges.

There are several kinds of mosquito which differ from one another in appearance and habits. Although only one kind carries malaria, it is well to wage war against all mosquitoes, because nearly all can carry some disease or other.

There are two tribes of mosquito very common in West Africa, the *Culex,* which is the kind most frequently seen and heard, and the *Anopheles,* which can carry the malaria germ. ... /

The differences between these two are as follows:–

	Anopheles.	*Culex.*
Eggs.	Lying flat and scattered on water, almost always in *natural* pools.	Floating vertically in a mass on water anywhere, in water tanks, cups, &c., as well as natural pools.
Larva.	Lying flat when at the surface of water	Hanging down at an angle from the surface of water.
Pupa.	Similar in both species.	
Imago.	Has tail end pointing in air when resting on flat surface, makes little or no sound when flying.	Has tail end parallel to surface it rests on, "sings" when flying.

In the males, the antennæ are bushy in both kinds. In the females, two small processes, one on each side of the proboscis, called the palps, are short in *Culex* and long in *Anopheles*. The *Anopheles* of West Africa has short dark bars on the front edges of the wings; the *Culex* has no special markings on the wings.

Among the many tribes of mosquitoes there is a family, *Stegomyia*, the members of which will be easily distinguished by their general appearance. They are striped black and white, and suggest a football costume. This is the mosquito which can transfer yellow fever from the sick to the healthy.

Everyone going to West Africa should make it his business to learn how to distinguish between *Anopheles, Culex,* and *Stegomyia,* and how to find and destroy them and their larvæ.

The importance of making war on all mosquitoes cannot be too strongly emphasised. From the life history of the mosquito, already described, it will be / seen that the insect can be most easily attacked in its water stage. This can be done by **permitting as little standing water as possible round dwelling-houses.**

Any small pools that cannot be drained or filled in should have a little cheap, thin oil (kerosene will do) poured on their surfaces once a week. The oil makes it difficult for the mosquito to cling to the surface of the water, and it also gets into insect's breathing apparatus and chokes it.

Water tanks and like must be carefully looked after; the ordinary lids scarcely ever fit with sufficient exactness to prevent mosquitoes from entering and breeding. Over the lids it is easy to fit canvas bags filled with sand, and this will be found to be one of the best ways of closing the apertures round the badly fitting lid of an iron tank. Water barrels should have a sheet of canvas placed over the top and fastened to the staves by short nails. The pipes and holes which enter the tank, for the purpose of letting water in or out, must be carefully attended to and sealed when not in use with wire gauze, sand bags, canvas, or other means which will prevent mosquitoes from entering.

The edges of any river, small stream, or ditch, near a house must be carefully cut and trimmed so as to prevent the formation of little stagnant pools and back waters in which *Anopheles* would readily breed.

All gutters should be kept clear of grass and weeds, as it is found that *Anopheles* shelters among them.

It is astonishing how soon a mosquito, and especially a *Culex,* makes use of any water it may find to breed in. It is usually necessary to stand each leg of a meat safe or table, on which jam, sugar, and the like are kept, in small tins of water in order to prevent ants from eating the food, &c. *Culex* always breeds in these tins if the water is not completely changed once a week, or / vinegar or something acting similarly added to it. Again, *Culex* will breed in the small cups of water used to keep a wet bulb thermometer moist, or in a water jug left in quarters which have been vacated for a short time, or in a water cooler which is not regularly emptied. An officer may go into the bush travelling for a fortnight or more, and when he comes back, if the water jug has not been emptied, he will often find his rooms full of mosquitoes.

It is, however, the *Anopheles* mosquito which is the more serious danger. There are two species which are common in West Africa, one brown, the other black-looking, and both of these, as already mentioned, usually breed only in pools of water which form naturally. Collections of water in manufactured vessels can, however after a time take on the peculiarities of natural pools, *e.g.,* if a new canoe gets some water in it after a shower of rain, *Anopheles* will not, as a rule, grow in this, although *Culex* will; but in the case of an old canoe, or a new one which has been left by its owner in one place for a couple of months, moss, grass, &c., accumulate round the sides of the contained water, and for all practical purpose the canoe forms a natural pool in which *Anopheles* will breed. They will also breed in the big wooden mortar in which natives beat up and mix their food, if this article is left for two or three weeks where water can get into it; and in a country where most journeys are made on foot it is no uncommon thing for a canoe or a house to be left uncared for during two months or more.

In the case of bamboo cut midway between two joints and stuck vertically into the ground to make railings or fences, the top of the stick forms a little cup and will hold water in which *Anopheles* will breed. It might be thought that such a small collection of water would dry up quickly; but, in the rains, grass and other vegetation are apt to grow up sufficiently high to / protect the top of the fence from the sun, and also from heavy downpours of rain which would wash out the larvæ.

These are only a few example of how water can collect and in time become a breeding place for mosquitoes. Everyone who looks about carefully will find many others. For example, the spouting round the roof of a European house may sink between two supporting hooks and form a cavity where water and débris can collect. A large leaf which in the dry season has had its edges curled up, like leaves in autumn in England, may be so lying when a shower of rain comes as to collect water and form a pool; mosquitoes have often been found breeding in such a pool.

Puddles, if exposed, may be dried up by the direct rays of the sun or washed out by a heavy downpour of rain, or the concussion of the drops of rain on the surface may seriously damage the larvæ, although these creatures can defy both sun and rain for a time by living in the mud at the bottom of a pool.

It is not, however, exposed pools that are the difficulty. They can be seen, and it is only crass folly not to deal with them. The difficulty is in finding out-of-the-way collections of water near fences, forks or roots of trees, and old drains, which often have long grass round them. Accordingly all grass and vegetation should be kept cut close to the ground for sixty yards, or, better, a hundred yards, round a European dwelling. A few ornamental plants and shade trees may be excepted if puddles are not allowed to form beneath them.

Instructions similar to the above have been given and are well know in most of the West African stations, but it is not unusual to find that they have not been carried out.

Clearing grass and bush, however, takes time, and in a new bush station it is imperative to have some / protection against mosquitoes immediately on arrival. An officer may take with him a portable mosquito-proof shelter in which he can sit and sleep. If he does not do this he should have a house made mosquito-proof. This can be done temporarily and quickly by fastening muslin over the window-openings and doorways, and also, if the houses be a native one, from the top of the walls to the adjacent roof, between which, in native houses, there is always a space.

A more satisfactory and permanent method is to cover the window-openings with wire gauze, and to construct, a mosquito-proof porch. The windows covered should be as large as possible. The porch should have a gauze door at each end. Any mosquitoes which have come in with a person will then probably stop in the porch and can be killed there. Failing a porch, doorways may be protected by two weighted curtains of muslin, so arranged as to allow a person to pass through the door by separating them, care being taken after passing through that they meet and cover the door. These curtains can be fixed to the top and sides of the doorway by nails.

Mosquito-proof houses and rooms have been objected to on the ground that they are stuffy; but stuffiness is avoided when the windows, &c., covered with gauze or muslin are sufficiently large. A mosquito-proof house can be made very light and airy when the building is a suitable one.

On sunny days the doors and windows should be opened. On dull days *Culex,* if breeding near, is liable to get in if the house is opened, although *Anopheles* will never be seen after 6.30 a.m. or before 6 p.m. unless the house is absolutely and closely surrounded by bush.

In a mosquito-proof room, really kept free from mosquitoes, no mosquito-net is required over the bed. / When a man is resident in a mosquito-proof house, has not been previously infected, and does not go out at night, he may dispense with quinine: but these conditions are rarely fulfilled, and it is in nearly all cases much safer to continue the use of quinine.

Finally any site selected for a European's house should be on high land, at least a quarter and preferably half a mile distant from a native town, without any resort of native children in the neighbourhood, and when possible not closely surrounded by bush. Where the bush is thick the level cannot be seen and it is not easy to decide which is the highest ground; the best plan is to choose the ground which keeps driest at the height of the rainy season. But if the highest land is near a swamp, it preferable to build the house on somewhat lower ground, and to have a good clearing between it and the swamp.

The ideal site is on or near the top of a hill, a mile at least from any swamp.

A most important fact, always to be borne in mind in traveling or in selecting a site for a house, is that the principal source from which the mosquito obtains the malaria parasite is the native children. Practically all native children may be regarded as infected with malaria, and therefore all *Anopheles* in native houses should be regarded with the greatest suspicion, and the neighbourhood of native children should as far as possible be avoided for European houses or camps. / ...

PERSONAL HYGIENE.
"Prevention is better than Cure."

The diseases and ailment chiefly to be guarded against in West Africa are malaria, dysentery, jiggers, prickly heat, and dhobie itch. These diseases and ailments are all caused by the presence of a special animal or vegetable parasite. A low condition of health predisposes to attacks by these parasites; therefore everything that tends to strengthen the body should be encouraged, and everything that tends to weaken the body avoided.

The sun, the wind, and the rain are three elements which may damage the body from without and so make it more susceptible to the attacks of parasites.

It is of paramount importance to **wear a helmet when in the sun**, and when possible to use a white umbrella (lined). Even if the sun is somewhat obscured by a haze, it is still necessary to wear a helmet.

The high temperature of the air causes the body to perspire after but little exertion, and even when not perspiring the body always has, in hot climates, a great volume of blood circulating just under the skin; consequently, if the wind blows strongly, the body, unless protected by suitable clothing, may lose a considerable amount of heat suddenly, and so have its vitality lowered. Similarly as regards rain, wettings are more liable to cause chills than in temperate climates.

Chills often induce attacks of fever in persons whose blood contains malaria germs.

Accordingly, a helmet, white umbrella (lined), flannel suitings, and a mackintosh are essential, and indiarubber boots are very useful. These articles cannot always be obtained on the coast. /

The three classes of essential precautions against malaria have been mentioned under that head. Two of them fall also under the head of personal hygiene.

1. Always carefully to use a good large mosquito net kept in thorough repair.
2. To take quinine systematically.

With regard to the first precaution, even the smallest holes in the net must be promptly mended, and the bottom of the net must be properly tucked in between the canvas of the bedstead and the mattress or blanket upon the sleeper will lie. The practice, usual in some places, of having the net weighted at the bottom and allowing its bottom edge to lie on the floor is a bad one, because mosquitoes often shelter in the day under the bed, and when the net is turned down they are inside it and attack the sleeper. Where there are mosquito rods or a frame above the bed, the net should be inside the rods or frame. It is no uncommon thing to see a man who imagines that he is getting the benefit of a mosquito

net when his net contains one or more holes or is not accurately arranged round
the bed at its lower part. It may be caught up on a chair or pair of boots and so
leave ample space for mosquitoes to get in. The net should be turned down and
tucked in at sunset or before. The details of the mosquito net are discussed in
Appendix A.

With regard to the second precaution, the advice given on page 9 should be
most carefully attended to. The **bi-hydrochloride** of quinine is one of the best
preparations. It is best taken dissolved in water. The tablets should be wrapped in
paper and crushed, and will then dissolve readily in a quarter of a small tumbler-
ful of water.

It is very important to have the bi-hydrochloride of quinine, as the bisulphate
is not nearly so soluble as the bi-hydrochloride. Euquinine, which is tasteless /

but more expensive, may be used instead of the bi-hydrochloride. Information about euquinine will be found in Appendix A.

Officers are specially warned of the danger of taking tablets dry like a pill. After a
while tablets often become hard, do not dissolve in the stomach, and are excreted
unchanged. The result is that the quinine does not enter the system, and that the
germs of malaria are not killed off when they get into the blood.

Some Old Coasters think that if a man takes quinine every day the drug will
lose its effect on him, and that he will therefore be in a sorry plight if he does get
fever. The newcomer may rest assured that there is no foundation for this belief.

A man's system is, as a rule, quite clear of a five-grain dose of quinine in less
than twenty-four hours, and it is for this reason that a frequent dose is so important.

It is wise to give personal servants a ten-grain dose of quinine once or twice
a week, both for their own benefit and to prevent them from infecting their
masters with fever.

Dysentery and other troubles are avoided by drinking only water that has
been boiled, and by taking care that all soups, tea and coffee, &c., are made with
boiling water.

Sometimes radishes and the like are grown by Europeans and eaten raw as is
the custom in England, but in all such cases water that has boiled must be used,
to wash the vegetables.

A pinch of permanganate of potash or some Condy's fluid should be put into
the bath water, and plenty of carbolic soap should always be used. The object of
/ this is to kill small fungi or even worms which might otherwise cause skin diseases. It is desirable when possible, to use boiled water for washing. Bath water
should be just warm, as cold baths are more liable to cause chills than in England,
and hot baths induce sweat.

Jiggers are most plentiful in sandy places. They are sand fleas which eat into the skin, usually about the toe-nails. They can be avoided by never walking about in bare feet and always keeping boots at a height above the floor when not in use, by having the bedroom floor polished with beeswax and turpentine, and by seeing that it is thoroughly swept daily. On getting into bed men often leave their slippers on the floor at the bedside; the next morning they thrust their feet into the slippers and proceed to dress, thinking that by wearing the slippers they will escape jiggers. But jiggers will walk into a slipper while on the ground empty. Slippers therefore should be placed on a chair by the side of the bed. Boots should be kept high on the top of boxes or hung by the tabs to nails in the wall.

Jiggers which have penetrated the skin must not be neglected. A description of how they can be removed is given in Appendix E.

Dhobie Itch is a skin disease usually but probably erroneously attributed to clothes becoming infected at the wash. Clothes may be thus contaminated in the rainy season, when there is little or no sun to dry them. Whether this is so or not, it is proper to insist that no native's clothes should be washed at the same time as a European's. The European at a station usually pay the washerman a substantial salary, and it is only fair that their washing should be kept distinct from any native's washing he may get. /

If this complaint is caught when returning to England, two or three sulphur baths can be taken, and will almost always effect a cure.

Officers should note the caution against sitting unprotected in the open air after six in the evening, given under the head "Work and Amusement," and the advice as to water and alcoholic drinks, given under the head "Food and Drink." /

CARE OF QUARTERS.

All furniture should be at least a foot from the wall of the room so that a servant can fan and dust behind it every day. If heavy furniture is placed close to the wall, as is usual in England, mosquitoes, &c., will hide behind it during the day. If clothes are hung on a wall they should be completely covered by a white cloth reaching to the ground, in order that mosquitoes may not hide in them.

The following rules, among others, apply to official quarters in Lagos and will be useful for the guidance of officers in other parts of West Africa:–

(1.) The occupant is responsible for the care and cleanliness of the quarters and compounds; the former should be adequately cleaned at least once a fortnight, and the latter swept and cleaned at least three times a week. (It is advised that thorough dry-scrubbing with a little bees-wax and turpentine, be adopted as the method of cleaning boarded floors.)

(2.) Window glass should be cleaned at least once a week; and jalousies frequently.

Jalousies should be opened and worked daily. (They are a favourite haunt of mosquitoes in the day-time.)

(3.) Responsibility for the care and cleanliness of furniture rests with the officer to whom it is issued and who has signed for it on the inventory form.

(4.) (i.) No rubbish, offal, or dirty water of any description should be thrown on the surface of the ground in the neighbourhood of a well for a distance of at least 10 yards from the latter. /

(ii.) To prevent leaves and dirt from being blown into the well by wind, the cover of the well should always be shut down except when water is actually being drawn.

(iii.) Tanks should be most carefully examined, at least once a month, and cleaned out if there is evidence of the slightest contamination by any vegetable or other substance.

(iv.) The first rain-water from a roof, after a period of dry weather, should not allowed to enter the tank.

(v.) Tanks must be kept free from mosquitoes (*i.e.*, they must be made mosquito-proof, and kept so).

See under the head "Malaria" for directions as to how to do this, and how to keep down mosquitoes in the neighbourhood of dwelling-houses. /

FOOD AND DRINK.
Never eat tinned food if you can get fresh.

In West Africa chickens are the chief fresh animal food, but they are very small. A good plan is to buy a number of live chickens, according to the size of the place they are to be kept in, and to give them a small feed once a day of rice, maize, or other grain. In a month they are much better eating, and well repay the trouble.

In many places the natives are unwilling to sell eggs because they prefer of keep them, either for sale in the more profitable form of chickens, or for use as offerings to the dead. Tinned eggs have been recently imported from England.

Beef, mutton, and goat-flesh, can often be obtained.

West African yams are large potato-like tubers and are of two kinds. Both are of a yellowish white inside, and the smaller of the two kinds has a pink layer just below the skin. The large are called yams simply, and the smaller coco-yams; the former are the better eating.

On the coast potatoes can be bought from the ships.

The pawpaw looks like a small vegetable marrow, but grows on a tree. When ripe it is eaten as a fruit; and when unripe it can be boiled and served like a vegetable marrow, from which when properly cooked it is practically undistinguishable.

There are several other vegetables which grow in West Africa. The best way to find them is to enquire of some intelligent native. For example, certain kinds of leaves, such as the young leaves of the coco-yam, can be chopped up fine and served like spinach. /

Banana, orange, pineapple, and certain kinds of plum, are common. Mango, guava, &c., grow in some places.

When traveling, biscuits may be used in the place of bread, but, when stationary, bread is easy to make (see recipes in Appendix D).

Beef should be firm, of a deep red colour, not flabby, sodden, or watery. The flesh should consist only of meat fibres, fat and gristle. There must be no minute white spots on or between the meat fibres.

Goat meat is paler in colour than beef and there is not much fat as a rule.

It is very important to know that a beast intended for food was slaughtered and that it did not die from disease.

A humane way to kill a bullock is to have the animal tied up by the head close to a tree or post, and then to shoot it with a revolver. The revolver should be held about six inches from the centre point of the frontal bone, *i.e.*, midway between the upper border of the eye socket and the lower border of the horn of the opposite side. The animal falls unconscious at once. It should be bled five minutes afterwards.

Fish is usually plentiful and good on the coast.

With regard to drink, water and palm wine are the two beverages of the country. Palm wine should not be drunk unless it has been seen collected, otherwise it is very likely to have been mixed with water from some infected pool or stream.

Water is the most wholesome drink; it may be filtered, and must always be boiled. It is important to use a filter of the best kind, and to have it cleaned and examine it not less frequently than once a mouth. The Berkefeld or the Pasteur-Chamberland can be recommended, but the ordinary carbon filters are worse than useless. The filtering can be left to a servant, but / the European should always go daily and **see that the water is actually boiled**. The vessel of boiled drinking water should then be covered up and placed to cool on a piece of wood in a soup plate full of water, to keep it free from ants.

Water, if muddy, should first be strained through a piece of linen, such as a handkerchief. If it is still thick and difficult to filter, it can be placed in a large basin and a little alum added to it, six grains to the gallon being the usual quantity. The alum causes all the fine particles in the water to sink to the bottom of the basin in about six or eight hours. Some people add a little lime also.

It is necessary to distinguish between straining water to get rid of solid matter suspended in it, and sterilising it to make it free from germs. It is difficult to keep any filters free from germs, and accordingly **water should be first filtered and afterwards boiled**.

Alcoholic drinks, if taken, should be consumed only at meals, and preferably at the evening meal. **Heavy drinkers should not go to West Africa, moderate drinkers should be very moderate there, and total abstainers should remain so.**

For a short list of suitable tinned foods and for cooking recipes, see the Appendices A and D. /

TRAVELLING AND BUSH LIFE.

In certain parts of tropical West Africa, a considerable amount of travelling is done on rivers by means of steam launches or native canoes.

When travelling in a canoe it is very important that Europeans should have an awning, at least two mats thick, over them to shelter them from the sun. The natives can easily arrange an awning by means of sticks cut in the adjacent bush.

Should a tornado be about to break, shelter must be taken in the bush, or at least the mat awning must be removed, otherwise there is grave risk of the canoe capsizing. The removal of the awning is necessary on such occasions in all small boats.

Land travelling is done on foot, in hammocks, and, in some parts of the interior, on horseback. There are railways in Sierra Leone, the Gold Coast and Lagos.

To prevent blistered feet on the march avoid tight boots and rub some nearly dry soap on the feet before starting; some people prefer vaseline or hazeline.

Loads must be kept within about 50 lbs., which, as has already been said, is the heaviest weight an average carrier can manage.

In getting ready for a march, the first thing to do is to have all the loads arranged in one line, about six feet from one another. The carriers are then chosen according to their strength and placed beside their loads. The strongest carrier should always be given the bed, mosquito net, and bedding. At the same time, it is very important that the bed load should be kept as light as possible, because the uncertainties of a march are / considerable, and the lighter the load the less handicapped is the carrier when he meets difficulties. The other loads are distributed to the carriers according to the importance of the load and the ability of the carrier to convey it.

If there is a good headman of the carriers, he will attend to these matters better than the European can.

It is best for the European to travel last; he can then be certain that no load is left behind, and, should any accident happen to a carrier, the European will soon come up to the place and can decide what is best to be done.

Most European on foot, without hammocks, will find ten miles a day a fair average march.

When one's clothes get wet on a march in the rains, the best plan, if the rain is still falling, is to make a fire under a shed and spread them on sticks above it, at a sufficient height to avoid blackening them with smoke. A sheet of corrugated iron, if obtainable, makes an admirable drying tray.

It is repeated here, as being a matter of prime importance, that the **site of a camp should always be as far as possible from a native town and native children**.

If, therefore, it is necessary to lodge in a native town, ask for the most isolated house that you can find on its borders.

The officer should be prepared to deal with the more common cases of sickness among carriers. They are particularly liable to get their feet cut with jagged pieces of stick, and these wounds should at once be attended to, for fear that the germ of lockjaw, which is always present on the ground, should get into the wound. For the method of treatment, see Appendix E. They are also apt to suffer from constipation. /

Mosquitoes are kept off to a certain extent by the smoke of a fire, but the safest plan is always to finish the march about 4 o'clock, so that the carriers and the European can eat before dark, and the European can get under the shelter of a mosquito net shortly after 6 o'clock.

A mackintosh cape is useful when marching in the bush in the early morning; it protects the shoulders from the dew dripping off the leaves.

A bush latrine can be made by digging a hole and placing across it horizontally, at a convenient height from the ground, a thick bough, supported at each end beyond the hole by means of Y-shaped branches. If necessary, it should be roofed in.

Care must be taken to prevent thefts of Government money when travelling. The cash boxes should be placed under a trustworthy guard, and should be fastened at night with a padlock and chain to an immovable object, close to where the European is sleeping, or to his bed. /

WORK AND AMUSEMENT.

The working hours in West Africa vary greatly in the different Colonies and Protectorates, but a good plan is to get up early and do as much work as possible before 11 a.m. This leaves the hotter part of the day for what is usually the smaller half of the work.

An early breakfast of, say, a rasher of bacon or an egg, with tea, is usually taken on first getting up in the morning, about 6.15. It is certainly of great importance never to go out without having first eaten at least a biscuit. The principal breakfast takes place as a rule about 11 o'clock, some men have tea about 4, and dinner is usually taken at 7.

A day's work in West Africa is much the same as a fair average day's work in England. If what has to be done is done regularly and with method, an officer will rarely have any serious difficulty in performing the duties.

In out-stations a great deal of customs, post office, and other administrative work is performed by native clerks, who daily make out papers which require for their completion to be examined and signed by the European officer in charge. Such papers should be dealt with at once whenever possible, as if they are put on one side for other work they may have to be dealt with in haste when the mail day arrives, and errors and occasionally defalcations may be overlooked. The errors may or may not have serious consequences in themselves, but in any case they cause needless work to the staff at headquarters and to the officer himself, while if defalcations are overlooked from carelessness the officer may have to make them good out of his own pocket. /

Officers who have to travel should always arrange their journeys so that the in-coming and out-going official mails are not neglected.

Twice at least in every month the routine office and storekeeping work should be carefully checked. It is not pleasant for an officer who works hard himself to find himself placed in an unfortunate position through the mistakes or neglect of his native clerk.

Officers will find it absolutely necessary for the proper conduct of business that correspondence registers and other official records should be carefully compiled and kept up to date, and that individual papers are methodically stored, arranged according to subject, number, or date. The Governor and any inspecting officers who may visit the station will ordinarily examine the books and call for correspondence to see that it is properly kept, or for actual use, and any long delay in producing papers called for is a sure sign that there is something wrong with the system or with the way in which it is being worked.

Officers in charge of cash should never leave their offices for the night until they have balanced the cash in the safe against the amount shown in the books.

Government stores should be regularly checked to see that they tally with the entries in the books regarding them.

Official books of record vary much in different places. Officers in charge of districts usually have to keep or superintend the keeping of the following books, or local equivalents for them:–

Correspondence registers, Treasury books, Law books with alterations appended, Court books, Standing Order book, Instructional files, Store books, Prison books, Transport book, Intelligence book, Officer's official diaries. /

Every officer should use a diary or some other means of bringing to mind duties which require to be discharged periodically, and things which should be done on particular days.

Games, chiefly golf, bowls, cricket, and tennis, are played in the late afternoon from about half-past four, at all events at the larger stations. Polo is played at Bathurst, Accra and in Northern Nigeria. In any case Europeans should always take brisk exercise every day equal at least to a two-mile walk.

After a walk or games men are apt to sit down in the open air to smoke and talk. But the practice of sitting after sunset in the open air without protection from mosquitoes is dangerous, because the evening is the very time when the *Anopheles* mosquitoes are most active, and therefore when malaria is most readily contracted. The evening should, if practicable, be spent in a house, room, or verandah, which has been made mosquito-proof. /

THE RETURN TO ENGLAND.

Shortly after leaving the Coast, particularly after leaving Sierra Leone, the northeast trade winds are met, and the liability of men returning from the tropics to contract chills when exposed to these winds is very great. They should be careful not to sit on deck in the light clothing that people are accustomed to wear in West Africa.

A man with a few malarial germs in his system may very easily induce their multiplication by contracting a slight chill, and so these germs (which had he exercised care would probably have become innocuous during his leave) may be the cause of serious illness upon the voyage. Accordingly heavier clothing should be worn when on board ship from the day of embarkation. The regular dose of quinine should be continued all the way home, and for six months afterwards, in order to kill off any malarial germs which might otherwise multiply.

Even though he has had no fever on the Coast, a man must not think that he is safe from fever when he leaves the place of infection. The malaria parasites contracted in Africa are not left behind when the African coast fades away on the horizon. They may live in the body for over two years after the return to Europe. Ignorance or neglect of this important fact has caused much sickness and not a few deaths. The majority of physicians who practise in tropical medicine in England are agreed that they see, case for case, severer cases of fever in England than they ever did abroad.

It is therefore a matter of paramount necessity to have warm clothing during the voyage home and in / England for some months, and to take quinine regularly every day during the voyage, and for at least six months in England.

To sum up:–

(1) Be careful of the change of diet when first getting on to the ship.

(2) Live regularly.

(3) Do not remain on deck after sunset without putting on an overcoat.

(4) Gradually put on thicker clothing as required.

(5) Avoid draughts and chills.

(6) Continue the regular use of quinine on the voyage home, and for six months after leaving Africa.

Lord Elgin, Colonies (General), *Circular Despatch. Dated 15th February, 1907, Relative to the Part Taken by Ex-Governors of Colonies in the Organization or Direction of Companies Formed to Operate in Territories which they were Recently Administering 1907* **[Cd. 3402] (London: Darling & Son, Ltd, 1907).**

THE SECRETARY OF STATE to THE GOVERNORS OF ALL COLONIES. (Circular.)

SIR,

Downing Street, February 15, 1907.

I HAVE the honour to inform you that during the past Session, questions have been put in the House of Commons with regard to certain cases in which ex-Governors of Colonies have taken a prominent part in the organization or direction of Companies formed to operate in territories which they were recently administering.[1] The publicity which has thus been given to those cases and the public comments which have been made upon them make it desirable that I should, without suggesting any impropriety in the action of those concerned, express my personal opinion with regard to such commercial ventures.

I have every reason to believe that the strongest motive which actuates a former Governor in engaging in a commercial enterprise in a Colony with which he has been connected is that he feels assured, from his intimate knowledge of the whole circumstances, that there are opportunities for development which will benefit the Colony, and that it is incumbent on him not to refuse to give the enterprise the support which his name and reputation must carry with it. A secondary motive, perfectly legitimate and honourable, may be that the enterprise may prove successful and co-operation in it remunerative.

At the same time, I cannot help feeling that retired Governors would be well advised in most cases to refrain from taking a prominent part in the management of Companies which are formed to develop for profit the natural resources of the territories which they have administered. I shall always be ready and anxious to defend the conduct of those who have given years of arduous and devoted work to the Empire; but the strongest and best-merited defence cannot always remove a false impression made by reflections cast on them; and I think myself, therefore, entitled, in the interests of the State and of the Colonial Service, to draw the attention of Officers Administering the Government of Colonies or Protectorates to the necessity for earnest consideration before taking part in any commercial undertaking of such a character.

I have, &c.,

ELGIN.[2]

The Officer Administering the Government of

Colonial Nursing Association, *Tenth Annual Report of the Executive Committee of the Colonial Nursing Association* (1906), pp. 1–21. Rhodes House Library Papers of the overseas nursing association. Brit emp s. 400, box 131, annual reports, item 1.

Patroness.

H.R.H. THE PRINCESS [*sic*] HENRY OF BATTENBERG.

President.

The LORD AMPTHILL, G.C.S.I.

Vice-President.

The Right Hon. SIR ALBERT HIME, K.C.M.G.

Hon. Vice-President.

LADY PIGGOTT.

Council.

Mrs. CHAMBERLAIN	The DUKE OF DEVONSHIRE, K.G.
The DUCHESS OF MARLBOROUGH	The DUKE OF BEDFORD, K.G.
The DUCHESS OF SUTHERLAND	The MARQUIS OF RIPON, K.G.
The COUNTESS OF SELBORNE	The EARL OF ABERDEEN, G.C.M.G.
The VISCOUNTESS KNUTSFORD	The EARL OF SELBORNE, G.C.M.G.
The VISCOUNTESS ST. ALDWYN.	
The LADY METHUEN	LORD GEORGE HAMILTON, G.C.S.I.
The Hon. Mrs. ALFRED LYTTELTON	LORD STANMORE, G.C.M.G.
LADY ALISON	Rt. Hon. SIR J. WEST RIDGEWAY, G.C.M.G.
LADY OSBORNE MORGAN	Rt. Hon. SIR G. TAUBMAN-GOLDIE, K.C.M.G.
ELIZABETH, LADY ORR-EWING	SIR FRANCIS EVANS, Bart., K.C.M.G.
LADY QUILTER	SIR DONALD CURRIE, G.C.M.G.
LADY BRUCE	SIR THOMAS SUTHERLAND, G.C.M.G.

LADY WINGFIELD
LADY BROOME

Mrs. F. DENNY
Mrs. FRED. DUTTON
Mrs. ROBERT PRICE
Mrs. SICHEL

Miss GEORGINA FRERE

SIR HENRY BURDETT, K.C.B.
SIR COLIN SCOTT-MONCRIEFF,
    K.C.S.I.
SIR HUBERT JERNINGHAM, K.C.M.G.

SIR ALFRED JONES, K.C.M.G.
MAJ.-GENERAL CHARLES ROBIN-
    SON, C.B.

Executive Committee.

The LORD AMPTHILL, G.C.S.I., Chairman.

Mrs. CHAMBERLAIN
The LADY BALFOUR OF BURLEIGH
LADY MUSGRAVE
LADY SENDALL

LADY OMMANNEY
LADY MITCHELL

Mrs. ANTROBUS

Mrs. ERNEST DEBENHAM

Mrs. WESTON DEVENISH
Mrs. LATTER
Mrs CHARLES ROBINSON
Miss ANDERSON
Miss HUTTON /

Miss MOWBRAY
Miss NAPIER
Miss ROSALIND PAGET
SIR ALBERT HIME, K.C.M.G., Vice-
    Chairman.
The Hon. THOMAS COCHRANE, M.P.
SIR EDWARD NOEL-WALKER,
    K.C.M.G.
SIR WILLIAM HAYNES-SMITH,
    K.C.M.G.
SIR PATRICK MANSON, K.C.M.G.,
    M.D.
C. T. BRUCE, Esq.
FRED. DUTTON, Esq.
H. J. READ, ESQ.
OLIVER WILLIAMS, ESQ

General Purposes Committee.

C. T. BRUCE, Esq., Chairman.

Sir EDWARD NOEL-WALKER, K.C.M.G.
Sir PATRICK MANSON, K.C.M.G., M.D.
H. J. READ, ESQ.
OLIVER WILLIAMS, Esq.

The LADY BALFOUR OF BURLEIGH.
Mrs. ANTROBUS
MISS HUTTON
Miss MOWBRAY

Nursing Committee.
MRS. WESTON DEVENISH, Chairman.

LADY MUSGRAVE
LADY SENDALL
LADY OMMANNEY
Mrs. ANTROBUS
Mrs. ERNEST DEBENHAM
Mrs. LATTER

Miss ANDERSON
Miss HUTTON
Miss MOWBRAY
Miss NAPIER
Miss ROSALIND PAGET

Sick Pay Fund Committee.
LADY OMMANNEY, Chairman.

LADY MUSGRAVE
LADY MITCHELL

Miss MOWBRAY
Miss NAPIER, Hon. Secretary.

Trustees.
The DUKE OF BEDFORD, K.G.
The EARL OF SELBORNE., G.C.M.G.
FRED DUTTON, Esq.

Bankers.
Messrs. BARCLAY & CO., LTD.,
19, Fleet Street, E.C.

Hon. Auditors.
Messrs. PRICE, WATERHOUSE & Co.,

Hon. Treasurer.
SIR EDWARD NOEL-WALKER, K.C.M.G.

Hon. Solicitor.
FRED. DUTTON, Esq.

Hon. Secretary.
MISS MOWBRAY.

Secretary.
Miss M. E. DALRYMPLE HAY,
Imperial Institute, S.W. /

THE SCOTTISH BRANCH.

President.
The LADY BALFOUR OF BURLEIGH.

Council.

The MARCHIONESS OF BREADALBANE

The MARCHIONESS OF LINLITHGOW

ANNA, COUNTESS OF MORAY

The COUNTESS OF ELGIN, C.I.

The COUNTESS OF KINTORE

The COUNTESS OF GLASGOW

The LADY REAY, C.I.

The LADY MOUNT STEPHEN

The LADY OVERTOUN

The LADY STRATHCONA AND MOUNT ROYAL

LADY MITCHELL THOMSON

LADY GRANT-DUFF, C.I.

LADY CHALMERS

Mrs. MAN STUART

LADY OLIVER RIDDELL

Mrs. MC LAREN

Mrs. A.A. GORDON

Mrs. HENRY M'GRADY

Miss LOUISA STEVENSON

The MARQUESS OF BREADALBANE, K.G.

The MARQUESS OF LINLITHGOW, K.T.

The EARL OF ELGIN, K.G.

The EARL OF KINTORE, G.C.M.G.

The EARL OF GLASGOW, G.C.M.G.

LORD MOUNT STEPHEN

LORD OVERTOUN

LORD STRATHCONA AND MOUNT ROYAL, G.C.M.G.

SIR JAMES FERGUSSON, BART., M.P., G.C.S.I.

SIR THOMAS LIPTON, BART, K.C.V.O.

COLONEL MAN STUART, C.B., C.M.G.

HENRY M'GRADY, ESQ.

SIR THOMAS R. DEWAR, M.P.

P.A. YOUNG, Esq., M.D., F.R.C.P.E.

JOHN A. DEWAR, Esq., M.P.

Executive Committee.
Chairman.

The LADY BALFOUR OF BURLEIGH.

The LADY KINROSS

LADY MITCHELL THOMSON

LADY CHALMERS

Mrs. STEWART CLARK

LADY OLIVER RIDDELL

Miss LOUISA STEVENSON

PRINCIPAL SIR W. TURNER, K.C.B.

COLONEL MAN STUART, C.B., C.M.G.

Nursing Committee.

The LADY BALFOUR OF BURLEIGH.

LADY MITCHELL THOMSON

LADY CHALMERS

Miss LOUISA STEVENSON

Miss HALDANE

P.A. YOUNG, Esq., M.D., F.R.C.P.E.

Joint Hon. Secretaries.
CHARLES F. WHIGHAM, Esq., C.A.
CHARLES L. DALZIEL, Esq., C.A.
46, Castle Street, Edinburgh.

Bankers.
MESSRS. BARCLAY & CO., LTD.,
19, Fleet Street, E.C. / /

RULES.

The Association is constituted under the Patronage of Her Royal Highness Princess Henry of Battenberg.

1. The name of the Association shall be "The Colonial Nursing Association."   I. Name

2. The object of the Association is to provide trained Nurses for the British Colonies and Dependencies and other British Communities abroad, both for private and hospital work.   II. Object

3. The Association consists of a President, Vice-President, a Council, an Executive Committee, such Honorary Officers as the Executive Committee may from time to time appoint, and Members.   III. Administration.

4. Subscribers of not less than 10/- annually, and donors of £5 and upwards, shall be members of the Association.

5. The number of members of the Council shall be in the discretion of the Executive Committee, who may at any time consult the Council, and for that purpose may arrange a meeting in such a manner as the Executive Committee may decide.   IV. Council

6. Members of the Council, unless elected at the Annual General Meeting, must be proposed and seconded by members of the Executive Committee, the name of the candidate and proposers to be entered in a book kept for the purpose. The vote for admission shall be taken at the next General Meeting of the Association.

7. The Executive Committee shall consist of the President, Vice-President, such of the Honorary Officers as the Executive Committee shall from time to time determine, and such other persons, not exceeding twenty-three in number, as may from time to time be thought fit.   V. Executive Committee

8. The President shall be Chairman of the Executive Committee, and preside at its meetings. In his absence the Vice-President shall preside. In the absence of both the President and Vice-President, the members of the Committee present shall elect the Chairman for the meeting. Seven members of the Committee present shall be a quorum for the transaction of business. /

9. The Executive Committee may employ any such paid officers or servants as they may deem necessary, and shall generally administer and conduct the affairs of the Association, subject nevertheless to any resolutions duly submitted and passed at a General Meeting.

10. The Executive Committee shall meet on the first Wednesday of every month at 12 o'clock, unless otherwise determined by resolution of the Committee.

11. A resolution passed at any meeting of the Executive Committee shall not be altered at any subsequent meeting, unless notice of the proposed alteration has been given in the circular convening the meeting, and the alteration is approved by two-thirds of the members present at the meeting at which it is proposed.

12. The Executive Committee shall have power from time to time to form Sub-Committees, and to delegate to them all or any of its own powers, and to revoke the same.

13. The Executive Committee may also create from time to time branch organisations of the Association in such localities and centres as may be thought desirable, and may appoint the officers to administer any such branch organisation, and prescribe from time to time rules under which the working of any such branch organisation shall be conducted.

14. The Executive Committee may fill up any vacancies in its own body, or amongst the Honorary Officers howsoever arising, the members or officers so appointed to hold office until the next annual general meeting after their appointment.

VI. Funds   15. The Funds of the Association shall be derived from donations, annual subscriptions and bequests.

16. All donations and bequests (unless special directions respecting the application thereof be given by the respective donors) shall, in the discretion of the Executive Committee, be applied either to form or increase the capital of the Association, or as revenue. All annual subscriptions, and all dividends and interest arising from capital, shall be considered as revenue. /

17. The Executive Committee may, in their discretion, from time to time, add to the Capital Funds of the Association by transferring thereto and investing any portion of the revenue.

18. The Executive Committee may, whenever in their opinion an urgent necessity for so doing exists, resort to the Capital for Funds to be applied to any of the objects of the Association, or to meet any deficit on Revenue Account, but no such application of capital shall be made without a resolution of the Executive Committee passed by a two-thirds majority at a meeting specially convened for that purpose, at which meeting not less than two-thirds of the members of the Executive Committee for the time being shall be present.

19. The property and funds of the Association, when invested shall be invested in the names of Trustees and in pursuance of a resolution of the Executive Commit-

tee. The first Trustees shall not be less than three nor more than five in number, and shall be appointed by the Executive Committee. When by death, resignation, or other cause the number of continuing Trustees shall not exceed two, an additional Trustee or Trustees shall be appointed at the next annual meeting, and the continuing Trustees shall, immediately after any such appointment, transfer all property and funds of the Association into the name of themselves and the new Trustee or Trustees.

20. The investments to be selected shall be entirely in the discretion of the Executive Committee, who shall also have absolute control over all the funds and property of the Association, and the Trustees shall be bound at all times to comply with any resolutions or directions of the Executive Committee in regard to such property and funds, and the investment, realisation or reinvestment thereof, and any such resolution or direction shall be a sufficient authority, and when complied with a complete discharge to the Trustees.

21. The uninvested Funds of the Association shall be kept in the name of the Association at a Banker to be selected by the Executive Committee, and all sums received on account of the Association shall be lodged with such Banker. Subject / to the direction of the Executive Committee, the uninvested Funds and the Banking Account shall be under the control of the Honorary Treasurer of the Association. All cheques on the Banking Account shall be signed by the Honorary Treasurer, and if so directed by the Executive Committee, countersigned by such other person or persons as the Executive Committee may, from time to time, by resolution prescribe.

22. A General Meeting of the Association shall be held once in every year upon such day as may be fixed by the Executive Committee, of which such notice shall be given, either by circular or otherwise, as the Committee may decide. VII. General Meeting.

23. At this meeting shall be elected the President, Vice-President, Council, Executive Committee, Honorary Officers, and an Auditor for the ensuing year.

24. The General Meeting shall be presided over by the President, or in his absence the meeting shall elect the Chairman.

25. The Executive Committee shall lay the Report for the past year before the General Meeting. Copies of the Report shall be circulated among the members of the Association in such manner as the Committee may decide.

26. If a General Meeting shall fail to elect the Council or Executive Committee, or all or any of the officers of the Association, the person or persons previously holding such office shall continue to do so until the next succeeding annual meeting.

27. All questions to be decided at a General Meeting shall be decided in the first instance on a show of hands. A declaration by the Chairman that a Resolution has been carried or lost shall be conclusive unless a poll be demanded by not less than five members personally present. If a poll be demanded, the manner and time for taking the same shall be entirely in the discretion of the Chairman. /

28. No person not recommended or accepted as a candidate by the Executive Committee shall be proposed for election on the Council or Executive Committee, or to any office under the Association, unless notice in writing of the intention to propose such person signed by the proposer and a seconder shall have been given to the Honorary Secretary at least fourteen days before the day of the meeting.

29. The ordinary business of the Annual General Meeting shall be the consideration and adoption of the annual Report and Accounts, and the election of the Council and Executive Committee and Honorary Officers. All other business shall be deemed special business requiring due notice.

VIII. Alteration of Rules.
30. The rules of the Association may, from time to time, be altered, revoked or added to, by resolution of the Executive Committee, passed by not less than two-thirds of the members present at an Executive Meeting, provided notice of the proposed alteration, revocation or addition has been given in the circular convening the meeting.

IX. Notice of special Business
31. Any Member desiring to submit a resolution on any special business must give to the Honorary Secretary notice in writing of the proposed Resolution, signed by the proposer and seconder at least fourteen days prior to the day on which the meeting is to be held.

Interpretation
32. In the construction of these rules, words importing the masculine gender shall include equally both sexes. /

COLONIAL NURSING ASSOCIATION.

REPORT.

THE Executive Committee of the Colonial Nursing Association, in presenting the Tenth Annual Report, have great pleasure in recording continuous and steady progress. Five new Private Branches have been started since April, 1905, and a former Private Branch has been revived under Government auspices.

Statistics of Work.
The total number of Nurses at work during the year has been 144; of whom 108 were employed by Government and 36 as Private Nurses.

Last year the total was 121; 94 being in Government and 27 in Private employment.

To meet the increasing demand many new Nurses have been added to the books. These Nurses, almost without exception, possess the certificate of the Central Midwives' Board, and the number of posts to which Nurses without this qualification can be sent becomes smaller year by year.

The new Private Branches have been started in places as far apart as **Lisbon, South Africa, and Tehran, Persia,** where the British communities have raised considerable funds to enable our fellow countrymen abroad to benefit in sickness by as efficient trained nursing as they would have found at home. The application from **Tehran** was received last October (1905), just when the troubles in Russia were at their worst,[1] and many difficulties and even dangers had to be encountered by the Nurse on her outward journey; she had, however, the great advantage of travelling under the escort of Dr. Odling (Physician to the British Legation, Tehran), and Mrs. Odling. The journey, a long and adventurous one even under ordinary conditions, was rendered doubly difficult by the railway strike, which delayed the / travellers for three days on the Russian frontier. The Executive Committee have learned with great regret of the death of Dr. Odling, which took place in February last; they cannot speak too highly of the kindness he showed in helping in the selection of the Nurse, and are most grateful to him and to Mrs. Odling for the care they took of her on the journey.

New Local Branches.

Owing to the outbreak of plague at **Zanzibar** last autumn the Association was asked to supply emergency Nurses, and sent out two, who worked there until January. Fortunately the outbreak was not a serious one, but the Committee were gratified to hear that the Nurses gave satisfaction both in their work and conduct.

South Africa.

In addition to these new developments of the work the Association has lately supplied a Matron and two Nurses for the Queen Victoria Hospital for Women, **Johannesburg,** a Nurse for the Maternity Home at **Salisbury, Rhodesia,** and has selected a Nurse for work with the **South African,** Church Railway Mission, in this case giving a grant to cover all expenses for the first year and guaranteeing a sufficient sum to meet the expenses of the second and third years if required. This Railway Mission work is a most useful one, ministering as it does to the very large British and Dutch population scattered along the South African railways, and the Committee feel that in making it possible for them to obtain the service of a skilled Nurse the Association is fulfilling one of its principal aims and undertaking a work which promises to develop largely in the future.

The Private Branch which has been revived under Government auspices is in the lonely and wind-swept **Falkland Islands** in the South Atlantic, and care has been taken by the Committee to select a Nurse well suited to the peculiar character of the work.

The Committee have, during the year, recommended two Nurses for the Government service at **Nairobi** in **East Africa** and one for **Entebbe** in **Uganda.**

New Government Posts.

As is well known, Uganda is suffering from a devastating epidemic of the / Sleeping Sickness, which has not only decimated the native population, but has now, unfortunately, begun to attack Europeans – amongst those who have contracted this mysterious complaint is a member of the scientific expedition recently sent out to study the disease.

Every effort has been made by the Schools of Tropical Medicine and other Scientific Societies in this country to investigate, and if possible discover the original cause of the malady (attributed to a parasite – trypanosoma – found in the blood of the patient), and already, owing to these researches, a certain measure of success has attended the treatment of the patients attacked.

The staff of the **Colombo** General Hospital has been increased by three Nurses and that of the **Kandy** General Hospital by one Nurse. In the **Federated Malay States** one of the nurses sent out in 1901, after completing a successful tour of service in **Selangor,** has now been transferred to **Pahang,** showing that the services of the Nurses belonging to the Association who are stationed in the Malay Peninsular are appreciated and that the demand for them is still on the increase.

Grants for Training. The great advantage to the Nurses of a course at the **London** or **Liverpool Schools of Tropical Medicine** is generally acknowledged, and the Committee would wish to take this opportunity of again thanking the authorities at both Schools for the very generous manner in which the Candidates recommended by the Association are received free of all cost for the three months' training.

For some years the Government have allowed a small grant of £3 to each Nurse attending the course, who subsequently takes service in any of the West African Colonies, and latterly the Governments of East Africa, Gibraltar and the Straits Settlements have also granted this allowance, the Committee have therefore decided to make the same grant from their own funds to all Nurses belonging to the Association who are willing to give the necessary time for this most useful addition to their training. /

Experience has shown that Nurses returning from abroad after three or five years' service, much appreciate a short course at some large General Hospital in this country with the opportunities this affords for bringing their professional knowledge up-to-date before taking fresh appointments in the Colonies. It was therefore decided to make arrangements for this course for any Nurse who had done good service abroad, and to allow in each case a grant to the amount of £10 to cover the expenses. The number of these grants will tend to increase and absorb a considerable sum, but the Committee feel sure that all who have practical knowledge of nursing will agree with them that the funds of the Association could not be employed in a more useful manner.

The grant to the South African Church Railway Mission mentioned previously, is £90 for the first year, whilst the further sum of £65 for the second year and £90 (which includes the homeward passage) for the third has been guaranteed.

Besides these grants, many advances are made from the funds to the Nurses, both for the purpose of obtaining special training (where a grant is not considered necessary) and also to enable them to procure their outfit for service abroad.

These advances, which vary from £5 to £20, and which last year amounted to upwards of £160, are made simply on the note of hand of the Nurses, and the Committee have always found that they are repaid with great punctuality and within the limit of time; which is usually a year.

The amount advanced for the outward passages of Nurses is also increasing yearly. During the past year £337 has been paid from the funds for this purpose.

Donations and subscriptions amounting to £14 14s. 6d. have been received during the past year for the Sick Pay Fund. These include a subscription of two guineas from the / Oporto Nursing Association. The Committee gratefully acknowledge their obligations to the English Ladies' Orchestral Society, who kindly gave a Concert in aid of the Fund at the Royal Horticultural Hall, Vincent Square, Westminster, on February 21st, 1906. The Concert was extremely successful, and resulted in a net gain to the Sick Pay Fund of £145 13s. 9d.

During the past year grants amounting to £44 3s. have been made from the Fund, and the Committee are glad to report that the help given is very much appreciated by the Nurses. One writes: "I should have had a very poor chance without it"; another: "It is almost worth while being ill to find out how kind people are." As the work of the Association expands, the claims on the Sick Pay Fund inevitably increase, and the Committee earnestly commend it to the notice of all interested in the well-being of Nurses employed abroad.

The following table shows the number of new Nurses sent out each year since 1897.

NURSES SENT OUT.

Year ended April 30th.	Government.	Private.	Total.
1897	3	3	6
1898	11	4	15
1899	14	2	16
1900	11	15	26
1901	24	5	29
1902	32	8	40
1903	24	11	35
1904	27	10	37
1905	37	13	50
1906	32	19	51
	215	90	305 /

A list of Nurses with details of their training and employment will be found appended to this Report, and attention may be directed to the fact there noted that several of the Nurses have now belonged to the Association for eight and nine years, and have, in some instances, completed as many as three engagements either in the same Colony or in different parts of the world.

It may be of interest to mention here briefly that the Association now selects the Matrons and Nurses for twenty different Crown Colonies and Protectorates in Central, East and West Africa, the Transvaal, the Eastern Crown Colonies, the Mediterranean Colonies and the West Indies, whilst the private Nurses are working in Bangkok, Ceylon, Costa Rica, Cyprus, Hong Kong, India, Japan, Lisbon, Mauritius, Oporto, Singapore, South Africa, Tehran and Rhodesia.

Many interesting particulars of the Work, received from the Nurses themselves and from other sources of information, are contributed monthly to *Nursing Notes*[2] which has for some years generously afforded a space in its columns for news concerning the Association, and all who may wish to know further details would find much to interest them in this publication.

Legislation of Officers.
The Committee announce with much regret that the Earl of Westmeath, who ever since 1899 has given most valuable service to the Association as Vice-President and President, has been obliged to sever his connection with it owing to his engagements elsewhere, and they would wish to offer him their sincere thanks for all he has done to further the work.

They have been fortunate in securing the services of Lord Ampthill to succeed him in the Office of President.

The Committee also regret the resignation of Viscount Ridley, who has acted as Vice-President for the past year, but was unable to continue his services owing to other claims on his time. They are glad to announce that Sir Albert Hime has consented to fill this office. /

Annual Meeting 1905.
By the kind invitation of the Duke and Duchess of Marlborough, the Annual Meeting last year, on June the 7th, was again held at Sunderland House. Her Royal Highness Princess Henry of Battenberg was present throughout the proceedings, and the Meeting, which was in every way most successful, attracted an audience of nearly 300 persons.

The President, the Earl of Westmeath, occupied the chair, and gave in the opening address details of the work carried on by the Association. The adoption of the Report was moved by the Right Hon. R.B. Haldane, M.P., and seconded by Sir Alfred Jones, who, in the course of his speech promised to give £250 to the funds of the Association for the current year, a promise which has been most generously fulfilled. Amongst the other speakers were: Lady Balfour of Burleigh, Sir John Rodger, Sir Patrick Manson and Mr. Fred Dutton.

It is obvious that the work of the Association must depend very largely on the subscriptions received, and experience has proved that a grant from the funds is often of the greatest use in starting the work; it not only shows the sympathy felt in this country but it tends to stimulate local generosity. One Honorary Secretary writes: – "We are most grateful to the Colonial Nursing Association for their kind offer, and we accept the gift with very many thanks. It is so encouraging to feel there is someone taking an interest in us at home."

Nor is the work merely represented by its expenditure. That part of its administration which organises the establishment of self-supporting Branches of the Association is perhaps equally, if not more, promising of vitality and permanence.

In conclusion, the Committee would wish to thank all those who have during the past ten years helped in making the work of the Colonial Nursing Association so successful.

The Tenth Annual Report shows yery [*sic*] plainly how that work, from small beginnings, has, owing to the great need for it, become one of far-reaching dimensions, and as the field of work broadens, so do new possibilities of useful development present themselves. /

Some of the posts are still in very truth "Outposts of Empire." Such names as Zungeru and Lokoja, Entebbe, Kuala Lumpur or Seremban must, to many ears, sound unfamiliar and outlandish, and might well attract the hearers to a much-needed study of the geography of the British Empire.

Each name, however, represents in greater or less degree a spot where men of our race are toiling hard, often in lonely and depressing surroundings, to drain the swamps and clear the bush, to raise the native races and to prepare the way for the civilisation and justice which always follow the British Flag.

To those who already know the work of the Association, each name also represents a spot where these same men can find the care and trained skill in nursing which they would have at home. To those who are not acquainted with the work the Committee would point out that the ideal of the Association is to have at least one Nurse, and, when circumstances and funds permit, a hospital with a trained Staff wherever the climate is most deadly and the work most lonely. Where disease is most rife, there the skill should be found to fight it on its own ground, and it is the work of the Association at home to see that nothing is lacking which can be provided to help in the fight for the lives of those who go out to serve the Empire.

By order of the Committee,

EDITH M. MOWBRAY,

Honorary Secretary. /

SIXTH ANNUAL REPORT
OF THE
SCOTTISH BRANCH
OF THE
COLONIAL NURSING ASSOCIATION,
For year ended April 30th, 1906.

The Executive Committee of the Council of the Scottish Branch have pleasure in submitting to the Association its Sixth Annual Report for the year ending 30th April, 1906. During the year the work of the Branch has again been satisfactorily carried on and the Committee are glad to be able to report that the number of subscribers and the amount of subscriptions has been well maintained. For the year under review the subscriptions and donations received amounted to £108 19s., as against £112 17s. 6d. for the previous year, being a decrease of £3 18s. 6d. Every endeavour is being made to widen the field from which subscriptions are received, and it is hoped that by this means the work of the Association may become better known and the revenue of the Scottish Branch maintained.

During the year the number of applicants interviewed has been larger than usual, and it is a source of gratification to the Nursing Committee that the London Office continue to approve of the recommendations made to it. Of the four applicants selected by the Scottish Committee, Miss A.G.A. Cadman was employed for special plague duty at Zanzibar, and since that engagement terminated has received an appointment at the Government Hospital at Colombo, while Miss E.J. Milne, has been appointed to the Tehran Branch of the Association, and the names of Miss M.H. Hall and Miss M. Foord have been placed on the books of the London Office as eligible for employment, when suitable vacancies occur. /

During the year reports have from time to time been received regarding Nurses recommended by the Scottish Branch in former years, and these have in all cases been most satisfactory.

It is with deep regret that the Committee have to refer to the death of Miss Flora Stevenson, LL.D., who has been one of the most active members of the Executive Committee of the Scottish Branch since its inception, and they desire to record their sense of the irreparable loss which the Association has thus sustained.

The Committee have to report that Lady Mitchell Thomson, of 6, Charlotte Square, Edinburgh, and Miss Haldane, of Cloan, Auchterarder, have been kind enough to give their services to the Association by becoming members of the Nursing Committee of the Scottish Branch.

It is desired to take this opportunity of again thanking the members of the Nursing Committee for their services in interviewing applicants.

KATHERINE BALFOUR OF BURLEIGH,
President Scottish Branch.   } *Joint Hon. Secretaries.*
CHARLES F. WHIGHAM,
CHARLES L. DALZIEL.,

Unpublished Memoir of H. B. Arber, Sudan Political Service, 1928–54. University of Durham Sudan Archive, H. B. Arber Memoirs, 736/2/1–27, pp. 1–6.

H.B. Arber[1] Sudan Political Service 1928–1954

Background

My parents were both of North London middle-class stock. My father's father was an architect and my mother's father the managing director of the music firm of J.B. Cramer[2] of Bond Street. My father made his living in business connected with the building industry, eventually becoming sales manger in a well-known paint firm. We lived throughout the First War on the Kent-Sussex borders and later moved to the lower Thames Valley.

My father's influence on me was considerable on the sporting side, giving me a lifelong interest in village cricket and in fishing, and introducing me to life on the river. My parents made considerable sacrifices to get a family of four, of which I was the eldest, educated in private schools. I went to a preparatory school Ovingdean Hall[3] near Brighton, following in the footsteps of a step-brother of my mother's, E.S.Wood, who later became Director of Stores at the Admiralty. From there I won a scholarship to Winchester, but as it was 12th on the list and meant waiting 2 terms, my father turned it down and I sat again for Charterhouse[4] where I won 3rd scholarship. There I read Classics, played cricket and was head of my house. From there I won an open scholarship in Classics to Wadham College Oxford.[5] There I read Lit. Hum., getting a good 2nd in Mods, but sinking to a regrettable 4th in Greats because I had become immersed in rowing. I was Captain of the College Boat Club, rowed in two Trial Eights (in one as No. 7 to the stroke of Arthur Hankin, with whom I was to go out to the Sudan), and just missed being a member of the Oxford 1928 crew[6] to which I was spare man.

At Oxford I was much under the influence of Maurice Bowra,[7] later the celebrated Warden of the College, and it was he, and not my father who sought commercial openings for me, who put the idea of foreign service into my head. This idea was made more precise by the influence of two Wadham men, a little older than me, B.V. Marwood and M.H.V. Fleming, who were in the Political Service already and on their leaves advised me strongly to try for it. Accordingly, while many of my Oxford friends were going for the ICS or the Colonial Service, I decided to try for the Sudan.

2. Joining

The Appointments Committee at Oxford put my name forward in the summer of 1928 and I was interviewed by two members of the Service who came up to make a preliminary selection (they were I think John Humphrey and Ewen Campbell). I was then summoned to a full selection board in London, chaired by Harold MacMichael,[8] and was lucky enough to be selected. (Years later, my wife and I had the luck to be lunching with Sir Harold MacMichael, High Commissioner, on D-Day 1944. My wife said to MacMick: 'I believe you were you were head of the board which selected my husband?', and he, looking down the table, said with a twinkle 'Well, we all make our mistakes'). In the autumn of 1928 the twelve of us who had been selected, attended a 3-month Arabic course at the School of Oriental Studies[9] in Moorgate where we were taught by H.A.R. Gibb.[10] I was lucky in finding that Arabic slotted easily into the channels cut by my classical education and I passed out top of the class with a good grounding in written Arabic. We were also given some lectures on the Sudan Penal Code. This period seemed just about right, long enough to / give us some basic knowledge, but not too long to blunt our expectation of getting out to the Sudan as soon as possible. But it meant of course that we were not given much background information, and had all to learn when we reached the country. We kitted out at Lawn & Alder,[11] but not with much more than camp kit and saddlery, and of course a super uniform with Wolseley helmet from Hawkes, since we were told we could get most of what we needed, particularly light clothes, in Khartoum.

3. First Impressions

My very first impressions of the country were a bit daunting. I had my watch stolen from my cabin by a Fuzzy docker, and then slept with my sleeper window open to wake up clogged with dust as we approached Atbara. But on arrival in Khartoum we were billetted in the Sudan Club and very well looked after. The memory of bulbuls snatching the biscuits from my early morning tea-tray and of kites mewing overhead is one I have never lost. We were looked after by Maurice Lush, then DACS(pers.),[12] with great helpfulness. We were given some general talks; we were bidden to call and drop cards on heads of departments; and we dined and played bridge at the Palace where Jack Morricon & I combined rather successfully against Sir John Maffey and A.J.C. Huddleston. We went to the Indian tailor, Ali Buck, for bush shirts and shorts; to Morhig for groceries and a case of the cheapest whisky (John Haig at 45p a bottle seemed expensive on £480 a year). Then we were given our postings and four of us were put on the train to the West, I to become ADC[13] El Obeid.

4. Assistant District Commissioner

Here I was very lucky. My DC[14] was C.H.L. Skeet and I was excited to be posted with him. With my father I had seen him playing as a member of Plum Warner's Middlesex XI which won the 1920 County Championship. He was one of the famous Twelve Apostles of 1920 and a wonderful man to start with; very patient and with that quietness which the Sudanese call 'barid', and I was to have a friendship with him which lasted down the years. The Mamur[15] was Khalafallah Khalid, later to become a prominent Khatmi politician;[16] the sub-mamur, Abdek Magid Abdullah, later to become a D.C.; the senior translator Mohammed Abu Rannat, later to become Chief Justice of the Sudan; and the junior translator Abdullah Wagiallah, an avowed nationalist who never wore European clothes, later to work with me in the Secretariat. Apart from Khalafallah who was rather stiff, no one could have asked for better trainers. For as I said earlier, we had to learn on the job, and the patience of this team with me as a raw and I suspect lightly know-all recruit, was kind and reassuring. Arabic lessons (for although I could read and write it, I could not speak a word) were arranged for me with Hassan Zahir, the local headmaster, and he again was kindness itself. In retrospect I think that my respect and liking for the Sudanese was fostered from the very outset by these good people.

Work in the Town Merkaz[17] was full and varied. Skeet put me early on to investigate a hashish case in which a whole 4-gallon petrol tin of the aromatic herb was placed on my desk every day; that did much for my Arabic. Abdel Magid, most charming of men, took me round the district on my first camel trek. He showed me how to ride a camel (although it is true that the first time I ever mounted I ended up the wrong way round to Geoffrey Hawksworth's delight); how to live in rakubas; but he did not tell me that even a brand new angareb[18] offered in one village would prove to be full of bed bugs. In the Bedeiria district outside / I met my first tribal leader, Sh. Hussein Zaki el Din, at that time Omda Umum of the Bedeiria, and formed a great liking for him, admiring his dignity, his charming smile and his tolerance.

Social lfe [*sic*] in El Obeid was full and interesting. I shared a house known as the Oven with Geoffrey and later with Robin Elles, who used to practise the bagpipes in his half. It was of course not only Province Headquarters (Gillan as Governor), but also Camel Corps HQ (A.R. Chapter); the SMO[19] and the Province Judge also lived there; and there was still a platoon of British troops who left that winter. Life was amusing and full, and I should think it would have been difficult to find a district which combined town work, outside work and life in a province HQ so well, and which introduced one to the other departments and the SDF[20] as well. The province staff were all outstanding personalities – Ned Mayall in Hahud, John Hamilton in Bara, Stuffy Armstrong in Umm Ruaba, Arthur Vicars Miles in Rashad and so on – and the pressure towards devolution and native administration was very strong.

When I had been there 6 months, Skeet went on leave and left me in charge, with G.N.I. Morrison, one of the Deputy Governors, keeping an eye on me (and taking me on a tour of the beerhouses and brothels by night as part of my education). Of those three months I remember mainly my first go of malaria and my inability to keep the books of the El Obeid Club. But the summer passed and Skeet came back from leave only to be transferred immediately to Dilling. He should have been succeeded by Arthur Oakley who however was recovering from a wound received in the Elliri Patrol, and so I found myself once again holding El Obeid single-handed until Arthur arrived in the next summer and I went on my first leave. I thus had a baptism of fire in a big town at an early age and it gave me confidence.

The district office in El Obeid was always busy, but in particular it had an immense amount of magisterial work on small cases; and with encouragement from the Mudiria[21] and the Province Judge (Artie O'Meara) I put up for the creation of a Town Bench, acting under the Penal Code with the powers of a 1st Class magistrate, and composed of leading notables. Apart from some spectacular quarrels among the members – I had to smooth over a scene in which Sh. Omer el Tinai called the venerable Sh. Nail Osman a coward – this proved an immediate success and took a great load off the merkaz. A small but humourous problem which I had to decide was the piping of the police guard from the merkaz across the maidan to the mudiria every day. I can not remember which Governor had started this custom and had the pipers trained, possibly Saville, but it was still working in 1929. By mid-1930 however we were reduced to one piper only, who was then caught up in a hashish case and ended up in the merkaz prison. But by special dispensation he was allowed out every day to put on his police uniform and pipe the guard over to the Mudiria. I imagine the custom died soon afterwards. I have written rather at length about El Obeid, but one's first district makes an indelible impression.

DAC Public Security & Intelligence Granch [*sic*]
DACS (Admin) Civil Secretary's Office[22]

After my first leave in the second half of 1930, a leave during which I had a reminder of my first go of malaria by being smitten with a real ague on Kempton Park Racecourse, I was transferred to the Secretariat in Khartoum and attached to José Penney's Branch of Public Security and Intelligence. I had hardly got there when I was detached for temporary duty in Port Sudan where Bill Clark was off sick. Here / there was an enormous amount of magisterial work and I tried over 100 small cases in 3 months. I can not remember what they were all about, but I do remember a prominent Yemeni merchant bringing his teenage son to my office and asking me to give him a good beating as he would not listen to his father. Did the merkaz have that reputation? Anyway, drawing on my experience of the Town Bench in El Obeid I proposed to the Commissioner (Col. Douglas Thompson) the creation of a similar body for Port Sudan, and this in due course came to pass after I had left. I also had my first experience of chairing a Business Profits Tax assessment board, sitting with the leader of the Indian community, Harkisondas Khooshal, and a leading Yemeni merchant, Gaafar el Yemeni. I was able to go down to Suakin to sleep a night in the Mehafaza among the tall crumbling buildings, made eerie by the subdued funds of women's voices from high up and the cries of cats from the alleyways. My three months in the sticky heat of Port Sudan had been very hard work, but I enjoyed it and was grateful for the chance of serving in the country's main port. We played cricket against visiting ships, I played polo under Major Bert Hibbert and, most important, was sought to play top squash by Eddie Burgess, then Deputy Commissioner. (there are so many stories about Eddie Burgess who was a great eccentric; how he took his piano to Darfur, how he always had his servant deck his sleeper with leopard skins when he boarded the train at El Obeid, how he took his Muscovy duck from Juba to Yei to be mated and then claimed travelling allowance for it, how in Post Sudan his garden was decked with coloured lights and always mistaken for the local nightclub).

Back in Khartoum I rejoined José Penney's office and became a lifelong admirer of him. I can not remember doing much useful work, but I learned Secretariat method. Sir Harold MacMichael put me on to writing a précis of the files dealing with the Kuku-Kakwa boundary in Mongalla Province, and then red-pencilled my draft like a don in college to teach me how to prepare proper minutes on the files. I was transferred for a short while to the Admin. side of C.S.'s[23] office and during the summer lived in the empty Palace as caretaker. But I formed many friendships in Khartoum and enjoyed the life as a young manabout-town. I still had for a while a nice grey horse which I had brought from El Obeid and raced it once or twice; and I had a model-T Ford which I bought for £12 and which had a kick like a horse in its starting handle. I wnet [*sic*] on leave in the late summer of 1931, travelling with John Hillard via Egypt. There was nationalist rioting in Cairo at that time and we were hurried through by the Agency and told to go down to Alex where we stayed in comfort at San Stefano until our Loyd Trestino boat sailed. After leave I had an enjoyable Khartoum winter season and soon after Christmas was told I was being posted to Mongalla Province as ADC Torit. This was something entirely new and I ran round Khartoum asking quwstions [*sic*] of those who knew the South, particularly friends in the Egyptian Irrigation like the Perrys and the Wallers who knew it well. All I heard reassured me and I set sail from the Mogren, travelling with Geoffrey Elliot-Smith who was going to the UNP,[24] in expectation.

ADC Torit

There began a period of five years which has made I think the most vivid impression on my memory in my life. As an arabicist and northerner I had at the age of 26 to learn something completely different, to serve under perhaps the most famous of all Southern DC's, Harry Lilley, and to live with and get to know intimately / Nilo-Hamitic tribes living in a wonderful district which combined small hills with the highest mountains in the Sudan, grasslands, swamps and that thorn savannah which is so typical of Africa; and which eventually, after it took in the Opari sub-district, stretched from the Kidepo River to the Nile. It offered somehow so rich a life to me at a most impressionable age that I have the material for a separate book about it.

Administratively Harry Lilley, with whom I formed an admiring and enduring friendship, had got the district very well organised. His was an authoritarian rule based on the strength of his personality, but the tales of his draconian methods were exaggerated and I think the Latuka knew that at heart he was a sentimentalist. One of the best known stories about him was that when the Latuka of Torit village, which was in sight of the merkaz, refused to go out on roadwork, he had them lined out face downwards across the village square and put two strong shawishes to start beating them from each end inwards. After they had got about three in, the rest, about 50 strong, jumped to their feet, laughed happily and rushed off to do the work. By the time I got there he had devolved authority on the chiefs, but hid personal power was there in the background.

There were chiefs, usually hereditary, of geographical areas and each chief had his court (usually called a lukiko after the Swaheli) trying cases in accordance with tribal custom with a clerk keeping court records. Much of our work was travelling round checking the court books coram publico and meeting the people. Appeals were referred to the central lukikos, B Courts, sitting in Idali, Torit and Ikoto, at which the DC presided with a panel of chiefs. Touring was made easy by the good roads and resthouses, many of which had been laid out originally by Lord Raglan[25] when he was DC and known to the Latuka as 'Obisekoi', meaning 'Straight path'. Our tours were geared to keeping the courts and poll tax records checked regularly, but we were not so busy that we could not go up into the hills fairly often where the climate was wonderful but few tribesmen lived. Lilley established a great chan [*sic*] of resthouses across the Imatong – I helped him locate one at Ibakhin above Lomo on the slopes of Mt. Garia –, planted coffee at Itibol, and eventually put some trout in the high Kineti river. Often we were escorting visitors from the North, but I found time to hunt a good deal and this gave me the opportunity to get to know the district and the people very intimately. / ... I learned Latuka from Fr. Muratori of the Verona Fathers, and eventually became sufficiently good at it to revise and enlarge with grammar Lord Raglan's original Latuka vocabulary.[26] We were encouraged by L.F. Nalder, the Governor, to gather anthropological information about the tribes, and I became very immersed in this, contributing much material about the Latuka and the Lango to his book.

Our attitude to the tribes, and indeed the attitude of all the old Southern DC's, was very district-proud and we thought our tribes better than anyone else's. But we were very paternalistic towards them, seldom shaking hands or accepting food as one did in the more egalitarian North where one would drink tea in the humblest tukl.[27] We thought it was our duty to help them preserve their way of life, providing law and order prevailed. I was sitting in my office at Torit once when an irate doctor from the Roan Antelope mine in S.A., passing through and staying in the resthouse, burst into my office and said: 'You ought to be ashamed of yourself, letting these people go naked'. It had never struck us so; nor at that time had it struck the Latuka who were proud of their traditional freedom of dress. In this way of thinking I was a supporter of Southern policy but not in favour of christianising them (indeed I was thankful at the end to be leaving the South when Martin Parr had become Governor with his militant christianity). But as a Northerner I suffered from a dichotomy [*sic*] of feeling in that having come from the more civilized and prosperous North I could not see how, unless by some miracle the old attachment to Uganda could be revived, the South could be kept separate and immunised from the North within the boundaries of one Sudan.

My stay there had to end and in the Spring of 1936 I was transferred back to Kordofan to the Eastern Jebels.

Sir Ralph Furse, Colonial Appointments Committee, 'Note by the Private Secretary (Appointments) on Liaison with Universities in the Self-Governing Dominions' (1929), Rhodes House Library, Furse Papers, MSS Brit. Emp. S 415, box 4/1, ff. 36–40.

COLONIAL APPOINTMENTS COMMITTEE.

Note by the Private Secretary (Appointments)[1] on Liaison with Universities in the Self Governing Dominions.

The idea is to supply the Dominion Universities with information about the Colonial Services and to provide better machinery for the selection of graduates of these Universities for the Colonial Services, without making the men come to England for examinations and interview.

To give effect to this idea I was sent to Canada in 1922 and visited the Universities of Australia and New Zealand, while attending the Empire Forestry Conference in these countries last year.

Arrangements of the kind described in paragraph 2 were made with the Canadian and New Zealand Universities and had the approval of the respective Governors General and Prime Ministers.

I was able to work out a parallel scheme with the Australian Universities, which was favourably received by the Prime Minister, Governor General, State Governors and Universities. Information on one point is still awaited before a decision in the case of Australia is taken.

There has been correspondence with representatives of some of the South African Universities and when the Secretary of State was in the Union last year he was led to understand that similar arrangements would be welcomed there. It has not, however, yet been possible for anyone acquainted with the work of recruitment to visit South Africa and it is considered that such a visit is essential to success. In the meanwhile a certain amount of liaison with / individual professors who can recommend likely candidates has been effected.

(2) The following short description of the machinery set up in New Zealand will serve for Canada and Australia also.

Each University appoints a member of its staff to act as Liaison Officer. He is supplied direct from the Colonial Office with printed matter giving information about the services, application forms etc. He becomes the centre of information about the services to all inquirers from his University, and, if he does his work well the personal adviser and friend of any intending applicant.

When he gets a definite application, he puts it before a Selection Committee, also appointed by the University.

This Committee decides as to whether or not it is prepared to vouch for the man's fitness for the services he applies for. If the answer is "no" the matter ends there. If "Yes" the Liaison Officer sends forward all the papers with the written report of the Committee to the Dominion Liaison Officer for submission to a Central Board of Selection appointed for the Dominion.

This Dominion Liaison Officer is the Administrative hub of the whole machine and the channel of communication about applications, and any special points arising in connection with the scheme, with the Private Secretary (Appointments) at the Colonial Office.

He gets the Central Board of Selection to / investigate any application recommended by a University. They make any enquiries they choose and also interview the candidate.

They have power to turn down any application, even when recommended by a University committee.

If they decide to recommend, the Dominion Liaison Officer arranges for the man to be medically examined as to fitness for tropical service and then sends the complete dossier, with the Central Board of Selection's report and medical report, to the Private Secretary (Appointments) at the Colonial Office.

The candidate is then considered along with applicants from elsewhere.

The Secretary of State for the Colonies reserves full powers of decision as to whether he will offer an appointment to any candidate or not.

(3) These arrangements have been made primarily with a view to the moral effect which they might ultimately produce in the Self-Governing Dominions. Their effect on recruitment was expected to be small, owing to the range of opportunities offered in the Dominions themselves, and in the case of Canada has fallen below my original expectations.

The main objects sought for, were as follows:–

(a) To remove any excuse for the idea that men from the Dominions, if suitable, were not welcomed in the Colonial Services.

(b) It is hoped that, over a period of years, a better understanding on the part of the Dominions of the problems and responsibilities to be faced in the

Colonial Empire might be fostered / by the fact that a certain number of their own men would be serving in various departments in different Colonies. Such men would normally return to their Dominion on leave, and might in some cases enter the public service of these Dominions or their mandated territories, after working in a British Administration.[x]

In the case of Australia and New Zealand it is hoped that the qualities sought for in candidates for these British Colonial Services, and the care taken over their selection, may have a favourable indirect influence on the methods of selection for the services in the mandated territories of these Dominions. Recruitment for these services is not believed to be on wholly satisfactory lines at present.

(Itd) R.D.F.

(d) Some indirect effect may also be produced on the system of selection for the Civil Services of Australia and New Zealand. The present arrangements discourage and almost, I believe, debar – the recruitment of men with a University education. This consideration appeared to carry weight with almost every University in the two Dominions, judging from my discussions with them.

(4) So far as recruitment goes the Canadian results have been very small. The machinery of the scheme has been used in the appointment of 18 men to positions in the Administrative, Education, Medical, Agricultural, Police, and Public Works Departments and in the following Colonies: – / Nigeria, Gold Coast, Kenya, Malaya, Mauritius, Hong Kong and West Indies.

3 have resigned and returned to Canada after a few years services. One was a failure and returned to Canada at once. 11 are at duty and 3 are undergoing training.

The authorities working the scheme in Canada have performed their duties of selection with care and an obvious desire to recruit only suitable men. Though the majority of men selected have not been up to the highest standard recruited from home, the selecting boards have only recommended one man in 7 years who turned out to be thoroughly unsuitable.

The machinery appears to be as satisfactory as can be expected, having regard to the difficulties involved by time and distances; but the selecting authorities necessarily lack full knowledge of what is required and in some cases appear to be too busy to give as much time to this work as would be desirable. The scheme appears to suffer from the lack of men in Canada willing and competent to promote recruitment by interesting likely undergraduates in the Colonial Services. An attempt is being made to improve matters in this respect.

---

x <u>Note</u>. Two Australians who have served in West Africa, (though selected before these arrangements (e) were made) are doing special public work under Mr. Bruce in Australia.

There is some reason to hope that greater results may be obtained in the other Dominions especially South Africa and New Zealand.

It is worth mentioning that 8 applications from the Dominions have been received this year for Colonial Agricultural Scholarships.

COLONIAL OFFICE,   (Sd) R.D. Furse.

June, 1929.

'Memorandum Showing the Progress and Development in the Colonial Empire and in the Machinery for Dealing with Colonial Questions from November 1924, to November, 1928' [Cmd 3268] (1928).

PART I. – GENERAL.
Colonial Office Re-organization.

THE most important event in the domestic history of the Colonial Office in recent years has been the separation of business connected with the self-governing Dominions from the organization for the control and supervision of the affairs of the non-self-governing Colonies, Protectorates, and Mandated Territories. In July, 1925, a new Secretaryship of State for Dominion Affairs was created, and as a result, the Dominions Office was set up to take over from the Colonial Office, business connected with the self-governing Dominions, the self-governing Colony of Southern Rhodesia, and the South African High Commission Territories (Basutoland, Bechuanaland Protectorate, and Swaziland); including also business relating to the Imperial Conference.

The Colonial Office continues to deal with the administrative work of the Colonies, Protectorates, and Mandated Territories, other than those for which the Dominions Office is responsible. Up till 1928, it contained seven Geographical Departments, the West Indian, Far Eastern, Ceylon and Mauritius, East African, Tanganyika and Somaliland, Nigeria, and Gold Coast and Mediterranean, dealing with the affairs of various groups of Dependencies; a Middle Eastern Division, which was established in March, 1921, to conduct business relating to 'Iraq, Palestine, Aden and Arab areas under British influence; and a General Department, concerned with the correspondence of a general and miscellaneous character, including questions relating to the establishment of the Colonial Office, the Dominions Office, the Office of the Crown Agents for the Colonies, and other subsidiary Departments.

A further measure of re-organization was effected as a result of a Committee appointed in 1927 by the Secretary of State,[1] with the Permanent Under-Secretary of State[2] as Chairman, to advise him as to any changes which were needed in the organization of the Colonial Office to enable it to undertake more effectively the increased burden of work which it was now experiencing in connection with the economic development of the Dependencies, and the need for a continuous application of scientific knowledge to the / various problems connected with that development, for instance, in the direction of medical, agricultural, educational, and other Services. Some twelve months later, the Committee were able to submit a Report, as a result of which certain modifications have been introduced into the organization of the Department, of which the principal are as follows:–

The branch of the Office which had dealt with affairs of general interest and concern to all or the majority of the Dependencies ("The General Department") has been considerably enlarged in order to enable it to deal more effectively with those scientific subjects in particular which require to be treated as single Empire-wide problems with particular local aspects according to the geographical area concerned. Moreover, the enlargement of this General Division in the Office will, it is hoped, facilitate the supply of information and advice by the Colonial Office to other Government Departments and public institutions on many scientific and administrative matters of which it has experience in the tropical field.

At the same time, the Committee did not recommend, nor is it contemplated, that there should be any disturbance of the main system of division of the work in the Office, namely on the basis of geographical areas, though one or two adjustments in the grouping of the Colonies as between the several geographical Departments of the Office have been effected, viz., the four West African Colonies have now been grouped together in a single West African Department, and the work connected with the Mediterranean Colonies has been transferred to the care of the Middle Eastern Division.

To ensure economy of the administrative staff, there have also been set up two sections of clerical staff, which will assume a large measure of responsibility for dealing with and disposing of the work and correspondence arising out of the employment and service conditions of officers in the Colonial Services, e.g., leave arrangements, pay, pensions, etc.

A further important innovation was the appointment of a *Chief Medical Adviser to the Secretary of State for the Colonies*. In 1925, the Secretary of State considered that the time had come when it was essential to supplement the existing machinery of the Colonial Office for dealing with medical and sanitary matters, and, after consultation with various eminent experts, he decided to ask the Treasury to agree to the appointment of a Chief Medical Adviser. In 1926, the Treasury sanctioned this appointment for a period not exceeding three years from the 1st of April, 1926. Dr. A. T. Stanton,[3] formerly Director of Government Laboratories in the Federated Malay States, was appointed to the post, and he took up his duties on the 1st August, 1926. /

The duties attaching to the post are more particularly as follows:–

(1) To advise the Secretary of State generally on all medical and sanitary matters in the Colonies and Protectorates, etc., and for this purpose to have access to all necessary departmental documents:

(2) With a view to the improvement of sanitation in the Tropical Dependencies, to ensure, so far as is possible, continuity of policy, co-ordination of action between different administrations, and the introduction of new ideas in the work of the Colonial Medical Services:

(3) To maintain a personal liaison and co-operation with other Government Departments and other bodies in relation to health work in the Colonies, and to keep in touch with the medical schools in the United Kingdom:

(4) To preside over the Colonial Advisory Medical and Sanitary Committee:

(5) To advise the Secretary of State on all questions relating to the personnel of the Colonial Medical Services:

(6) To assist in the interviewing of candidates for appointment as Medical Officers in the Colonies, and to be a member of the sub-committee on Colonial Medical appointments:

(7) To advise on all changes in the regulations and conditions of employment of Colonial Medical Officers.

The post of *Economic and Financial Adviser to the Secretary of State for the Colonies* was created in 1927. It is of a temporary character, terminable at any time at six months' notice. The appointment took effect from the 1st of October, 1927, when Sir George Schuster,[4] K.C.M.G., C.B.E., M.C., formerly Financial Secretary to the Government of the Sudan, was selected for the post.

The duties of the post comprise the tendering of advice on any subjects with an economic or a financial bearing. While the officer's position is purely advisory, he is expected to be of service to the Secretary of State by assisting at or undertaking interviews, or by partaking in negotiations on specific matters. His services are also available for the Crown Agents for the Colonies.

[...]

Recruitment and Training of Candidates for the Colonial Services.

1. Administrative Service of the Tropical African Dependencies.

In 1926 training courses for selected candidates for these Services – in which normally a hundred or more vacancies may be expected annually – were instituted at Oxford and Cambridge with the unanimous approval of all the Colonial Governments concerned. In the first instance these courses were of two terms' duration, but it has now been decided to extend them to cover a full academic year. These courses (which have taken the place of a much shorter course formerly held in London) provide probationers with a valuable training in a variety of subjects including Indian, Mohammedan, and English Law and Procedure; Anthropology; Tropical African History and Geography; Tropical Hygiene and Sanitation; Surveying and Field Engineering; Tropical Agriculture and Forestry. It is hoped that they will also have the effect of stimulating recruitment by attracting the attention both of the University authorities and of undergraduates more and more to the careers offered in the Colonial Services. Evidence of their beneficial effect in the latter respect is indeed already to be seen, both in regard to the numbers and in regard to the higher average intellectual standard of candidates.

2. Colonial Services Clubs at Oxford and Cambridge.

In view of the considerable number of probationary officers in the Colonial Services who undergo preliminary courses of instruction of various sorts at Oxford and Cambridge, it was decided, on the recommendation of a Committee appointed as a result of the Colonial Office Conference, 1927, to assist financially from the funds of Colonial Governments in the establishment of club premises at Oxford and Cambridge which would enable these probationers in the various Services overseas to meet together not only for social purposes, but also to hear informal addresses from principal Government officers on leave from the Colonies and to learn something of the conditions and circumstances of their future work in the Colonial Service. Accommodation in the clubrooms has also been provided for a library of books and literature relating to the Colonies, including the volumes of Laws, the annual reports, and other official publications of the Oversea Governments.

3. Forestry.

Full advantage has been taken of the facilities afforded by the Imperial Forestry Institute which was set up in 1924 at Oxford on an experimental basis. At this Institute officers receive valuable postgraduate training either before taking up their duties or subsequently during leave. Courses have also been attended when on leave by officers who were selected since the war but before the / founding of the Institute. The Institute is also providing training in certain instances for specialist forest officers. Facilities for such training did not exist before in this country.

4. Agriculture, and Scientific Services connected with it.

An authoritative Committee was set up in 1924 under the chairmanship of Viscount Milner,[5] who was succeeded on his death by Lord Lovat,[6] to enquire into and report upon the recruitment and training of officers for these Services.

This Committee presented an interim Report in 1925, as a result of which a system of *Colonial Agricultural Scholarships* was instituted, the first selection taking place in 1925. There are about 20 scholarships a year. They are normally held for two years, the first being spent in this country, and the second usually at the Imperial College of Tropical Agriculture,[7] Trinidad. The scholars form a pool from which vacancies can be filled in the year their scholarships end. Men are selected and trained with an eye both to specialist appointments and to appointments in general agriculture, and the training is varied to suit each case on the advice of an expert committee.

This scheme is still at an experimental stage, but the reports received are encouraging, and it may safely be said that it is already attracting to the Agricultural Services men of a higher standard than the average obtained in the past. Moreover, the scholars will have had two years' training in subjects chosen to fit them for their work, over and above the qualifications usually held by candidates for these Services.

5. Survey.

As the standard of recruitment for Survey appointments had not been regarded as satisfactory, a course of one academic year under the School of Geodesy at Cambridge followed by a period of practical work under the Ordnance Survey[8] at Southampton, was instituted on an experimental basis in October, 1925, for probationers selected for Ceylon. This scheme was also adopted by Malaya in 1927, and Nigeria in 1928. In the case of the other Colonies concerned the existing course of instruction for probationers at Southampton was extended in 1927 from two to six months' duration.

6. Educational Services.

On the recommendation of the Advisory Committee on Native Education in Tropical Africa it has recently been decided to institute a training course in Education for selected candidates for certain junior appointments in these Services. The first course of this kind will begin in London in September, 1928, under the control of Professor Percy Nunn, Principal of the London Day Training College; there will be provided special instruction, including educational psychology and practical teaching; in conjunction / with the existing professional course at the College. The course is designed more especially for selected candidates who have had but little, or no, previous experience of educational work. Its duration will be one academic year.

7. Statement showing the number of candidates appointed by the Secretary of State in the years 1924–1927.

	1924.	1925.	1926.	1927.
Legal	11	12	7	16
Administrative	72	85	103	101
Police	32	19	30	19
Educational	43	46	76	64
Financial	9	10	20	18
Marine	8	8	7	8
Medical	84	129	97	121
Veterinary	5	8	16	9
Agricultural	17	27	23	42
Forestry	20	16	13	11
Survey and Geological	12	15	15	19
Scientific Specialists (*e.g.*, Botanical, Entomological, Analytical).	25	14	9	18
Miscellaneous (*e.g.*, Game Wardenships, Secretarial posts).	14	17	8	14
	352	406	424	460
Agricultural Scholarship	–	16	17	15
	352	422	441	475
The number of candidates selected in addition to the above who –				
(a) withdrew	53	69	66	70
(b) were found medically unfit	6	24	20	16

[...]

PART II. – STATEMENT OF PROGRESS AND DEVELOPMENT IN THE VARIOUS GROUPS OF DEPENDENCIES.

A. WEST AFRICA.

1. Nigeria.

Since 1924 the outstanding development work in Nigeria has been the completion and opening to the public service of the Eastern Railway from Makurdi to Kaduna with its branch to the tin mines. As a result a total of over 300 miles of new line has been thrown open to traffic, and the mileage of railway in Nigeria raised to 1,600. A vigorous programme of railway construction was being investigated even before the completion of this railway, and further branches are under construction, one running eastwards from Kano for about 140 miles and one northwestwards from Zaria in the direction of the country round Gusau and Kaura-na-Moda. Surveys for other branches have been carried out, and construction may be begun in several directions as soon as the lines on which work is now proceeding are finished. The construction of the largest bridge in Africa has been sanctioned in connection with the Eastern Railway. It was at first hoped to work the trains across the River Benue by means of a train-ferry, but shifting sand-banks began to cause alarm, and it was eventually decided that the construction of a bridge was a necessity. The work has been entrusted to Messrs. Arrol and Sons, and the cost will be just under £1,000,000. The bridge is designed to serve not only as a railway bridge but as a road bridge as well in order to supply a very necessary link between the roads north and south of the Niger and Benue. The Nigerian Government has also embarked upon an active policy of road construction, the goal aimed as being between 400–500 miles of new first-class road each year. In the financial year 1924–25 the sum provided for road maintenance was £50.000. In the current year no less than £126,000 was provided for that purpose, so that the provision has increased by two-and-a-half times. The way in which roads have developed the trade of the country is shown by the imports of motor-cars and motor spirit. In 1924, 971,000 gallons of petrol were imported and in 1927 the total had risen to 3,268,000 gallons. Indeed, to such an extent is the consumption of petrol increasing in West Africa that some of the great oil companies are busily preparing a bulk depot and filling station at Lagos. The number of cars and lorries imported is rising rapidly, and in 1927 1,869 cars and lorries entered Nigeria. It is interesting to record that the Morris firm supplied more vehicles than the Ford.

The completion of the new wharves at Apapa has done much to improve the facilities of the Port of Lagos, but the main work there must for many years be the carrying-out of the programme / laid down, by the Engineers. At Port Harcourt, Nigeria's other main outlet, a new installation has been provided to deal with exports of coal. It is hoped that this will come into operation in the early part of next year.

Development activity in Nigeria has been fostered in many ways. Since the completion of the electric light and power station at Lagos, electric light schemes have been considered for other main centres, and during the past three years schemes have been sanctioned and are now under construction for Port Harcourt and Kaduna, while others are being actively investigated. Water supplies have been installed or are under construction at Oyo, Port Harcourt, Enugu, Kaduna, Kano, and other places.

Agriculture is the mainstay of Nigeria's prosperity. Government attention is devoted largely to endeavouring to improve gradually the native crops and the native methods of agriculture. Experience has shown that it is by no means always wise to attempt to introduce new methods or to induce the Nigerian farmer to attempt to grow new crops. A research station has been at work at Ibadan for several years and in 1926 sanction was given for the establishment of a second laboratory and research station in the Northern Provinces near Zaria. Perhaps the outstanding feature of the work of the Agricultural Department has been the successful introduction of a new variety of native cotton adapted to the conditions of the Southern Provinces. The experiments which have proceeded since 1924 have, it is hoped, reached a successful termination, and cotton of this new type is now available for farmers. The main industry of Nigeria is still palm oil and palm kernels. The efforts of the Agricultural Department have been directed to inducing the native producer to improve the quality of his product, and various cheap forms of machinery have been devised to assist him. At the same time, in order to enable Nigeria to meet the situation created by the establishment, of oil-palm plantations and a factory industry in the Far East, the Nigerian Government has prepared a scheme under which assistance would be given to firms which wish to erect modern machinery in the palm belt.

An active campaign of research has been instituted by the Veterinary Department of the Northern Provinces and has already met with substantial success in controlling the ravages of rinderpest. Research is now beginning to be directed towards the improvement of the stock thus rescued from disease.

In medical research great advances have been made. A special party has been engaged for the past three years on special work in connection with sleeping sickness and problems connected with the tsetse fly and its relations both to man and to animals. The staff of the Medical Research Institute, Lagos, has been more than doubled, though some difficulty is found in securing officers of the special types desired.

In the field of general administration an important step was taken in 1927, when sanction was given to the Governor's proposal / that the whole of the Southern Provinces should, be brought into line and that native administrations should be set up throughout the entire region. This has involved the introduction of direct taxation in the Southern Provinces, half of which goes to the native administrations and half to the Government. The tax is small, ranging from 3s. to 8s. per adult male per year.

2. – Gold Coast.

During the period of years under review, work on the great new harbour at Takoradi has been carried on without interruption. The Harbour was formally opened in April, 1928, but its opening for traffic was delayed until December. It is now in full activity though Sekondi is still used for some commodities.

As regards railways, the Central Province Railway, running across country for a distance of 99 miles, has been laid out and carried to completion, while surveys have been made of two distinct routes for a railway to penetrate to the extreme northern frontier.

The mileage of roads maintained by the Public Works Department has been increased from 1,241 miles in 1924 to 1,700 miles, while the mileage maintained by the native communities has increased by a thousand miles in the same period. It is now possible by rail and motor to travel from one extremity of the Gold Coast to the other in five or six days without discomfort, and the number of stores and trading stations being opened up even in the remoter parts of the

Northern Territories shows that in the Gold Coast trade rapidly follows communications.

The main feature of the Gold Coast is always its cocoa export. The crop now amounts to nearly half the entire world's output, and in 1926 231,000 tons were shipped.

The prosperity of the people leads to increased demands for assistance in many ways, more especially in the two directions of medical and sanitary work and of education. The Medical Department has shown itself fully alive to the need for increased activity: while in 1924 expenditure under the various medical heads amounted to £263,000, this had risen to £320,000 in 1928-29. Within the last two years an intensive campaign against leprosy has been instituted, while a special staff of European Lady Medical Officers deals with the various problems of child welfare at the main centres of population.

As regards education, the construction and opening of the Prince of Wales's College at Achimota[9] probably represents the most far-reaching educational experiment in any part of the world in modern times. This College hopes to provide a secondary education on modern lines not only for the people of the Gold Coast but indeed for the people of West Africa generally. An immense sum of money (over £600,000) has been spent, on this, and from the numbers of pupils who apply to enter and the enthusiasm of the staff there appears to be little doubt that it will achieve this object. /

In the administration of the Gold Coast a very important change was made in 1925 when Provincial Councils of Chiefs were set up. At the same time, the Legislative Council of the Colony was remodelled and provision made for increasing electoral representation, though such representation must as yet be the exception rather than the rule. The Provincial Councils of Chiefs first met with some little opposition, chiefly due to misunderstanding. But the opposition now appears to be diminishing, and the Governor reports that the Provincial Councils continue to do valuable work.

3. – Sierra Leone.

The development of Sierra Leone has been hampered in recent years by the need for the strictest economy. Nevertheless a programme has been prepared for the construction of a number of roads which are necessary if the country is to be opened up. Sierra Leone is supplied with main arterial railways and the question is one of providing access to the railway for produce from the surrounding districts. In the Protectorate of Sierra Leone roads in the sense in which they are known in the Gold Coast and in Nigeria were largely unknown, but within the past four years some 200 miles of first-class road have been constructed and are available for motor traffic. A scheme has been prepared for linking up these roads and for the construction of pioneer roads which will, it is hoped, prove suitable for modern motor-cars adapted to rough country, and when the preliminary scheme now in progress has been carried out Sierra Leone will have quadrupled its road mileage.

A Geological Department was established in Sierra Leone in 1926, and the activities of the new Department have already resulted in discoveries of iron ore, gold, and platinum. It is not as yet possible to judge the economic value of these discoveries, but preparations are in hand for the energetic working of the iron deposit.

In the realm of agriculture the construction of a new agricultural college in the Protectorate at Njala was begun in April, 1926, and is now nearly completed. This college aims at turning out agricultural officers with a sound training and also giving the Education Department the necessary experience in agricultural methods. During the first three years, efforts have been made to encourage the cultivation of swamp rice with the object of giving economic value to what have been considered waste and uncultivable tracts of territory. A research division has been established in the Agricultural Department, and work has been carried out on investigations of local problems.

One of the amenities of Freetown, the capital, is the Hill Station, and a special railway was constructed many years ago to transport residents to and from their work. With the construction of an improved motor-road the railway's usefulness has departed, and approval has now been given for the abandoning of the railway / service and its replacement by a motor-omnibus service from Freetown to the Hill Station.

As regards general administration, the outstanding feature in Sierra Leone has been the abolition of the last trace of slavery. This was due to the discovery of an unexpected flaw in the Colony's legislation. Among the inhabitants of the Protectorate what is called, quite irregularly, "domestic slavery" had been in existence and an Ordinance was passed in 1926 which it was believed abolished even this. In the summer of 1927, however, the Full Court delivered a judgment which held that the status of slavery was recognised by law. Measures were immediately taken to remedy the oversight, and the last trace of slavery was abolished by a special Ordinance passed in September, 1927, with effect from the 1st January, 1928.

4. – Gambia.

The Gambia is a small strip of territory alongside the river of the same name and is virtually an enclave in French West Africa. Like Sierra Leone it is wholly agricultural, and its prosperity depends almost entirely upon the crop of groundnuts. Recent financial returns are as follows:–

Year.	Revenue.	Expenditure.
	£	£
1924	208,613	203,635
1925	189,086	271,836
1926	214,181	213,643
1927*	232,423	281,760
1928†	241,821	281,474

*   Revised estimates.
†   Estimates.

Of the expenditure, £50,000 was an appropriation to form a reserve fund to meet possible contingencies.

The conditions for the Gambia being what they are, endeavours to develop it consist almost entirely of agricultural work and investigations of various kinds in connection with the staple crop of the Colony. A new agricultural station has been established at Cape St. Mary, and the Director of Agriculture with his staff has done much good work in investigating matters affecting the groundnut crop and in endeavouring to introduce improved methods of handling.

In the Protectorate, roads are being constructed in places where they are likely to be beneficial, but the river provides an excellent navigable waterway from one end of the Gambia to the other. On it the Government maintains two steamers and a large motor-yacht.

An electric lighting scheme has been completed for the town of Bathurst, and the town is now lit in the most modern style. Work / is being conducted on reclamation of the low-lying swamp areas adjacent to the town, and it is hoped that substantial progress will be made in view of the more powerful dredgers working at it. Bathurst already has a water supply.

5. – St. Helena and Ascension.[10]

The revenue of St. Helena is insufficient to meet its expenditure, and the Colony is dependent on grants-in-aid from the Imperial Treasury for any development works of a special nature; in consequence many projected works of development have to await the provision of funds. Work is in progress on the repair and reconditioning of the principal Government buildings, including the Governor's residence at Plantation, and the Castle and Civil Hospital at Jamestown. It is hoped during the current year to carry out improvements on the roads, thereby rendering the introduction of motor-transport possible. Improvements are also being carried out in the water-supply, both for the service of the Island and for the supply of water to shipping. Arrangements have been approved for a visit from an engineer of standing to advise on these questions. A horticultural officer has been appointed, and it is hoped in the near future to take steps for the development of agriculture and forestry in the Island.

The main industry is the cultivation of "New Zealand flax," and varying quantities of fibre and tow have been regularly exported.

At Ascension, concessions have been granted for the working of phosphates, guano, and lava, and for the curing of fish, though operations have not yet reached a large scale.

B. – EASTERN AND CENTRAL AFRICA.

General.

The Parliamentary Commission to East Africa, under the Chairmanship of Mr. Ormsby Gore,[11] reported in 1925,* and subsequent development has been largely influenced by its recommendations. The Report drew attention to the desirability of greater co-operation between the various British Administrations in East Africa, and in this respect has had important consequences. In 1926 a Conference of East African Governors was instituted, with a permanent Secretariat, the first meeting being held at Nairobi in January of that year. In the same year other Conferences were held at Nairobi, one of which was attended by the legal officers of the Governments, another by agricultural, veterinary, and other scientific officers. As a result of these Conferences greater / uniformity has been achieved in many matters, such as the legal codes and the conditions of service of European officers, whilst a stimulus was given to collaboration amongst those engaged in scientific research.

In 1927, His Majesty's Government appointed a Commission, under the Chairmanship of The Bight Hon. Sir E. Hilton Young, G.B.E., D.S.O., D.Sc, M.P., to visit East Africa and enquire into the possibility of federation or other means of closer co-ordination between the several British Governments in Eastern and Central Africa.†

In 1925 the Eastern African Dependencies Trade and Information Office was opened in London at Royal Mail Buildings, Cockspur Street. The objects of this Office are to furnish information regarding East Africa to all those interested, whether from the point of view of trade, settlement, or travel.

The Palestine and East Africa Loans Act, passed in 1926, authorises a guarantee by His Majesty's Government in respect of loans up to £10,000,000 to be raised by the Governments of Kenya, Uganda, Northern Rhodesia, Nyasaland, and the Tanganyika Territory for the following purposes: –

Railways;

Harbour construction and port improvements;

Roads and other development works, including scientific research.

---

*   Cmd. 2387.

†   The Report of the Commission has been presented to Parliament (Cmd. 3234).

1. – Kenya, Uganda, and Zanzibar.
I. – GENERAL.

Kenya. – The native councils which were created in 1924 have proved their utility, and afford an excellent means of interesting the natives in the government of the country. They have voted considerable sums for education, veterinary and forestry services, etc. The boundaries of the Native Reserves were gazetted in 1926, and a Bill has been framed to provide for the vesting of the control and management of the land in the Reserves in a Native Lands Trust Board. The position as regards native labour has, on the whole, greatly improved during the last few years. The Government has in contemplation a scheme for further land settlement. A number of important enquiries have been completed, notably a Commission under Mr. Justice Feetham of South Africa,[12] to report on schemes for Local Government in Nairobi and Mombasa. In Nairobi and other centres important public works have been undertaken, the services of Sir Herbert Baker[13] having been employed as Architect.

The Turkana Province, formerly part of Uganda, was incorporated in Kenya in 1926. An important step towards solving the / question of frontier raids is the acceptance in 1928 by the Abyssinian Government of liability for compensation in respect of damage done by raiders.

Uganda. – Uganda experienced a "boom" year in 1925, when its exports exceeded £5,000,000, but this has been followed by a period of depression due to the fall in cotton prices and the partial failure of the crop. There is, however, reason to believe that the set-back is only temporary. Tin mines have recently been opened in the Western Province, and prospecting for oil is in progress around Lakes Edward and Albert.

Zanzibar. – In addition to the fall in the price of cloves, its staple crop, Zanzibar has to face increased competition from other clove-producing countries and also from synthetic substitutes for clove oil. Careful consideration is, however, being given to the organization of the clove industry and to the development of other resources.

On the death of Sir Robert Coryndon[14] in 1925, the arrangement by which the Governor of Kenya also held the Office of High Commissioner for Zanzibar was terminated, the latter office being abolished. The British Resident at Zanzibar is now responsible directly to the Secretary of State for the Colonies.

By the Zanzibar Councils Decree, 1926, the Sultan created Executive and Legislative Councils for the Protectorate.

II. – FINANCE AND TRADE.

The following are comparative figures of the estimated Government revenue for 1924 and 1928: –

	Kenya. £	Uganda. £	Kenya and Uganda Railway.	Zanzibar. £	£
1924	1,932,172	1,007,394	(1924)	1,386,032	416,308
1928	2,859,404	1,369,200	(1927)	2,278,660*	538,392

*   Plus £153,256 revenue from Mombasa Port.

The proceeds of the loan of £3,500,000 voted by Parliament in 1924 were devoted to the extension of communications. In November, 1927, Kenya successfully floated a loan in London of £5,000,000 5 per cent, stock (out of which the Parliamentary loan has been repaid), and a further loan of £3,500,000 4 ½ per cent stock was raised in May this year. With the concurrence of the Treasury, the Government of Uganda is to take advantage of the Palestine and East Africa Loans Act, for important works including the extension of the Railway from Jinja to Kampala, water-supply in Kampala and elsewhere, improved road communications, and a Human Trypanosomiasis Research Institute.

In 1927, by the abolition of duty on goods re-exported from Kenya and Uganda to Tanganyika and vice versa, the last obstacle to complete free trade between these counties was removed. /

The principal articles of export from Kenya and Uganda are cotton, coffee, maize, and sisal; and from Zanzibar, cloves.

The following tables summarise the trade position in the years in question:–

(a) IMPORT AND EXPORT TRADE.

	IMPORTS. Kenya. £	Uganda. £	Zanzibar. Rupees	DOMESTIC EXPORTS. Kenya. £	Uganda. £	Zanzibar. Rupees
1924 ...	4,038,914	1,975,307	29642000	2,239,614	3,897,395	18746000
1925 ...	4,195,724	2,677,764	27510000	2,724,629	5,097,215	20138000
1926 ...	4,197.657	1,964,174	24503000	2,414,341	3,596,045	15203000
1927 ...	4,947,569	1,819,961	23615000	3,086,916	2,310,300	16496000

(b) PERCENTAGE OF IMPORTS FROM AND EXPORTS TO GREAT BRITAIN.
(Kenya and Uganda only.)

	1924.	1925.	1926.	1927.
Imports...	39.90	38.06	37.12	38.34
Exports...	42.80	56.40	49.50	47.40

III. – COMMUNICATIONS AND TRANSPORT.

By the Kenya and Uganda (Transport) Order in Council, 1925, the railways, steamer services, and harbours of Kenya and Uganda were vested in a High Commissioner, under whose authority the communications of the two countries are directly administered. The Office of High Commissioner is held by the Governor of Kenya for the time being.

The development of communication has been rapid. The main line now runs through to the Nile and Lake Victoria, the first train to Jinja having been driven through by the High Commissioner in January, 1928. The extension of the line from Jinja to Kampala, the commercial capital of Uganda, has been authorised. By means of the Lake Kioga and Lake Albert steamer services and the Masindi Port - Butiaba motor service, the Railway administration maintains through communication with the Belgian Congo and the Sudan, while a branch from the main line at Tororo towards Soroti, which will eventually cover the same area, is already open as far as Mbale. Several branch lines feeding development areas and native reserves have been opened in Kenya. Two deep-water wharves are now available at Kilindini; two more are under construction and the construction of a fifth has been authorised. Road construction has been continuously undertaken both on the mainland and in Zanzibar and Pemba.

On the 14th June, 1928, a direct wireless service, known as the Kenya Radio, was opened between this country and Nairobi, serving both Kenya and Uganda. /

IV. – RESEARCH.

An International Sleeping Sickness Commission under the auspices of the League of Nations was at work in Entebbe from January, 1926, to June, 1927. Arrangements have been made for the continuance of its work by British scientists under Dr. H. Lyndhurst Duke, O.B.E., Deputy Director of Laboratory Services, Uganda, who also presided over the International Commission.

The Agricultural, Veterinary, Entomological, and Mycological Conference held at Nairobi in 1926 was attended, by representatives not only from British East Africa, but from South Africa, the Empire Cotton Growing Corporation, and dependencies of other European Powers.

A number of distinguished experts have been called in to advise the Government of Kenya, among them Professor Sir Rowland Biffen[15] of Cambridge, who was invited to study the possibilities of producing types of rust-resisting wheat.

V. – SOCIAL SERVICES.

Great efforts have been made throughout the years since the war to increase and improve the educational, medical, agricultural, and veterinary services and to bring them, into closer relation with native needs. Notable landmarks in educational development have been the opening of Makerere College for natives in Uganda,[16] and of the Jeanes Training School for Native Teachers in Kenya.[17] The stimulus given by the visit of the American Phelps-Stokes Education Commission in 1924 has been actively maintained, and the figures given below indicate the increased efforts which have been made since 1924 to provide adequate social services of all kinds:–

		Amounts provided in Estimates	
		1924.	1928.
		£	£
(1)	MEDICAL. –	126,943	206,601
	Uganda	116,513	154,658
	Zanzibar	37,561	51,679
(2)	EDUCATION. –		
	Kenya	63,399	168,546
	Uganda	20,839	51,385
	Zanzibar	9,850	20,596
(3)	AGRICULTURAL AND VETERINARY. –		
	Kenya	87,659	145,768
	Uganda	49,037	62,886
	Zanzibar	68,472	100,630 /

2. – Tanganyika Territory.

Tanganyika has shown striking development in all directions. The country had been devastated by war, famine, and pestilence and needed generous assistance from the Imperial Exchequer when it first came under British administration. In 1923-24 the total revenue was £1,315,188, and the deficit, met by Imperial loan, was £92,220. In 1927–28, the revenue was expected to reach £2,377,700, and to yield a surplus available for permanent public works of over £200,000, after paying interest and sinking fund on all loans for development from Imperial funds. The volume of trade increased from £4,757,930 in 1924 to £7,112,640 in 1927. Transit trade with the Belgian Congo increased in the same period from £693,092 to £1,493,010.

The general economic development of the Territory is reflected in the large increase in exports of all kinds. Its exports of sisal (the chief export of the Territory.) reached a total of 33,012 tons in 1927 (to the value of £1,160,735) as compared with exports of 18,428 tons in 1924 and 20,834 tons in 1913. Exports of cotton, almost wholly a native crop, have tended to fluctuate owing to changes of prices and uncertain weather conditions; but a record total of 109,450 centals of pounds was exported in 1926 and 88,272 centals of pounds were exported in 1927. There have been large increases in the export of coffee, which is grown both by natives and by non-natives. In the areas in the Southern Highlands recently thrown open for European settlement experiments are being made in the cultivation for export of tobacco, tea, and maize.

A large part of the Territory's wealth consists in the stock, numbering nearly 5,000,000 head, held by native tribes, some of whom, like the Masai, are purely pastoral. Great efforts have been made by the Government Veterinary Department to improve the quality of the stock and to eradicate disease. The campaign against rinderpest, which, during and immediately after the War, threatened to exterminate the whole of the native stock, has, in particular, proved most successful, and the ultimate suppression of the disease is in sight.

European settlement has steadily developed. In particular, areas amounting to nearly 200,000 acres of land in the Iringa Province, which were previously lying idle and were used by no one, have been leased during the last three years for non-native occupation. Occupation is limited to areas of not less than 2,000 acres in order to avoid the possibility of an influx of settlers with inadequate capital. A large area of unused land has also been leased on the lower slopes of Mounts Meru and Kilimanjaro.

Mining is developing steadily. Gold, diamonds, mica, salt, ochre, and garnets are already being worked; while coal and copper deposits, are under investigation.

Much of this general economic development has been made possible by the provision of improved transport facilities, which / are being financed, for the most part, from the East African Guaranteed Loan. Foremost amongst these is the extension of the Central Railway from Tabora to Mwanza, 238 miles away on Lake Victoria. This extension, which was completed in August, 1928, gives the rich and populous country between Shinyanga and Mwanza direct access to the sea, and is the first link between Victoria and Lake Tanganyika. An especially pleasing effect of the new line is that it has permitted a reduction of the small military force maintained by the Territory. The Tanga-Moshi line in the north of the Territory is being extended to Arusha, and will tap a rich coffee area. The whole of the railway system has been re-equipped with new workshops, rolling stock, etc., while large sections of the permanent track have been relaid with heavier material. In addition, surveys have been made of routes for two projected further extensions of the Central Railway – one from Manyoni to the Iramba Plateau, and the other from Dodoma towards the Rhodesian border in the south-west through the Southern Highlands.

The facilities for the handling of cargo, etc., at Dar-es-Salaam Harbour have been greatly improved by the extension of existing wharfage and the provision of new cranes. In addition, surveys of the Harbour have been made with a view to the adoption of extended schemes of reclamation and construction of further wharfage. A regular steamship service is now maintained on Lake Tanganyika by the SS. "Liemba," a German vessel sunk in the lake during the war, which was subsequently salved and reconditioned.

A programme of road development of some hundreds of miles in extent, as approved by the Guaranteed Loan Committee, has been carried out; and this has made possible a great diminution in the use of native porterage, a wasteful and unpopular system of carriage.

Political development has also been notable. A Legislative Council, on which there are seven Unofficial Members, has been established; the Territory has been re-organized on a provincial basis; and a complete system of indirect administration through Native Courts and Native Councils has been set up. This system has proved highly successful in working. The native authorities deal with such matters as local road, agriculture, stock improvement, prevention of disease, etc. Minor criminal and civil cases are disposed of in the Native Courts; while each native authority has its own Treasury which controls expenditure. It has been found that the native authorities command public confidence, and that their institution has led to an increased sense among the native peoples of responsibility for their own welfare, especially in matters of public order, education and medical services. In consequence, crime has decreased and reductions have been made in the Police Force. /

Thanks to the increased funds at its disposal, it has been possible for the Government largely to increase the provisions made for education, medical, and other social services. The European Education staff has been increased, and works in the closest co-operation with the education authorities of the Missions, who now receive increased grants-in-aid 'from Government funds. An Educational Code was drawn up after consultation with mission authorities and was first introduced in 1928. Advance in education has led to the formation of an African Civil Service with established terms and regular promotion; while increasing numbers of skilled artisans are becoming available both for private and for public work.

In medical work special attention has been given to the training of Africans as dispensers, sanitary officers, and medical assistants; while continuous efforts have been made in the investigation and eradication of native diseases, such as yaws. A special staff is at present undertaking the intensive study of the health of a particular tribe in the Kahama area, in the endeavour to obtain some reliable statistics as to native development, etc. A Labour Department was formed in 1926, with the object of watching over the conditions under which native contract labour is employed. Two valuable reports have been published by this Department, and labour-camps have been established for the assistance of natives travelling to or from employment.

The problem of combating the advance of the tsetse fly has engaged the serious attention of the Government. A special research staff of nine scientists has been appointed and is engaged on a detailed investigation of the habits of the fly with a view to determining the methods likely to succeed in checking its advance. The Veterinary Pathologist has been seconded for special research work on the possibility of producing, by injection or other means, certain breeds of cattle which will be immune from trypanosomiasis. Extensive measures of bush-burning and land-clearing have been undertaken in the Shinyanga district; a large area has been freed from the fly by this means, and is once more occupied by native stock.

It was decided in 1926 that the former German Agricultural Research station at Amani (in the Tanga district in the north of the Territory) should be re-opened as a Research Station for the whole of the East African Dependencies, to be maintained by contributions from each of the Governments concerned. A Director was appointed towards the end of 1926, and, after making a tour of investigation throughout the East African Dependencies, he submitted a scheme for the re-establishment and future working of the Station, which has been adopted. A staff of twelve officers has been appointed and is at work at the Station. Considerable progress has been made in the preliminary work of re-construction and re-equipment; and a comprehensive programme of research has been begun. /

3. – Nyasaland.

The progress of Nyasaland has been seriously hampered up to the present by expensive and irregular communications with the rest of the Empire, one factor in which is the absence of a bridge or other means of maintaining uninterrupted railway communication for expeditious transit of goods across the Zambesi River to Beira. This question has seriously engaged the attention of His Majesty's Government during recent years, and in 1926, on the recommendation of the East African Guaranteed Loan Advisory Committee, a special Commission was appointed to report on the possibility of constructing a bridge across the Zambesi, of extending the existing railway system from Blantyre to Lake Nyasa, and generally on the economic possibilities of the Protectorate. In the light of the information thus obtained a survey for the proposed railway extension was carried out during 1927, and in 1928 a further examination of the proposed bridge site was made by experts. The results of this investigation are now being studied.

A programme of road development financed from Guaranteed Loan funds was also commenced in 1927, the completion of which will occupy three years.

The need for developing social services in the Protectorate has not been lost sight of and the provision of increased funds for these objects is now under active consideration with the Treasury. An Education Code has been introduced and has been adopted by the missionary societies, to whom increased grants-in-aid for educational services are now being made by the Protectorate Government. Since 1922 the European population has increased by twenty per cent., while the taxable income of the community has been nearly doubled.

Owing to the impetus given by the stabilization of British preference for Empire-grown tobacco at 2s. per pound, a satisfactory development has taken place in the production of tobacco, exports of which increased from 7,044,175 lb. in 1924 to 15,466,032 lb. in 1927. Though a slump has seriously affected the market for bright leaf tobaccos, dark tobacco has continued to be absorbed fairly readily. The total volume of trade has increased from £1,131,711 in 1924 to £1,899,330 in 1927, while in that year exports exceeded imports by £22,408, whereas in 1926 imports had exceeded exports by £119,968.

A permanent Geological Survey has been established, which has already made useful additions to water-supply and knowledge of local resources. As a result of the Survey's examination of mineral occurrences, a Syndicate is about to investigate fully a number of promising areas.

A gradual improvement in the financial position of the Protectorate has taken place in spite of the difficulties already referred to, and on the 21st December, 1927, there was a surplus balance of / £134,169 as compared with a deficit of £7,704 on the 31st March, 1924. Further information in regard to the financial position may be obtained from the figures in Appendix III.[18]

4. – Northern Rhodesia.

Northern Rhodesia was taken over from the British South African Company in 1924, and seems likely to become one of the most important mining centres in the Empire, especially as a source of copper.

The European population, which was 3,634 in 1921, is now about 6,000, and is increasing steadily: 1,016 Europeans having entered the Territory during 1927 to settle as compared with 740 in 1926 and 470 in 1925. Its increasing importance has been recognised by the introduction of an elective element into the Legislative Council. The first elections were held in 1926.

The mining industry is expanding, and employs each year an increasing number of European and native personnel. The construction of two branch railways from the main line to serve important mines is shortly to be commenced. The increase in the imports of the Territory from £662,642 in 1924 to £2,061,999 in 1927 was mainly due to importation of mining equipment.

Concurrently with the growth of the mining industry, the last four years have seen a considerable development in the tobacco industry, especially in the Fort Jameson area and in the farming districts adjoining the railway line. The grant of preferential treatment to Empire tobacco has done much to assist this industry, as also the campaign conducted by the Empire Marketing Board to induce consumers in this country to purchase Empire products, and, in spite of a temporary slump in the tobacco market, the future of the industry is full of promise. In this connection the recent investigations carried out by the Imperial Economic Committee in regard to the growth and marketing of tobacco in the Empire should prove of considerable assistance.*

At present other agricultural production is chiefly absorbed either by local industries or by mining centres in neighbouring territories; the establishment of a Central Agricultural and Veterinary Research Station at Mazabuka, the construction of which was commenced in 1926 from funds to be provided from a loan under the Palestine and East Africa Guaranteed Loans Act, 1926, is an important step towards the development of agriculture in Northern Rhodesia. Experiments

---

* *See* Ninth Report of the Imperial Economic Committee, on the marketing and preparing for market of Tobacco: July, 1928 (Cmd. 3168).

are being made at Mazabuka to obtain a cotton plant which will resist some of the diseases and insect pests encountered in the endeavours made during the last few years with the assistance of the Empire Cotton Growing Corporation to encourage the growing of cotton on a commercial basis in the Territory. /

With Guaranteed Loan funds an extensive programme of road improvement and development was also commenced in 1926, and an interesting experiment is being made in carrying out an air survey of the Zambesi River and its larger tributaries with a view to investigating their possibilities as water-ways.

The general development of the Territory alluded to above is reflected in its financial progress. When Northern Rhodesia was taken over from the British South Africa Company it was necessary for His Majesty's Government to furnish annual financial assistance to the Protectorate revenues by way of a loan-in-aid from Imperial Funds. It has now been found possible to dispense with this assistance, and a portion of the loans so made has been repaid. The improvement in the financial position of the Territory has enabled approval to be given in 1927 for a revision of the salaries of European officers in the service of the Government to bring their salaries into general conformity with those paid by the Governments of the other East African Dependencies. The financial progress which has been achieved is illustrated by the figures of revenue and expenditure in Appendix III.

5. – Somaliland.

The history of British Somaliland may be said to have begun afresh with the overthrow of the Mullah[19] in 1920. Since that date, peaceful conditions have, for the most part, prevailed in the Protectorate, though, during recent years, the action taken by the Government of Italian Somaliland to disarm certain tribes under their jurisdiction has necessitated military measures of a precautionary character by the Somaliland Government in the neighbourhood of the frontier.

The nature of the country and the nomadic character of its inhabitants preclude any immediate or extensive agricultural development in the Protectorate. There has, nevertheless, been a tendency in recent years on the part of the natives in the western part of the Protectorate to begin to grow their own food crops, and the appointment of a Director of Agriculture has been made in order to afford them advice and assistance.

The main wealth of the natives consists of sheep, cattle, and camels, and the staple exports from the Protectorate are live-stock and hides. A small Veterinary Department, with a Veterinary Officer at its head, was set up a few years ago, and has been doing good work in dealing with stock diseases and in giving instruction as to the preparation of skins.

The development of the mineral resources of the country has received much consideration in recent years. A Government geologist has been appointed and has carried out a mineral survey in the Protectorate. Negotiations which have for some time taken place with a Company for the investigation and working of the oil deposits in the country have recently terminated in the conclusion / of an agreement. The mica deposits have also been investigated, and the grant of a concession for mining salt is in course of negotiation.

The revenue of the Protectorate is small, depending almost entirely on import duties, and the financial resources of the local Government are limited. It has, however, been found possible to undertake certain major public works during the past few years, including the construction in Berbera of a new hospital. This was opened in June, 1925. Extensive road construction has also been carried out, roads from Berbera to Hargeisa and from Burao to Erigavo in the east of the Protectorate being the more important of the new roads built. The construction of these new roads and the increasing adoption of motor vehicles have revolutionized transport arrangements in the Protectorate during the last few years.

R. D. Furse, Colonial Office Conference, 1927, 'Recruitment and Training of Colonial Civil Servants. Memorandum by the Private Secretary for Appointments', National Archives, Kew, London, CO 323/982/5, ff. 1–12.

Section I – Introduction: Scope of Memorandum and point of view from which it is written.

This Memorandum deals with recruitment since the Armistice for those branches of the Colonial Service for which men are selected by the Secretary of State personally with the assistance of his Private Secretary (Appointments). A table of these services, showing the number of appointments made annually in each is given in the Annex. From this it will be seen that – broadly speaking – the memorandum covers initial recruitment for all services expect (a) Eastern Cadetships, which are filled on the recommendation of the Crown Agents for the Colonies. These two groups are dealt with in separate memoranda* which have been prepared by those concerned Minor appointments and educational appointments open to ladies for which the Board of Education recommend candidates, are not included.

The Private Secretary is responsible only for recruitment from outside the Colonial Services. He therefore does not deal directly with questions of promotion and transfer and although he has been called upon to recruit for a number of senior appointments – especially in Education and in Scientific Departments – he is mainly concerned with recruitment for the junior grades.

2. The main object of this Conference, as I understand it, is to promote co-operation between Colonial Governments and the Colonial Office by the interchange of opinions and of information. The majority of its members represent individual Colonial Governments. The natural tendency of these Governments must be to look on recruitment mainly from the standpoint of their own Colony. It is

---

* C. O. 40 and C. O. 41.

probable too that the pressing needs of the moment may often bulk most largely in their eyes. I have therefore thought it would prove the most helpful course if I drafted this memorandum quite frankly from the standpoint that comes natural to me; that is, from the point of view of those who are responsible for supplying the needs not of one Colony or branch of the Service but of the many; who have opportunities of applying to one Colony or Department experience gained in connection with others, and who are increasingly coming into touch with the various sources of supply and with the factors, favourable and unfavouable, which affect it. The nature of our work, in fact demands a comprehensive view, so far as recruitment is concerned, of the Services as a whole.

3. Further, as I have been responsible for recruitment under successive Secretaries of State since February, 1919, as well as having shared in that responsibility between 1910 and the outbreak of war, I have thought it advisable to put this memorandum in the form of a personal statement: and more particularly so because some of the opinions expressed are my own and must not necessarily be taken to commit anyone else. /

Section II. – Recruitment since the War and consideration of factors which have affected it.

4. The period since the Armistice has confronted us with certain exceptional difficulties. For our purpose it falls into three main divisions. The first covers the years 1919-21, and was marked by heavy and often urgent demands for men, to make up for lack of recruitment during the war and to meet the needs of the mandated territories.[2] As against 248 appointments made in 1913, 295 were made in 1919, 551* in 1920, and 387 in 1921; or an annual average of 411. To meet these demands we had to rely almost wholly on the abnormal sources provided by demobilisation and subsequent retrenchments in the fighting Services. The ordinary peace-time sources of supply were practically unproductive, because the Universities, Agricultural Colleges, and so on, required three years or more from the end of the war before they could resume their normal output. As a consequence although there were very large numbers of ex-service men clamouring for posts, there was a serious and unavoidable shortage of properly trained candidates for all technical and specialized Services. Our work in this period mainly consisted in a rather desperate effort to sift out the heterogeneous mass of ex-service candidates and to meet, as rapidly as possible, the urgent demands with which we were bombarded from practically every Colony and Department. It was complicated by the lack of trained material for technical services, such as agriculture; by the fact that the age of so many ex-service candidates was necessarily greater than is normally preferred and by the difficulty, in

---

*   But for the delay occasioned by having to organize recruiting machinery, etc, a number of these would probably have been made in 1919.

many cases, of deciding whether the strain, to which the man had been subjected in the war rendered the danger of selecting him for tropical service too great. These complications were aggravated by shortage of staff at this end and by the pressure under which the work had to be done.

5. The second period – 1922 – was marked by a heavy slump in recruitment caused by widespread financial depression. The number of appointments fell in that year to 174: and in some Colonies, such as Kenya, retrenchment of existing staff was carried out. The effect of this slump was very bad. Not only were better men turned away than some of those selected both before and since, but the confidence of some of the training centres was shaken.* In the highly specialised department of Forestry, for example, our recruitment has not yet recovered from this blow.

6. The third period runs from the end of 1922 to the present time. Recovery began in the autumn of 1922, but was only gradual. 233 appointments were filled in 1923, 352 in 1924; 406 in 1925 and 424† last year. Demand therefore, has shown a steady rise up to a figure greatly in excess of the immediate pre-war period. Special features of the year or two have been (i) increases in the administrative staff in Tropical Africa; (ii) a large increase in the demand for Educational officers [76 Educational appointments were made in 1926 as against 46 in 1925, and we have 55 such vacancies on hand at the moment]; and (iii) the creation of a number of scientific posts mainly in connection with agriculture.

   During this period the abnormal war-sources of supply have practically dried up. On the other hand, the Universities and training Colleges have resumed their full annual output. /

7. It has therefore become possible during the last two or three years to take stock of the position and to get a better idea of the relation between supply and demand, under conditions which might be expected to be fairly permanent. It became clear that definite measures would be needed if the increased demand in regard to both quantity and quality was to be met, and if the higher training required to cope with recent developments was to be provided. I will deal with these measures later, but, before doing so, I should like to invite attention to certain factors which have considerably influenced recruitment, and which had therefore to be taken into account in considering measures for its improvement.

8. There seems to be a lack of enterprise and a tendency to stay at home amongst the post-war generation. This has been commented on at the Headmasters Conference and elsewhere and has, I believe, been noticed by the Civil Service Commissioners, who recruit for different groups of services. This tendency may be largely due to a temperamental reaction from the war, but there appear to be

---

*   See paragraph 32 f. of Report of Lovat Committee (Cmd. 2825) – circulated in Conference Paper C. O. 10.[3]
†   In addition, 16 Agricultural scholars were selected in 1925, and 17 in 1926.

other factors at work; though in discussing them I know that I am on difficult and, possibly, controversial ground, and can only give my opinions for what they are worth. The kind of man who usually proves most fitted for the Services under discussion needs certain personal qualities and an educational background mainly to be found in the type of family which has been most severely hit by the war. The loss of his father or elder brother may strengthen the desire to keep a boy at home. Beyond this we have the undoubted fact of the limitation of families; and it was generally the younger sons of large families who went overseas in the past. Economic pressure has also made it harder for such families to send their sons to a University. Fewer of them, therefore, get the type of education we prefer, and, as, for climatic reasons, we cannot usually send a man out till he is 21½, those who cannot go to a University tend to drift into other employment before we can take them. It must also not be forgotten that we lost 30,000 officers killed in the war. The effect of such a wholesale destruction of leaders cannot be made good in a short time, and it is men with the qualities of leadership whom we especially need. Finally, it is, I think, generally accepted that business firms are far more alive than they used to be to the value of the type of man we seek to attract. We have therefore to face a far stiffer competition from this quarter than in pre-war days, and the greater financial rewards, which a business career offers, are doubly attractive in these times of economic stringency.

9. In the second place, a higher general standard of quality is demanded; and here I may perhaps be permitted to say that the utmost importance has always been attached to obtaining men of the highest quality that circumstances allowed. In pursuance of this policy it has quite often been decided to leave vacancies unfilled for some time, if the available material was unsatisfactory and there was reason to hope that better candidates could be secured by waiting. This has been the principal cause of the delay which has not infrequently taken place in filling vacancies; but I hope that, in view of the interest at stake, the Conference will endorse the policy which has been followed.

The demand for a higher standard has been shown principally in three ways:–
 (a) As development progresses there is a growing need for high intellectual ability among recruits for the African Administrative Services, without any relaxation of the necessity for insistence on those qualities of personality and character which are essential to the proper handling of natives.
 (b) Whereas in pre-war times the other departments had, on the whole, to be content with a somewhat lower personal standard, it is now recognised that many of them, for example, the Educational, Agricultural, Forestry, and Veterinary Services, need men of similar standing in this respect to the Administrative staff, with the addition of professional qualifications.

(c) It is clear to anyone looking at the whole field that recruitment for scientific departments has entered on a new phase. In a number of important Colonies, particularly in Tropical Africa, Agriculture and the kindred arts of Forestry and Animal Husbandry have reached a stage where their problems call more and more for the application of a higher degree of scientific knowledge and skill. This entails a higher standard of scientific attainment in all officers entering the Service and creates a greatly increased demand for the specialist and the research worker. It is also providing opening for workers in certain specialised branches of science, for which we have hitherto hardly recruited at all; as for example, bio-chemistry, soil-science, genetics, and various branches of forestry research.

10. As against this increase and intensification of demand, we have to compete with the adverse general factors which I have tried to outline. Above all we must face the fact that the development of the non-self-governing Dependencies is advancing much faster than is realised by public opinion at home. Neither the young men, who should be our recruits, nor their parents or teachers – perhaps not even we ourselves – yet realise the important part which these Dependencies as a whole already play in the economy of the Empire: still less the far greater part which they are destined to play, if properly developed even within the official lifetime of any one entering the Service.* The rapidly expanding range of opportunity for responsible and interesting work, which these Services will offer, are by no means fully grasped. † Equally apparent is the failure to appreciate the vital part which science and scientific research must play if these territories are to be fully developed.†

11. We have had accordingly to face a demand for:–
   (a) About 60 percent more men per annum than in prewar days;
   (b) A higher standard of quality;
   (c) More, and better, training.

It therefore became progressively clearer:–

(1) That special steps must be taken to stimulate recruitment, and to make the fullest possible use of the material available.

(2) That in regard, at any rate, to certain scientific departments there were not enough young men of the right personal stamp and general education who were undergoing appropriate training to fit themselves for these services and had the intention of competing for them. In summing up their conclusions on this

---

*   This aspect of the question is fully with in paragraphs 12-23 of the Lovat Committee's Report.
†   See paragraph 25 of the Report of the Research Special sub-committee of the Imperial Conference 192. (Cmd. 2769).

point, in connection with agricultural recruitment the Lovat committee ended by saying:–

"In short the supply from which to select does not exist, and must be created."*

(3) That in certain directions the normal curricula of the training institutions did not fully provide for our requirements. Consequently, that, until our annual demand / was sufficiently stable and sufficiently well known to make it worth the while of these institutions to modify their systems of training in the required directions, it would frequently be necessary to supplement such training by providing special post-graduate instruction for our probationers.

(4) That in recruiting for such a service as Education, it would no longer be possible to rely on the candidate with professional experience, but that we should have in the main to recruit the "raw material" as it left the Universities, and train it ourselves.

In the next section I propose to outline the principal steps which have, so far, been taken to make good these deficiencies. It will be seen that, as experience was gained, various schemes have been devised to stimulate recruitment, to encourage men to take up appropriate lines of study in the training centres, and to fill gaps in their training by post-graduate instruction.

Section III – Steps taken since the Armistice to improve Recruitment and Training.

12. I will deal first with measures of general application, and then with special steps designed to help particular branches of the Service. The former can be conveniently grouped under two heads:–

(a) Steps taken to attract recruits, and

(b) Those designed to make the best use of the men who apply.

13. Under (a) the following points may be noted. The salary scales of many departments have been raised. The information provided with regard to the Services has been greatly improved. The pamphlets dealing with appointments and conditions of service have been largely rewritten, and in some cases considerably expanded. They are frequently revised and reprinted in order to keep them up to date. In addition much fuller information in regard to particular vacancies is now prepared for circulation to recruiting centres and to individual inquirers. We have gradually built up a widely extended system of liaison with the University Appointments Boards and with educational authorities at the Universities. Agricultural Colleges, Medical Schools, and similar institutions, who may be in

---

*   Paragraph 38 of the Committee's Report.

a position to recommend suitable candidates. Our list of such correspondents covers several institutions in the Dominions as well as those in the British Isles. It is being continually extended, and we now have well over 100 correspondents on our standing list for the distribution of pamphlets or the notification of vacancies as they occur. We also communicate with the headmasters of over 100 of the leading schools with regard to vacancies in the police forces of the Eastern and West Indian Colonies, whose minimum age limit permits us to consider applications from boys of 19.

In addition, we have made extensive use of advertisement in the Press in respect of particular vacancies. Here, however, it is necessary to use discretion, for experience has shown that in regard to some classes of appointments advertisement merely leads to a large number of applications which on investigation turn out to be worthless. Much time is thereby wasted, and this method should only be resorted to, in such cases, if all others fail.

14. *(b)* Use of available material. – The vital importance of securing the best men that circumstances permit has been clearly recognised: and it is obvious that the greater the difficulties of recruitment the more important it is to make the / best use of the material available. No pains have therefore been spared to obtain trustworthy information as to the record and qualifications of those who apply, and to judge of their suitability on grounds of personality and temperament. This is done by personal interview and confidential enquiry. I do not propose to go into details; but I doubt if the time-honoured phrase still used in our despatches to the effect that the candidate's personal referees have been communicated with gives an adequate idea of the thoroughness of the methods now used, or of the labour which they imply.

Apart from this investigation, which we conduct ourselves, very complete arrangements have been made for obtaining expert advice on the professional suitability of candidates for technical services. Arrangements now exist whereby the opinion of a recognised expert, or of an expert committee, is obtained in the case of every candidate who seems worthy of serious consideration, for all scientific services; medical, agricultural, entomological, forestry, and so on. In all such cases the candidate, if in this country, is interviewed either by a committee, at which experts are present, or by an expert and ourselves independently, the two results being afterwards compared. We also obtain valuable assistance from these advisers as to where best to look for candidates for specialised vacancies. Similar assistance is given us in respect of many educational vacancies by the Secretary of the Advisory Committee on Native Education, himself an ex-Director of Education in Africa, or by members of the Committee. Much valuable assistance is also obtained by consultation with heads of Colonial departments, and other experienced officers, when on leave. Their advice is sought as to filling vacancies which exist, or are expected, in their departments; we arrange for them to interview the most promising candidates and examine their papers; in some cases also they are good enough to visit the Appointments Boards, &c., at the Universities and talk to men who are making enquiries about the Service and who may often be turned into definite applicants by getting first-hand information from someone with local experience.

As it has become possible to do so, we have concentrated in our hands recruitment for a number of appointments which were formerly undertaken mainly by others. The advantages of such concentration are twofold. Those who have a large field of opportunities before them can often make use of a candidate in a department other than that for which he first applies. They can also frequently apply the lessons gained in connection with one Colony or department to the problems presented by others.

Finally, we do what we can to check the results of our recommendations, as a guide to future selections. We examine all the confidential reports on officers in the Service. Should an officer selected prove unsuitable, the case is carefully gone into, in order to try and discover where the mistake in selecting him was made. Every opportunity is also taken, so far as circumstances permit, to consult experienced officers in the Service as to how the men sent to their departments have turned out, and as to the type of man they will require in future.

In these and other ways, which it would take too long to enumerate, our general machinery has been continually improved, as experience has been gained; but no one realises more clearly than we do the need for further improvement.

15. Certain other definite steps have, however, been taken to stimulate recruitment and to improve training in connection with particular branches of the Service, and I will deal with these roughly in chronological order. /

16. *Forestry.* – Forestry was taken up because its position was in many respects the most unsatisfactory. Previous to the war there had been no common standard of recruitment, and a number of officers had been selected whose scientific training on entering the Service was not up to the standard required by present day conditions.

In 1919 there were a number of vacancies for which practically no trained candidates were immediately available. To encourage applications a training grant was made to assist students in the last year of their forestry course at approved Universities, the men being selected as probationers for our Forest Departments, subject to their completing their University course satisfactorily. From 1920 onwards, this has enabled us to insist on the possession of a degree or diploma at a recognised University school of forestry, a standard not previously attained by several men who had entered the Service.

In 1921 an interdepartmental committee, representing the Forestry commission, the India Office, and the Colonial Office, reported that the courses provided by the Universities were not in themselves sufficient for forest officers in Government departments, and should be supplemented by special post-graduate training. They recommended that a central training institution should be set up for this purpose. The proposal was temporarily dropped owing to the need for economy. It was revived at the Empire Forestry Conference of 1923, and endorsed by the Imperial Economy Conference of that year. As a result the Imperial Forestry Institute was set up in 1924 at Oxford on an experimental basis for five years, and placed under the control of Professor R. S. Troup, C. I. E., F. R. S., Professor of Forestry at Oxford, and formerly of the Indian Forest Service.[4] At this Institute our officers receive valuable post-graduate training either before taking up their duties or on their first leave. Courses are also attended by officers, who were selected since the war but before the founding of the Institute, as they come on leave. The Institute further provides for special or "refresher" courses for officers who have been for some years in the Service and arranges for the training of specialist forest officers. Facilities for such training did not exist before in this country, and the Malay States, when they required a research officer in 1921, had to secure the services of an American, because it was impossible to find a candidate in the British Empire qualified to hold the appointment. It was foreseen, when the Institute was started, that the need for trained specialists would shortly be felt. This has already begun to be the case. The Institute has lately been asked to train two specialists for Nigeria, and more posts of this nature are now to be created.

Much more, of course, needs to be done, but in regard to Forestry it is possible to say that a higher standard of scientific knowledge is now required of all our junior forest officers than was attained before the war by any of them, save in exceptional cases.

Facilities have thus been provided for the common training of our forest officers, and for bringing them into touch with each other; for the provision of "refresher" and special courses, and for the training of specialists. None of these advantages existed before 1924.

17. *Agriculture, and Scientific Services connected with it.* – The case of the agricultural departments was next taken up.

In 1920, on the recommendation of the Committees appointed for the purpose, considerable improvements had been effected in the salaries of agricultural officers and information with regard to the improved careers offered had been widely broadcast in / the training centres. By these means it was hoped that satisfactory recruitment would be ensured as soon as these institutions had had time to resume their normal output of graduates. An improvement did certainly take place, but it was insufficient to meet the growing demand. An authoritative committee was therefore set up in 1924 under the chairmanship of Viscount Milner, who was succeeded on his death by Lord Lovat. This Committee produced an interim Report in 1925 with special application to recruitment and training. Its full Report, which embraces wide questions affecting Research and the organisation of agricultural departments, has lately been published,* and has been circulated to members of the Conference. (C. O. 10.)

As a result of the interim Report, a system of Agricultural Scholarships was instituted, and the first selection took place in 1925. There are from sixteen to eighteen scholarships a year. They are normally held for two years, the first being spent in this country, and the second usually at the Imperial College of Tropical Agriculture, Trinidad. The scholars form a pool, from which vacancies can be filled in the year their scholarships end. Men are selected and trained with an eye both to specialist appointments and to appointments in general agriculture, and the training is varied to suit each case on the advice of the expert committee which interviews the candidates. In general the scholars destined for specialist appointments do one year's work under an expert in their own line; the men for administrative posts normally take a year's course at the Agricultural Economics Research Institute at Oxford, together with certain instruction in genetics, practical plant-breeding, statistical methods, and both seed and crop testing at Oxford and Cambridge. During their second year both classes obtain, in Trinidad, an introduction to agriculture under tropical conditions.

This scheme is still at an experimental stage, but the reports received on the progress of the men selected are encouraging, and I think it may safely be said that it is already attracting to the Agricultural Services men of a higher standard than the average obtained in the past. Moreover, they will have had two years' training in subjects chosen to fit them for their work, over and above the qualifications usually held by candidates for these Departments.

It will, too, be possible in future to vary the training in particular cases to suit the requirements of any highly specialised appointments, which it may be desired to create and which it would be difficult to fill satisfactorily from the open market. This can, however, only be done if the Colonial Government concerned gives at least two years' notice of its desire to create such a post.

18. *Survey.* – The standard of recruitment for Survey has not been satisfactory. As an experiment, a course of one academic year under the School of Geodesy at Cambridge, followed by three months' practical work under the Ordnance Survey at Southampton, was instituted in October, 1925, for probationers selected for Ceylon. Only two or three men have so far attended this course; but it appears to have attracted some attention in the University and has led to

---

*   Cmd. 2825.

inquiries with regard to our survey appointments from a few Cambridge men, who appear to be of a caliber much above the average of previous candidates. Should this course prove satisfactory the question of its extension to other Colonial Survey Departments will be considered. In the meanwhile the existing short course at Southampton, which has been proved insufficient, is being expanded to one of six, or, in certain cases, eight, months. To enable the training / to be done at the right time of year only one examination will in future be held per annum. To bridge the temporary gap in recruitment which this change will entail an extra examination is now proceding. This was widely advertised and has attracted a fairly numerous field.

19. *Administrative Services in Tropical Africa.* – As far back as 1920 we had considered how best to ensure a good supply of candidates for these Services when the abnormal source provided by demobilization should have dried up and peace conditions should have again reasserted themselves.

The policy here has always been to select the best material available wherever it may be found, and the administrative staffs have in practice been drawn from a great variety of sources. At the same time it was clear from our records that the Universities of Oxford and Cambridge had for several years before the war supplied a very considerable proportion of these staffs. Experience had also shown that the life and education that these residential Universities provide produce a considerable number of men fitted for successful work among native races; provided that their attention, and that of their advisers at the Universities, can be sufficiently drawn to the openings for such work, which the Colonial Services offer.

A training course for candidates selected for the administrative services was previously held at the Imperial Institute in London,[5] where the selected probationers were out of touch with any important source of recruitment. It was thought possible that, if this course could be held at Oxford and Cambridge, the presence in the Universities of men select for these Services, and the fact that various faculties of the University would be definitely responsible for their training, would have the effect of attracting the attention of the Universities authorities, and of the older undergraduates, more and more to the careers offered by the Colonial Services. It was hoped that in this way recruitment would in course of time be permanently improved.

The possibility of the Universities undertaking this training was accordingly discussed with both Oxford and Cambridge, but before a decision could be reached the slump of 1922 intervened. Administrative vacancies in that year fell to 18, and it was decided to shelve a scheme which was designed to increase recruitment, and which must necessarily prove more expensive than the existing arrangements. When, however, recruitment revived and steadily increased through 1923 and 1924, it was decided to revive these proposals. The Universities agreed to undertake the training, and the scheme was unanimously approved by all the Colonial Governments concerned.

The new courses started at Oxford and Cambridge in October last. The syllabus was framed generally on the lines of that previously in force at the Imperial Institute. Two subjects, tropical medicine and accounts, are still taught in London by the previous lectures. The remaining subjects are taken at the Universities.

To make these arrangements possible, two selections are held a year instead of three; the selection in the spring, which under peace conditions was never likely to produce many candidates, being dropped. A large selection is held at the end of the summer, when most of the men who have graduated at the Universities in that year are available. A smaller selection is held at Christmas. Men selected in the summer take the Michaelmas and Lent terms at the University, and those selected at Christmas the Lent and Summer terms. The lectures in the Lent term are common to both groups. The two reserved subjects are taken in London by both groups during the Easter / vacation. The men of the first group are therefore available to proceed to duty in May, and those of the second group about July.

As I have said above, the syllabus followed is, in general, that previously in force. It is possible, however, to give more time to certain subjects, particularly anthropology. In addition, two experiments have been tried at Oxford. A series of lectures on Colonial history, with special reference to the treatment of dependent races, has been given by the Beit Professor of Colonial History, Professor Coupland.[6] In addition, Mr. K. N. Bell, M. C., the Beit Lecturer in Colonial History, who has done invaluable voluntary work in connection with the social welfare of the probationers, has conducted a series of discussion on matters of Imperial interest. The Colonial agricultural scholars in residence at Oxford, and the Forestry probationers, take part, as well as the Administrative cadets. Much keenness has been displayed at these discussions, and they have formed a useful, informal meeting ground at which cadets can get to know each other and their future colleagues in other departments.

The second experiment has been an attempt to see whether training could not be given during this course which would assist the Administrative officers in their subsequent relations with the more technical departments. So far this has only been attempted in connection with Forestry and at Oxford, where the presence of Professor Troup and the fact that he was training the Colonial Forestry probationers lent itself to the experiment. Professor Troup has delivered a series of lectures to the Administrative probationers. In these he has made no attempt to train them as pseudo-Forest officers, but has endeavoured to give them some information as to the main principles on which the Forest Departments work; the reasons why forest conservation is important, the utility of forests, their principal produce, and the main lines of Forest policy and administration. In brief, the intention of this course is to give the junior administrative officer an idea of what his colleagues in the Forest Departments are "up to"; the reasons why they may ask him for leave to do things the object of which may not be apparent to him; and, in general, to show him how he can best co-operate with them.

Professor Troup has reported that he considers this instruction likely to be of definite use; that the men have shown intelligence and keenness, and that he believes that as a result of the course they will be in a much better position to appreciate the Forest officers' point of view. He recommends that these lectures be continued each year. If this experiment proves successful, it might be possible to extend it in other directions as opportunity offers. The fact that we now have at Oxford men in training for Administrative, Forestry, and Agricultural Services, and at Cambridge for Administrative, Agricultural, and Survey Services, may lend itself to useful developments in cross-training of this kind, as the whole scheme develops.

Apart from the regular instruction, arrangements have been made for Governors and experienced officers to visit the course while on leave and to hold informal talks with the probationers; giving them first-hand information as to the kind of life and the nature of the work which lies ahead of them, and answering their questions. At these meeting it is often possible to arrange for University dons and for undergraduates, who may be thinking of entering the Colonial Service later on, to be present. By these means interest is aroused and recruitment may be stimulated, at the same time as instruction is given to the probationers. Mr. Ormsby-Gore[7] has visited both Universities. Mr. Alexander, of the Southern Nigeria Administration, has visited Cambridge: and Sir Herbert Stanley. Mr. Letham, of the / Northern Nigeria Administrative Service, and Mr. Dundas, Secretary for Native Affairs in Tanganyika, have visited Oxford.

It will be appreciated that these Administrative courses are still at a very early stage at the Universities, and are in many respects experimental. Considerable improvements can probably be effected as experience is gained, and there are several difficulties in regard to both accommodation and training which must be overcome. I venture to suggest that, if they can spare the time, a small conference should be arranged between the representatives of the Tropical African Governments now in this country and representatives of the two University Committees, at which such questions might be profitably discussed.

It is too early to tell what effect these courses may have on recruitment in Oxford and Cambridge, but there is evidence that other steps which have been taken to stimulate interest have borne fruit. From 1925 onwards recruitment from these Universities has definitely improved. The intellectual standard is appreciably higher. The majority of University candidates possess honours degree and, apart from a number who have been taken for Educational posts, between thirty and forty men who possessed a first or second class honours degree entered the Administrative Services in 1925 and 1926.

20. *Medical Services.* – Recruiting for the Colonial Medical Services in the years immediately after the war was in a highly unsatisfactory state. Consequent upon the losses in killed and disabled, and the lack of new entrants at the medical schools, there was a shortage in the supply of qualified doctors and, on account of the longer time required for qualification, the effect of this shortage was felt over a longer period than in other technical services.

On the other hand, the demand for doctors at home was greatly increased, mainly owing to the expansion of various social services. New territories were added as a result of the war and the medical services of some of the older Colonies underwent rapid development. In addition to these unfavourable conditions another factor has adversely affected recruitment, for, while home conditions of service, especially in the matter of salaries, were quickly adjusted to the law of supply and demand, many Colonial Governments lagged behind in this matter. For some years, therefore, prospects in the Colonial Medical Services generally were relatively unattractive, and in some of them they remain so.

The conditions of recruitment are now easier. The supply is greater and the demand for the home services is less. The following table shows the numbers added to the Medical Register during each of the past ten years:–

Year.	Number added.	Year.	Number added.
1917	1,134	1922	1,983
1918	1,077	1923	2,482
1919	1,322	1924	2,796
1920	1,457	1925	2,570
1921	1,760	1926	2,120

The total number of names on the Register on 31st December, 1917, was 43,819, on the same date in 1926 the number was 52,614.

The quality of the applicants now coming forward for the Colonial Medical Services has sensibly improved. Active measures have lately been taken to bring the attractions of these services more prominently to the notice of recent medical graduates and it is hoped that it will soon be possible to exercise a greater freedom of choice in the selection of candidates and so to raise the standard of qualifications, personal and professional, required for entry. /

21. *Educational Services.* – The active policy now being followed in regard to the education of Africans has led to a sharp rise in recruitment. The Advisory Committee on Native Education has endorsed the policy, which so far as possible had been pursued since the war, of recruiting men whose education and outlook are similar to that desired in Administrative candidates. It is, of course, unavoidable that this should impose an added strain on recruitment for both services, especially at a time when both are expanding.

The Committee has also accepted the view that it will be necessary to recruit from untrained candidates, as soon as they leave the Universities and before they have become committed to a teaching career at home. They have recommended that such candidates should be given special instruction before taking up their duties, and the possibility of organizing probationary courses of instruction is being explored.

22. *Veterinary Services.* – The position is not satisfactory. The question of taking steps to improve recruitment and training, on somewhat similar lines to those recently adopted for agriculture, is now under consideration.

23. *Eastern and West Indian Police.* – Steps have been taken each year to bring the careers offered by these Services to the notice of the principal public schools. The field for the annual selection this summer is considerably larger than before; but it has been decided to arrange for more intensive propaganda in the autumn and winter. A despatch has recently been sent to the Governor of the Straits Settlements, asking that fuller information with regard to conditions of life and service in Malaya should be prepared. It is probable that the other Governments concerned will be approached in a similar sense, and we hope that it may be possible to supplement this written information by arranging for officers on leave to give lectures in, at any rate, a certain number of schools.

Section IV. – Future Progress.

24. It would be premature to discuss in detail schemes for future development; but perhaps I may be allowed to suggest certain general lines on which progress might be made and in which we need the co-operation of Colonial Governments.

(a) *Training Schemes.*

25. A great deal more work is required before the various schemes for probationary training, outlined in Section III, can be made fully efficient. Some of these have not yet been started and none of them is more than three years old. Time will in any case be needed before the full effect either of the training which they give or of the influence which they may have on recruitment can be properly gauged. It will be of great assistance if Colonial Governments will from time to time report on the general efficiency of the men they receive, and on the value – or otherwise – of the various kinds of training which they have been given. It is to be hoped, too, that they will give as much encouragement and opportunity as possible to men like the Agricultural Scholars, when they join the Service; for the success of such a scheme will largely depend on the accounts of life in the Colonial Services sent back to the training centres by the men who are selected during its early years.

The question whether any of these training courses should be supplemented by short courses after arrival in the Colony has also to be considered. The Gold Coast Government is organizing such a course for its administrative officers.[8]

The ideal would seem to be that subjects of general application and those which can be best taught at a University should be taken beforehand, / and the more practical subjects and those of local application after arrival in the Colony. In any case it must be realised that there are limits to what can be taught before the man reaches the Colony, and time must be given him to "find his feet."

In connection with training a word should be said on the subject of study leave. The need for such leave has been a good deal emphasised recently, particularly in connection with technical services, and arrangements have just recently been made with, for example, the Commonwealth Fund,[9] to enable Colonial officers to compete for their valuable travelling scholarships. Full advantage cannot, however, be taken of such opportunities, unless Colonial Governments can see their way to recommend specially suitable officers from time to time, and to give those selected sufficiently generous conditions in regard to leave, &c.

(b) *Propaganda.*

26. Full recruitment will not, I think, be secured until the prevailing ignorance with regard to the Colonies and their services has been overcome. For this we need a sustained educational campaign. Two methods can be used. The best results will, I believe, in the long run be achieved by what I may call the indirect method; that is to say, by the influence of good books and articles dealing with matters of general interest. For I think that these have a greater and more lasting influence on the thoughtful type of candidate and on the people who train and influence him.

We cannot, however, wait for the results of this method, though I hope it will be employed. It will also be necessary to make a more direct attack. This can best be done by lectures and informal addresses delivered in the training centres. The best men to deliver them are our own officers when on leave, for they can speak with up-to-date and first-hand knowledge. I hope it may be possible before long to make arrangements whereby Colonial Governments should notify us periodically of officers who are coming on leave and whom they think suitable for the purpose. It is obviously desirable that they should be carefully selected. I hope too that it may be possible to grant them a certain amount of extra leave and adequate lodging and traveling allowances.

Owing to the need of meeting immediate demands, such work of this kind as has so far been done has been mainly confined to the Universities, and efforts in these quarters need extending. I feel, however, that, with an eye to the future, we should do similar work in the more important schools.

A word of warning is necessary. Anything in the nature of a recruiting appeal or of "touting" for men must be avoided. The aim should be to educate, to lay stress on the importance and interest of the work to be done by officers in the Service, on the fact that only the best men are needed and that it is an honour to be chosen. Secondly, it is very important to guard against any temptation to represent conditions of service as in any way better than they are, or to minimize the risks or disadvantages of tropical life. Any attempt to do either – whatever temporary advantage it might bring – would ultimately recoil on our heads with double force. Thirdly, I think that missionary work of this kind should be done under the general direction of those responsible for recruitment. Only in this way will it be possible to avoid the risk of too many fishermen flogging the same water, possibly on behalf of rival services; and even of contradictory statements, misunderstandings, and possible / friction. A good deal of mischief has before now been done by well-meant efforts of the kind, where this precaution has not been taken.

(c) *Conditions of Service and Regulation of Demand.*

27. Responsibility for work under (*a*) and (*b*) must mainly rest with us at home. But I think it is fair to say that the success of recruitment ultimately depends on the Colonies themselves. In the long run they will get the recruits they deserve. They must rely on the inherent attractions which their services offer to the type of man they need, and on their capacity so to frame their policy that demand does not outrun supply.

28. It would be impossible here to discuss the adequacy or otherwise of the very varied conditions of service now in force. Considerable improvements have been effected in many directions since the war. There is undoubtedly room for more; and of some appointments it may truthfully be said that the less they are advertised the better for the Service as a whole.

29. On the other hand, it may be worth while to emphasise the need for regulating demand. For good recruitment it is of prime importance that a definite policy should be laid down and adhered to. Only on this basis can demand be kept even from year to year and due notice of special requirements be given. This gives confidence to boys, parents, and teachers that an adequate number of posts will be forthcoming if the necessary training is undertaken. Recruitment has been greatly hampered in recent years by uneven demand, and delay and disappointment caused by failure to give sufficient notice.

    The following examples of what is required may help. If you want to get men as they leave the Universities, it is clear that the majority will be forthcoming after the degree examinations in the summer and very few between January and July, Schoolmasters, again, are usually available in August on the conclusion of the school year. If secured at any other time, they almost always have to give at least one term's notice to their headmasters, and are therefore not available for some months after selection. If these and similar factors are remembered by Colonial Governments, they will be saved much disappointment at delay in getting what they ask for. In general it will be of the most assistance if we can be given as long notice as possible and as much latitude as possible to secure the best man when he is available.

30. In the case of specialised Services long notice is particularly necessary. The Forest Service, an important one in itself, is a good example. The training of a Forest officer is highly specialized. Very few good openings for him exist outside Government service. Consequently the number of men who take up such training is mainly regulated by the number of Government appointments likely to be available when the training is finished. Under present conditions our Forest officers do three years at a University school and one year at the Imperial Forestry Institute. In consequence it is practically impossible to meet a sudden extra demand, such as was made shortly before the last annual selection by one Colonial Government, unless there has been an unexpected slump elsewhere. I do not believe (and I am supported by the conclusions of a recent conference with the Forestry professors) that recruitment for this service will ever be fully satisfactory until Colonial Governments can put us in a position to tell the Forestry schools of our probable needs three, and preferably four, years before the men are wanted. The Colonial Governments concerned were asked to give us an annual estimate of this kind in 1923, but, except in one or two cases, the response has not been sufficient. /

31. I must, however, gratefully acknowledge that in general the Colonial Governments have shown great readiness to meet us over matters affecting recruitment. If co-operation is still imperfect, it may largely be due to our not having yet brought the facts sufficiently home to them.

R. D. FURSE.
April, 1927.

NOTE. – Many of the points touched on in this Memorandum are more fully dealt with in the Report* of Lord Lovat's Committee on Agricultural Services, which has been circulated to members of the Conference, and in the Report of Lord Balfour's Research Special Sub-Committee of the Imperial Conference (1926). "Part II – Man-Power."† Though both these Reports are specifically concerned with Scientific services, much of what they say applies to recruitment and training generally.

---

*   Cmd. 2825.
†   Cmd. 2769.

ANNEX.

Statement showing the number of Candidates appointed by the Secretary of State with the assistance of the Private Secretary (Appointments) in the years 1913 and 1919–1926.

–	1913.	1919.	1920.	1921.	1922.	1923.	1924.	1925.	1926.
Legal	10	11	21	10	3	8	11	12	7
Administrative	82	108	179	90	18	67	72	85	103
Police	13	44	45	32	17	14	32	19	30
Educational	19	13	37	43	39	30	43	46	76
Financial	15	27	31	21	4	12	9	10	20
Marine	4	8	10	4	4	2	8	8	7
Medical	67	44	73	63	41	49	84	129	97
Veterinary	7	4	23	10	7	7	5	8	16
Agricultural	11	9	25	29	10	12	17	27	23
Forestry	1	4	33	26	3	11	20	16	13
Survey and Geological	2	0‡	30	32	9	5	12	15	15
Scientific Specialists (e.g. Botanical, Entomological, Analytical)	9	9	26	18	9	6	25	14	9
Miscellaneous (e.g. Game Wardenships, Secretarial posts)	8	14	18	9	10	10	14	17	8
	248	295	551	387	174	233	352	406	424
Agricultural Scholarships	–	–	–	–	–	–	–	16	17
	248	295	551	387	174	233	352	422	441
The figures in brackets give the number of candidates selected in addition to the above who either withdrew or were found medically unfit.	(111)	(152)	(93)	(39)	(41)	(59)	(93)	(86)	

‡ The Private Secretary was not concerned with the selection of Surveyors in 1919.

Gordon Guggisberg, 'Memorandum by the Governor of the Gold Coast'. National Archives, Kew, London, 'Recruitment and Training of Colonial Civil Servants', CO 323/982/5, f. 4.

ˈCOLONIAL OFFICE CONFERENCE.
MEMORANDUM BY THE GOVERNOR OF
THE GOLD COAST.[1]

HEAD A. (1). RECRUITING AND TRAINING OF COLONIAL OFFICE CIVIL SERVANTS.

1. However good the system of training recruits for the Civil Service in England may be, local training courses carried out on arrival in the Colony are essential. In the case of Technical Departments, such as the public Works and Railways, the local course need only be very brief provided that sufficient care has been taken by the recruiting agents to engage men properly trained in their respective professions.

In the case of the Medical Service, however high his professional qualifications may be, the newly arrived Medical Officer should spend six months in a large and up-to-date hospital on his arrival in the Colony. Two great advantages are secured, the officer gaining first-hand and valuable experience from the Resident Medical Officers and Surgeons of the hospital in dealing with local tropical diseases; and, what is equally important, with an alien race. The value of this knowledge of the characteristics of the people among whom he is to practise his profession cannot be over-estimated, for experience has shown that success either in Medicine, Surgery, or Sanitation in a tropical country depends as much on the confidence which the native places in the Medical Officer as on the latter's professional skill. /

The value of this local training of newly joined Medical Officers has been fully proved in the last three years in the Gold Coast, but the system can only be fully successful if there exists a large, up-to-date, and efficiently staffed Colonial Hospital, such as that at Accra.[2]

In the Education, Agricultural, Forestry, and Veterinary Departments, the local training of newly arrived recruits is essential. This training has been greatly facilitated in the Gold Coast by the existence of local Agricultural, Forestry, and Veterinary Training Centres. Experience of the local conditions under which the four services are conducted is gained, and also of the best methods of dealing with the Chiefs and people, instruction in the last-named subject being given by the Secretary for Native Affairs or other specially qualified Political Officer. It is essential in all three services mentioned that the vernacular should be learned, and a period of at least nine months is therefore necessary for local training in the four Department named. This system is now being started in the Gold Coast where experience has shown the great disadvantages arising from ignorance of the local language.

2. With regard to the Political Services, experience in the Gold Coast in the past seven years has shown the serious disadvantages which have followed the abandonment of the old Political Cadet system. About five years ago, after ascertaining the views of the best Political / Officers, the system of four months' training at Headquarters of newly arrived officers was adopted. Experience of the working of this system showed that it was invaluable but that the time was not long enough. The following carefully organised system has therefore been adopted and stands this year:–

(a) The average number of vacancies occurring annually in the Political Service from ordinary causes are estimated, between ten and twenty per cent added for unforeseen casualties, and the Colonical Office is informed. In initiating the system, at least eighteen months' notice of the number required must be given.

(b) The Colonical Office arranges for each annual batch of Cadets to be sent out by the same steamer.

(c) The Secretary for Native Affairs, or some specially selected senior Political Officer, will be entrusted with the supreme charge of the batch for a period of twelve months.

(d) The first three to four months will be spent at Government Headquarters, where a thoroughly systematic course of instruction will be given by the Secretary for Native Affairs with the assistance of / native teachers in various languages, and by Heads of Departments or officers selected by them.

(e) The course at headquarters will include:–

(i) Languages.
(ii) Practical Anthropology.
(iii) The Constitution of the Colony (and its Dependencies if any); the principles of Native Constitutions, Institutions and Customs; the sta-

tus of the various Chiefs and their Councils; and the relation between the Central Government and the native administrations.

(iv) Court work, local legislation, etc.

(v) Treasury work.

(vi) Office organisation and correspondence, based on the standard system of the Colony.

(vii) Elementary instruction in local policies, e. g:– Agricultural, Forestry, Transport, Sanitation, and Educational, as a basis for future co-operation with the technical officers concerned.

(viii) Lectures on the general trade and revenue of the country.

(ix) Lectures on any particular Government policy peculiar to the country, such as employment of the local natives in the Government Service, Government's attitude towards the colour question, etc., etc. /

(f) On completion of the first part of the course at Government Headquarters the Cadets will be sent to stations where they will have the best opportunity of continuing their language studies and of practising the vernacular with the local inhabitants. This part of the course will last from eight to nine months, thus completing the whole year's training.

(g) The second part of the course will be broken by the Cadet being sent periodically for a week or two to a district headquarters, and once to a provincial headquarters, where, while continuing his language study, he will obtain direct instruction from the Political Officers of those stations in his practical duties.

(h) During the second part of the course the Cadets will still be under the supreme charge of the Secretary for Native Affairs, who will visit them periodically. The senior Political Officers of the localities where the officers are stationed will, in co-operation with the Secretary for Native Affairs, carefully watch the progress of the Cadets in language and in obtaining experience of their practical duties; and will generally study their personal characteristics.

(i) At the end of the year the Cadets will be required to pass the Lower Standard Language Examination, failing which their services will be disponsed with. This is essential. /

3. Finally with regard to the local training of newly arrived officers, it cannot be too strongly emphasised that ability to speak and understand the vernacular is essential to the success of the Political, Education, Agricultural, Forestry, and Veterinary Services of a British West African Colony.

To this should be added the Medical and Sanitation Services, especially the latter, but under the present conditions governing that service, and owing also to the frequent transfers between the different Colonies, the idea is impracticable of attainment. /

(j) Finally, the relative seniority of the Cadets in each batch should be determined at the end of the year by the Secretary for Native Affairs in conference with those Political Officers under whom the Cadets have been working during the second part of their course. The fact of their relative seniority depending on the results of their course is an incentive to the Cadets which should prove invaluable.

(k) With regard to the above course for Political Cadets, experience has shown that one year is the minimum time in which a sound elementary knowledge of the language can be obtained when the other subjects which have to be studied are considered. Any suggestion of employing the Cadets as Political Officers before the completion of the year should be firmly turned down. The newly joined officers should therefore be definitely designated "Political Cadets", and not called "Administrative Officers", "District Officers", "Assistant District Commissioners", or by any other title used in the Political Service which they will eventually join. If this is done it will usually be found that local legislation prohibits the exercise by them of any powers allotted to Political Officers.

Colonial Office Conference, 1927. Summary of Proceedings, 'Recruitment and Training of Colonial Civil Servants', House of Commons Parliamentary Papers [Cmd. 2883] (1927), pp. 12–17.

VI. RECRUITMENT AND TRAINING OF COLONIAL CIVIL SERVANTS.

(*a*) The Conference had under consideration a comprehensive memorandum* dealing with recruitment since the Armistice for those branches of the Colonial Services for which men are selected by the Secretary of State with the assistance of his Private Secretary (Appointments). Major R. D. Furse,[1] who, as Private Secretary for Appointments, had been responsible for recruitment under successive Secretaries of State since 1919, was present during the discussion.

This memorandum shewed that during the post-war period great difficulties were faced in satisfying the requirements of Colonial Governments. There had been a demand for (*a*) about 60 per cent. more men per annum than in pre-war days; (*b*) a higher standard of quality in personnel; and (*c*) more, and better, training. It had therefore become evident

(1) that special steps must be taken to stimulate recruiting and to make the fullest possible use of available material;

(2) that in regard to certain scientific and technical departments there was a scarcity of candidates with the requisite personal qualifications and general as well as specialized education;

(3) that the existing curricula in training institutions, whence the supply is drawn, were not fully in accordance with Colonial requirements.

The memorandum then detailed the general steps taken during this period to improve recruitment and training, e.g., by general increases in salary levels, by developing a widely extended system of liaison with the University Appoint-

---

*   See Appendix II. in Cmd. 2884.

ments Boards and other educational authorities, and by extensive use of advertisement in the Press in respect of particular vacancies.

An account was next given of various specific schemes for improving the supply and training of recruits for particular services, / e.g., the administrative, forestry, and agricultural departments, which either had been inaugurated or were under consideration.

The general lines on which it was thought that recruitment for the Colonial Services could best be developed in the future were also discussed, including (*a*) various training schemes, (*b*) extended publicity work, and (*c*) efforts to ensure longer notice being given where possible of prospective demands by Colonial Governments.

The Members of the Conference expressed their high appreciation of the work done since the war in connection with recruitment, in spite of the foregoing difficulties, and of the type of candidate which had been selected for appointment to the Colonial Services in recent years, particularly in the case of the administrative services in the Tropical African Dependencies. They were of the opinion that it was vital to the interests of the Colonial Empire to maintain the quality of the personnel of the various Services at the highest possible level.

In particular, the Representatives of the African Dependencies welcomed the transfer of the Tropical African Services Course to the Universities of Oxford and Cambridge.[2] There appeared to be good ground for believing that the presence at these Universities of men selected for the Colonial Services undertaking post-graduate courses would have the effect of attracting in an increasing degree the attention of the University authorities and the undergraduates to the possibilities of careers in the Colonial Services.

Recent experience had, however, shewn that the conditions under which the Tropical African Services probationers were at present living at both Universities were not entirely satisfactory. There had been difficulties particularly in regard to accommodation. The Conference therefore formed a Committee, consisting of Representatives of the Tropical African Dependencies and Major Furse, to investigate on the spot the question of the existing accommodation difficulties at Oxford and Cambridge, and to see in what way these could best be removed. If and when it was found possible for any useful proposals to be put forward, it was understood that they would be sympathetically considered by the Colonial Governments concerned.

The Conference felt that they owed a special debt of gratitude to those members of the University staffs who had shewn so much personal interest in making a success of these experiments.

On the question of recruitment for the Colonial Services generally, several Members of the Conference emphasized the importance of efforts being made to organize and grade the establishments in the various branches of the Services

in such a / manner as to ensure throughout an avenue of promotion with a sufficiently attractive number of highly paid posts to which to look forward.

The Conference recognized the value of an educational campaign in this
country to overcome the prevailing ignorance with regard to the Colonies and
their services. They approved generally of the methods proposed in the memorandum, e.g., lectures and informal addresses delivered in the training centres
by carefully selected officers when on leave. The importance of interesting the
Public Schools, as well as the Universities, in the work of the Colonial Services
and the careers which they offer was fully appreciated.

As regards the future, the Conference realised that successful recruitment
would depend partly on the better regulation of the annual demand. In the case
of most services, and particularly in the case of a specialized service such as Forestry, long notice of requirements was essential.

Members considered that Colonial Governments should endeavour where
possible to give four-or even five years' notice of their requirements in respect of
appointments in some of the more specialized services. It was further understood
that the Governments of the Tropical African Dependencies would be prepared,
so far as the administrative services, and all Governments interested so far as forestry services are concerned, to allow the Private Secretary for Appointments to
recruit two or three candidates each year in excess of anticipated requirements.
In this way a small reserve pool would be created, from which recruits could be
selected for appointment to smaller Colonies where unexpected vacancies, had
occurred. If these smaller Colonies did not require these additional recruits, the
larger Colonies would undertake to absorb them.

The following is a statement showing the number of candidates appointed by
the Secretary of State with the assistance of the Private Secretary (Appointments)
in the years 1913 and 1919–1926: –

	1913	1919	1920	1921	1922	1923	1924	1925	1926
Legal	10	11	21	10	3	8	11	12	7
Administrative	82	108	179	90	18	67	72	85	103
Police ..	13	44	45	32	17	14	32	19	30
Educational	19	13	37	43	39	30	43	46	76
Financial	15	27	31	21	4	12	9	10	20
Marine	4	8	10	4	4	2	8	8	7
Medical	67	44	73	63	41	49	84	129	97
Veterinary	7	4	23	10	7	7	5	8	16
Agricultural	11	9	25	29	10	12	17	27	23
Forestry	1	4	33	26	3	11	20	16	13
Survey and Geological	2	0*	30	32	9	5	12	15	15 /
Scientific Specialists (e.g., Botanical, Entomological, Analytical)	9	9	26	18	9	6	25	14	9

Miscellaneous (e.g., Game Warden-ships, Secretarial posts)	8	14	18	9	10	10	14	17	8
	248	295	551	387	174	233	352	406	424
Agricultural Scholarships	–	–	–	–	–	–	–	16	17
	248	295	551	387	174	233	352	422	441
The figures in brackets give the number of candidates selected in addition to the above, who either withdrew or were found medically unfit	(111)	(152)	(93)	(39)	(41)	(59)	(93)	(86)	

*   The Private Secretary was not concerned with the selection of Surveyors in 1919.

(b) Recruitment for certain Eastern Cadetships.

The Conference were informed that the recruitment of officers for the Cadet Services in British Malaya and Hong Kong by the system of open competitive examination had proved unsatisfactory in recent years. There was a very serious shortage of qualified candidates, attributable among other reasons to

1.   the increased demand for University graduates in business, both at home and abroad; and

2.   the largely increased number of posts with similar prospects in East and West Africa, which can be obtained without a competitive literary examination.

It was explained that the Governor of the Straits Settlements had accordingly been asked for his views on a suggestion that Malayan Cadetships should, for an experimental period, be filled by the system of appointment by selection already in force for the Tropical African Services.

It was generally agreed that this position required early consideration by the Governments concerned.

(c) Appointments made through the Crown Agents,

The Conference considered the arrangements for recruitment for the Public Works and Railway Departments in the Colonies, which were described by Lieutenant-Colonel J. F. H. Carmichael, one of the Crown Agents for the Colonies.

Colonel Carmichael explained that the selection of suitable officers for these Departments was often a matter of great difficulty. In the first place the salary offered was frequently inadequate to attract men possessing the requisite qualifications and experience. Again, there was a special difficulty in those cases where men were required for temporary employment only, particularly on constructional works, in that there was no promise of further employment and a man found it difficult to obtain re-employment in England after absence for some years abroad. /

Every endeavour was being made by the Crown Agents to improve the quality of the men recruited, and it was believed that an improvement had in fact taken place since the war.

It was suggested that the second difficulty might be surmounted by the institution of a Provident Fund such as exists for the benefit of employees of the railways in East Africa and in India. Such a Provident Fund system is in operation in regard to the Crown Agents' technical staff, where it has proved most beneficial. The system enables a good man who can better his position to take up employment elsewhere; and this in turn attracts to the Office other candidates, who realise that their predecessors have been able to secure good appointments.

Conversely, this system would, if applied in the Colonies, enable local Governments to dispense with the services of employees no longer required, without inflicting hardship on them. In technical services, it is obvious that there are great advantages in maintaining a constant flow of promotion, as it tends to prevent men from getting out of touch with modern practice, which in engineering is continually being modified.

The Conference discussed Colonel Carmichael's proposals at some length. There was general agreement that the establishment of the Provident Fund system might be beneficial to recruiting for the Railway and Public Works Departments in the Colonies, etc. It was recognised that such a system could not be applied to officers already serving, except with their consent, and that, as some officers would no doubt prefer to retain their established pension rights, there would be two systems operating concurrently for a period of years: The Provident Fund scheme would, however, be made compulsory in the case of new entrants, so that it would eventually supersede the other system. The Conference recommended that the Colonial Office and the Crown Agents should investigate the whole question further with a view to devising a scheme which, if acceptable to Colonial Governments, could be made the basis of general application for the future.

The following is a summary of vacancies from the 1st January to the 31st December, 1926, in appointments made through the Crown Agents: –

Accountants and Storekeepers	23
Architects	9
Artisans (Workshop): Fitters, Turners, Erectors, Boilermakers, Mechanics, Locomotive Foremen, etc.	66
Clerical	37
Draughtsmen	10
Engineers (Public Works)	129
Engineers (Railway)	27 /
Engineers (Electrical)	28
Engineers (Marine)	10
Foremen of Works	128
Foremen, Posts and Telegraphs	7

Locomotive Drivers	37
Lunatic Attendants	7
Masters and Mates	11
Police and Prison Officers	203
Platelayers	10
Printers and Linotype Operators	5
Sanitary Inspectors	34
Traffic Department: Assistant Traffic Superintendents, Traffic Inspectors, Station Masters, Guards	23
Miscellaneous	32
	836

W. Ormsby-Gore, MP Speech for a Meeting with Vice Chancellors and Headmasters at Board of Education (1928). National Archives, Kew, London, CO 323/1021/20 f. 6.

Speech for Meeting with Vice Chancellors and Head Masters at
Board of Education, on 24th October, 1928.
by
The Rt. Hon. W. Ormsby Gore,[1] M.P.

The number of new appointments made by the Colonial Office to the various Colonial Services has been steadily rising since the War, and is likely to increase. The number of individuals in the United Kingdom appointed by selection in 1924 was 352, and in 1927 was 475. I will not analyse this total, but I should like to mention that of last year's figures 121 were Medical Officers; 101 Administrative Officers; 42 Agricultural Field Officers; 18 Scientific Specialists for the Agricultural Department; 11 for the Forestry Department; 9 for the Veterinary Departments. These figures do not include personnel required for the Sudan Services, which are under the Foreign Office; nor do they include the Administrative officers for Ceylon and Malaya, who are appointed as a results of the Civil Service Examination (Eastern Cadetships); nor do they include the engineers, &c. for the Railways and Public Works Departments, recruited through the machinery of the Crown Agents for the Colonies.

The steady expansion of numbers is due to the rapid development of the Colonial Empire, and more particularly of the Tropical Colonies. We have to man the services for over thirty separate Governments who together form the Colonies, Protectorates and Mandated Territories. Collectively they comprise / an area of 2,000,000 square miles, i.e. about twenty times the size of Great Britain. The total population for whose progress and welfare we are responsible, is just over fifty millions, of whom approximately forty millions are Africans by race. The overseas trade of these Colonies has trebled in the last twenty years and its principal expansion has been since the War. It now amounts to £500,000,000 sterling.

Practically the whole of this wealth is represented by agricultural production. In recent years quite half the new appointments were new ones, i.e. were demanded by the increase of staff and not for replacements. Looking to the future the main increases are likely to be in the Agricultural, Veterinary and Education Departments as the principal effort on which we are now engaged is the application of science to the development of the potential resources of the Tropics. So far from this period of expansion showing any signs of ending I think it is only just beginning.

Nearly all our Agricultural Departments are under-manned both in quality and numbers. The same is true in an even greater degree with regard to the Veterinary Services. Further the proportion of what are called research workers in comparison to general field officers is likely to increase. We are committed to the establishment of a chain of Imperial Research Stations in the Tropics, and additional central Bureaux for the dissemination of scientific information and experience.

During the last few years the Colonial Office have taken between sixty and seventy men annually, excluding Medical Officers, who required biological / training as the most essential part of their qualifications. Even in connection with the expansion of the medical work I should perhaps say that in addition to Medical Officers we require bacteriologists, biochemists and entomologists for the manning of the Medical Research centres.

Of the sixty or seventy men required for the Agricultural, Veterinary and Forestry Services, not more than one third are required to be scientific specialists in a particular department of biological science such as mycologists, entomologists and economic botanists.

If I analyse the 1927 figures I find we took:–

  7 botanists and mycologists
  8 entomologists
  6 marine and other zoologists
  22 agricultural field officers
  7 crop or produce Inspectors
  3 horticulturists
  3 agricultural chemists
  12 forestry officers
  9 Veterinary officers

From this it will be seen that our requirements are seldom for chemists but are in the main in the biological field. In this latter field there is a shortage both in quantity and quality. When I use the word "quality" I refer not to their attainments in the particular branch of biology in which they specialise, but in general biological training in, particularly, what is called the ecological outlook.

The Schools and Universities are turning out large numbers of chemists and physicists but an / inadequate number of young men with a broad biological training. Even among those who have had some biological training too much attention seems to have been paid to systematic botany, anatomy and zoology, and too little to both plant and animal physiology.

In regard to financial assistance, the principal feature has been provision at the public expense for free post graduate training. Since 1925 we have awarded 68 Agricultural Scholarships. These scholars have been drawn from 59 different Schools and from 21 different Universities and Agricultural Colleges. Of the Universities and Colleges, Cambridge has provided 12 scholars, Glasgow 8 and Wye 7.[2] 62 have been for 2 years' post graduate study and 6 for one year. Up to 1933, by which time the position will have to be reviewed, funds are now available for at least twenty such scholarships per annum.

There is one other point which I may mention. Owing to the gradual improvement of facilities for instruction about tropical matters and for the collection and dissemination of information about them, there are an increasing number of scientific appointments in this country being made from the ranks of those with tropical experience. The staffs of Kew Gardens,[3] the Bureaux of Entomology and Mycology,[4] the Imperial Forestry Institute[5] and the Agricultural Adviser to the Colonial Office supply examples. Entry, therefore, into the Colonial Service may not always necessitate permanent absence from this country. /

We recently had a Committee on the Veterinary requirements of the Empire and we are going to propose a system of post graduate scholarships for veterinarians. I use the term "veterinarian" advisedly because in the development of the animal husbandry of the Tropical Empire we want men qualified to deal not so much with the curative treatment of sick cattle as with the prevention of disease, animal genetics and animal nutrition. Such scholarships will take two forms:–

(1) for members who have obtained their qualifications from the Royal College of Veterinary Surgeons[6] with a view to their taking a general post graduate science course, and,

(2) for science graduates of a University in order that they may become qualified veterinary officers.

In general men are required both for research and investigation on the one hand, and for administrative duties on the other. For the first, in which there is at present the greatest shortage of candidates, the best brains are essential. Candidates for both spheres must be of such a type that they will hold their own with other administrative colleagues, with European settlers and planters, and with the native population. In fact they must have qualities of self-reliance and leadership. Hitherto too many of the candidates applying have drifted to us towards the end of their University career after considering some other occupation. We want to see a regular flow of candidates coming forward of a quality capable of taking a First or Second Honours Degree, who have been aiming at an appointment in the Colonial Services since the age of 17. /

Quite apart from the posts which we have to offer to men who have undergone biological training at school and University, I want to take this opportunity of emphasizing the vital importance of some knowledge of biological science to all men who are going to be called upon to serve in the Tropical Empire. Only a fortnight ago one of our ablest young officers of the Education Department of the Northern Provinces of Nigeria came to tell me that he had spent his leave in endeavouring to acquire some elementary knowledge of biology. He was at University College, Oxford, where he had read Greats. He found himself faced with the responsibility of initiating and starting education in a Province in Northern Nigeria, inhabited by approximately one million fairly primitive Africans, whose whole economic and social life depended upon agriculture, and for whom life itself was dependent upon preventing the spread of tropical diseases. He told me that experience of some years in that country had convinced him that the one point of contact between his mind and those of the natives, and the only hope of building up an educational system, suited to their requirements and comprehension, lay through the biological sciences, e.g. through the laws of life of plants, animals and men. He had done some chemistry at school but no other form of science then or since.

Nature in our tropical possessions is amazingly bountiful but also amazingly destructive. In tropical development, where we take a hand in the most intense warfare of nature, when man has to live in far closer / contact with nature and the elementary forces of nature than he does in a civilized urbanished community, where human beings are killed like flies by malaria, sleeping sickness, hookworm and all the range of tropical diseases, and their domestic stock by fly-borne and tick-borne diseases and epidemics and scourges unknown in this country, progress of agriculture depends absolutely upon the conquest of pests, breeding immune varieties of crop, and the study of the scientific inter-dependence of different types of crop.

I sometimes wonder how many of the European officers serving in different capacities in the Tropics know about Pasteur[7] and his dynamic discoveries in the world of bacteriology and protozoology? And yet on those discoveries has been virtually built up the whole of the possible application of western science to the conquest of the tropics.

In the last ten years I have visited 22 tropical Colonies, and if I am to be truthful I must confess that it was not so much the shortage of scientific workers - though that is everywhere apparent - that struck me so much as the amazing ignorance of the educated laymen. I remember on one occasion a scholar of Balliol informing me in the presence of one of our malariologists that he still questioned the assumption of science that malaria is due to the mosquito, and he expressed himself as confident that malaria lived in the ground. This so shocked me that I asked several other leading people in the Colony what they thought. I found that they did not think at all! I am afraid I bored the whole Legislative Council of the / Colony by giving them in Layman's language a full account of the life history of the malaria parasite and all its metamorphoses in the body of man and the mosquito respectively, and I think I finally convinced them that the malaria parasite cannot continue a chain of life without both mosquito and the human body.

This particular Colony has spent literally millions of pounds on hospital accommodation and only a few paltry thousands on the prevention of malaria, and when I was there there was loud complaints about the inefficiency of its railway. I asked the General Manager what was the trouble and he informed me that twenty per cent. of his railway staff were down with malaria!

The main fact of the matter is that the present curricula of both Public Schools and Universities, from which we draw our staff for the Tropical Empire, neglect the teaching of the one branch of science which is the link between the mechanical or inorganic science on the one hand and the humanities on the other, and the link between agriculture on the hand and personal and public hygiene on the other, which has a more important bearing on economics than any other subject.

Finally, may I give you one example of the economic side of this questions? During my last Colonial tour this year I incidentally visited the Dutch Island of Java and there I found, among many other remarkable things, an Agricultural Research Station at a place called Pasoeroean, devoted solely to the problems of the sugar crop.

Java is, as you know, the second largest producer of sugar of any country in the world. Within the last two years the work at Pasoeroean has put anything from 15 per cent / to 20 per cent on to the output of sugar per acre. The area of land available for sugar cultivation is limited and therefore the whole effort has been to get the maximum possible yield. This sudden increase in the productivity of the Java sugar fields is due to the rapid introduction of a new cane. This cane, the highest yielder yet discovered in the world, is entirely the result of laboratory research. It is the result of cross fertilization of different sugar canes with a wild reed growing in the marshes of Java, which wild reed contains no sugar at all but provides

(1) increased strength and rapidity of growth
(2) immunity to various local diseases
(3) greater rapidity of ripening

Its production involved, of course a fundamental knowledge of cytology and mendelian genetics. It is on this sort of work that the whole of the future economic progress of he British Colonial Empire depends, but it requires a whole team of scientific workers trained not so much in the inorganic sciences as in the biological sciences.

I understand that a Committee of the British Association under Chairmanship of Sir Richard Gregory,[8] the Editor of "Nature", is shortly producing a special report on the improvement in the curricula of biological teaching in Public Schools and Universities. Doubtless this will be laid before you for consideration, and all I can say is, speaking on behalf of the Colonial Office and the Colonial Empire, that in the future it is in this direction that the leading educational institutions in this country can help us most.

Colonial Agricultural Service, Report of a Committee Appointed by the Secretary of State for the Colonies, House of Commons Parliamentary Papers [Cmd 3049] (1930).

IV. – COLONIAL AGRICULTURAL SERVICE.

46. As we stated in the Introduction to this Report[1] we have felt obliged to make an important departure from the recommendations of the Conference Committee, and from our own Terms of Reference, in regard to the formation of a "Colonial Agricultural Scientific and Research Service," which we have found to be perhaps the most important – certainly the most complex – of the questions referred to us.

The meeting of the Imperial Agricultural Research Conference in London last October enabled us to obtain the views of the representatives of both the specialist and the administrative sides of agricultural work in the majority of the Colonies, and we took full advantage of this exceptional opportunity – an opportunity, we may remark, which was not open to the Colonial Office Conference or to the Conference Committee.

The evidence obtained from this source forced us to the conclusion that whatever the advantages of doing so – and there were in our opinion very real advantages – the formation of a Colonial Agricultural Research Service without the inclusion of any agricultural officers, as proposed by the Conference Committee, would be attended by unjustifiable risks.

47. In the first place it is in practice very difficult to draw an accurate dividing line between specialist and agricultural officers. Men on each side of any such line may be found to be doing work which really belongs to the other, and it has indeed happened in the past that some of the most valuable advances in scientific knowledge have been initiated by agricultural officers and based on their observations in the field, to be subsequently developed and improved upon by the specialist staff.

Again, many officers who nominally belong to the specialist branch of their Department have of necessity to devote a considerable part of their time to administrative duties, and a further difficulty is caused by the fact that many, if not the majority, of the higher administrative appointments are held by officers who started their career as specialist officers. /

Secondly, we feel that to exclude agricultural officers from the unified Service might increase the tension and widen the breach which already exists to some extent (as indeed it does in most professions) between the specialist and the general practitioner.

Finally, we fear that this exclusion might adversely affect the prospects of recruitment for the agricultural branch of the Services. We hold that the agricultural branch has done far too valuable work in the past and is far too important a factor in the development of agriculture to warrant the taking of these risks.

We unanimously recommend, therefore, the following proposals for the creation of a unified Service which will include a proportion both of the specialist and of the agricultural officers now serving in Colonial Agricultural Departments.

Formation of Colonial Agricultural Service.

48. We recommend that a "Colonial Agricultural Service" should be formed, which should be divided into two wings, "Specialist" (i.e., Research) and "Agricultural" (i.e., Administrative).

Our detailed proposals regarding the organisation and classification of the Service can best be seen by a study of the following Diagram and Tables:– /

COLONIAL AGRICULTURAL SERVICE.

A. Chief Agricultural Adviser and Assistant Agricultural Adviser.

Specialist Wing.	*Agricultural Wing.*
B. Certain members of Council when fully developed; members of staff of Council, Imperial Bureaux, Imperial Institute, Empire Marketing Board, etc.*	G. Directors and Deputy Directors of Agriculture, etc.: about 30 posts.
C. Officers on special missions, study-leave, etc.	
D.D. Superior Staff of Central Research Stations.	
E.E. Scientific Specialist Officers serving in Colonies.	H. Potential Administrators, i.e., Agricultural Officers who show exceptional promise and are given "Brevet" rank and unified Service rates of pay.
F. Other Specialist Officers, e.g., in cotton or sugar, or in Agricultural Economics, etc.	
	Line of Admission to Service.
Specialist Officers in Colonial Agricultural Departments.	Agricultural Officers in Colonial Agricultural Departments.

*   These officers might belong to either Wing of the Service, but for purpose of convenience they are shown together on the Specialist Wing. /

TABLE P.

Proposed Salary Scales applicable to both Wings of Unified Service.

Class I.	£2,000 – £50 – £3,000.
Class II.	£1,500 – £50 – 2,000.
Class III.	£1,350 – £50 – £1,500.
Class IV.	£1,200 – £50 – £1,350.
Class V.	£l,000 – £50 – £1,200.
Class VI.	£750 – £50 – £1,000.

TABLE Q.

Rates of Pay drawn during early years on existing Long Scales of Principal Colonies.

Year.	East Africa.	West Africa.	Ceylon Both. Agricultural.	Specialist.	Malaya Beth. Agricultural.	Specialist.
	£	£	£	£	£	£
1	480	600	480	600	500	490*
2	500	630	480	630	530	490
3	520	660	480	660	560	560
4	540	690	510	690	600	595
5	560	720	540	720	630	630
6	580	750	570	760	660	665
7	600	780	600	800	690	700

*   Assuming entry at 24. /

TABLE R.

Existing Salaries attached to certain Senior Specialist and Agricultural Appointments, showing Class in unified Service Scales within or below which the maximum of each would fall.

Appointment.	Salary.	Class in unified Service Scales.	Notes
A. – *Specialist.*	£		
Director, Amani Institute	1,500	III	
Director, Singapore Gardens	1,050–35–1,190	V	
Mycologist, Ceylon	1,000–50–1,200	V	
B. – *Agricultural.*			
Director of Agriculture –			
Malaya	1,680*	II	
Ceylon	1,400–50–1,550	II	
Nigeria	1,600†	II	
Kenya	1,500	III	

Appointment.	Salary.	Class in unified Service Scales.	Notes
Uganda	1,350	IV	
Tanganyika Territory	1,350	IV	
Zanzibar	1,250	IV	
Gold Coast	1,200†	V	
British Guiana	1,200	V	
Trinidad	1,150	V	
Palestine	£P. 1,100‡	V	
Nyasaland	1,100	V	
Deputy Director of Agriculture –			
Kenya	1,100	V	
Nigeria	1,100†	V	
Assistant Director of Agriculture –			
Nigeria	1,050†	V	
Director of Agriculture –			
Mauritius	1,000§	VI	
Fiji	800–25–1,000	VI	
Jamaica	800–50–1,000	VI	
Barbados	1,000	VI	
Sierra Leone	1,000†	VI	
Deputy Director of Agriculture –			
Gold Coast	1,000†	VI	
Tanganyika Territory	1,000	VI	
Palestine	£P. 750–25–950‡	VI	
Uganda	960	VI	
Director of Agriculture –			
Gambia	600–920	VI	
Assistant Director of Agriculture, Zanzibar	840–40–920	VI	
Deputy Director of Agriculture –			
British Guiana	875	VI	
Nyasaland	840	VI	
Director of Agriculture –			
Cyprus	600–25–750	VI	
Bermuda	600	VI /	

*   Plus Temporary Allowance.
†   Plus Duty Allowance.
‡   Plus Expatriation Allowance.
§   At normal exchange rate, of Rupee.

Scales of Salary.

49. It will be seen that we propose that both the Specialist and the Agricultural wings of the Service should have common scales of salary, graded by classes. The number of officers in either wing who may at any moment be in one or other class of the salary scale will depend upon circumstances.

We contemplate that the two wings should normally be independent of each other for purposes of promotion, but it should, of course, be open to the Secretary of State, on the advice of the Council, to transfer an officer from either wing to the other at any time in his career, provided the officer desired such a transfer.

We propose that the salaries should be basic rates, common to the whole Service in whatever Colony the officer is employed. Since, however a unified Service implies the liability to transfer we propose that local compensation allowances should also be paid in certain Colonies, as was recommended by the Conference Committee in paragraph 62 (*b*) of their Report,* in order to safeguard an officer against any direct loss on transfer to a post where conditions are less favourable, e.g., owing to climatic conditions or to the cost of living.

50. In certain Colonies local allowances are already given, e.g., in West Africa and Malaya, and these might serve as a basis upon which a complete system can be evolved. We recommend that the Council should consider this question with a view to the matter being taken up with the Colonial Governments concerned at as early a date as possible.

It should, however, be clearly understood that these local allowances will be paid directly by the Colony and not from the Central Fund.[2]

Provident Fund.

51. We endorse the recommendation of the Conference Committee that retiring benefits for the members of the Service should be secured by a Provident Fund Scheme. It appears to us that such a scheme would greatly facilitate transfers, particularly in the case of officers in the Specialist wing, where mobility is most needed, and we feel that its institution will be generally welcomed.

We have accordingly consulted the Crown Agents for the Colonies, who have been examining the question with particular regard to recruiting for Colonial Railway and Public Works Departments in accordance with the recommendation of the Colonial Office Conference.

52. Although we have been unable, in the time available, to work out a detailed scheme we recommend that the following main principles should be adopted, it being always understood / that no officer admitted to the Service should thereby suffer as regards his financial prospects on ultimate retirement:–

---

*   Cmd. 2883, page 37. /

(*a*) That, on the admission to the Service of an officer already in the service of a Colonial Government, his pension rights as at that date should be surrendered and his account in the Provident Fund credited with a suitable lump sum in compensation;

(*b*) That an officer admitted to the Service should come under the Provident Fund Scheme as from the date of admission: while in the Service he would he required to contribute to the Fund a definite percentage of his salary and a similar amount should be contributed from the Central Fund;

(*c*) That (i) an officer who at the time of his admission to the Service contributed to an approved Widows' and Orphans' Pension Scheme should be required either to continue his contributions to that scheme, if the provisions of the scheme allowed, or to insure his life with an approved Society; and (ii) an officer who did not then contribute to any approved scheme should be required to insure his life with an approved Society. In either case the contribution or premium could be deducted from an officer's contribution to the Provident Fund;

(*d*) That a detailed scheme to give effect to these proposals should be prepared with the assistance of the Crown Agents, who should ultimately be responsible for the investment of the Fund and for the keeping of the individual accounts;

(*e*) That in due course the Agricultural Committee of the Council should appoint a Sub-Committee to advise on questions arising in connexion with the scheme in consultation, when necessary, with the Colonial Office.

The proposal in (*c*) is framed with a view to meeting cases where an officer dies at a comparatively early age, when the amount standing to his credit in the Provident Fund would be considerably smaller than the amount which would have been secured to his dependants if, instead of contributing to the Fund, he had devoted a like amount to the payment of premiums on an Insurance Policy.

The question of the percentage which should be adopted under (*b*) must be decided on the advice of experts. For present purposes we have taken a provisional figure of 12 ½ per cent. on each side and our estimates have been prepared on that basis.

As stated in the Conference Report, special arrangements may be necessary in particular cases during the transitional stages, but we do not consider that any insuperable difficulties will be met in changing from a Pensions to a Provident Fund basis.

Leave.

53. In paragraph 62 (*b*) of their Report* the Conference Committee proposed that the ordinary local leave regulations should / not apply to officers in the unified Service. This proposal only had reference to officers engaged on research and was based on the great importance of ensuring continuity of work, a point to which we have already called special attention.

We are of the opinion that officers in the Service should, as a general rule, be granted leave in accordance with the local regulations. These regulations have been framed with due regard to the maintenance of health, which should be the primary consideration. If continuity of work is to be ensured, we consider that this should be done by gradually making the necessary increases in staff rather than by interfering with leave regulations in any way which might prejudice an officer's health.

We fully endorse the recommendation in paragraph 139 of the Agricultural Report† regarding the provision of adequate facilities for study-leave, and we have made allowance accordingly in our estimates of cost.

Passages on Leave and Transfer.

54. We recommend that the cost of an officer's passages on leave and on transfer and the cost of family passages on transfer, as recommended below, should be defrayed from the Central Fund.

In view of the liability to compulsory transfer which membership of the unified Service implies, we recommend that in all cases where a married officer is transferred he should be given free first-class passages for himself, his wife, and his children, from his old station to his new by the most direct route, or, alternatively, the equivalent in cash.

It is well known that in many cases the expenses incurred in transfer press very heavily on individual officers and, as one of our main objects in framing the scheme is to make transfers as easy as possible, we attach great importance to the above recommendation.

We consider that a uniform practice in regard to family passage allowances on leave should be adopted, and we recommend that this matter should receive the attention of the Council when established. These allowances would, of course, be paid from the Central Fund.

*	Cmd. 2883, page 37. *
†	Cmd. 2825, page 58. /

Admission to the Service,

55. We recommend that the admission of an officer to the Service should be approved by the Secretary of State on the advice of the Council, and that an officer should be eligible for admission at any period while he was proceeding up the "long scale,"* provided he had passed the usual probationary period and had been confirmed in his appointment. /

No officer at present serving should be compelled to join the Service against his will, but we consider that an officer who for any reason did not enter the Service, while retaining his eligibility to rise to the maximum salary of the post or long scale in which he was then serving, should *ipso facto* be rendered ineligible for further promotion.

We do not think that officers should be permitted to submit applications for admission to the Service. Their claims should automatically be considered by the Council as occasion arises, and in this connection we strongly support the recommendations contained in paragraph 157 of the Agricultural Report† regarding the form of the Confidential Reports to be adopted. In particular, we think that it should be definitely stated in these Reports whether or not an officer is recommended for promotion.

We consider that the Council should in due course be requested to advise whether any clause should in the future be inserted in offers of appointment to candidates whereby they would undertake to enter the Service if required to do so at any time in their career.

We contemplate that admission to the Service should be gradual, even up to the initial maximum. It is clear that the Council will need time to acquaint themselves with the capabilities of existing officers, and it is probable that personal visits to all the Colonies will be necessary before full information can be obtained.

Promotion.

56. As we have stated above we propose that the two wings of the Service should normally be independent of each other for purposes of promotion. We do not consider that admission to the Service should in itself entitle an officer to rise to a higher class. Every officer entering the Service can count on rising to a salary of £1,000 per annum, in addition to any allowances which may apply, but promotion to a higher class should depend on merit, and should be by selection.

To ensure flexibility the Secretary of State could admit or promote an officer to any point in the incremental scale of any class.

---

*   Or "time-scale," *i.e.*, the scale providing continuous increments over a period of 15 to 20 years, subject to passing efficiency bars at certain points./

†   Cmd. 2825, page 65. /

Numbers of Officers to be admitted to the Service.

57. Our decision to recommend that a proportion of agricultural officers should be admitted to the unified Service necessarily involves a reduction in the number of specialist officers to be admitted, if the figure of cost envisaged by the Colonial Office Conference is to be adhered to.

In considering the number of possible admissions to the two wings we have been guided by two main considerations:–

(*a*) Mobility, i.e., the power to send an officer where he is most needed, which the Service provides, is generally more / important in the Specialist than in the Agricultural wing. In the case of the latter it is only needed in connection with Directors and Deputy Directors, or with specially promising men earmarked for promotion to such posts.

(*b*) We consider that the prospects held out by the unified Service, especially in regard to the scope which it offers for a varied career as against service in watertight Agricultural Departments, are likely to prove particularly attractive to the genuine research officer. Men with the true flair for research are rare, and there is great and increasing competition for their services on the part of large industrial concerns both in this country and abroad.

We recommend therefore that the number of specialist officers to be admitted should be greater in proportion to the total number of such officers in the Colonial Services than in the case of the Agricultural wing. That is to say, a larger proportion of junior officers should be admitted. It is, for instance, important that junior officers on the staff of Central Research Stations should be members of the Service.

It will be realised that the number of officers who can in fact be admitted to the Service at any time will depend on the funds available. Our detailed estimates regarding the numbers who can be admitted at the start will be found later in this Report; we have based them on the general proposals as to finance which were made by the Conference Committee, but we contemplate that the Service should expand as the revenue of the Central Fund increases.

Directors and Deputy Directors of Agriculture.

58. We are of the opinion that all Directors and Deputy Directors of Agriculture should normally be members of the Colonial Agricultural Service, but we are not in a position to say whether all the officers at present holding, such posts are in fact fitted for admission to the Service.

It is clear that the automatic inclusion of an officer with inadequate qualifications would adversely affect the prestige of the Service, and we feel, too, that individual officers would probably set a higher value on admission, if it were granted on the grounds of personal merit rather than by virtue of the post they happened to hold. At the same time we think that it would be unfair to throw upon the Council; at the very start of its career, the onus of advising on its own responsibility that a given Director should not be admitted.

We recommend therefore that the Council should only submit the names of existing Directors and Deputy Directors to the Secretary of State for admission to the Service on the definite recommendation of the Governor of the Colony concerned.

We appreciate that a Director or Deputy Director who was not admitted to the Service would probably wish to retire from his / post, and we consider that provision should be made to facilitate the retirement of such officers on liberal terms, as was recommended by the Conference Committee in paragraph 71 (*b*) of their Report.*

Grading of Directorships of Agriculture.

59. Directorships of Agriculture should normally be graded by the importance of their respective Departments. Such posts should, we think, be divided, with the assistance of the Council, into categories which should be subject to review at stated periods. If at any time it was desired to give any additional reward to exceptionally good officers in low-grade posts, this could be done by a system of personal allowances, provision for which might be made by establishing a small pool of money at the disposal of the Council.

At the same time we consider that the Secretary of State should have power in special circumstances to send a man of any class to any Colony, irrespective of the existing grading. We believe that this might prove a great help to the smaller Colonies. To take an example:– a small Colony now has a Director who would come under Class VI. Supposing it became clear that great results might be hoped for if that Colony's Agricultural Department were thoroughly reorganised, a Class IV Officer might be sent for a period of years to pull it into shape, but, when this had been done, a Class V or Class VI officer might be capable of "carrying-on." The same principle could be applied in regard to specialist officers.

Interchange and Transfers.

60. We fully endorse the emphasis laid by the previous Committees on the necessity for making flexible arrangements for the transfer of officers between Colonies or between Colonial Agricultural Departments and Central Research Stations. We wish to go further and to recommend that the Council should explore the possibility of arranging that certain posts at home, for example, on

---

*   Cmd. 2883, page 39. /

its own staff, at the Imperial Institute, the Empire Marketing Board, or at one or other of the Bureaux, should be held by members of the unified Service. We believe that it would be of the greatest value if opportunities could thereby be offered for a spell of service at home to selected officers which, apart from giving them a welcome change from tropical conditions, would bring them into touch with the progress of scientific and other knowledge in this country. We believe that the institutions to which they were attached would equally gain, and that important advantages would be derived by maintaining a flow of officers with first-hand knowledge of different parts of the Empire to and from those institutions at home which were especially concerned with their development. /

We recommend that this proposal should be adopted in principle and that its practical possibilities should be considered by the Council.

We recommend that the Chief Agricultural Adviser and the Assistant Agricultural Adviser should be members of the Service, and we have included other such appointments in our diagram (see group (B)), even though it may, not be possible to make them for some time to come.

Economic and other Specialists.

61. In our opinion officers who specialise successfully in, the culture of particular crops, such as cotton, tobacco, or sisal, or in such matters as Agricultural Economics or Cooperative Marketing, are likely to prove of increasing importance. We feel that they have an equal right to the title of "specialist" and to a place in the Service with their colleagues who are specialists in such subjects as entomology, and we have accordingly provided for them in group (F) in our diagram. Appointments in this group would be open to any suitably qualified officer, whether previously serving as a specialist or as an agricultural officer.

Potential Administrators.

62. We attach particular importance to what we may call the group of "Brevet-Administrators," group (H). Men admitted to this group should be officers of a few years service who have shown exceptional promise. Once admitted to this group they should be specially watched and encouraged, and every opportunity should be taken to assist them to qualify for eventual promotion to a Directorship or Deputy Directorship. Admission to this group would, in fact, be comparable to the grant of Brevet rank in the Army, with the additional advantage that, in most cases, as will be seen from Table Q, it would in itself improve the financial position of the officer concerned. /

We believe that the formation of this group would be a great encouragement to all ambitious junior agricultural officers from the start of their career, and should lead to a higher standard of efficiency in future Directors and Deputy Directors.

In this connection we wish, once again, to lay emphasis on the importance of the Agricultural wing and the consequent need to provide its members with adequate prospects of promotion within itself, so that they may not be led to think that if they want to get on they must necessarily abandon administrative work and attempt to qualify as specialists.

General Observations.

63. In framing the foregoing recommendations we have kept the following broad considerations in mind. /

The proposal to create a unified Service of any sort originated with the Colonial Office Conference of 1927, and from a study of their discussions it seems clear that the Conference had two main ultimate objectives in view. In the first place, they definitely approved in principle the eventual formation of a Colonial Research Service, covering Medicine, Forestry, Veterinary Science, &c., as well as Agriculture. Secondly, they wished to see the ultimate unification of at any rate all the more highly-trained elements in the Colonial Agricultural Services, whether agricultural or specialist; but they came to the conclusion that practical considerations made it necessary to confine unification in the first instance to the specialist or research branches.

It will be seen that our proposals mark a definite advance on those of the Conference towards the second of these objectives, since they provide for an immediate start with the unification of the agricultural as well as of the specialist branches, and are so framed that all officers in the higher grades in the Agricultural Departments can eventually be brought into the new Service.

64. The admission of agricultural officers to the Service might at first sight appear to add to the difficulty of realising the Conference's other ideal of a Colonial Research Service. We do not however feel that this will be so in practice. The Conference in advocating the creation of a Colonial Research Service regarded such a Service as a means to an end, and not as an end in itself. Their object was to ensure thereby full cooperation between the various scientific Services, and so to clear away obstacles that, for example, an entomological problem could be attacked with the most effective and economical use of the entomological resources of the Agricultural, Medical, and Veterinary Departments, and not merely by one of them alone or by each of them independently; or again, that in dealing with some problem of exceptional importance, like Trypanosomiasis, in which the cooperation of many Departments was essential to success, such cooperation should be as free and efficient as possible.

We have divided the Colonial Agricultural Service into two wings – a Specialist (or Research) and an Agricultural (or Administrative) wing. We believe that, if it is found possible to adopt a similar procedure in the event of other scientific Services being reorganised, cooperation between the Specialist wings of different Services could easily be secured, especially if methods can be found for properly coordinating their efforts in dealing with common problems.

We feel, too, that jealousy and friction will be obviated and cooperation made easier if the Specialist wing of each Service is generally of equal standing in respect of such matters as salary scales, status, and scientific training. We believe that the measures advocated in this and the two previous Reports / and the measures which, from our common discussions, we understand that your Veterinary Committee are likely to propose, will do much to equalise the position of the Agricultural and Veterinary Services in respect of training and status, and to bring them into line with the hitherto more highly developed Medical Services.

65. We would also call particular attention to the salary scales which we propose. We have endeavoured to make our provisions with regard to them as flexible as possible, not only with an eye to the Agricultural Service, but in the hope that they may be found suitable also for the Veterinary or other scientific Services, if in the future it may he decided to adopt unification in those Services also. The scales suggested may at first sight seem to be high, but we are convinced of the absolute necessity for framing them on bold, simple lines. The Reports of other Committees, and notably that of the Research Special Sub-Committee of the Imperial Conference, 1926,* have emphasised the fact that a Service, to be successful, must rely on its own inherent advantages to attract the best recruits. Schemes to induce men to offer themselves for a Service, such as the grant of scholarships, are valuable and often essential, when neglect of the Service has rendered such measures necessary. But they can only be temporary expedients. To produce permanent results the Service itself must be so organised and so paid that it will be worth the while of the best men to enter it for its own sake, and to take any necessary training at their own expense, and equally worth the while of training institutions to provide the necessary courses of instruction.

66. The raising of the standard of future recruitment for the Colonial Agricultural Services to the highest possible level is perhaps the most important objective which we and the Committees which have preceded us have had in view. Our proposals with regard to organisation and training will, we believe, have an important influence in this direction, but we are convinced that, if the very best men available are to be attracted to the Service, adequate prospects must be provided for them, and in saying that we mean both financial prospects, and prospects in the sense of a wide and varied career which will call the best out of each man and will in itself attract ability and ambition. It is the lack of these ultimate prospects, rather than any inadequacy of initial salaries, that at present hampers recruitment for Colonial Agricultural Departments.

* Cmd. 2769, pages 299–320.

Moreover, as has been shown in the previous Reports, and particularly in the Introduction to the Report of the Conference Committee* and in the appendices to the Agricultural Report,† the wealth of the Colonies is mainly derived from agriculture. The salaries of other branches of the Colonial Services depend, / therefore, largely upon the efficiency of the agricultural staffs and it will not be illogical if the remuneration of these officers, provided that their qualifications are sufficient, should be at least as high as that of any other branch.

67. This brings us to a further point. If this section of the Report is carefully studied in conjunction with the diagrams and tables it will be seen that, though the salary scales provide for the possible promotion of selected officers up to a maximum of £3,000 per annum, the number of officers to be admitted to any grade can be strictly governed by the scope of the work to be done and the merit of the individual. Reference to Table R and to the Staff Lists will also show that at the start the majority of officers affected could, if desired, be admitted to a scale with a maximum of £1,000 per annum, plus any compensatory allowance in respect of Provident Fund contributions, and need not be promoted above it, unless the nature of their work and their own qualifications justified such action. /

On the other hand, we understood that you wished us so to frame our proposals that they should be capable, of serving as a basis for a permanent organisation of the Agricultural Service. The Agricultural Report has shown the rapid growth of trade with the Colonies in recent years and the vital importance of agriculture to that trade and to Colonial prosperity. It has also shown the possibilities of very much greater prosperity and growth, if agricultural development is fostered by an efficient and well organised staff. We have therefore deliberately framed our scheme of salaries so as to allow for what we believe to be the inevitable growth in the scope and importance of the Colonial Agricultural Service.

V. – FINANCE.

68. We have carefully considered the method by which the Council and the unified Service should be financed, and we have come to the unanimous conclusion that that portion of the total cost which will fall upon Colonial Governments, should be provided by means of a percentage cess upon Colonial revenues. It is, in our opinion, of the first importance that provision should be made for the automatic expansion of the Service, and that a definite financial basis should be adopted on which the future development of the scheme may be planned. At a later date, possibly at the next Colonial Office Conference, it may be desirable to review the position in the light of the experience which will then have been gained, but for the present we are agreed that a percentage is the most satisfac-

---

*   Cmd. 2883.

†   Cmd. 2825. /

tory course to adopt. Colonial revenues have been steadily increasing during the last few years and if, as we hope and anticipate, the present rate of increase continues it will be possible thereby to maintain an equally steady rate of expansion in the Service. /

[...]

VI. – CONCLUSION.

80. In this Report we have refrained both from emphasising the advantages of the scheme and from dwelling on the prospects / of future progress which it offers. Throughout our inquiries, however, we have been conscious of the vast possibilities of agricultural development in the Colonial Empire, towards which the creation of a single Agricultural Service is an important step.

The welfare and progress of agriculture is to-day the most vital concern of almost every Colonial Administration. The prosperity of the people, the trade, and, not least, the revenue of each Colony is mainly dependent upon its agricultural production. Agriculture, in fact, may be said to be *the* main industry of the Colonial Empire, and on the efficiency of agriculture depends therefore not only the food supply of the population, but, indeed, all economic and social progress.

Science does not stand still, and the country which lags behind in the application of the latest scientific knowledge to the practice of agriculture must suffer a loss which cannot be estimated. The failure to provide for efficient and up-to-date agricultural research may mean not merely serious annual losses on crops but indeed the loss of a whole industry to a country or group of countries: on the other hand, the provision of such research may mean the gain to a country of a new industry or at any rate the retention of an industry which would otherwise be lost. Such are the large issues at stake.

The figures which were given in the two previous Reports, and to which we have already referred, show the great expansion in Colonial trade which has taken place during the present century. That expansion still continues, and in 1926 the total trade of the Colonies with which we are here concerned, which amounted in 1906 to £157,000,000, had grown to £485,000,000.

Rapid and striking as this development has been, we are as yet only witnessing its infancy. As we have already shown the trade of the Colonies depends at present on the agricultural activities of 50,000,000 people, a number which is small in proportion to the territory they inhabit, and its full development is still to come.

81. The proper organisation of the agricultural resources of the Colonial Empire must always depend first and foremost on the supply of properly trained and qualified staff. It is our considered opinion that the creation of the Colonial Agricultural Service will in itself put recruiting on an entirely new basis. The Service will offer a wide and varied career, which will afford its members the

opportunity of doing the best work within their power and of receiving full recognition for that work, while, on the financial side, the scales of salary which we have recommended, and which approximate to those paid to scientific officers in private employment, should not fail to attract the ablest recruits. We have deliberately included a class with a maximum salary of £3,000, although, as we have already stated, we do not contemplate that officers should be promoted to this class until their own qualifications and the importance of their work justify such a course. But we are confident that it will be found / possible, and indeed necessary, to appoint more and more officers to this class as agriculture develops in the Colonies, and we see no reason why the ambitious recruit of to-day should not hope to be the Class I officer of twenty or thirty years hence.

82. Nor will the benefits of this scheme be confined to either the richer or the poorer Colonies. It is to the former that the best men will eventually gravitate, as they will find there the highest paid appointments; and those Colonies will benefit by securing the services of the most highly qualified officers who will, in addition, have had considerably wider experience than it is generally possible for them to acquire under present conditions. On the other hand, the smaller Colonies will gain by having as their Directors of Agriculture picked officers in the unified Service on their way up to the highest posts, who will not, as so easily may happen to-day, lose touch with the progress of agricultural practice and science and, if we may use the word, stagnate, without hope of promotion or of recognition. These Colonies will also benefit from the special investigations or missions which they cannot at present afford and which will in future be provided for them, if necessary, from the Central Fund.

83. All Colonies will benefit alike from the general *apercu* of the agricultural situation as a whole which the Advisory Council will be qualified to give. The Council will be able to draw fully upon all sources of information, such as Imperial Bureaux or Correspondence Centres at home, Central Research Stations abroad, or the published results of investigations in foreign countries such as those of the Department of Agriculture in the United States of America or the Research Stations in the Dutch East Indies. Their knowledge will be world-wide, and the advice based on that knowledge which they will be able to give to the Secretary of State and to Colonial Governments will be such as no other body which exists to-day can equal.

84. This brings us to a further point. From our own discussions and from those which we have had with your Veterinary Committee, two important principles of organisation have emerged – the need for promoting free and well-directed cooperation between the different scientific Services when a problem of common interest is to be solved, and the need for giving each Service its proper status and prestige.

We believe that the former can best be secured, first, by providing machinery for coordinating effort and exchanging information on the lines of the Advisory Council which we have recommended for the Agricultural and Veterinary Services, and, secondly, by making the training and conditions of service approximately similar in each Service, so that they may regard each other as members of a common scientific corps.

We consider that the status and prestige of individual Services can, in the main, best be fostered by two provisions. In the / first place, the Secretary of State should have professional advice with regard to each of them available in this country, whether in the form of an individual Adviser or a Council, or, as in the case of agriculture, of both. Secondly, each Service should, in any Colony where its importance justified such a course, be placed under its own professional head, who should act as its spokesman.

85. We would wish, in conclusion, to repeat once more that the scheme which we have recommended is not meant either to stereotype the lines of future development or to limit in any way the efforts of individual Colonies. We would strongly object also to any suggestion that the officers in the unified Service should be placed under a central authority. We do not contemplate that the Council should exercise executive control in any way whatever, and it is essential that in his own Colony each Governor should retain unimpaired his authority over the members of the Service, who will, of course, be subject to the local disciplinary and other relations. Nor do we suggest that the Council should themselves communicate with Colonial Governments on questions of policy or general administration: it may indeed be convenient for individual members of the Council to communicate direct with officers in the Service overseas on technical questions not involving policy in connection with any particular work on research, but even then it is important that copies of the communications should be sent, if only for information, to the Director of Agriculture concerned.

86. We do not deny that difficulties may be found in initiating the organisation which we have recommended, and it would be unduly optimistic to hope that in the first instance the scheme will be found to be invariably fair in its incidence. But we are confident that in considering our proposals Colonial Governments will have regard not only to their own individual needs and interests but also to those of the Colonial Empire as a whole. The Colonies have before them great opportunities of making a real contribution to agricultural knowledge and science, and if full advantage is to be taken of these opportunities it is essential that they should act together and join in a great cooperative effort. The Colonial Empire is a unity in itself, and we claim that in the field of Agriculture that unity can best be shown through the scheme of organisation which was approved in principle by the Colonial Office Conference and which has been set out in detail in this Report. /

The Committee consider themselves fortunate in having secured the services of a particularly competent Secretary in the person of Mr. Creasy. The Committee wish to place on record their appreciation of his industry, tact, and ability.

LOVAT, *Chairman*.

W. ORMSBY GORE.

J. B. FARMER.

H. C. SAMPSON.

A. S. HAYNES.

A. T. STANTON.

R. D. FURSE.

E. B. BOYD.

GERALD CREASY, *Secretary*.

8th February, 1928.

[Warren Fisher], Report of a Committee on the
System of Appointment in the Colonial Office
and the Colonial Services, House of Commons
Parliamentary Papers [Cmd. 3554] (London: Her
Majesty's Stationery Office, 1930).

PART I.
THE COLONIAL SERVICES.[1]

I. The Colonial Empire.

The territories which fall within the sphere of the Colonial Office cover an area
of about two million square miles – nearly twice the size of British India – and
contain a population of nearly fifty millions – nearly twice the total population
of the oversea Dominions. Except for some 160,000 square miles with four millions of people, these territories lie wholly within the tropics.

In these areas the administrative systems are sometimes described as The
Colonial Service, as though they constituted a single Service with uniform terms
and common conditions. Such an illusion does not survive the most cursory
examination. As a matter of fact the Secretary of State for the Colonies has to
deal with the affairs of more than fifty distinct governments. Each, whether it
deals with a population of many millions in a territory as large as Central Europe,
or with a few thousand people in a remote island group, has its own administrative and technical services, its own scales of pay and conditions of leave, passage
home, and pensions.

These territories, since they include units of every size and economic importance in every corner of the globe, show a remarkable variety of conditions of
life and material equipment. Some have achieved self-government in a greater
or lesser degree, while others are under direct official control. They include
Colonies proper, which are British territory, Protectorates, Protected States,
Mandated territory, Leased territory, and a Condominium. In some of them

there is an intelligent and influential public opinion and a well-informed Press, while others remain relics of an earlier world.

In an Empire so widely scattered and so curiously varied, the extent to which the Services of the different territories recruit their staff from the mother country must obviously depend upon their size and wealth and the degree in which they are able to draw for their officials upon the local population.

The Colonial Services have immeasurably increased in importance of recent years, through the remarkable development of many of the Dependencies in material wealth, and consequently in the standard of living, through the wider interests which this increased prosperity has brought to them, and through the greater / mobility of the population owing to improvements in transport. This development is for the most part a very recent thing. The overseas trade of the Dependencies has trebled in the last twenty years. The sum of the Government revenues has increased from ten and a half millions sterling in 1900 to twenty-five and a half millions in 1913, and seventy-two millions in 1927.

This development had already begun in the period immediately preceding the Great War. The years of war were in most respects a time of stagnation. The rate of development was not maintained; there was inevitably a check in recruitment for the Colonial Services; and at the end of the War many Dependencies were in the position of "countries of arrears". But from the Armistice onward their advance has been rapid. Moreover, the administrative area of the Colonial Empire has been extended through the acceptance by His Majesty of certain ex-enemy territories under the Mandate system.[2]

Along with the economic development there has been evolved a new sense of responsibility for the welfare and education of the native peoples in the tropical territories and Protectorates of the Crown. It is now a truism that the duty of trusteeship is the guiding principle of Colonial administration, and this principle has a very real application to our enquiry. To a large extent the services which at home are supplied by private or municipal enterprise fall to be carried on in the Dependencies by the Colonial Governments themselves. With the increased resources now available those services are continually extending, not only in connection with the material improvement of life, the preservation of peace and order, improved medical facilities and measures for public health, but in the direction of the provision of education for different types, the study of social anthropology, the revival or protection of native forms of culture, and every activity which can promote moral and intellectual progress.

With these new purposes the public Services have endeavoured to keep pace. In extent and complexity they have grown out of all comparison with their position thirty years ago, or even just before the War. The sum of the expenditure by the Colonial Governments on all their activities in 1929 was estimated at

£68,000,000, as compared with an expenditure of £19,000,000 in 1909.* In 1909 the total staffs of all Government branches numbered approximately 93,280, while in 1929 the corresponding figure was 220,770. This contrast was reflected in the figures / of the staff required from this country; in 1909 the appointments made to the Colonial Services from home were 657: in 1929 they numbered 1,076. For a true comparison it should be noted that many classes of appointment which twenty years ago were normally filled from home are now staffed locally. The contrast is not merely a matter of numbers: modern conditions demand also a generally higher standard of personal, educational, and professional qualifications, and in addition the employment of men with scientific and special attainments of a kind not previously to be found in Colonial service.

Bearing these facts in mind, we can appreciate the diversity and complexity of the work for which the Colonial Office is now responsible. The rapidly changing situation overseas has required many developments in the reorganization of that Office, of which we desire to mention in particular three recent instances. The first is the appointment to the Office of specialist advisers on certain subjects: in 1926, a Chief Medical Adviser: in 1927, an Economic and Financial Adviser: in 1929, an Adviser on Tropical Agriculture. The second is the institution of special Standing Committees to secure expert advice on matters of growing importance to the Colonies, such as education, medical research, and tropical agriculture. The third is the institution in 1927 of periodical conferences at the Colonial Office of Colonial Governors, or their deputies, with British Ministers and the principal members of the permanent staff of the Department. We understand that twenty-six Colonial administrations were represented at that Conference, and that the list of subjects on which there was a free exchange of views included such matters as the recruitment and training of Colonial Civil Servants and the whole general conditions of service overseas. This Conference elicited evidence of the highest value, and we shall venture to refer in later pages of this Report to certain of the views recorded in the published summary of its proceedings (Cmd. 2883).[3]

The Colonial Empire has therefore become a problem of the first magnitude, both on the quantitative and the qualitative side. Its geographical area has been largely extended, its wealth is advancing every year, and the duties of government have been increased in number and immeasurably increased in complexity. On the political side we are labouring to establish a regime which seeks

---

*   It is worth while to contrast their expenditure for certain branches of public activity in the same two years:–

	1909.	1929.
Administration	1,066,000	4,831,000
Medical ..	1,149,000	6,211,000
Education ..	557,000	3,970,000
Public Works	3,773,000	17,713.000 /

to preserve what is best in the traditional native culture, rather than to provide a cleared ground for the establishment of a ready-made alien polity. Such a purpose demands a high degree of knowledge and understanding on the part of the administrators. On the economic side we have to bring to bear the latest results of scientific research on the development of wealth, which is important not only to the Colonies themselves, but also to the Empire and to the world. Most of the greater problems of the Colonies to-day are problems of applied science. Obviously, in a field so intricate and so fateful, the organization of the Government Services demands the most scrupulous care. /

II. The Present System of Appointment to the Colonial Services.

A. THE APPOINTING AUTHORITY.

In the Colonial Regulations there are laid down certain rules of general application to the Dependencies, regarding appointments to public offices, and the limits within which Governors have power to make appointments in the public service of their territory without the prior approval of the Secretary of State. These rules are directions given by the Crown to Governors for general guidance and do not constitute a contract between the Crown and its servants. In general the appointments to public offices are made by letter signed by the Governor or written by his direction, except in the case of Judges of the Supreme Court, who are appointed in His Majesty's name by an instrument under the Public Seal of the Colony.

The effect of such regulations is that the Governor may make appointments to offices of which the initial emoluments do not exceed £200 a year: to offices with initial emoluments above that figure but less than £400 a year he may appoint provisionally and subject to the Secretary of State's approval. In neither case, however, does this power of a Governor extend to the selection of persons not resident in the Colony. All appointments to offices of which the initial emoluments exceed £400 a year rest with the Secretary of State.

In certain Dependencies local variations of a minor character have in fact been authorized by the Secretary of State in the direction of extending the Governor's powers – both in respect of the limit of £400, and of the appointment of persons locally domiciled or domiciled in neighbouring Dominion territory, e.g., appointments to Northern Rhodesia from South Africa, and to the Western Pacific Islands from Australia and New Zealand. In particular Colonies, where there are locally domiciled candidates suitable on personal and educational grounds for appointment to the higher offices, it will be understood that, although the general regulations apply without variation, the appointment of a local candidate recommended by the Governor would normally be approved by the Secretary of State.

Subject to what has been written above, the power of selection lies with the Secretary of State, while the actual appointment rests on a letter of appointment from the Governor which the officer receives on his arrival in the Colony. In dealing with the various existing systems of appointment we propose to divide the subject into the system of entry into the Colonial Services, and the system of selecting officers already members of a Colonial administration for promotion and transfer to a vacancy in their own or in another Colony. /

B. – THE SYSTEM OF ENTRY.

Apart from the system of local recruitment, generally for subordinate appointments, there are various methods by which candidates outside a Colony may enter into the various branches of the Colonial Administrations.

(*a*) *The Civil Service Commission* in London hold an annual competitive examination for the Home and Indian Civil Services and for Eastern Cadetships. These Cadetships are appointments to the administrative services of the Governments of Ceylon, the Straits Settlements, the Federated Malay States, and Hong Kong. The Civil Service Commission also hold an annual qualifying examination for appointments in the commissioned grade to the Police Service of Ceylon. For the benefit of Ceylonese candidates for the Ceylon Service, the examinations are held concurrently in Ceylon. Except in the case of Ceylon appointments, successful candidates at these examinations are offered appointments at the direction of, and on the authority of, the Secretary of State for the Colonies. In the case of the Ceylon Cadetships, candidates successful in the examinations in London are offered appointments by the Secretary of State, and those successful in the examinations in Ceylon by the Governor. There is a similar practice in the case of the Ceylon Police Service, after the selections have been made from among the candidates qualifying at the examinations.

The examination held by the Civil Service Commission for Engineering appointments in the Home Post Office Service is publicly announced to be also a qualifying examination for engineering appointments in the Posts and Telegraphs Department of Nigeria and the Gold Coast. Successful candidates desiring such oversea appointments are engaged by the Crown Agents for the Colonies.

(*b*) *The Crown Agents for the Colonies* select candidates for appointments of a technical character, such as qualified engineers for Colonial Railways, Public Works, Posts and Telegraphs, and Marine Departments; also for certain posts requiring technical training, such as mechanics, works' overseers, linotype operators, sanitary inspectors, draughtsmen, and locomotive drivers; and for other subordinate appointments, such as European police non-commissioned officers and constables, clerks, foremen, etc.

In all cases of appointments made by the Crown Agents the successful candidate is engaged for a term of years by a written engagement concluded with him by the Crown Agents acting on behalf of the Colonial Government concerned.

(c) *The Private Secretary (Appointments) to the Secretary of State for the Colonies* selects and recommends to the Secretary of State outside candidates for a first appointment in the Colonial / Services.* By this system the great majority of appointments in the higher branches of the Colonial administrations are made, except where in particular cases vacancies may be filled by the transfer or promotion of officers already serving in a Colonial Administration. For instance, the Private Secretary is concerned with appointments in the Administrative Services of all the Dependencies except those mentioned in (a), and of all medical, agricultural, financial, legal, forestry, survey, and other professional and scientific posts, where special qualifications are demanded, except those mentioned in (b) and (d).

In assessing the merits of candidates, the Private Secretary is able to obtain advice and assistance from the specialist Advisers at the Colonial Office, from men of eminence in the various professions, and from senior Colonial officials who may be on leave or recently retired.

A statement of the qualifications, record, etc., of the candidate recommended is submitted to the Secretary of State for his approval, and, subject to his consent, the offer of the appointment is made by letter from the Colonial Office.

If the appointment is of a permanent nature, the selected officer is usually required to serve on probation for a period of one, two, or three years according to the Colony concerned.

(d) *Other Departments of the Home Government* are from time to time asked to select and recommend candidates for certain appointments in the Colonial Services, principally those in which are required qualifications and experience of a sort which can best be looked for in the Home Public Service. The principal instances are as follows:–

> *War Office.* – Military personnel for the local Forces in the Colonies. Appointments, however, in the Royal West African Frontier Force and the King's African Rifles are made by the Secretary of State with the advice of the Staff Officers of those Corps in the Colonial Office, and with the consent of the War Office to the employment in Tropical Africa of the personnel selected.
>
> *General Post Office.* – Postal and telegraph personnel.
>
> *Board of Customs.* – Customs officers of the Superintending grade.

---

*   It should be understood that the Private Secretary (Appointments) has the assistance of a not inconsiderable staff, and presides over a highly organized branch. /

Board of Education. – Assistant Mistresses, and certain other Educational personnel – particularly elementary school teachers and teachers possessing commercial or technical qualifications.

Home Office. – Prisons superintending personnel.

Air Ministry. – Meteorologists. /

We may mention here also the system of selection by the Overseas Nursing Association[4] in London of Nurses and Nursing Sisters in the hospitals and Medical Departments of the Colonial Governments.

In all these instances the names of candidates recommended as suitable for appointment are communicated to the Colonial Office, and the appointment is offered to the selected candidate by the direction of the Secretary of State. If more than one name is submitted, an order of preference is customarily stated by the Department concerned. In the classes where the recruitment is of some volume, special arrangements exist for making the final selection where the name of more than one suitable candidate is submitted.

In the case of the Board of Education selections, that Department arranges for candidates to be interviewed by a Board, which includes a suitable person with experience of the Colony concerned and/or a member of the Colonial Office.

In the case of military personnel an arrangement exists by which a consulting officer (who is an officer with personal experience of the local Force concerned) is nominated by each Colony to advise the Colonial Office on the final selection out of the names recommended by the War Office.*

In the case of personnel recommended by the General Post Office the custom of the Colonial Office is to arrange for a selective interview to be carried out by the Crown Agents for the Colonies.

Where officials serving on the pensionable establishment of the Home Service are selected for appointments in the Colonial Services, it is the custom for them to be seconded in the first place for a period of a few years. At the end of this time they may either decide to return to the Home Service or, if the Colony desires it, to be definitely transferred to the Colonial Administration.

It will be seen from this statement of the existing systems of entry into the Colonial Services that the problem of securing the quantity, quality, and variety of the staff needed to maintain and promote the efficiency of the European element, which is the controlling element in these Administrations, is one that has called for diverse methods, and for co-operation on a considerable scale with various authorities at home. We have laid no emphasis on the assistance, which according to our evidence has been ungrudgingly given by University authorities, by heads of educational establishments, by men of eminence in professional,

---

* This as already stated does not apply to the Royal West African Frontier Force and King's African Rifles. /

scientific, and technical circles in this country, and by Governors and senior Colonial officers either on leave or after their retirement from / active service overseas. Under any system such co-operation and advice must remain of the greatest value; and we wish to put on record from the evidence we have received that, for the success of the recruiting effort for the Colonial Services, the Colonies are under a very real obligation to the authorities and individuals who have served the Colonial Office and the Crown Agents in this connection.

We propose to comment in turn on each of these systems of entry, apart from the system of appointment of local candidates by the Governor to the subordinate grades of the Public Service. On that matter we offer no observation, except that a proper system must depend not only on the quality and quantity of the suitable local candidates available, but also on the existence and intelligence of a local unofficial public opinion, and on the peculiar local conditions to which the system of appointment must be adapted.

(*a*) *Open competitive examination.* – On the evidence submitted to us, there is nothing in the experience of appointments under this system to the Eastern Cadet Services which would justify us in recommending that the present system of appointment by competitive examination under the control of the Civil Service Commissioners should not be maintained for those branches of the Service to which it at present applies. This is not the place to argue the general merits of the system of competitive examination, but we may note that it has a certain special value as a method of appointment where parallel recruitment is being carried on from candidates at home and in a Colony.

(*b*) *Selection by the Crown Agents for the Colonies.* – Among their functions as the agents of Colonial Governments in a great variety of important commercial, financial, and other business, the Crown Agents carry out the duties of selecting and engaging certain classes of staff for service overseas. Prior to July, 1911, vacancies under the Colonial Governments thus filled were those of marine officers and engineers, clerks, store-keepers, policemen, and others of a subordinate character, the total number per annum being below one hundred. This number excluded the candidates selected and recommended by the Consulting Engineers under the arrangement at that time in force. Candidates for various technical appointments connected with the survey, construction, and maintenance of roads, railways, harbours, electrical undertakings, sanitary drainage, water works, public works, etc., were filled by the Crown Agents on the recommendation of their Consulting Engineers. In July, 1911, however, this system was replaced by an arrangement whereby the Crown Agents, with the assistance of their own technical staff and of responsible Colonial officials when available, should select candidates for most of the appointments of a technical character. /

The following figures show the number of appointments filled in the various Departments in 1909 and in 1929, and the totals for the years 1922 to 1928.

Department.	1909*	1929
	No.	No.
Railway	134	130
Public Works Department	88	118
Posts and Telegraphs	12	26
Marine	28	30
Printing	2	2
Medical and Sanitation	4	3
Veterinary and Forestry	–	5
Survey	18	4
Police	13	†229
Irrigation	3	–
Miscellaneous (Laboratory Assistants, Fire-Brigade Officers, Clerks, Foremen, etc.)	40	100
	342	647

Year.	Total.
1922	350
1923	447
1924	588
1925	672
1926	726
1927	612
1928	772

*   These figures include all candidates engaged by the Crown Agents, whether the actual selection was their own work or that of the Consulting Engineers.

†   Of this total 185 were recruited for a special emergency in Palestine. /

While these figures show the increased scale of recruitment in recent years, it is necessary to explain that the later figures represent a greatly increased proportion of higher-grade fully-qualified personnel in relation to the total appointments made.

Vacancies are usually advertised in the Press by the Crown Agents. On being selected for appointment a candidate is engaged on a written agreement for a term of years, unless it is a case of / seconding from the Public Service at Home to one of the Dependencies. In the case of technical appointments, the selection is made by a board composed of a senior member of the Appointments Branch of the Crown Agents' Office, a technical assistant attached to that Branch, and a senior Colonial Official when available. When Consulting Engineers are employed, candidates are interviewed by them and recommended to the Appointments Branch. They are then interviewed by a senior member of the Branch, and the candidates selected are thereupon engaged by the Crown Agents on behalf of the

Government of the Colony concerned. Candidates for non-technical appointments are selected in the same way, but without a technical assessor.

The results of the selections by the Crown Agents are, according to the evidence which we have received, quite satisfactory. Some criticism was offered on the ground of delays in filling appointments and in a very few instances we were informed that some complaint was made that occasionally a candidate had been selected who was unsuitable from the point of view of temperament and personality. The terms of appointment and the qualifications stipulated are strictly laid down by the Colonial Governments in their instructions to the Crown Agents respecting each vacancy, and if, as sometimes happens according to our information, the emoluments offered are below the market rate, or the qualifications stipulated are too exacting in view of the material available, either delay must be expected, or a candidate will be appointed who is not in all respects up to the standard. This system of selection by the Crown Agents does not require that the names of the selected candidates should be submitted for the Secretary of State's approval. They exercise their power of appointment on behalf of a Colonial Government by virtue of their position as that Government's Agents. We take the view therefore that, both as regards their status and their practice, they are, as far as concerns their appointments work, an authority independent of the Secretary of State – a position to which we attach importance.

The Crown Agents possess many special advantages which aid them in these duties. They have available in their Office very complete information as to the nature of the works going on in each Colony, the special local conditions of concern to engineers, and the equipment locally available. They are in close and constant touch with their Consulting Engineers, who can assist in the assessment of candidates' technical qualifications. They are also in close touch with senior technical officers of the Colonial Governments, who may be on leave. They are able to establish their own most useful contacts at home which directly assist recruitment. For instance, we may refer to the scheme arranged with the Great Western Railway Company for the seconding on trial of members of the staff of that railway to the Railway Services of Colonial Governments. /

We do not recommend any alteration in the system under which such appointments to the Colonial Services are made, but we think it right to take this opportunity to offer certain observations.

The recruitment of qualified technical officers is peculiarly open to competition from private employment, and this has been especially in evidence recently with regard to electrical engineers. The qualifications usually stipulated for by Colonial Government, for instance in the case of young civil engineers, are both the possession of a University degree, or a similar professional qualification, and some period of practical engineering experience. We can well understand that often it may not be easy to find candidates satisfying these conditions, who at the same time possess the personal qualities needed for public service in the Colonies. It seems to us possible, however, that sufficient information is not yet available at likely sources, such as Universities and Technical Colleges, where prospective candidates could be informed of the opportunities in the Colonial Services open to young engineers, after qualifying and obtaining some practical experience in their profession. We suggest also that it would be an advantage if a waiting list or pool of applicants found to be qualified and suitable for appointment could be established, from which vacancies could be filled as soon as notified.

We have the further observation to offer that recruitment by Colonial Governments in all of the branches of the Services with which the Crown Agents are concerned seems to be of a spasmodic and irregular character, though its total annual volume is considerable. It is beyond doubt that the field of candidates might be improved and enlarged if it were possible for the Colonies to indicate their requirements, even if only their minimum requirements, in a bulk requisition, presented some months before the actual selection of candidates was imperative.

In particular branches of engineering work – for example, railway construction – where experience is not generally to be obtained in this country, we recommend that Colonial Governments should offer appointments of a cadet type. This would make it possible to engage young engineers on the completion of their professional studies, and then send them overseas to acquire a practical knowledge of the particular branch of engineering required.

Apart, however, from these special observations, we do not hesitate to give it as our opinion that any real improvement in the quantity and quality of the fully-trained engineering personnel required for the Colonial Services must depend on an improvement in the general rate of emoluments offered. Our evidence shows clearly that in view of the cost and duration of an engineer's training the financial inducements usually offered by the Colonial Services are not adequate. /

(*c*) *Selection by the Secretary of State for the Colonies On the recommendation of his Private Secretary* (*Appointments*). – The nature and approximate number of the appointments; made on the recommendation of the Private Secretary in 1929 is as follows:–

Administrative	115
Medical	107
Educational	62
Agricultural	35
Police	33
Survey and Geological	17
Financial	15
Forestry	13
Scientific Specialists (e.g., Botanists and Chemists)	13
Legal	11

Veterinary	11
Marine	1
Miscellaneous (e.g., Game Wardenships, Secretarial posts, Mining Appointments)	16
	449
Agricultural Scholarships*	22
The number of candidates selected in addition to the above who –	
(*a*) withdrew	65
(*b*) were found medically unfit	14
Total submissions made to the Secretary of State	550

*   The Agricultural Scholarships are scholarships maintained by contributions from the funds of the Home Government and the Colonies, which are awarded by the Secretary of State on the recommendation of the Private Secretary to candidates with suitable attainments in the science of agriculture, who undertake to accept appointments in any of the Colonies which may be offered to them on completing a special scholarship course of instruction (generally two years) in Tropical Agriculture. /

The method of selection for the appointments enumerated above, is that a candidate is required to supply the necessary detailed information as to his record – education, experience, and / so on. His referees, tutors, or employers are communicated with. Then he is summoned to London for a personal interview with the Private Secretary or one of the Assistant Private Secretaries, and in many cases an additional interview with one of the specialist Advisers at the Colonial Office, or with some other experienced consultant whom the Private Secretary customarily or occasionally asks to advise him in the work of selection.

In the case of legal, educational, agricultural, and audit appointments, it is the custom for the specialists in these subjects at the Colonial Office to interview candidates, apart from the interview with the Private Secretary or a member of his staff; and to present to the Private Secretary, as a matter of advice their impression of the relative merits of candidates, both from the point of view of their professional qualifications and their personal suitability.

In the case of medical appointments candidates are interviewed by a Medical Appointments Sub-Committee, comprising the Chief Medical Adviser at the Colonial Office, two specialists in Tropical Medicine not members of the Colonial Office, and one of the Assistant Private Secretaries. This Sub-Committee has before it all the detailed information of candidates records, etc., and makes its recommendations to the Private Secretary. In practice the large volume of these appointments continually being made has led to the majority of interviews being conducted by the two Colonial Office members without the presence of the two outside specialists.

In the case of forestry appointments there has been since 1925 a Forestry Examining Board to examine and report on the technical qualifications of candidates. The recruitment of qualified forestry officers takes place once annually, and the selection work does not therefore require continual meetings of the Board throughout the year. The Board's method is to interview candidates by arrangement with the Private Secretary (Appointments), and to present each with a series of technical forestry questions, to which they are required, to give not full written answers but the headings of answers. The Board then conduct a *viva voce* test. The Board's reports are confined to the candidates' technical knowledge of forestry, and are in the form of official reports to the Under-Secretary of State at the Colonial Office. The Board is thus not solely in an advisory position to the Private Secretary, although the responsibility for the final recommendation to the Secretary of State of a candidate for appointment rests with him.

We may at this stage refer also to the schemes which have been promoted recently to facilitate applications for Colonial appointments from suitable candidates in the Universities in the Dominions." For Canada, Australia, and New Zealand arrangements are already in force. Briefly, the machinery is for each University to appoint a member of its staff to be the Liaison Officer with the Private Secretary (Appointments) in / London, by whom he is supplied direct with information about the Services, application forms, etc. He thus becomes the centre of information in his University. He places the applications of candidates before a selection committee appointed by the University. If this committee is prepared to support the application, the Liaison Officer submits it with the Committee's report to the Dominion Liaison Officer for consideration by a Central Board of Selection appointed for the Dominion, which interviews the candidate. If the Board decides to recommend him, the candidate is medically examined as to fitness for tropical service, and the report of the Board and of the medical examination is sent to the Private Secretary in London for the candidate's merits to be considered along with those of applicants from elsewhere.[5] The system is still in its infancy, and the actual results of these arrangements, measured by the number of successful candidates, have not so far been important; but we agree with the view that on other grounds it is a sound policy and may well open up in time a field of recruitment of considerable value.

Among the most important of the branches of the Services for which the Private Secretary conducts the selection work are the Administrative Services in the Tropical African Dependencies. The vacancies are filled by group selections in August and September of each year. Recruitment is now on a greatly increased scale, as would be expected in connexion with the increased development of the Territories concerned. The figures for the last few years are

107 in 1926,
98 in 1927,
118 in 1928,
106 in 1929.

The majority of the successful candidates are recruited from the Universities. The sources of supply are as follows:–

	1926.	1927.	1928.	1929.
Universities	71	83	88	89
Service (K.A.R. & R.W.A.F.F.)	9	3	5	6
" Others	10	5	9	5
Local and Promotions	7	4	6	5
Miscellaneous	10	3	10	1
	107	98	118	106 /

Of the 17 non-University candidates in 1929, 13 had experience of dealing with native races in one way or another.[*]

There is no specialist adviser inside or outside the Colonial Office to participate in the selection work for these appointments, as is the practice with professional and technical vacancies. Nor are there any precise categories which could with advantage be laid down to govern the qualifications necessary for candidates for the work of Administration. The special needs are a liberal education, a just and flexible mind, common-sense, and a high character, and there is no calculus by which these endowments can be accurately assessed. But the Private Secretary and his staff, from their continuous close contact with the oversea Governments, are able to form a judgment of the type of endowment required and from the precise and detailed information in the records of the candidates, and evidence obtained from the Universities and elsewhere, they have a reasonable basis on which to found their assessment, supplemented, as this is, by personal interviews and special enquiries on particular points.

The evidence which we have received from Governors and senior officers of the Colonial Services, especially in Tropical Africa, leaves no room for doubt

[*]   The following is an analysis of the recruitment from the different Universities:–

	1926.	1927.	1928.	1929.
Cambridge	34	42	45	25
Oxford	20	37	39	48
Trinity College Dublin	6	2	1	9
Edinburgh	1	2	–	2
London	3	–	1	–
Glasgow	2	–	–	1
Aberdeen	2	–	–	–
Belfast	–	–	–	1
Durham	–	–	–	1
Liverpool	–	–	–	1
St. Andrews	–	–	–	1
Sheffield	1	–	–	–
Dominions Universities	2	–	2	–
Total	71	83	88	89 /

that the present method of selection has satisfied these authorities. There is, indeed, abundant proof that the standard of selected candidates has in recent years steadily improved. The work of your present Private Secretary (Appointments), Major Furse,[6] and his staff, is held in the highest esteem by the Colonial Governments.

Nevertheless, the work is of such extreme importance that it is necessary to consider whether the methods now in use do not need to be reinforced. The conditions of work in the Colonial Services are often exhausting, and a tropical climate has a testing effect upon health and character. Whole tribes and areas may / suffer disastrously from a single error of judgment on the part of one European officer. The future development of the Colonies depends upon the professional and technical competency, the integrity, and the initiative of those who administer them. The method of selection, therefore, demands the most careful study. It should be at once rigorous and elastic; it should search the widest field for the best candidates; it should provide no ground for suspicion that the best men are not selected; above all, it should have some assurance of continuity.

The present system is open to criticism, first and foremost, as being, at any rate in theory, a system of patronage. The Minister for the time being has the sole power, through his Private Secretary, over the selection of candidates. Even so, the appointments made are on such a scale that no Secretary of State in recent years has been able to take any appreciable share in the work of comparing the merits of rival candidates. It would be a rare case in which more than a single name for each vacancy, with brief particulars in support, was submitted, to him for approval The Private Secretary is assisted in his selection work by a number of Assistant Private Secretaries. Technically, both the Private Secretary and his assistant may be replaced on each change of Minister, though in practice in recent years the Appointments staff has been retained by successive Secretaries of State. We cannot escape the conclusion that, if seriously challenged, such a system could not in theory be defended. At the same time, we feel that we should be doing the system and those responsible for it less than justice if we did not add that the fact that it has not so far been called in question is a striking testimony to the work of Major Furse and his colleagues, and to the confidence felt in it by successive Ministers.

Our own decided view is that the existing arrangements should be replaced by a system of recruitment at once more authoritative and more independent. For a variety of reasons we find ourselves unable to recommend the system of open competitive written examination. Such a test for many of the appointments now dealt with by the Private Secretary would clearly be unsuitable. So far as the African Administrative Services are concerned, we are satisfied that it would be inexpedient, at any rate under existing conditions, to rely on the test of written examinations.

Our recommendation, in the case of all appointments made through the machinery of the Private Secretary is that the appointing staff cease to be in the position of private secretaries to the Secretary of State, and that the Appointments branch be incorporated in the Colonial Office as a permanent part of a Personnel Division of that Office. The duties of the branch would be to continue all the activities of the present Appointments Branch – the liaison work with possible sources of recruitment and the preliminary sifting of candidates, with a view to submitting for each vacancy a short list of suitable names from which the final selection would be made by a Colonial Service Appointments / Board, to be set up as a standing independent Board. The Board's selections would be submitted to the Secretary of State, on whose authority the appointments would then be made. We recommend also, that the Board shall have the oversight of the machinery of recruitment for first appointment and shall have the power to suggest changes of method to the Secretary of State.

In considering the composition of such a Board it is necessary to avoid any proposal which would have the effect of delaying the appointments work. Though the recruitment for certain important branches of the Services is seasonal, there is, nevertheless, a not inconsiderable number of submissions to the Secretary of State being made throughout the whole year. It may be useful to give the figures for the last three years:–

	1927.	1928.	1929.
January	26	43	25
February	29	35	22
March	32	40	28
April	24	21	27
May	50	26	22
June	35	31	51
July	68	82	106
August	73	111	143
September	75	94	54
October	53	41	29
November	40	34	16
December	56	34	26
	561	592	549

An analysis of these figures shows that the bulk of the appointments to the Administrative, Educational, Agricultural, Forestry, and Police Services are made in the months July to September, but the appointments to other branches, and particularly to the Medical Services, are more evenly distributed throughout the year. The Colonial Services Appointments Board must therefore be composed in such a way as to enable it to meet at regular intervals throughout the year – probably two or three times a month – with more frequent sessions in the summer months.

We recommend that the Board consist of a Chairman and two other persons all of whom should be nominated by the Civil Service Commission, and one of whom should have had recent experience of service in the Colonies.

An impression, which is in need of correction, exists that for appointments in which a University standard of education is needed, candidates are mainly sought from Oxford or Cambridge. We have made a careful examination on this point. The / total figures for the three years 1927–29 of successful University candidates selected by the Private Secretary for the main classes of post for which University men are normally selected are as follows:–

Cambridge	211
Oxford	198
London	108
Edinburgh	91
Glasgow	48
Trinity College, Dublin	41
Dominions and Overseas	35
Aberdeen	34
Agricultural Colleges	30
Birmingham	16
Leeds	14
Liverpool	13
Belfast	12
Bristol	12
St. Andrews	11
Wales	11
Durham	10
National University of Ireland (and Royal College of Science for Ireland)	8
Reading	7
Sheffield	5
Exeter University College	1
Nottingham University College	1
Total, Oxford and Cambridge	409
Total, other Universities	518
Grand Total	927

An analysis of these figures shows that for medical appointments, the Medical Schools in London were by far the largest source of supply: for Forestry, Edinburgh was the principal source; for Agriculture, Wye College.[7] For the aggregate of the scientific appointments (except medical) of a specialist and research type for the years 1927–29, London (including the Imperial College of Science) comes first with 16 appointments out of 71: Cambridge and Edinburgh 9 each: Oxford 7: Leeds and Dominion Universities 4 each: Aberdeen and Glasgow 3 each: Birmingham, Liverpool, St. Andrews, and the University of Wales 2 each: and one each from Durham, Manchester, Midland, Sheffield, Bristol, Nottingham, Trinity College, Dublin, and the Royal College of Science for Ireland. /

For the Education Services, an analysis of the appointments made on the selection of the Private Secretary shows that in 1927 Cambridge produced a great majority of successful candidates, while in 1928–1929 Oxford led by a large margin. In the last year London took second place and Cambridge third. For the Tropical African Administrative Services, as shown earlier in this part of our Report, Oxford and Cambridge in 1929 provided 73 out of the 89 successful University candidates. For appointments in the non-scientific Services as a whole, for which recruitment is mainly from the Universities, the results for the last three years are: Oxford 173, Cambridge 168, other Universities 91.

These figures serve to show that there is no real ground for the suggestion that the older Universities have anything like a monopoly of the Colonial appointments. In the matter of certain classes of specialist posts, neither Oxford nor Cambridge is the chief source of recruitment. For appointments in the Administrative Services, however, which are in many ways the most attractive and important, the two older Universities provide by far the greater number of successful candidates, and for this we believe there are cogent reasons. At the older Universities there is a long tradition of public service overseas. For India, Egypt, the Sudan, and the Diplomatic Service young men have for many years been taken principally from Oxford and Cambridge.

Under a system of selection it is not surprising that these two Universities have been regarded as the main recruiting centres for the Colonial Administrative Services, attributable no doubt to the personal qualities which those in high office in the Colonies associate with students at these seats of learning and their confidence in the schools from which students flow to them.

Though they would not claim that the qualities which they regard as essential in an administrative officer, namely vision, high ideals of service, fearless devotion to duty born of a sense of responsibility, tolerance, and above all the team spirit are a monopoly of the products of the Public Schools and Oxford and Cambridge, they undoubtedly believe that administrative recruits drawn from these sources are more certain to possess them than those drawn from schools and universities about which they know little. Another factor has to be taken into account, the new Universities have specialized in training students for the professions, for example medicine, engineering, science, education. It was inevitable, therefore, in the post-war period of expansion of the Colonial Services, that the efforts of the small recruiting staff under the Private Secretary (Appointments) should have been concentrated on those centres where the quickest results could be obtained. Oxford and Cambridge were clearly the most promising as regards the Administrative Services, other centres – in particular the Universities of London, Edinburgh, and Glasgow – were looked to for well qualified recruits for the Medical, Scientific, and Agricultural services. /

Nevertheless, the fact that it is mainly from the universities other than Oxford and Cambridge that the supply of recruits for the Colonial specialist services is obtained proves that there is no general disinclination on the part of students of these universities to embark on a career overseas. We are of opinion, therefore, that a greater effort should now be made to attract such students for administrative service, and to remove any impression which may exist amongst them that as candidates for that branch they are at a disadvantage in competition with Oxford and Cambridge men. We do not, however, mean to suggest that suitable applicants are likely to be recruited from other centres in such numbers as may be expected from Oxford and Cambridge. That the preponderance of candidates selected from those two Universities does not necessarily arise from a system of selection, as opposed to one of written examination, is illustrated by the fact that of the 35 successful European candidates at the open competitive examination in 1929 for the Indian Civil Service, 27 were drawn from Oxford and Cambridge.

The increased urgency of recruitment since the War has been recognized by the increase of the Private Secretary's establishment. In 1919 the Private Secretary (Appointments) was given two temporary assistants; in 1923 a junior member of the established Civil Service in the Colonial Office was attached to the Appointments Branch; in 1926 the addition of one temporary Assistant and one more junior member of the Colonial Office staff was sanctioned. Apart from these, additions have been made from time to time to the clerical staffs of the Branch. But in each case the additional staff was sanctioned in order to give some relief to pressure of work already existing, and in these circumstances the bulk of the recruiting effort has been naturally directed towards centres from which experience proved that the best and quickest results could be expected. We suggest that it might be worth consideration whether, for the purpose of assisting in the task of interviewing, the existing practice of making use of carefully chosen officers of the Colonial Services while on leave should not be still further developed; This might be done by forming a panel of such officers from which one or more could be selected from time to time to take part in the work according to their convenience and to the number of vacancies to be filled.

We are confident that the staff organization required for the new Appointments Branch of the Personnel Division of the Colonial Office, which we propose should be set up, will be established on a basis sufficiently broad to ensure that there shall be no ground for such criticism as we have indicated above; and that on this special work – special in the sense that it must be done by a staff possessing the special capacity needed both for assessing the personal qualities of applicants and for the wise and sympathetic handling of *persons* as opposed to *subjects* such as / Treaties, Finance, Communications – a sufficient expert personnel will be employed on a scale commensurate with the importance of the issues at stake.

We would repeat our former recommendation that in building up the revised organization it is most desirable to perpetuate the excellent tradition of the present Appointments Branch and that therefore full use should be made of the experienced staff at present employed in it.

We have suggested that the field of recruitment for the Colonial Services should be extended so as to embrace all the home Universities and if possible the Universities in the Dominions. The officers of the Appointments Branch, while maintaining the already established connections with the older Universities, through the students' societies, the Appointments Boards, and the heads of University Faculties, should be encouraged to stimulate the interest of students and university authorities in other centres in Colonial appointments. Recruitment at Oxford and Cambridge has been greatly assisted by the personal visits of Major Furse, Colonial administrators on leave, and the political and administrative heads of the Colonial Office where they have been able by arrangement through the Appointments Boards to address groups of students on the opportunities for careers in the Colonial Empire. There can be no doubt that visits of this kind are especially valuable aids to recruitment, and we advise that every effort should be made to develop the practice in the other universities. Much, too, might be done to direct a flow of desirable candidates from the civic and provincial universities to the Colonial Services by means of informative articles written by recognised authorities for College Magazines and the journal of the National Union of Students; we have every reason to believe that the last-named body would be willing to give active assistance to the Colonial Appointments Branch in putting before students the facts relating to Colonial Appointments.

We should like to stress one other point in connection with the recruitment work; we feel that the effectiveness of the Appointments Branch will be conditioned to a certain extent by the first-hand knowledge of life in the Colonies possessed by the Appointments staff at the Colonial Office. It is important therefore that they should be given every opportunity by means of visits to Colonies to acquire this knowledge.

(d) *Appointments made by the Secretary of State on the recommendation of other Government Departments.* – We do not advise that any alteration in the system of selection for these classes should be made, where in fact an independent authority does already carry out the work. In any cases which may arise of a Department recommending to the Colonial Office a short list of qualified candidates, by which we mean more than one name, leaving the final selection to be carried out in the Colonial Office, we recommend that the selection should be placed in the hands of / the Colonial Service Appointments Board, unless other arrangements, such as those for Military and for Posts and Telegraphs personnel, already exist for an independent authority to undertake the duty. On a comparatively minor aspect of these appointments, we recommend that the Appointments Branch in the Colonial Office should handle the correspondence with other Government Departments regarding vacancies of this nature. In the case of the Overseas Nursing Association, however, we see no reason for any alteration of the existing routine practice, by which the several Geographical Departments of the Colonial Office transmit to the Association the requisitions of Colonial Governments, and effect the appointment of candidates recommended by the Association.

C. – PROMOTIONS IN THE COLONIAL SERVICES.

Apart from the recruitment of fresh candidates to the Colonial Services our terms of reference require us to consider the system of filling appointments by the promotion or transfer of officers already serving.

This is in the main a matter which concerns the more senior appointments, but it not infrequently happens that quite junior appointments in those Colonies where the staffs are larger, the prospects better, and the range of salaries higher, are filled by the transfer of officers from other Colonies.

The machinery at the Colonial Office for dealing with promotions and transfers consists of a Promotions Branch, which is a branch of the General Division.[8] As regards administrative staff, the work occupies the part time of a Principal and an Assistant Secretary, the latter being of the same status as the Heads of the several Geographical Departments of the Office. The Promotions Branch is responsible for recording the annual confidential reports "by each Governor on the officers of the local Service; the individual applications for transfer which any officers may make; and all other available information, bearing on the professional qualifications, record, experience, personal qualities and inclinations of all officers who may either of their own motion be applicants, or in the view of their Governor or of the Colonial Office may be deserving of consideration for promotion in the "Colonial Service," whether within or without the Colony in which they may be serving. We mark the expression "Colonial Service," since in this connexion alone do we find it officially sanctioned as though there were a single Service and not a number of separate, independent Services, a problem with which we deal particularly in Part III of this Report.

Many of the vacancies occurring in all grades of a Colonial Administration are of course filled by local promotion. But, as stated earlier in our Report, the Secretary of State's approval is needed for all except relatively subordinate appointments, and / this requirement gives the opportunity to consider, along with those of any local officer recommended by the Governor, the relative merits of officers who are in the service of other Colonies. In many instances the Governor himself may recommend that a vacant appointment should be filled from outside the Colony.

An officer already serving in one of the Colonial Administrations is, rightly in our opinion, regarded as having a prior claim to consideration over an applicant from outside the service, provided that both are equally suitable according to the qualifications required. It happens therefore that, in the case of many vacancies not only in the higher ranks of a Colonial Administration but also in appointments of a junior character which are usually filled by the selection of outside candidates, a notification of the vacancy may be sent in the first place to the Promotions Branch of the Colonial Office by the particular Geographical branch concerned in order that they may consider whether in their lists there are suitable officers in any Colonial Service who would be attracted by the vacant appointment. The total number of vacancies referred to the Promotions Branch in 1929 was 322. If the Branch have no names to put forward from their lists, the vacancy will be remitted to the Private Secretary, the Crown Agents, or whoever may be the appropriate recruiting authority for selecting an outside candidate. If there are suitable names forthcoming from the Promotions Branch, the vacancy will be placed before a standing Office Committee – the Promotions Committee – for a recommendation to be made. In practice, if there are only one or two names, a selection would be made by consultation between the Departments concerned, and a recommendation made to the Secretary of State without reference to the Committee.

The appointments of Governors and Colonial Secretaries are not dealt with by the Promotions Committee, but are the subject of advice given direct to the Secretary of State by the Permanent Under-Secretary of State, after consultation with the Assistant Under-Secretaries. The Committee are, however, frequently asked to advise upon the relative merits of possible candidates for the smaller Colonial Secretaryships. Special lists of the senior officers of the Colonial Services deserving consideration for such promotion are kept in the Promotions Branch for the convenience of the authorities mentioned.

The Promotions Committee meets once a week, if the business so requires. It consists of an Assistant Under-Secretary of State (Chairman): the Legal Adviser: the Assistant Secretary in charge of the Promotions Branch: the seven Assistant Secretaries in charge of the Geographical Departments: an Assistant Secretary of the Dominions Office: the Private Secretary (Appointments): and the Principal concerned in the Promotions Branch. In addition, according to the nature of the vacancy, the appropriate Specialist Adviser attends the meeting; in the case of an Engineer vacancy, one of the Crown Agents or a member of his staff. /

The members of the Committee, having already received from the Promotions Branch a statement of particulars of the vacancy and the names of candidates, including any local officer recommended by the Governor, with a summary of the information about each, meet and on a majority vote make a selection for submission to higher authority. If they consider none suitable, they may recommend that the vacancy be remitted to the recruiting authority for an outside candidate. If there are good outside candidates known to be available, the Committee may in any instance be notified of the particulars of such candidates to assist them in their comparative view of the Colonial Service candidates.

In 1929 the number of vacancies considered by the Promotions Committee was 103. The total number of vacancies filled by transfer was recorded in the same year as 70.

On the basis of the evidence we have received we have certain criticisms and proposals to make under this head. As a result of a Report by a Colonial Office Committee, which in 1927 considered the question of the organization of the Department, the Promotions Branch of the Colonial Office was reorganized and its efficiency improved. In particular our evidence suggests that the presence and interest of the several Specialist Advisers appointed during the last few years have had very appreciable results in improving the Promotions work so far as concerns their particular branches. Nevertheless, though we gladly recognize the excellent work which has been done by the existing Promotions staff, there are still improvements which might be effected, but which would require some slight increase of staff for their fulfilment. The provision of such a staff is involved in the proposals of this Report.

We have formed the opinion, from our own investigations and from the statements of many witnesses, that the system of annual confidential reports on officers which are rendered by the several Governors, though adequate in theory, has in practice not always proved satisfactory. We are given to understand that, in the case of certain Colonies, these reports have in the past been received only after a considerable interval of time, and sometimes not at all, and that in some cases only the senior officers of the Administration are thus reported upon. We need hardly emphasize how desirable it is that such Reports should be rendered regularly and fully in the case of all officers who might, however remotely, be considered as possible candidates for promotion or transfer.

It may be convenient at this stage to record a suggestion which we believe to be worthy of support, that the various authorities at home and overseas who have to concern themselves with Promotions work should, in the case of vacant appointments in the Administrative branch, include in their review of possible candidates any suitable officers of technical departments who have shown exceptional capacity of an administrative order, and who would like to be considered for such transfer. /

Our attention has been called to the great importance of the closest co-operation between the Promotions Branch and the other Departments of the Colonial Office, and to the necessity of the Promotions Branch being furnished with very complete information and personal knowledge regarding the officers noted on their lists. We are in full agreement as to the importance of this point.

The Colonial Regulations while requiring all officers of the Colonial Service to report in writing their arrival home do not, on account of the large number of officers coming on leave and of the fact that their homes are scattered all over the country, definitely require such officers to report in person at the Colonial Office, but nevertheless many senior officers in fact make a practice of doing so. In so far as this is not done already, we think it desirable that with the enlarged Promotions Branch which we propose, it should be the normal procedure for the Geographical Departments of the Colonial Office to keep that Branch informed of the arrival on leave of all officers noted on the lists for promotion or transfer, in order that, if it should be so desired, these officers may be requested to call and interview a member of the Promotions Branch. The Promotions Branch would in this way not have to rely solely on a chance visit from such officers. We are convinced that the more an enlarged Promotions staff is able to obtain information and advice from Governors, Heads of Departments, and other senior officials when they are available in this country in person, the easier will it be to make the best use of the personnel in the Colonial Services. We think that our proposals will enable more to be done in this direction than has been possible with the existing staff.

We are aware of the great difficulties in the way of inter-Colonial promotions due mainly to the fact that each territory maintains its own independent Service. We are also aware that a complete assimilation of the conditions and terms of service in all the several territories has been regarded as impracticable. Some territories are large and rich, others are small and poor; the local climate, local cost of living, and a hundred other circumstances hinder, and to some extent prevent, uniformity throughout the Dependencies. All these difficulties give the central handling in the Colonial Office of the question of inter-Colonial promotions a special importance. The comparatively short career of a European in the Tropical Colonial Services – some 30 years of active service at the most – calls for a policy of the early and rapid promotion of the best officers in whatever Colony they may receive their first appointment, if the fullest use is to be made of them in high positions of responsibility. The constant need to improve the quality and prestige of Colonial service requires that it should offer a career in which the prizes go to merit, and the only value of seniority is the value of the experience which it has brought. In Part III of this Report we make a recommendation as to the organization of the Colonial / Services which, in the light of the evidence received, is in our view a matter of principal importance for the furtherance of this policy.

The recommendations which at this stage we make about the Promotions organization are designed to ensure

(1) that there will be no risk of omitting to note officers who are deserving to be considered for promotion in any of the higher appointments in the Dependencies;

(2) that the most complete information may be obtained and recorded about them, so that on the occurrence of any suitable vacancy the work of selection shall not be hampered;

(3) that individual vacancies are not handled in the Promotions Branch as isolated occurrences, but as part of a large general plan to secure that the most suitable officers of the Colonial Administrations are appointed to such posts as will be to the best advantage of the Service;

(4) that on this special work – special for several of the reasons which we have already mentioned in the case of the Appointments Branch – a sufficient expert personnel may be employed on a scale which will enable considerably more detailed attention to be given to it than can safely be looked for under the existing arrangements.

We recommend that the Promotions Branch in the Colonial Office be separated from the General Division and form a section of the Personnel Division, the creation of which we have proposed. To this Personnel Division we propose elsewhere that, besides the Appointments and Promotions work, there shall also be entrusted certain other business at present allocated to the General Division, which relates particularly to matters of personnel in the Colonial Services, discipline, pension, honours, etc.

Regarding the existing Promotions Committee itself, we suggest that it should be reorganized on a smaller scale. As a standing Committee for its present purpose we believe that a body of 13 persons, with the addition of one of the Specialist Advisers in certain cases, is too large for the effective weighing of the rival merits of candidates. We have been informed that the advantage of having as members the Heads of each of the seven Geographical Departments is that it goes some way to ensure that there is present at the Committee some one person at least who has personal knowledge of each of the candidates under consideration, and that they constitute a valuable "jury" for arriving at a fair selection from the names before them. We believe that the first of these advantages should more properly be looked for from the staff of the Promotions Branch, in so far as it is a case of knowledge pertinent to the candidate's comparative suitability for promotion, and under the new arrangements which we propose we should in due course expect an enlarged Promotions Branch to be in / a position to supply it. We recommend that the existing Committee should be replaced by a much smaller body, presided over by the Permanent Under-Secretary of State or his Deputy: and we suggest that the Heads of Departments and Specialist Advisers particularly concerned in any vacancy should, as necessary, be invited to attend the meetings in an advisory capacity.

D. – The Highest Offices.

In concluding this part of our Report we venture to offer an observation on the subject of the appointments to the highest offices in the Colonies.

We have referred to the special method adopted in considering persons for the appointment of Governors of Colonies, and we are aware that in the majority of cases such appointments are the prizes given to the best officers of the Colonial Services as the culminating opportunity of their overseas careers. The outstanding influence and importance of the Governor in his Colony is such that only the most proven and experienced men can be regarded as suitable for such appointments. We therefore recommend that the quest for Governors should first be made among officers holding high appointments in the Colonial Services, and that only after the qualifications of such have been fully considered should the question arise of an appointment from outside the Service. We believe that such a declaration of policy would be a valuable encouragement to, and would increase the prestige of, the whole overseas Service. [...][9]

PART III.
UNIFICATION OF THE COLONIAL SERVICES.

I. – The Present Position.

At nearly every stage of our enquiry we have been faced with the difficulties arising out of the independence of each Colony's Service and the lack of a central control securing a reasonable relation between the salary schemes and other terms of service in the different Administrations, except in respect of certain services regionally grouped. The general situation is that in the past each Territory has set up its own distinct Service, and, subject to the approval of the Colonial Office, has laid down its own terms for its own staff. From time to time a successful effort has been made to co-ordinate to some extent the terms of service in neighbouring Colonies, for instance in the West African and the East African groups. In the Straits Settlements and the Malay States, too, there has been introduced an increasing element of combined Services for the whole of Malaya.

The question of creating a general Colonial Service was discussed at the instance of Mr. Joseph Chamberlain[10] in 1899, but the project was allowed to lapse in the face of the obstacles which presented themselves. In his view at that time the principal obstacle seemed to be the severity of the tropical climate in certain Dependencies, which made it impracticable to include those Territories within a single Colonial Service the members of which would have to accept the liability of serving in any region. In the last 30 years, however, the advance in the science of tropical medicine and in the provision of sanitary services in West Africa has effected nothing less than a revolution in the resisting power of Europeans to climatic conditions. We may quote a passage from Mr. Ormsby Gore's[11] report on his visit to West Africa in 1926 (Cmd. 2744):–

"When the cause and the method of transmission of malaria was discovered by the great work of Sir Ronald Ross and Sir Patrick Manson, the first great step was taken to make the conditions of life in West Africa more possible for Europeans. It is difficult, less than thirty years after that discovery, to realize with what scepticism it was at first received, and further to realize the difficulty which medical and administrative officers had, and indeed still have in places, in getting the danger of the mosquito adequately recognized. However, with the aid of anti-mosquito measures, and the regular use of quinine as a prophylactic, the risk of malaria in the main centres is now becoming less and less every year. The results of these measures, of sanitation generally, of improved houses and of wider knowledge of the causes of disease, are reflected in the steady decrease in the death-rate of the European officials, which has fallen from 20.6 per thousand in 1903, to 12.8 per thousand in 1924, while the invaliding rate has dropped from 65.1 to 21.7 per thousand in the same period."* /

In 1901, in order to make the conditions of service for Medical Officers in West Africa more attractive, it was decided to amalgamate the separate Medical Services of the six West African Colonies and Protectorates into a single West African Medical Staff, with liability to serve in any Territory in the group and with uniform terms of service for all members of the Staff.

In 1910, the model of the West African Medical Staff was referred to a Colonial Office Committee for the purpose of considering to what extent the Services of the East and West African Dependencies could with advantage be assimilated on the lines of the Medical Services. That Committee in an Interim Report made the following observations:–

"There is no room for doubt, we think, as to the desirability of introducing some measure of uniformity in the rates of salary attached to similar appointments in the different Colonies; and such a reform is especially desirable in the case of the administrative services, with which this report is mainly concerned, in view of the fact that these services are now recruited from batches of candidates who are selected from one list, undergo an identical course of training, and in many cases are not allotted definitely to their appointments, except as between West Africa and East Africa, until their two months' course of preliminary training is on the point of completion. In regard to the question of interchange there is, however, room for considerable doubt. Here it becomes a question of balancing against the advantages resulting from a wider range of experience the disadvantages of the loss of local knowledge acquired in a par-

---

*   The death-rate and invaliding-rate have continued to show a marked reduction: in 1929 they were respectively 7.7 and 10.1 a thousand.

ticular Colony. These factors, we think, may operate differently in the lower and higher ranks of the service. In the case of junior officers, who have to deal with practical administrative details rather than main lines of policy, the value of an officer's services may, we take it, be held to vary in direct ratio to the extent of his local experience. In the case, on the other hand, of an official of high standing, who can draw freely upon the knowledge of his subordinate staff in matters concerning local conditions and local practice, a wide experience may be of much higher account than local knowledge acquired at first hand. We recognize that these principles are only applicable within limits and subject to reservations, but we consider that they render impracticable any question of complete interchangeability in the lower ranks of the service, while on the other hand, we feel assured that in the higher ranks a measure of interchange intelligently directed is likely to conduce in the long run to greater efficiency, although occasionally, it may be, at the expense of temporary embarrassment."

It is not apparent from the Committee's Report that they envisaged the possibility of a unified service for the African territories. A later passage of the Report runs:–

"We have already stated our opinion that greater uniformity might with advantage be secured in rates of pay in the various Colonies and Protectorates. In support of this proposition we can, so far as the administrative services are concerned, advance no stronger argument than to call attention to the existing meaningless diversities. ..."

Since the War the rapid development of the scientific services has brought especially into prominence the urgency and difficulty of recruiting the increased specialist staff required, and a series of Committees on individual branches of the Services have pressed for a more rational organization of the Colonial Services. /

As a result of the Report of a Committee in 1920 (Cmd. 939), an amalgamation of the Medical Services of the East African Territories under the title of the East African Medical Service was carried out, and a corresponding step taken also in the Territories in the Malay Peninsula under the title of the Malayan Medical Service. In 1921, the West Indian Medical Conference meeting in British Guiana adopted a resolution in favour of the unification of the West Indies Medical Services, though without effect.

In 1920, also, a Committee reported on the Colonial Veterinary Services (Cmd. 922). As regards grading and salary scales that Committee recommended "as great a degree of uniformity as possible" between Tanganyika Territory (then recently brought under British civil administration) and the East African Protectorates; and as regards interchangeability of staff between neighbouring Colonies they reported in the following terms:–

"With a view to offering brighter prospects of promotion and advancement to the members of the smaller veterinary departments, your Committee recommended that, where possible, the system should be introduced whereby the staffs of neighbouring Colonies and Protectorates would be interchangeable. This would secure to all officers of those departments the prospect of rising to higher and more responsible positions, wherein not only would the remuneration earned be greater but their work also would be more scientifically valuable."

The Colonial Medical Services Committee to whose report we have already referred (Cmd. 939) stated that the ideal organization would be as a unified Service, but they considered that it was not at present possible. The difficulties which gave rise to this impression were set out as follows:–

". . . .each Colony is a separate Government and

"(*a*) Pays its own Medical Officers with funds derived from local taxation, with the exception of a few cases where local revenue is supplemented by a grant-in-aid from the Imperial Treasury.

"(*b*) In some Colonies the selection of candidates for medical appointments is made by the Secretary of State, whereas in others only the senior officers are so appointed, the junior officers being recruited locally and appointed by the Governor.

"(*c*) There is a wide divergence between the salaries paid on first appointment in the various Colonies. In some Colonies the salaries of the Medical Officers must be regarded as retaining fees to local practitioners for doing certain Government work, and not as remuneration for whole time appointments.

"(*d*) Racial difficulties obtain in some Colonies to a greater extent than in others.

"(*e*) The regulations as to private practice and the opportunities for such practice differ very widely.

"(*f*) In most Services the appointments are pensionable, but in a few they are not. Moreover, pension scales are not uniform.

"(*g*) The regulations as to leave and passage differ widely in the various Colonies.

"(*h*) In many Colonies knowledge of one or more local languages is very desirable." /

The advantages which the Committee saw in unification may be summarized as:–

(*a*) the recognition of the Colonial Medical Service as a distinct branch of the public Medical Service of the Empire:

(*b*) the enhanced status of the Colonial Services in the view of the medical profession:

(c) an increased attraction for recruiting purposes.

The Committee did definitely recommend that the term "Colonial Medical Service" should be adopted forthwith for appointments purposes, with if possible a single system of entry by competitive examination common to all the public Medical Services, viz., Royal Navy, Army, Royal Air Force, and India "as is done by the Civil Service Commissioners for the various Offices of the Civil Service." Other recommendations of this Committee were:–

(a) that failing a completely unified Service the Colonial Medical Service should be organized in groups corresponding to the grouping of the Dependencies according to the geographical divisions of the Colonial Office:

(b) that the complete assimilation of the Medical Services in East and West Africa should not for the present be considered on account of the prevailing economic conditions:

(c) that the policy of the unification of services and amalgamation of neighbouring units should be adopted wherever possible:

(d) that throughout the Colonial Medical Service a uniform nomenclature should be adopted for the designation of medical appointments:

(e) that the interchange of officers in the Colonial Medical Service should be facilitated alike in the interest of the officers and the Service, and that all reasonable expenses of transfer should be met from public funds:

(f) that a further review of the Colonial Medical Service should be undertaken after five years in the light of the experience gained in order that, if justified, further steps might be taken towards the formation of a 'still more' unified service.

The next important stage in this question was reached at the discussion of the subject by the Colonial Office Conference in 1927 – the first Conference of its kind to be convened by the Secretary of State for the Colonies. We quote from the published Summary of Proceedings of the Conference (Cmd. 2883):

".... there was a widespread feeling in many Dependencies, and particularly in the smaller Colonies, that in present circumstances, owing to the fact that there was no unified Colonial Service, officers, particularly in the scientific and technical branches, laboured under serious disabilities in the matter of transfers and had in many cases few or no prospects of ultimate promotion. The prevalent opinion was succinctly set out in the following extract from one of the memoranda:

'While co-ordination of political machinery in the non-self-governing Colonies is manifestly impracticable and doubtfully desirable, there would seem to be considerable scope for closer / co-ordination in the administrative system; not so much in matters of procedure but in respect of the higher personnel of the local Administrations in all departments, administrative and technical. Individual Colonies tend to become watertight compartments: the business of Government is conducted in a well-worn groove: there is not sufficient diffusion of experience and specialized knowledge to secure the steady development of this group of units as a whole. Transfers of officers seem to be opportunistic rather than systematic. The poorer Colonies have no regular facilities for calling for the advice of visiting experts in matters in which they cannot afford to employ a full-time man. Officers in the technical services in particular feel themselves hemmed in by local influences and may and often do succumb to them. They are out of touch with their colleagues in other Colonies, and there is little to promote inter-Colonial *esprit de corps* or a sense of Empire service. The general atmosphere, in short, is provincial rather than Imperial.' "

The Conference appointed a Sub-Committee to frame a scheme for the creation of a Colonial Scientific and Research Service, available for the requirements of the whole Colonial Empire. In their Report to the Conference (which is an enlightening document on the whole organization of the scientific branches of the Colonial Services), the Sub-Committee supported the principle of the ultimate creation of a unified Colonial Research Service, through the development of separate unified Research Services in the different branches of science, Medical, Agricultural, Forestry, and possibly Veterinary. The Sub-Committee recommended that the time had come for the organization of a Colonial Agricultural Research Service, and the Conference approved the general principles and objects of such an organization, and requested the Colonial Office to appoint a Committee to work out the details. The Conference also agreed that the question of wider grouping of services should be explored service by service, in order to ascertain what might be suitable areas for its application.

In 1928, the Colonial Agricultural Service Committee, appointed by the Secretary of State in pursuance of the recommendation of the Conference, made its Report (Cmd. 3049) in which was recommended the creation of a unified Colonial Agricultural Service, to include not only Research staff, but all qualified officers who might be selected out of the Agricultural Departments of the Colonial Governments.[12] The Committee proposed a definite scheme of salaries for this unified Service, and we draw attention especially to their view that the creation of the Service, with its prospect of a wide and varied career, would in itself put recruiting on an entirely new basis.

In 1929, there appeared the Report of the Colonial Veterinary Service Committee (Cmd. 3261) which recommended the creation of a unified Service, graded by classes, with a proposed scheme of salaries. In particular Colonies, where specially severe climatic conditions or the high cost of living called for some special rate of emoluments, the Committee proposed that local allowances should be given in addition to the basic rates of salary. /

II. Difficulties of Unification.

We have referred to this series of Reports in order to show that expert opinion is evidently moving towards the view that the present system of individual self-contained Services in each Colony has had its day. The increased specialization of staff and the need for specialist advice is responsible for a growing recognition of the limitations imposed by the maintenance of a system which had its value under other conditions.

The difficulties which have been hitherto regarded as forbidding such a project may be briefly set down:–

(1) the difference in the climatic and other conditions of life in the several Dependencies;

(2) the difference in the scale of salaries and other terms of service of officers serving in similar branches of the several Colonial Administrations;

(3) the personal inclinations of many officers for service in particular Territories;

(4) the consideration that, in the case of many branches of the Colonial Services, and particularly the Administrative branch, the efficiency of officers requires them to be conversant with the language, customs, etc., of the local peoples;

(5) the reluctance of many of the Colonial Governments to support any appreciable modification of the existing system of self-contained Services for each Colony, and their power in certain cases to reject financial or other proposals which have been hitherto regarded as necessary steps towards any unification.

Before we offer our observations on these objections in detail we desire to state unreservedly that there is a real value in a merely nominal unification of Colonial Services, considering the authority which the Secretary of State is in a position to exercise over appointments and terms of service. There is probably in present circumstances not so much movement of officers in the Indian Civil Service from one Provincial Administration to another or between a Province and the Government of India as there is inter-Colonial movement of officers in the Services of the different Dependencies. But the Colonial Services are deprived of that advantage and prestige which by reason of its being a unified Service accrues to the Civil Service in India. We venture to think that a part at least of the recruiting value of the Tropical African Services Course at Oxford and Cambridge[13] is derived from the impression thus conveyed of an "African Civil Service."

III. Advantage of Unification.

There is in existing circumstances a considerable measure of inter-Colonial transfers more particularly in the senior appointments. It may be fairly said that the highest appointments / in the Colonial Services are under the present system open to any officers recognized to be of outstanding merit. But what is to our mind a matter of doubt is whether, particularly in the smaller or more remote Colonies, officers of special ability do obtain recognition, or obtain it in time, by having the chance of showing their capacity in sufficiently responsible positions. We believe that the chief advantages to be gained from a unification of the Colonial Services would be –

(1) A wider recognition of the principle of the inter-Colonial movement of officers particularly in the professional and technical branches of the Service;

(2) The increased prospect of a career of oversea public service unlimited to a particular Dependency or a particular regional group of Dependencies, and of promotion on the ground of merit to the highest appointments in the Colonial Service;

(3) A great addition to the prestige of Colonial service, with its consequent effect both on recruitment and on serving officers.

These are not merely attractions in the interest of recruitment, but sound and essential principles to be applied in the interest of keenness and efficiency of the Public Service. As an ideal, unification has, as we have shown, received at least lip service on many previous occasions. Some of the practical difficulties which years ago loomed so large do not now appear so formidable, while fresh obstacles which now obstruct the road might then have been brushed aside. But the need of efficient service, the penalties of failure, the complexity of the Government machine, the opportunity of results of first-rate importance, all these are greater now. If a more economical and, in our opinion, more effective organization is to be achieved, the present is not the time for it, for, if we delay, it may become for ever impracticable.

If the objections we have mentioned are examined, we would first draw attention to the fact that by various means the rigour of life in the tropic for Europeans has been very appreciably mitigated. Recent experience shows that the deterrent effect of, for instance, the climate of West Africa has not to anything approaching the old degree the adverse influence on recruitment and transfers. It still admittedly exists, particularly in the minds of parents, but it is no longer a formidable hindrance. In the case of Colonial Agricultural Scholars, who are required to undertake that on completing their scholarship term they will accept appointment in any of the Colonies, we understand that it is rare to find an applicant who declines the offer of a scholarship on account of the liability to serve in West Africa. As for transfers / and promotions, of the last fifty offers made (the information was received at the end of January) two were declined for health reasons*

To the objection that terms and conditions of service in the different Dependencies show so much variety, we would reply that it has been in fact found possible to remove many of the "meaningless diversities" which at one time existed and that very considerable progress has been made in the assimilation of the terms and conditions of service in the four West African Colonies and in the East African group. As between East and West Africa there is sufficient relation between the terms of service, the scale of salaries, etc., to enable transfers to be carried out without undue difficulty. In Tropical Africa a sustained if not intensive effort had been directed to obtain a measure of uniformity. The results suggest that some relation between the scale of salaries and other terms of service, not necessarily in the sense of the adoption of identical schemes, could be also expected if a similar effort were to be directed to the Colonial Empire as a whole. This view is supported by the recent successful attempt to remove an old difficulty in respect of pensions for mixed Colonial service, and further by the testimony of those expert Committees which have, in the case of the Agricultural and Veterinary Services, recently considered it practicable even to recommend the adoption of a uniform scheme of salaries throughout all the Dependencies.

As regards the personal inclinations of officers for service in a particular Territory, this factor must naturally remain prominent so long as separate Services exist for each Colony, with the impression that the prospect of ultimately obtaining a transfer is remote. In a system of unified Services one need not hesitate to assume that such personal inclinations (which could in practice be met to an extent no less than is possible at present) are not so likely to be pressed. The need for a knowledge of the local language and peoples, especially in the case of the Administrative staff, is a difficulty which we appreciate. But it is not a difficulty in the way of a unification of the Colonial Administrative Service. The same difficulty exists for instance in India, while there is probably as much variety in local languages in Nigeria as in the whole of the rest of the Dependencies put together. We do not for a moment suggest that, during their early years of service, officers of such branches of the Services as the Administrative or Police should be normally moved from one Colony to another. Possibly in the case of such officers some minimum period of service in the Colony of first appointment should be usually required before a transfer would be considered. For the higher appointments, a personal knowledge of local languages and peoples / is, according to the evidence before us, not so essential as the selection of the best

* One concerned a transfer from South Africa to East Africa and the other from the West Atlantic to West Africa.

officers from the widest field. The wider an officer's experience the more adaptable he may be expected to show himself in regard to local conditions at first novel to him, while at the same time he is equipped with a store of comparative knowledge. Nor do we suggest that the system should be carried to the length of becoming a positive hindrance to the local promotion of officers of first-rate ability. Our recommendations elsewhere in the Report – in the matter of the long salary scales for instance – will have made it clear that we have no such intention. Our sole object is to remove obstacles to the promotion of the best officers wherever they may be serving.

The last of the difficulties set out above – that which may arise from the apprehensions of certain Colonial Governments – seems to us to be the one which most calls for attention. We have already quoted the passage in the Report of the Colonial Office Conference (1927) which explained the prevalent opinion in the Colonies of this question. We make no suggestion as to the degree of political autonomy which each Colonial Government at present or hereafter may enjoy. Our plea for the realignment of the Colonial Services is directed only to the "rationalization" of the staff organization as it concerns the personnel normally recruited in this country. Our sole aim is to assure the maintenance and improvement of the quantity and quality needed for the Public Service overseas, and the efficiency and prospects of service officers. We believe that our proposals are calculated to raise the prestige of the Colonial Service, and to secure, as far as is humanly possible, that the best officers shall have the chance of rising to the top. Participation in a scheme of unified Services would, it seems to us, bring substantial benefits to all Colonies which rely for their supervisory personnel on recruitment from home. For the smaller Colonies it would have additional and special advantages.

The proposals which we make involve in the first place the recognition of a single Colonial service, and in the second place, within this larger whole, the unification of special services such as Agriculture, Medicine, Education, etc.

It is an issue of the very first importance from the point of view of Colonial development. Much of the information on which it rests cannot be present in the minds of Governors or their advisers overseas, since it related particularly to questions of Home recruitment, and to the difficulties of individual Colonies. It is therefore a project which can be best promoted from home, and in which the Colonial Office must naturally take the initiative. Unification does not, as we have already suggested, necessarily involve undue interference with the local staff in any Colony. The Colonial Audit Service is an example of a service which calls for virtually no interference in practice with the Governor's control of the staff / of his Administration*

---

*   We recognize. of course, that both the position and work of the Colonial Audit Service is of a very special character. Virtually, it constitutes a staff of officers appointed by the Secretary of State to audit on his behalf the accounts of Colonial Governments.. Nor is

We recommend that this considered proposal be brought to the notice of the Governors and other Colonial representatives for discussion at the forthcoming Colonial Office Conference. The support of the oversea Governments is, we recognize, essential if the project if to be launched under conditions favourable to its success. Thereafter a Committee should, we suggest, be appointed to draw up a complete and detailed scheme for each branch of service, together with the general and special regulations which would be required to bring the new policy into effect. /

PART IV.
SUMMARY OF RECOMMENDATIONS.

1. In the case of all appointments now made through the machinery of the Private Secretary (Appointments) the appointments staff should cease to be in the position of Private Secretaries and the Appointments Branch should be incorporated in the Colonial Office as a permanent part of a Personnel Division of the Office.

2. A Colonial Service Appointments Board, consisting of a Chairman and two members – all to be nominated by the Civil Service Commission – should be set up as a standing, independent Board for the final selection of candidates for all such appointments, their selections being submitted to the Secretary of State on whose authority the appointments would then be made. The Board should also have the oversight of the machinery of recruitment for all first appointments.

3. The Promotions Branch of the Colonial Office should be separated from the General Division, and should be developed as a section of the proposed Personnel Division.

4. The Promotions Committee should be reorganized on a smaller scale.

5. The selection of Governors, prior to consideration should be given to the suitability of officers holding high offices in the Colonial Services.

6. The long salary scale system should be retained but
   (a) the scales should be prolonged up to £1,000 in cases where at present they stop should of four figures by a small margin.

---

a provision of central funds an essential first stage, though some scheme of related salary scales would be involved, and would, in certain instances, we think, require an inconsiderable revision of existing salary schemes in particular Dependencies. Similarly, some assimilation of other terms of service would be needed, such as leave and passage conditions, and in particular, the grant of free passages to officers on transfer. The terms of future appointments would have to provide that appointment would be to the Colonial Service in one of its particular branches for duty in the first instance in a territory stated, but with a liability to serve in future anywhere within the Colonial Empire.

(b) Above some middle point in the scale a number of posts of suitable importance should be designated as higher-grade posts to be filled by selection on the sole basis of merit from all officers on the scale whether in the upper or lower half.

7. Free passages on leave should be granted to officers and their families by Colonial Governments.

8. The arrangements for the various courses of instruction should be carried out in the proposed Personnel Division of the Colonial Office.

9. With regard to the Tropical African Services Course, it is desirable to aim at creating an effective link between the separate courses by means of a combined examination in the subjects of instruction common to each course. The desirability of instituting parallel courses at centres other than Oxford and Cambridge should be borne in mind in relation to the scale of recruitment.

10. Every encouragement should be given to the development of arrangements for study leave whether at home or in Colonial Territories.

11. Every encouragement should be given to the fullest interchange in practice between the Secretariat and the rest of the Administrative Staff in a Dependency.

12. A longer term of duty than is customary at present should be adopted in the case of officers of the Colonial Services who are attached for temporary service in the Colonial Office. The system should be developed, so as to permit of the attachment of senior as well as junior officers, and of an increase in the number of officers concerned.

13. The members of the Administrative staff of the Colonial Office who in accordance with the existing policy are to be afforded an opportunity of gaining overseas experience early in their careers should be given opportunities subsequently of renewing their personal impressions of tropical conditions.

14. A single Colonial Service should be created, and within this larger whole unified special services should be organized with the necessary degree of assimilation of the terms of service in the separate Dependencies.

In conclusion we desire to record our very real feelings of gratitude to our Secretary, Mr. G. E. J. Gent, whose wide knowledge of the subject matter of our enquiry and unfailing resourcefulness have been of the greatest assistance to us.

N. F. WARREN FISHER (*Chairman*).
HESKETH BELL.
JOHN BUCHAN.
A. G. CHURCH.
J. B. FARMER.
R. W. HAMILTON.
R. S. MEIKLEJOHN.
CYRIL NORWOOD.
WALTER R. B. RIDDELL.
H. A. ROBERTS.
R. R. SCOTT.
G. J. F. TOMLINSON.
S. H. WILSON.

G. E. J. GENT,
   Secretary.
24th April, 1930

'Recruitment in Colonial Service', *Nature*, 125:3164 (1930), pp. 917–20.

A SHORT time ago a Committee was appointed, under the chairmanship of Sir Warren Fisher,[1] to report on the "System of Appointment in the Colonial Office and the Colonial Services"; its report, which has been recently issued, merits careful consideration. In an opening section attention is directed to the extraordinary diversity of the territories administered by the Colonial Office, covering an area of two million square miles, practically all within the tropics, with a population of nearly fifty millions. Although often alluded to as the 'Colonial Service', in effect there is no such thing, as the Colonial Secretary has to deal with the affairs of more than fifty distinct governments, ruling territories in size from as large as Central Europe down to remote island groups; conditions of life, material equipment, and economic factors being entirely dissimilar.

Recruitment to fill the government posts in these diverse governments has developed in the past in a haphazard fashion under varying conditions, depending more on the ideas of a local governor for the time being than upon those of the authorities in Great Britain. Since the Armistice, matters have greatly improved and the number of posts has increased. In 1909 the appointments made by the Colonial Office numbered 657; in 1929 they rose to 1076, and this in spite of the fact that many classes of appointments, which were normally filled from Great Britain twenty years ago, are now staffed locally. But the Committee insists on the fact that this is not merely a matter of numbers. "Modern conditions demand also a generally higher standard of personal, educational, and professional qualifications, and in addition the employment of men with scientific and special attainments of a kind not previously to be found in the Colonial Service." It is the Committee's recommendations on this latter part of the problem which it is proposed to consider here.

It will be necessary, however, to summarise briefly the excellent exposition given in the Report of the present system of appointment to the various Colonial Services (it is not proposed to dwell on the internal administration of the Office at home), and the recommendations made for its improvement. Apart from local recruitment, the selection of home candidates for employment in the

Colonial Services is made in four chief ways: *(a)* The Civil Service Commissioners in London hold periodical examinations for the selection of candidates for Eastern Cadetships (administrative appointments in Ceylon, / Malaya, Hong-Kong, etc.), for the Ceylon police and for the post and telegraph services in Nigeria and the Gold Coast; *(b)* the Crown Agents to the Colonies select and appoint on behalf of Government candidates for technical posts, such as railways, public works, and so on, the selected men serving for a term of years; *(c)* the Private Secretary (Appointments) to the Secretary of State, aided by a strong staff, selects and recommends to the Secretary of State outside candidates for a first appointment in the Services; *(d)* other departments of the Home Government are asked, where necessary, to select from their staffs men with the desired qualifications to fill certain appointments overseas. These departments are the War Office, Post Office, Customs and Education, Home Office and Air Ministry.

It will be evident from the above résumé how varied have been the methods which have grown up with the object of securing quantity, quality, and variety of the staff required to carry on the great area administered from the Colonial Office.

We are here concerned with the great variety of appointments, by far the larger number annually, the selection for which is carried out, and, as the Committee emphatically emphasises, admirably carried out, by the Private Secretary (Appointments)[2] and his staff. The Private Secretary and staff have always been able to obtain the advice and assistance of specialist advisers, both from the Colonial Office and the universities and from men of eminence in various professions, and lastly from senior Colonial officials on leave or recently retired. The Committee places on record that the selection of candidates has at all times been undertaken with the greatest care and that the Colonial Governors have expressed entire approval of the type sent out. The Committee is also at pains to show that the idea, which has prevailed in some quarters, that Oxford and Cambridge have been specially favoured in this selection is not borne out by facts. The bulk of the appointments in administration have gone, for various demonstrable reasons, to these two universities; but London and the Scottish universities have provided the largest number of men for appointments in medicine and scientific departments, Edinburgh being specially mentioned as "the principal source" for forestry.

Whilst fully acknowledging the successful manner in which the selection of candidates is carried out, the Committee considers it undesirable that it should continue to be performed by a staff of private secretaries to the Secretary of State. It recommends that this staff should cease to be in the position of private secretaries and that the appointments branch should be incorporated as a permanent part of the Personnel Division of the Colonial Office. In addition, it is recommended that a Colonial Service Appointment Branch, consisting of a chairman and two members nominated by the Civil Service Commissioners, should be set up as a standing independent branch for the final selection of candidates whose names are put forward by the appointments branch, and that the names of those selected be then submitted to the Secretary of State, on whose authority the appointments will be made. It is also suggested that the promotions branch should be reorganised on a smaller scale and be a section of the Personnel Division. There can be little doubt that these are excellent suggestions, and if put into effect they will greatly strengthen the hands both of selectors for first appointments and also of those dealing with that important question of promotion. On the able recommendations of the Committee on the latter question space will not permit further digression; but in the future interest of the Service they merit careful consideration.

One other recommendation of the Committee requires mention before the scientific services are considered. The question of the unification of the Colonial Service is discussed. The Committee points to the hardships of officers on small cadres in the smaller dependencies, and admits all the objections which have been put forward – differences of salary, leave, pension, climate, customs and language of the people, and so forth; it recognises the reluctance of Governors and others to any change. After a consideration of all the objections, the Committee remains convinced of the importance of unification and recommends that a single Colonial Service should be formed and that, within this larger whole, unified special services should be organised, such as agriculture, forests, medicine, education, and so forth. As the Committee correctly points out, this issue is of the very first importance: "Much of the information on which it rests cannot be present in the minds of Governors or their advisers overseas, since it relates particularly to questions of home recruitment and to the difficulties of individual Colonies".

The question of the technical and specialist research officers remains to be considered. The Committee states that

> "many of the officers appointed to scientific and technical services such as agriculture, forestry, veterinary, medical, and so forth, are qualified to undertake research work of a fundamental character, and some officers are appointed in the first instance / for the specific purpose of carrying out research work on urgent problems confronting a particular service. In the ordinary course, however, an officer appointed to the agricultural service with special knowledge of plant diseases or insect pests, would rank for promotion in the higher grades in that service along with officers engaged in more general and less systematised duties, and would not necessarily confine himself to work of a specialised character throughout his service."

The statement that "many" of the officers appointed to the above services "are qualified to undertake research work of a fundamental character" would, for some of the services, scarcely be admitted at the universities. Twenty per cent would probably be too high a percentage. Experience has also shown that a young officer, on first appointment, should have a few years of executive work *before* being detailed for research. This will prevent his making recommendations, when he takes up research, which the executive officer knows to be impracticable. But this type of research officer, as the Committee points out, belongs to a definite service, will go up the grades of that service, will not necessarily confine himself to research all his service, and has a chance of securing the prizes of his own service. His social position is also assured as a member of a service.

The other type of research officer is perhaps of even greater importance – the whole-time specialist. As the Committee must have realised, this type has so far received scant attention. His value is not called in question. He is in demand. The universities could say in how great demand. They are aware that Government has now to compete in this market in some directions with the wide-awake commercial people. These specialist research officers are selected on the understanding that their whole service will be devoted to their particular line of research. It is contemplated that their work will be of such a character that any results they may obtain will be applicable in many parts of the Colonial Empire. Some of them may find it practicable to pursue their investigations in one particular research institution. Others may find it necessary to conduct their researches in different parts of the Empire, attached either to a research station or to a scientific department. In the normal course of things it is neither to be expected nor would it be desirable that their advancement should be conditioned by the occurrence of vacancies in the higher ranks of services other than their own. The Committee states that "it does not follow that such a service should be graded like other colonial services, for each individual in it must determine his own line of research in his particular sphere of work". In this connexion the Committee says:

> "In our opinion Research Officers should be encouraged by means of special inducements in the way of salaries and other terms of service to continue their long-range investigations. These terms should, in our opinion, be at least equal to those which they would be likely to obtain if they were prepared to abandon purely research work for more general duties."

Clearly there are considerations other than salaries to be taken into account in dealing with the research officers, and we should have preferred the Committee to have been more specific in its references to this class. It would be disastrous for recruitment if the research officer were to remain 'no man's child', which would mean that he would not enjoy the social position which attaches to the services in the Empire-circles overseas (and is of importance out there). The man may not care about this, but when he marries his wife will, and Government will lose a good man. An example may be quoted. Soon after the formation of the Agricultural and Forestry Research Institutes at Pusa and Dehra Dun,[3] India, by Lord Curzon,[4] a representative from each centre met by chance and discussed prospects. In reply to some remark, the Pusa man ejaculated, "Yes, your position is very different. You belong to a Service. We at Pusa do not." Dehra Dun was staffed from the Indian Forest Service. The Pusa specialist returned home shortly afterwards and was a great loss. That conversation took place more than twenty years ago!

A possible way out of this difficulty, it may be suggested, would appear to be to appoint each specialist research officer (for example, of the type serving in Malaya and Tanganyika) to one or other of the scientific or technical services (to which his investigations most nearly correlate) and then second him for research work, on the understanding that his service would be spent on such work: much as Royal Engineer and Military Medical officers are seconded for civil duty and remain seconded for the rest of their service. High salaries, higher than the Colonial Office could afford to offer, will not tempt, or if tempted retain, the right stamp of man unless the social conditions of life are assimilated to those of the Services. Incorporated in a Service, seconded with staff pay as specialised research officers, would, it is believed, remove the existing disabilities and secure in increasing numbers the type desired for this increasingly important work, The Committee thus alludes to this work: /

> "On the economic side we have to bring to bear the latest results of scientific research on the development of wealth, which is important, not only to the Colonies themselves but also to the Empire and the World. Most of the greater problems of the Colonies to-day are problems of Applied Science."

Possibly, however, the Committee wishes the research service to be a separate entity, under the general administrative control and supervision and responsible alone to an officer at the Colonial Office, linked through him with the various Imperial Bureaux which have recently been established, and through them with the British Dominions. This is the underlying assumption in the various reports on colonial research to which the Committee refers, and particularly that of the sub-committee which reported to the Colonial Office Conference of 1927 on the possibilities of the creation of a Colonial Scientific and Research Service, available for the requirements of the whole Colonial Empire; in other words, the creation of an Imperial Service, financed out of an Imperial fund, to replace a number of water-tight provincial services which have too long been dependent on individual Colonial governments, most of which have hitherto given little indication of their appreciation of the value of long-range research.

Colony and Protectorate of Kenya, *Pensions Committee, Interim Report* (Nairobi: Government printer, 1928), pp. 1–11. Rhodes House Library Papers, 753. 17 s 2/1928 (1).

PENSIONS COMMITTEE.
INTERIM REPORT.

1. The Committee was appointed in February, 1927, with the following terms of reference:–

Terms of Reference.

(i) To advise the Government as to the posts which should in future come under any of the following:–

(*a*) A free pension scheme.

(*b*) A contributory pension scheme.

(*c*) A provident fund scheme.

(*d*) Any other analogous form of provision.

(ii) To estimate the annual cost to Government of their recommendations if put into effect on the basis of the present staff.

2. The Committee interpreted its terms of reference as including an examination of the general features of the various schemes mentioned and of their application to the requirements of the Colony. It was, indeed, found to be impracticable to frame any recommendations on the terms of reference without a close analysis of the meaning and effect of each such scheme.

Examination of the scheme

3. The Committee came to the conclusion at an early meeting that the difficulties which are at present encountered by the Government in making a satisfactory and logical differentiation between pensionable and non-pensionable posts would be increased rather than diminished by the creation of further categories into which the Service should be divided, and determined, therefore, to concentrate its attention on one such further category only.

4. The essential difference between a contributory pension scheme and a provident fund scheme is that in the latter the benefit to the contributor is in the form of a gratuity and in the former of an annuity.

Contributory pensions and provident funds

For practical purposes, the Committee came to the conclusion that the benefits to be derived from any scheme applied in the Colony as an alternative in part or in whole to a free pensions scheme should approximate in form to those granted under a free pensions scheme. The Committee, therefore, examined the possibility of inaugurating a contributory pension scheme as opposed to a provident fund scheme.

5. The opinion of the Committee is that any alternative to the existing free pension scheme should be in the form of a contributory pension scheme. The Committee trusts that this recommendation may be regarded as disposing of the third and fourth sub-titles of its first term of reference.

European officers' pensions

6. The rules governing the grant of pensions to European pensionable officers have been crystallised since the appointment of the Committee in the European Officers' Pensions Ordinance, which took effect as from the 1st April, 1927. That Ordinance sets out the conditions for the grant of pensions in a form which, the Committee believes, has been adopted generally throughout the Colonial Service. In the course of this report the Committee will have occasion to recommend certain modifications in this law, and it is given to understand that no objection will be raised in principle to making a departure from the common form by way of an amending Ordinance, should consideration of local circumstances demonstrate the benefit of such amendments.

Non-European officers' pensions.

7. The rules governing the grant of pensions in the case of non-European pensionable posts have not yet appeared in the form of an Ordinance. They are to be found in various State documents collated and summarised in the Kenya Code of Regulations.

8. The Ordinance and Regulations, however, cover one part only of the problem connected with the grant of pensions. The selection of posts whose holders shall be entitled to pensionable status, either personally or by virtue of office, presents considerable difficulty. This part of the problem is complicated / by anomalies at present existing not only as between posts of a similar standing in different Kenya departments, but also as between posts of similar rank, standing and responsibilities in different Dependencies.

9. One part of the Committee's duty, therefore, has been to examine the various posts in the Service with a view to the detection of such anomalies and to frame recommendations to meet each case.

Finance.

10. There remains to be considered an essential aspect of the problem, upon which the selection of pensionable offices and the adoption of regulations governing the grant of pensions to a large extent depend, namely, that of finance. It is unnecessary to emphasise the importance of the financial aspect. The acceptance

of commitments by way of pensions payable in future years must be regulated by the capacity of the Colony to meet its anticipated liabilities in this direction.

11. In a country whose development and Civil Service are undergoing rapid expansion, the effect of an enlarged pensionable staff on the Colonial Budget is delayed, and in this lies a danger because the financial obligations entered into on the creation of a new pensionable appointment are not reflected in the Budget concerned.

12. The estimate of pensions and gratuities, exclusive of pension contributions for Army Officers and payments under the Widows' and Orphans' Pensions Scheme during recent years has been as follows:– *Pension payments.*

Year.	European Staff.	Non-European Staff.	Total.
	£	£	£
1906–07	312	63	375
1909–10	842	322	1,164
1914–15	2,733	537	3,270
1919–20	5,834	1,484	7,318
1920–21	13,618	2,051	15,669
1921	16,055	4,085	20,140
1922	23,708	5,008	28,716
1923	27,500	7,524	35,024
1924	45,918	11,405	57,323*
1925	51,652	14,839	66,491
1926	57,575	15,832	73,407
1927	62,105	17,961	80,066

*   This considerable increase in pensions paid may largely be attributed to the retrenchment carried into effect in 1922 and 1923.

13. These figures show a rapid rise in the Colony's annual pensions commitments and the increase, in the Committee's opinion, will become more pronounced within the next ten years, when the effect is felt of the considerable expansions of staff which took place during the four years before the war, coupled with the privilege, extended to Civil Servants who joined during that period, of voluntary retirement after twenty years of service. It must also be remembered that there have, of recent years been large increases in emoluments generally throughout the Service, and that the effect of these revisions of salary have not yet been fully reflected in the amount paid annually in respect of pensions and gratuities. *Pensions commitments growing.*

14. There is, unfortunately, no accurate method within the knowledge of the Committee by which pension commitments on the basis of a known pensionable establishment can be gauged. The normal rule in force throughout the Colonial Service is to estimate annual commitments of this kind at fifteen per cent. per annum of an officer's salary. The Committee takes this to mean that the annual *Future pension commitments.*

investment of a sum calculated at fifteen per cent. of the annual salaries of pension-able officers would suffice to defray pension commitments when they fall due. /

15. On this basis, the annual commitments at the present day in respect of pen-sionable posts now on the establishment amount to approximately £85,000 per annum. On the same basis, the commitments reflected in the East Africa Protec-torate budget twenty years ago were about £17,000 per annum, or one-fifth of present commitments.

16. Some estimate of the Colony's pension liabilities on the present establish-ment may perhaps be gauged from these figures. The average pensionable emoluments of an officer have increased by about seventy per cent. during the past twenty years. During that period some of the increase in average pension-able emoluments has been reflected in the amount of pensions paid, but, after making allowance for this, it may be calculated that the pension commitments entailed by the present establishment will amount to a figure between £180,000 and £200,000 per annum in twenty years' time.

17. The Committee regards these figures as an indication of the burden which the Colony will be called upon to meet in future years, and as emphasising the importance of limiting increases in future commitments of this kind. It is clearly necessary that considerations of economy should be borne in mind in the fram-ing of pensions regulations, in the application of these regulations to the Service, and in extending the number of posts to which the privilege of pensionable sta-tus is granted.

Liabilities already incurred.

18. These can be no question of attempting to reduce those commitments by altering the conditions on which pensions are granted to members of the Ser-vice who are now working under the present regulations. Such liabilities as have been incurred must be met when the time arrives, but the Committee feels that examination of the financial effect of the present pensions regulations discloses a prospective burden on the finances of the Colony sufficiently great to warrant a close scrutiny of the terms in respect of pensions upon which candidates are recruited in future.

Concerted action in East Africa desirable.

19. The pensions regulations in force form an integral part of the terms of service in any Dependency, and it is in Kenya's interest to make the conditions of service in Kenya as attractive as those in force in other East African Dependencies. The Committee, therefore, hopes that it will be found possible for concerted action to be taken throughout the East African Territories, and recommends that the Conference of East African Governors be asked to consider this possibility.[1]

20. The Committee is aware that competition for candidates is not confined to the East African territories, but feels that consideration of some alternative to

the present free pensions scheme, which is only partial in its application, should not be deferred on that account. The Committee believes that if an alternative scheme is adopted throughout Eastern Africa the effect on candidature for posts in East Africa will be practically negligible.

21. The Committee understands that it has already been agreed between the Governments of Tanganyika, Uganda and Kenya that the terms of service in these territories shall so far as is practicable be similar. This agreement strengthens the Committee's view that concerted action is desirable throughout Eastern Africa in respect of any modification in the pensions regulations.

22. The Committee is anxious that the terms of service in force in Kenya should be such as to attract the best men and to retain their services for the Colony when they are here. Free pension rights form a very material consideration to officers, and it is on these grounds that the Committee hopes that concerted action will be possible among the East African group of Territories. At the same time the Committee feels that even if concerted action fails to eventuate, a contributory pensions scheme should be introduced in Kenya. In view of the advantages which exist in Kenya in other directions the introduction of a contributory pensions scheme for Kenya alone would not, in the opinion of the Committee, place the Colony in a position of such disadvantage as would outweigh the financial benefit derived from such a scheme. /

23. The Committee considers that, if the introduction of a contributory pensions scheme fails to eventuate, the list of offices which carry free pension privileges will have to be very carefully pruned and the extension of present privileges to future appointees will have to be restricted. *Present pensions list*

24. The Committee finds that the present regulations in force in East Africa, which permit of retirement at the age of fifty and are calculated at the rate of one four-hundred-and-eightieth of pensionable emoluments for each complete month of pensionable service, compare very favourably with the regulations in force in the Dominions and in the rest of the Empire. *Age of retirement*

25. The Committee is glad to learn that the regulation which allowed an officer to take his pension on retirement after twenty years of service has not been retained among the provisions of the European Officers' Pensions Ordinance, and will not be applicable in the case of future appointments to the pensionable staff.

26. In spite of the varying climatic conditions encountered in different parts of Kenya, the Committee is of opinion that the age of retirement might well be increased to fifty-five throughout the Service, and recommends that a European civil servant should be entitled to retire on pension on his own initiative, or should be required to retire if called upon to do so, at the age of fifty-five years, or after thirty years' service, whichever comes first.

27. The Committee believes that with the development of East Africa and the rapidly growing amenities of civilisation, it will be in exceptional cases only that retirement before the age of fifty-five will be necessary or desirable on grounds of health of impaired capacity, and in this belief it considers that it is a mistaken policy to encourage the retirement at an earlier age of an officer whose experience and local knowledge fit him in a peculiar degree to serve the Colony efficiently.

28. The recommendation on this point is, therefore, a general one, and is intended to apply whether or not an alternative scheme for the grant of pensions or gratuities is adopted. The Committee considers that such a regulation could be introduced in Kenya whether or not the other Dependencies in Eastern Africa adopt a similar rule, and hopes that an amending Ordinance to give effect to it will be introduced in Kenya as soon as possible.

Basis of comput-
ing pensions

29. The Committee has also had under consideration the question of whether a continuance of the present rate on which pensions are calculated (i.e., one four-hundred-and-eightieth of pensionable emoluments for each complete month of pensionable service) is justified by the facts of the case. On this matter it feels that concerted action throughout East Africa is desirable and suggests that this question should be considered by the Governors' Conference. Its recommendation in regard to Kenya is that the rate on which pensions are calculated should be one six-hundredth of pensionable emoluments for each complete month of pensionable service.

Present
anomalies

30. The generosity of the present free pensions regulations adds greatly to the difficulties of removing anomalies which are known to exist in the division of the staff between pensionable and non-pensionable appointments. It appears probable that the intention underlying the pensions regulations is that all civil servants appointed to the permanent staff should, after serving the best part of their life in the Service, be able to retire on a reasonably adequate pension; and for so long as a free pension scheme is in force anomalies are bound to occur unless pensionable status is withheld only from those who occupy purely temporary posts.

31. The removal of anomalies by making additions to the pensionable staff to cover all but purely temporary posts would be a simple matter if the financial effect of such procedure were to be ignored, but, as the Committee has observed, the liabilities already incurred in respect of pensions are very large and cannot lightly be increased. Every effort should, in fact, be made to reduce such commitments in the interests of future generations. /

Financial aspect.

32. From the financial point of view the present system may be summarised as follows:–

Any addition to the pensionable establishment creates a contingent liability which will fall due in from twenty to thirty years. By virtue of the grant of free pension privileges the salary offered initially can be and is smaller than that which would have to be offered if the appointment carried no pension privileges. No provision is made for money to be placed in reserve against the future pension liability. By this means some portion of the revenue of future years is hypothecated in the creation of this new post.

33. It is of course true that by this expedient new and valuable services can be introduced at the present time to a greater extent than would be possible otherwise, and this factor is of importance in a country undergoing rapid development. At the same time, there is no reason to suppose that development will not also be progressing rapidly in a quarter of a century, when the necessity for setting aside large sums to defray pension liabilities may be found to limit the scope of other services.

34. These considerations lead the Committee to recommend that an attempt be made to safeguard future interests by the annual investment of money for which provision should be included in the Expenditure Estimates, and the Committee is of the opinion that some such procedure should be adopted whether a free pension scheme or a contributory pension scheme is in force.

Pensions fund.

35. The Committee observes that such a course was discussed in that portion of the report of the Committee on Pensions and Passage Expenses of Colonial Officers which deals with the institution of a central pensions fund. That Committee felt that there were serious objections to the establishment of a centrally administered pensions fund through which the various Colonies in the Empire would be invited to insure their pension liabilities, but added:–

> "The primary object of providing for pensions through a fund is to secure that the cost of accruing pensions is met by the generation to which the service of the officials concerned is rendered, and is not left to be borne by a subsequent generation. Such a fund is usually established by a single service or organisation to provide for its own employees."

36. Having referred to the difficulty encountered at the outset on account of the provision which would have to be made for the accrued liability in respect of service anterior to the establishment of the fund, a liability which would have to be met over a term of years in conjunction with the charge for current service, that Committee contemplated that:–

> ". . . it might be expedient for individual Colonies to examine the probable trend of their pension commitments with a view to possible rearrangement of finance on such a basis."

On this point, as is stated in the report, that Committee was not called upon to express an opinion.

37. The present Kenya Pensions Committee has endeavoured to examine the financial aspect of pension liabilities from this point of view, and recommends that steps should be taken to rearrange the Colonial finance on the basis outlined.

38. It has been stated that on the basis generally adopted in calculating the value of free pension privileges, the annual commitments of the Colony at the present day amount to approximately £85,000 per annum. If free pension privileges were to be extended to all permanent posts, the figure would be considerably greater. It requires but little acquaintance with the present colonial budget to realise that the addition to the Expenditure Estimates of a reserve fund amounting to £100,000 per annum to be invested against future pension liabilities, would cause considerable embarrassment. And yet this figure is not greatly in excess of the provision that has now to be made / annually to meet pension liabilities incurred in the past. If a reserve fund of this description had been started at the beginning of this century, departmental expenditure would to some extent have been restricted, but the present colonial revenue would have been sufficient to bear the cost of present services together with a reserve to meet the pension liabilities entailed by the present staff. The inauguration of a pensions reserve fund at the present time, intended to meet the full pension commitments in respect of the present pensionable staff, would have the effect of restricting departmental expenditure for a generation, because money would have to be found both for the reserve fund and also to meet past pensions commitments, but thereafter past pensions commitments would disappear and accumulations from the reserve fund would suffice to defray pension liabilities. In thirty years at four per cent. money more than trebles.

Effect of altera-
tions suggested.

39. It is, however, clear that the possibility of placing annually to a reserve fund a sufficient sum of money to defray future pension liabilities depends upon the amount involved. Consideration of the sum which would be required on the present basis leads the Committee to the conclusion that the present pensions regulations are altogether too generous for this to be done. The Committee believes, however, that the alterations which have been suggested in previous paragraphs of this report in regard to the age of retirement and rate at which pension is calculated would materially reduce the sum required; because the period over which contributions are made in respect of each officer would be increased, there would be five more years in which the contributions would be accumulating at compound interest, and the number of years during which pension was drawn would be reduced. Actuarial statistics are necessary before the effect of these alterations can be assessed with accuracy. For present purposes it will be sufficient to assume that the annual pension liabilities incurred in respect of each pensionable officer would be decreased from, say, fifteen per cent. to, say, twelve per cent. of his annual salary.

40. The effect of making provision in Estimates for an annual contribution to a pensions reserve fund is attained in the case of a contributory pensions scheme if the amount of assistance which the State contributes towards that scheme is provided for in annual Estimates and invested together with the money received from contributors. In the event of a contributory pensions scheme being introduced, the Committee recommends that this procedure be adopted, so that, apart from unforeseen circumstances or abnormal conditions, the necessary provision for meeting commitments under the scheme may be made in advance.

Contributory pensions scheme.

41. The Committee recommends that the feasibility of introducing a contributory pensions scheme applicable to the whole permanent service, to the complete exclusion of a free pensions scheme (apart from commitments already entered into in respect of persons now on the free pensions list) should be examined. It has itself examined the regulations governing the contributory pensions scheme in force in South Africa, but it is unwilling to frame definite recommendations on the matter until it is informed whether or not the Government is prepared to approve in principle the introduction of such a contributory pensions scheme.

Recommendations.

42. The Committee recommends that this principle be adopted and that actuarial enquiries be then made as to the manner in which such a scheme could be introduced for the European permanent service on the assumption that the benefits under the scheme should approximate as closely as possible to those given in the European Officers' Pensions Ordinance, 1927, with the modifications proposed in paragraphs 26 and 29. This enquiry would show what percentage of each permanent officer's salary would have to be contributed and invested in order to cover commitments under the scheme. The question of the percentage to be borne by the State and that to be borne by the officer concerned could then be determined and a decision could be reached showing whether or not the introduction of such a scheme was justified by the facts of the case. /

43. Actuarial enquiries are necessary before this can be done, and these entail expense. The Committee is, however, of the opinion that a strong *prima facie* case exists for making such enquiries, and that these should be carried out as soon as possible.

44. The Committee has considered the manner in which such a scheme could be applied to the Kenya Service, as required by the first term of reference, which instructs the Committee, *inter alia*, to advise Government as to the posts which should in future come under:—

Division of Service.

    (a) a free pension scheme, or
    (b) a contributory pension scheme.

45. Such a division of the Service implies the separation of posts into three categories, for there must in any case always be a number of temporary appointments which would not carry pension privileges.

Effect of two categories of pensions.

46. The Committee believes that the inauguration of a contributory pension scheme operating in conjunction with a free pension scheme would be found to create a difference in the terms of service applicable to various posts which could not be justified logically. A mass of anomalies would be immediately apparent, anomalies which could not be explained, and which could only be removed by giving way, gradually perhaps, to applications from contributors to be placed on the free pensions list.

47. Each such application, when granted, would lead to further anomalies, and the same remedy would follow. In short, the division of the permanent service into two categories, those under a free pension scheme and those under a contributory pension scheme, must inevitably lead to the whole, or practically the whole, of the permanent service coming under the former, unless some ready and justifiable means of discrimination could be laid down, and this the Committee has been unable to devise.

48. It would, in any case, be uneconomical to set in motion all the machinery necessary to the working of a contributory pension scheme unless a considerable proportion of the Service was to participate, and it is clear to the Committee that if the two schemes were in simultaneous operation there would be but a small number of contributors.

Alternatives.

49. There are two alternatives – the first, to enlarge the free pensions list so as to make the application of free pensions equitable and to remove existing anomalies by laying down that permanent appointments should, in general, automatically carry pension privileges; the second, to abolish the free pensions list entirely and to introduce a contributory pension scheme throughout the permanent service on the principles suggested above.

50. The Committee has attempted in an earlier section of this report to show that the pension commitments in respect of the present staff are far greater than a casual glance at the Estimates would indicate and has expressed its opinion that these liabilities should not lightly be increased. It holds the view that the grant of pensions on the present generous scale to large numbers of civil servants must in years to come have a crippling effect on the development of the Colony, and that the number of posts on the free pensions list should, on financial grounds, be reduced rather than increased. It is unable, therefore, to recommend any such extensions of the free pensions privileges and adopts the latter alternative.

51. The Committee recommends that in the event of a contributory pensions scheme being approved in principle and found feasible in practice, the contributory scheme should apply to the case of all appointments made to the posts mentioned in Appendix I,[2] that the present free pensions scheme should then be discontinued and should only be applied in the case of those individuals who are holding pensionable offices prior to the introduction of the contributory pension scheme, and that the contributory scheme should be on a compulsory basis. /

Compulsory contributory pensionsscheme.

52. The Committee has already suggested that it is desirable that the Government of Kenya should propose that the question of introducing a contributory pension scheme in complete eventual replacement of a free pension scheme should be discussed by the Conference of East African Governors, the object being to inaugurate an agreed contributory pension scheme throughout East Africa.

Concerted action desirable.

53. In making proposals for the inauguration of a contributory pension scheme, the Committee has assumed, without the assistance of actuarial calculations, that the benefits to be conferred will on balance represent the accumulation of twelve per cent. of a contributor's salary per annum. The Committee proposes that this should be obtained by a contribution of five per cent. from the officer and of seven per cent. from public funds. It considers that the State could not equitably call upon an officer to contribute more than five per cent. of his salary for this purpose.

Contributions by contributing officers.

54. The figure of twelve per cent. has, however, been postulated on the assumption that the age of retirement is increased to fifty-five following the recommendation made by the Committee for application to the Kenya Service, and that the basis on which pension is calculated is altered from one four-hundred-and-eightieth to one six-hundredth of the officer's pensionable emoluments for each complete month of pensionable service.

55. As the preliminaries necessary to the introduction of a contributory pension scheme must in any case take time, the Committee has examined the list of posts appearing in the Kenya Estimates with a view to the removal of certain anomalies and to the limitation of free pension commitments which might otherwise arise in the interim.

Interim pensionable posts.

56. In Appendix II the Committee has prepared a list of those posts which should, in its opinion, remain on the free pensions list pending the introduction of a contributory scheme.

57. This list has been prepared subject to the following reservations:–
    (i) that the interests of those persons now serving in a pensionable post will not be affected; (ii) that the list is contingent upon the eventual introduction of a contributory scheme and does not represent the list of posts which the Com-

Reservations.

mittee considers should be pensionable if no contributory scheme eventuates; and (iii) that the intended effect of the recommendations on this matter is to limit the growth of further free pension commitments pending the introduction of a contributory scheme.

Anomalies. 58. In preparing the list shown in Appendix II, the Committee has taken into consideration the various cases which have been represented to it as anomalous, and has made recommendations for certain posts to be added to the list of posts which at present carry free pension privileges. It has made these recommendations with one object in view only, namely, the removal of an existing anomaly which in the Committee's opinion should not be allowed to continue in justice to the office concerned and in the interests of efficiency.

Contributory pensions scheme. 59. It will be observed also that the Committee has not included in the interim pensions list certain posts which are now pensionable. The Committee wishes to reiterate that these recommendations do not apply to individual present holders of such offices, but only to new appointments to these offices during the period when a contributory scheme is under consideration. As will be seen from Appendix I, each office so deleted from the free pensions lists as an interim measures appears in the list of offices to which the benefits of a contributory pension scheme should apply, with the exception, of certain offices which must in the near future be under municipal control.

Interim proposals. 60. In considering the posts which should be included in the interim free pensions list pending the introduction of a contributory scheme, the Committee has attempted to reduce future pension commitments as far as / could be done without prejudice to the general efficiency of the Service and without affecting conditions of service in the more responsible posts which might, as vacancies arise, be best filled by selection from outside the Colony. In respect of such posts, the effect of the Committee's recommendations is to maintain the present conditions of service so that the field of selection in the interim will not be affected.

Appendix II. 61. Appendix II is accompanied by certain explanatory notes which have reference to the following recommendations.

Officers on long grades. 62. The Committee recommends that officers appointed in the future to a post on the interim pensions list on a long grade rising to above £600 per annum should not be on the pensionable establishment until they have passed the efficiency bar at £600 per annum.

63. This recommendation is intended to cover the case of future appointments of District Officers, Assistant Treasurers and so on, who are appointed on a long scale, starting at less than £600 per annum and rising to £720, £840 or £940 per annum, as the case may be. The Committee considers that pending the introduc-

tion of a contributory scheme, pensionable status should not be granted to such officers until an extended trial of their attainments has proved their efficiency and considers that the efficiency bar at £600 per annum, which will be reached in the ordinary course of events after from eight to ten years' service, provides a suitable opportunity for judging whether free pension privileges should be granted in each case.

64. The Committee recommends that the five years' period of probation at present in force for technical officers should be extended to cover scientific and professional appointments, including the posts of Medical Officers, Sanitation Officers, Magistrates and Crown Counsel.

Professional and technical officers.

65. This recommendation is intended to safeguard the interests of the Colony by enabling such an officer's work to be examined for two tours before definite appointment is made to the permanent and pensionable establishment. It will be observed that the probationary period suggested for such officers before appointment to the pensionable staff is not so protracted as that suggested for the non-technical or non-professional portion of the Service.

66. The Committee adds to these recommendations a general recommendation in consonance with present practice, that non-pensionable service immediately followed by service in a similar capacity in a pensionable office should qualify the officer concerned for pension calculated in respect of both his pensionable and non-pensionable service.

Non-pensionable service followed by pensionable service.

67. The Committee has been able to frame recommendations for an interim free pensions list pending the introduction of a contributory scheme in the case of all departments except the Post Office and Telegraphs Department. Appointments to that department are made to a large extent from among persons trained in the English Service who have been granted pensionable status in that Service and the Committee feels that while it would have wished to frame recommendations in respect of European posts in this department on lines similar to those it has adopted in the case of other departments, it is unable to do so in present circumstances.

Post Office and Telegraphs Department.

68. At the same time, the Committee considers that it is important to develop the Post Office and Telegraphs Department in Kenya as a Service filled more and more by local recruitment, as is done in many other Colonies, and trusts that it will in time be found possible to break away to such an extent from reliance on the English Service for recruits as to enable the Post Office and Telegraphs Department in this country to come on to a contributory scheme basis on the lines proposed by the Committee for the Kenya Service as a whole.

69. The Committee understands from the Postmaster General that steps have already been taken to break away to some extent from reliance on the English Service by recruitment in South Africa, where pensions are granted on a contributory basis. /

Cost of contributory pensions scheme.

70. The Committee estimates tentatively that the annual cost to Government, on an establishment similar in numbers and salaries to the present establishment, but contributing compulsorily to the pensions scheme, of a contributory pension scheme on the lines suggested would be in the neighbourhood of £40,250 per annum for the European permanent service and perhaps £52,000 in all if a scheme on similar lines were to be extended to the permanent non-European Service. By this the Committee means that by the annual investment of such a sum, calculated as being seven per cent. of the annual salary of contributing officers, together with the investment of the five per cent. of salaries contributed by the officers concerned, a sum of money should accumulate sufficient to defray all payments by way of pension and gratuity in time to come with the exception of those payments which might be specifically stated in the scheme itself to be payable from revenue.

Initial annual expenditure small.

71. If a contributory pension scheme is introduced the sums to be provided in Annual Estimates to meet commitments under it will be small at first and will grow gradually as the number of officers entering the Service on the contributory basis increases – on the retirement or transfer of those now on the free pensions list. The Committee feels, therefore, that a contributory pensions scheme can be introduced without any great disturbance to the Colony's annual financial programme.

Calculations tentative only.

72. In making all calculations referred to in this report, the Committee wishes it to be understood that the data have not been examined by an actuary and that the figures given are intended as an indication only.

Effect of extending pension benefits to members of permanent staff not now pensionable.

73. Approximately eighty-three per cent. of the personal emoluments paid to the present European permanent establishment, as shown in Appendix I, is paid to officers at present pensionable, and the application of a contributory pensions scheme to the whole permanent European portion of the Service would therefore increase the total liabilities in respect of pensions by about twenty per cent. Contributions received from contributing officers would, however, on a basis of five per cent. of salary, reduce the commitments falling on the State by approximately £28,750 per annum, and this would more than cover the increased liability incurred on the extension of pension rights.

Commitments in respect of present free pensions and proposed contributory scheme compared.

74. An examination of the pension position on the basis of the Estimates for 1928 and on the assumption that total pension commitments will amount to

twelve per cent. of annual salaries gives the following figures in respect of the European portion of the Service:–

Pension commitments in respect of European establishment at present pensionable (12 per cent. of salaries) approximately   57,500

    Pension commitments in respect of the European establishment proposed for contributory pensions scheme–

(Appendix I):

(a) Contributed by the officer concerned approximately   28,750
(b) Contributed by the State, approximately   40,250
– 69,000

75. The liability of the State is, on this basis of calculation, reduced from £57,500 per annum to £40,250 per annum, or by thirty per cent., while at the same time anomalies existing among officers on the permanent establishment in respect of pensionable status are removed. /

Liability of State.

76. The Committee has endeavoured in this interim report to emphasise the need for caution in respect of the Colony's pensions commitments. It recommends the eventual adoption of a contributory pensions scheme in order to reduce these commitments for the future, and it has indicated the offices to which such a contributory scheme, if found feasible, should apply. At the same time, it has put forward a list of posts which should be regarded as free pensionable posts in the interim, pending the introduction of a contributory pensions scheme. The Committee wishes to make it clear that this list of posts is put forward with this object only in view. In the event of a contributory pensions scheme being found impracticable, the Committee considers that the present free pensions list will require re-examination, that the terms of service respecting the grant of free pensions will have to be reviewed, and that the question of providing in Annual Estimates money to be invested against future pensions commitments will require more detailed consideration.

If contributory pensions scheme not found feasible present free pensions regulations, etc., require review.

77. In the interests of the Colony's finances and of the Service as a whole, the Committee urges the adoption in principle of a contributory pensions scheme and recommends that actuarial enquiries be made in regard to the details of a contributory pensions scheme which would confer upon European contributors benefits similar to those provided for in the European Officers' Pensions Ordinance, 1927, with the amendments proposed in paragraphs 26 and 29. Pending Government's decision on the principle, and the result of the actuarial enquiries, the Committee considers that no useful purpose would be served by an examination of the question of pensions to the non-European portion of the Service.

Further enquiry postponed pending decision on contributory pensions scheme.

78. The Committee desires to pay tribute to the valuable assistance rendered to it by the Secretary, Mr. G. R. Sandford.

(*Signed*) –
R. CLIFTON GRANNUM, *Chairman.*
H. E. SCHWARTZE,
CONWAY HARVEY,
J. E. S. MERRICK,
A. WALTER,
F. W. KNIGHTLY,
Members.
Nairobi,
5th March, 1928.
G. R. SANDFORD, *Secretary.*

B. Malinowski, 'Memorandum on Colonial Research' (1927). Rhodes House Library Papers, J. H. Oldham Papers, mss Afr. S 1829, box 2, file 2, 'Research. Memoranda – Interviews', ff. 55–64.

NATIVE RESEARCH.
Notes of Conversation with Professor Malinowski[1] 2nd December 1927.

The main problems in Africa affecting the native races in contact with white civilisation are three:

(1) The question of economic co-operation between races.
(2) Questions of political and legal administration.
(3) The moral and intellectual development of the native peoples.

All these are in reality bound up together. There is need for a study not only of native, but also of European sociology. The subject has not yet been tackled by anyone.

Such a question as how much land the natives really need demands a very careful enquiry into native economy along lines which have as yet been hardly even mapped out. Native conomic [*sic*] methods are bound up with their social organisation and the whole subject is a very delicate one, not by any means capable of a simple solution (of. Malinowski's article in the Economic Journal, March 1921).[2]

A study is needed of the relative advantages and disadvantages of the two methods of exploiting the resources of the territory – (1) through white capital and (2) through native production.

In regard to the third question noted above a great deal of present education assumes in fact that the native mind is a tabula rasa. Anthropologists of the old school are hardly aware of the new methods. Functional anthropology is concerned with the question how things work rather than how they came to be what they are. /

MEMORANDUM ON COLONIAL RESEARCH

The Problem.

You want to point out the need of a new research which would deal with questions of race, population, the administration and economic development of natives, as well as the adaptation of European culture to their Society. Such a science of colonial politics has already its forerunners in pamphleteering and propaganda work, part of which sentimentally defends the interests of coloured people, while the other part demands repressive measures against the dangers of race. The real research should stand in the same relation to the present partisan discussions as scientific economics, jurisprudence, theory of finance, politics and education stand to our own pamphleteering and political journalism. The expert in colonial policy ought to have at least the same chance as the expert in hygiene, economics and education.

The conflict of race and culture is rapidly becoming the burning problem of world politics. Anthropology, which purports to study races and cultures, should obviously provide some directing principles or at least a dispassionate and scientific attitude towards the issues. Yet old-fashioned antiquarian and historical anthropology is here of little use and we need, within our science, a resetting of problems and a far greater interest in the working of human institutions, customs and ideas, rather than retrospective speculations about their origins and vicissitudes.

The Practical Issues.

The political official in the Colonies has to secure safety and peace within the tribe and outside; legislate and administer justice; regulate the relations between settler and native; control economic development; and inaugurate or supervise moral, intellectual and practical education. Apart from any direct enterprise or activity of white settlers and their government, the mere contact of western and native culture produces a profound change in the latter, which affects the biological welfare of the race. It is therefore primarily problems of population, jurisprudence, / political organisation, economic and adaptation of culture on which a new type of anthropological study should concentrate.

Population.

Survival is the first condition of welfare to a race. The rapid disappearance of some native tribes is notorious. Reliable statistical observations associated with a sociological study of settlement, of village life, of the conditions of native hygiene are essential as a starting point for a control as to whether the new influences are beneficent, i.e., lead to increase of population or otherwise. A science of population begins to grow with regard to civilised communities. It would be very important to apply it immediately to those races where a rapid decrease and at times uncontrollable increase of population may create different but equally serious difficulties. Research in this subject is obviously necessary and perhaps might be recommended as the first approach to the adoption of science and application of it to colonial policy. Besides medical training, a knowledge of statistics and sociology would be necessary; above all the anthropological attitude of mind which does not ignore the outlook and cultural setting of the natives, and readily imagines that European cleanliness and sanitary methods can be directly applied to a stone-age society. A few useful books on the subject have already been published, to mention only Rivers and others' Essays on the Population of Melanesia,[3] Roberts' Population Problems of the Pacific,[4] Pitt Rivers' The Clash of Culture and Contact of Races.[5] As far as I know, these problems have not been specifically discussed with regard to Africa.

Economics.

The economic development of native areas is undoubtedly the primary motive of colonization. It can be done either directly or by native enterprise controlled by Europeans. The latter system, indirect development, seems to involve fewer difficulties and it seems to be the preferred system in the Dutch colonies. (In Java only / 7% of the land is alienated to Europeans; 55% are under native cultivation, 20% are not used and 18% are occupied by commercially exploited forests. (In Celebes indirect exploitation is almost the exclusive method.) The decision as to whether direct or indirect exploitation as a general policy is preferable requires careful and scientific, that is competent and dispassionate, study.

a. Direct exploitation.

A substantial transfer of land from natives to the white settlers is first necessary. This, as is well known, is one of the main causes of trouble on a large scale and lasting for generations. Very rarely it has been scientifically ascertained how much fertile land can be spared by the natives without injuring their economic organisation. Competent research into native systems of land tenure and of economic organisation should be vigorously advocated as one of the important functions of any department dealing with lands and exploitation. Even after the question is settled, how much land can be transferred, there arises another as to the equitable methods of purchase. Only a correct, anthropological knowledge of the various rights of ownership in land, of the native modes of alienation and of the economic, moral and religious relation between man and soil could lead to a complete avoidance of the more or less serious difficulties associated with all these transactions.

But land is not enough. Native labour is a natural asset of a colony and here direct exploitation is a source of chronic difficulties. Labour has to be recruited in all colonies by devices more or less objectionable; it has to be safeguarded by types of contract which always implies temporary loss of liberty; it has to be maintained during the term of service under artificial conditions of life. Recruiting, which, from slave-raiding and black-birding to the milder forms of "baiting" and "pressure", has always been open to criticism, could be made much less irksome by knowledge of what natives really need and how they could be innocuously induced to serve. The Government, who should control 'recruiting', 'baiting' and 'pressure' should have some impartial and realistic knowledge about what has taken place: about the promises and inducements offered to the natives, about their psychology in yielding to them, about the reaction which follows. /

The contract of labour should be considered from the point of view of duration, payment and possibilities of making it self-continuing. As regards payment, it is questionable whether high wages benefit the native in the long run. But the amount, the nature and the manner of payment is an important point for study in colonial economics. In the matter of time of service and possibilities of automatic re-enticement to work, the interests of the employer and of healthy tribal native life are obviously at variance. Long periods of absence estrange the native from his own community and lead to the formation of an amorphous, demoralised coloured population. Such a big black reserve of unskilled labourers is in my opinion the greatest future danger for Africa.

An impartial enquiry into this problem by a student who has no vested interests and is not a sentimentalist at the same time for the native and has a sense of economic realities, might disclose invaluable facts and hints for future conduct of affairs.

The arrangement of life for plantation hands is obviously a matter for social and moral as well as for biological hygiene. The addition of anthropological training to purely medical knowledge in supervising conditions must be advocated. Any serious and irremediable evils of a sexual, hygienic or moral nature might be signalled as another argument against direct exploitation of colonies.

b. Indirect exploitation.

This for many reasons has been advocated and adopted in some colonies, above all by the Dutch. Here, however, anthropological research (of a new type) is even more necessary than in direct exploitation. For here the natives must be stimulated and constantly controlled by people who have to understand native psychology, native custom and the principles of native organisation. Native production must be considerably increased; it will have to be constantly guided; the surplus will have to be purchased or levied; and the use to which natives put their gain will also have to be watched. For an increase of European wealth may become as dangerous and paralysing to further effort as it can be made stimulating and beneficial. /

The study of primitive economics recently taken in hand by a few anthropologists, has revealed that natives, by very complicated systems of production and distribution and an effective organisation of labour, produce a considerable surplus of goods, used for display and ceremonial purposes. Such a surplus could be easily directed to other channels while Europeans could satisfy native ambition and adapt their services to somewhat modified native requirements. Some such arrangements on a small scale I was able to study myself in Melanesia and they seem to exist also in several districts of Dutch East Indies. I think that the permanent collaboration between Europeans and semi-detribalised natives, such as the Maoris of New Zealand, the surviving Indian tribes in N. Central and S. America are also based on this type of arrangement. Under competent initiative and anthropological guidance, a similar form of co-operation could still be arranged on a large scale in order to develop indirectly the industries of some African tribes.

Indirect exploitation however presents immense and insidious difficulties. The natives may not easily take to increasing their production. Should they be forced? Should they be stimulated by taxation? By economic baits and organised festivities? Here a comparative study of methods already employed – by the Dutch for instance – and research into local conditions might provide us with useful indications. If successful, indirect production would give considerable wealth and power to the natives, which also would have to be watched. I believe that a sociologist with vision and training in economics, political science and the new type of "functional anthropology" could, after a study of local conditions in each colony reach concrete and valuable conclusions.

Politics.

The value of research and of having anthropological experts attached to a colonial administrator would probably mainly consist in that a scientifically trained mind would provide a dispassionate, disinterested attitude which comes from the study of human nature. It might be added that the existence of such an impartial and disinterested expert opinion might be sometimes useful for the administrator / or politician when he deals with such delicate questions as the limitation of the number of asiastics in Africa.

Native Jurisprudence.

The Administrator has to graft our law on to the tribal organisation, he has to administer the resulting mixture; he has to supercede old justice by new. This is largely done in the interests of Europeans who have to deal economically with natives, acquire land, sign contracts and feel safe and secure from moral shocks.

The reformer, who improvises a new tribal constitution, knows the white side of the question, but what about the native side? To the native, his sacred traditions are being upset, his religious values desecrated, his whole tribal constitution turned topsey-turvey. It could be easily demonstrated that none of the colonial constitutions have been drafted with a careful consideration of such fundamental principles of tribal law as the unity of totemic clan, mother-right or classificatory kinship, to take only the foundations of typical primitive tribal constitution.

But even considered as a faulty compromise, a body of native regulations can be administered in a less or more irksome manner. The official must know the principles of social anthropology, he must understand the difference between father-right and matrilineal succession; he must grasp typical native forms of counting descent, inheritance and succession. He must have a clear idea of clan organisation, totemism and the various relations between primitive religion and social order. It is impossible to administer law and justice in a society, with an entirely false view of its constitution. A general knowledge of primitive social organisation can be acquired in an ordinary course of social anthropology. But a specific understanding of the problem of primitive law is more difficult, for here the older anthropology has been under the sway of certain dogmatic assumptions. Even now such a generally acknowledged authority as Rivers speaks about "universal primitive communism", "absence of individual rights and claims", "undifferentiated legal codes", "absence of civil law" and "spontaneous submission to tribal tradition". In <u>Crime and Custom</u>[6] I have tried / to show that these assumptions are not valid even with regard to Melanesia, on which area mainly they have been framed. In that book also I have tried to show what exactly the legal mechanisms in my field of study are, and, from an administrative point of view, it would be possible to show where European administration could safely tamper with native law and where it should leave it alone. Scientific research into the legal mechanism of various African tribes, with special consideration of what forces really make the native obey his tradition, could easily be recommended to colonial authorities. The whole question of direct v. indirect rule which seems to be considered as the real issue in internal administration appears to me incorrectly framed. Indirect administration, that is the establishment of native chiefs, is worthless if this authority does not spring from tribal feeling and if their rule is not in the spirit of tribal tradition. Whom to choose and how to instruct him to rule can only be done by people who have a knowledge of the real tribal law and native feeling. Correct anthropological research would establish, I believe, against the preconceptions of many older anthropologists, a complex system of traditional rules which in every tribe could be distinguished as rules of law, morality and manners. They differ as to the manner in which they are sanctioned. Law is enforced by certain losses consequent upon failure and premiums following a satisfactory fulfilment. Rules of morality are sanctioned by feeling and emotion, at times also by super-natural punishment. Good manners are maintained because of the shame attached to any deviation from them. Anyone who has dealt with natives extensively knows how important it is to be acquainted with their code of good manners; and how hopelessly ridiculous or odious a man becomes to them when they come to regard him as a boor and a bounder. It is also important from another point of view to know what they mean by good manners and to understand how deeply attached they are to them, that is, in order to avoid tampering with them juridically. This applies also obviously to morality. Native religion enters as deeply into tribal organisation and culture as civilised faith does with us. An abrupt prohibition placed on certain customs because they appear to us unhygienic, offensive or improper, very often shakes the whole structure of tribal law and morality, when a gradual and tactful way of allowing the custom to fade out of existence would lead to the same results without the attending evils. /

It might be useful to mention that in the Dutch colonial service, a two years course is required of all colonial officials for the study of the customary law (adat) of their possessions (Of. van Vollenhoven "Het adatrecht van Nederlandsch Indie", 1918; Kleintjes "Het Staatsrecht van Nederlandsch Indie", 1927).[7] Both as regards the European regulation and the customary law of their colonies, they are fully aware that it not only must be taught to the colonial official but made an object of scientific research.

On education and missionary work.

Here there is no need for me to pass any remarks. Where research is necessary no one is better aware than some intelligent modern missionaries, and above all your organisation.

The real point as far as I can see to be brought home to responsible people in E.Africa is whether the colonies are to be run for the immediate enrichment of a handful of present white colonists or for the future generations of white and coloured alike. The problem of future de-tribalised coloured and bastardised labour is, I believe, a very serious one. I think that in this matter both sides, the Delamerite and the sentimentalist a la Norman Leys are wrong. A comparative study of conditions in E. Africa, S.Africa and the United States – taking as a comparison perhaps also Liberia, the W. Indies and Hayti – seem to show that the more civilised the negro, the more serious his problem. When big masses of white and coloured are in contact, bastardisation must occur, and if, as is inevitable you draw the line of colour at the top end, you immediately introduce a pariah cast, discontented, rebellious and essentially subversive. The more white and civilised the U.S.A. negroes become, the more irksome and unjust will they feel their present treatment by the whites. The S.African labour problem is equally serious. If I were dealing with a capitalist and conservative element in E.Africa, I would enquire what they imagine to be the future of a detribalised, mixed up and bastardised population there. The native, unless he dies out, has a disconcerting tendency to increase very rapidly. He has either to be educated up to our standard, or kept in cultural subjection or both. Is the educated Hindu a / success? Is the whole rather virulent question of independence of India at present not largely due to a too sudden westernisation of the Hindu, and to his "detribalisation"? Personally I feel convinced that the only sensible policy in Africa would be to re-establish as far as possible the old tribal system, not to drive rapidly and forcibly the native out of his own culture and resolutely to oppose the rapacity of the white settler who is preparing for his descendants a future similar to that prepared by the southern slave magnate in importing African slave labour to the States.

Language.

Language is closely associated with culture, and in any form of education the teaching of the language of the higher culture is as necessary as the knowledge of native language is indispensable for the understanding of native culture. Even here, apart from the study of the local tongues, scientific research should be taken into account with regard to what language should be chosen as the official general tongue for education, justice and administration. In many colonies, an intermediate usually simplified form of Arabic, an artificial or "pidgin" form of English or a mixture like Swahili is adopted. In the interests of uniformity as well as of efficiency some comparative study of these various problems should be undertaken in East Africa.

December 1927.
(Signed) B. MALINOWSKI.

Margery Perham,[1] 'A Re-Statement of Indirect Rule, Africa', *Journal of the International African Institute*, 7:3 (July 1934), pp. 321–34.

THE outstanding point about British Africa to-day is the extension of the indirect system of administration. This is the more remarkable because, in the decentralized position of our territories, such extension is the result of free adoption on the part of the different governments. It is the endorsement of the system, after long experience, by practical administrators. Yet in England it has lately been subject to a considerable amount of criticism. The object of this article is to re-state indirect rule in the light of these criticisms, in the hope of rebutting what is misinformed and incorporating what is constructive.

I must begin by defining indirect rule in order to concentrate the argument and avoid certain diversions which have generally been used to describe, not a general principle of government, but a particular and local form of its application. The expedient by which a conquering people makes use of the institutions of the conquered is as old as history. There are circumstances which, if only for a time, make it unavoidable. Direct government in the fullest sense may be practicable where neighbouring and culturally intelligible people are annexed, but it is out of the question when the agents of a distant nation are first confronted by a numerous and primitive people. An effective administrative grasp is checked by lack of power, and even more of knowledge, and the situation imposes on the rulers at least a tacit recognition of existing laws and customs.

It is often in history that a virtue has been consciously made of this necessity, and a system dictated by the convenience of the ruler prolonged in the interests of the ruled. It has happened more than once in the history of the British Empire because the expedient is particularly congenial to the national temperament. Nowhere, however, was the expedient so consciously and systematically developed as by Lord Lugard in Northern Nigeria.[2] It does not, as some critics seem to maintain, detract from his achievement that it was begun in / response to circumstances, or that examples of similar, though less considered, response can be found elsewhere. By trial and error over a series of years he and his staff built up a practical administration adapted to the immediate needs of the country as they saw them. It was a definite and yet a highly adaptable system which incorporated native societies as subordinate units of government. It gave statutory authority, in accordance with the varying capacity of the tribes, to native courts, native authorities, and later, to native treasuries. It appeared as the years went on that Lord Lugard and his officers had built even better than they knew. A series of *ad hoc* enactments and instructions developed into a 'corpus' in which principles applicable far beyond the Western Sudan could be distinguished from their local application. But it was not until later that, in characteristic British fashion, the chief architect and others began to find a philosophical explanation for what they had done, and to realize how readily their system could be informed with the new scientific spirit. The system, like others of our constitutional inventions, is not weaker but stronger for this sequence of development, and it is strange that some critics should have turned this also into a reproach.

More than one critic has contrasted indirect rule unfavourably with the equalitarian and assimilative policy of Victorian humanitarians and the administrators they influenced. An examination of this view will throw useful light upon our subject. The Victorians, it is said, looked upon native society and saw that it was bad. They set to work with a will to civilize it. The new theory of administration has weakened this will and has even induced officials and teachers to aim at preserving rather than superseding native culture; it has therefore come to act as a drag upon natural and desirable progress. The reply is that a growing knowledge of African society has taught us a new respect for it. We begin to understand how African cultures were integrated and so to recognize the functions of certain customs which seemed to our grandfathers the perverse aberrations of the heathen. We identify in miniature and under primitive disguise the elements common to all human societies, and we begin to question whether those elements, instead of being wholly destroyed, might not be re-expressed in forms more serviceable to the needs of to-day. We can see by example that what one of our African governors / has called the 'killing-out' of a culture, or even of selected items in it, may be an injurious process. A tribe which is made to feel that its customs are ignored or despised by its white rulers loses its self-respect and sinks into apathy or bitterness. The loss of social energy is the more complete because our society is unable or unwilling to absorb the individuals into which an African community may be disintegrated by our contact.

Those who deplore the new theory of administration are apt to regard anthropology as its evil genius. They contend that the anthropologists, and those whom they infect with their point of view, are so deeply absorbed in their reconstruction of the past that they begin to exaggerate its value and to denounce all those changes which spoil the scientific completeness of their reconstruction. Their views are eagerly appropriated by administrators who have their own reasons for desiring to stereotype African conditions. They may be pedants who like to pose as exclusive authorities upon obscure tribal cultures: they may be prompted by lethargy to prefer the tractable savage to the restless semi-literate: they may be romanticists who admire the dignity and aesthetic simplicity of their beloved primitives.

It might seem unnecessary, especially in this Journal, to attempt a justification of anthropology, or to pay serious attention to a depreciation of scientific knowledge as an aid to government. The earlier anthropologists were very legitimately concerned to record primitive cultures before European influence obliterated the picture. Any regret they may have expressed at the gaps change had made in their records were quite unavailing. And to-day, as is well known to readers of this Journal, anthropologists are beginning to study the phenomena of change itself, and that in no hostile spirit. As for the failings of officials, human beings will always justify these in current scientific language if they can, and pedantry and lethargy in so far as they exist will not be exorcized by prohibiting the study of anthropology or introducing more direct forms of government.

The prejudice expressed by many educated Africans against anthropology deserves more serious attention. It is natural that the newly self-conscious African should be quick to suspect attitudes of superiority, and he unfortunately believes himself to be singled out as the subject for a specially humiliating form of study. It is regrettable that / the branch of sociology directed towards primitive society should have a separate name as it allows Africans to ignore the amount of what is really anthropological study that Europeans direct upon each other, and which is increasingly valued as an assistance to government. There is a tendency for the educated African to challenge the anthropologists with his own interpretation of native society. Nothing could be of more value than authoritative anthropology from an African with the proper training and impartiality. Unfortunately the candidate for civilization is too often unwilling to face squarely the backwardness of his own people. He is hardly able yet to adopt a scale of values that does not accord contempt to primitive cultures and uncritical laudation to the first instalments of an alien civilization, and his first essays in anthropology are sometimes written with the object of exalting his past or of disproving the need of European tutelage. However deeply we may sympathize with his position, we must conclude that unqualified Africans are unlikely to add much to the knowledge upon which policy outside their own usually urban areas must be founded. This is not to say that their views are not politically of the greatest importance; indirect rule, may, indeed, stand or fall according to the expression it affords to the political energies of the educated class. The time will come when Africans will turn eagerly to the records of anthropology. We may hope they will never find themselves in the melancholy position of some Maoris whom I saw visiting a European anthropologist in order to learn from him what was the day sacred for planting and what was the magic which should be made over the seeds.

The exponent of indirect rule, though he may not commit himself to a contradiction of the Victorian estimate of African culture, is definite on the question of how and how fast it can be changed. The estimate of time is important, because of its effects upon policy. Many able men in South Africa clung almost to the end of the century to the belief that savagery would wither away at the very touch of civilization. It was only necessary to remove or incapacitate chiefs, to prohibit certain customs and to send a few magistrates and missionaries into a reserve, and civilization would automatically set in. A few years after their appointment we find these agents reporting with impatience and regret that the tribesmen are still clinging to their heathen practices. / The condition of these same reserves after some fifty years or more of such influence is a comment on this early hope and upon the methods it suggested.

I am not suggesting that conditions in these reserves had remained unchanged, but that change had not been progress. Indeed, the answer to those who fear that indirect rule means the preservation of the past is that such preservation is quite beyond the powers of any administration, direct or indirect. What government has the power and the knowledge to prevent men from adapting their culture to the many and drastic changes we have made in their environment? When the South African Protectorates are cited as an example of a preservative policy what is really meant is that the peoples there have not been helped to make a successful adaptation. It is true that most of those concerned with the Protectorates, European and African alike, made their plans in the conscious hope of being able to preserve tribal institutions, but in a world in which every aspect of native life was changed, sometimes obviously, sometimes more subtly, they succeeded in preserving only the form and not the content of the old society. And, thus preoccupied, they neglected the task of guiding adaptation. But this Protectorate policy has nothing in common with indirect rule. It is a policy of non-interference, of proffering advice, of leaving two parallel governments to work in a state of detachment unknown in tropical Africa. Under indirect rule native institutions are incorporated into a single system of government and subjected to the continuous guidance, supervision, and stimulus of European officers.

For the sake of the argument I have divided what was really one: the attitude of the nineteenth-century humanitarian to native culture arose from his absolute confidence in his own civilization as a substitute. This confidence has been set to its advantage against what has been called the cultural agnosticism of to-day with the wavering front it turns towards barbarism. We may regret, but we cannot regain, this confidence. It is out of our power to stop the whirling of the European roundabout in order to give an impression of stability to backward races. And is it not possible that our relations with Africa will be none the worse for the tempering of arrogance with a little humility? The change is not likely to go too far. There may be moments in Africa when a prosperous agricultural scene takes on such Arcadian / colours to a European whose mind holds pictures of ugly and stricken urban areas in his own country that he may be tempted to deny the superiority of his own civilization. But this is a feeling which, if he argues the subject out honestly with himself, is unlikely to become a rational conviction.

This slightly less confident attitude towards our own civilization is by no means a refusal of it to the African or a denial of his capacity to share in it. Indirect rule is based upon a juster appreciation than was possible before of the possibilities of assimilation. Where this has gone farthest it is generally the result of strong or prolonged European influence, generally in combination with economic prosperity. Is this influence or this prosperity likely to be spread very rapidly outside certain head-quarters and lines of communication in the near future? The achievement of the urban lawyer or trader in civilizing himself in one or two generations is very important for his own pride and prosperity and as an indication of the capacity of his race, but it gives us no standard by which to gauge the future advance of his fellow millions. There will, at least, be an interval for them, and even the most ardent assimilator would surely not have it an empty one.

Those who turn back to the Victorian's point of view may sometimes fail to distinguish his belief that rapid cultural substitution was possible and desirable with his advocacy of just and equal treatment for subject peoples. They charge the indirect school and the anthropologists with playing into the hands of repression by supporting a policy of differential treatment and of offering a spurious scientific reason for indefinite political subordination on grounds of colour. It may be admitted that nothing but the possession of full citizenship will secure Africans from injustice and discrimination in a mixed state. But the issue is not a simple one. We differ from the older view to-day, not in denying the right to equality, but in having learned from experience that, in the stage of development reached by the majority of Africans, equality offered in the same form to white and black means that the one receives the substance and the other the shadow. This differential policy is not easy to administer, and lends itself easily to misuse in the interests of a selfish and negative plan of segregation. Yet it is strange that segregation and indirect rule should have been confused. The policy of segregation is of course that of the mixed / territories, and here indirect rule has never been applied. If we except the small white element in Uganda and Tanganyika we can say that it was originated and has flourished in the purely native territories. Its successful execution demands an atmosphere of trust and friendliness with a patience and knowledge which a white community in the ardour of pioneering can hardly hope to achieve. Such a community does not readily hand over to Africans the important administrative and financial responsibilities which characterize indirect rule. It would, indeed, be roughly true to say that in British Africa indirect rule obtains in obverse ratio to the amount of white settlement. Where it has been applied to Africans in close contact with

European colonists, as with the Wachagga of Kilimanjaro, the indirect school might claim that it seems likely to prove more effective in helping them, not only to protect their rights, but also to civilize themselves than has the so-called 'identity' policy applied to the South African Ciskei.

Indirect rule is more vulnerable from the exactly opposite side. There is some truth in the complaint that it fails to preserve African societies and distorts their development in the attempt to adapt them. This arises from a defective knowledge of the societies in tutelage, less excusable now than in the past, and from forcing functions upon institutions quite unfit to perform them. Numerous examples can be quoted of attempts to turn African chieftainship with its peculiar attributes and its numerous limitations into an autocracy or, more often, a bureaucratic agency of the foreign power. This important criticism cannot be evaded because it strikes more effectively upon direct rule, where little attempt is made to study, and still less to reanimate, African institutions. It concentrates attention upon the central feature of indirect rule, its claim to assist adaptation. Anthropological study of this process has hardly begun, and meantime we are left to speculate whether it is possible by any exercise of political art to carry over a primitive institution into the modern world and there help to mould it into a new form. It is argued on the one side that African institutions are incapable of such adaptation: on the other, that it is by the clumsiness of our very attempts that we spoil their great inherent qualities. Dr. Rattray[3] deplores our neglect of the natural democracy of the tribal system, and two Africans, Mr. Mockerie,[4] speaking of the Kikuyu people, and Chief Tshekedi,[5] of the Mangwato, maintain / the same view. They are speaking of a democracy based upon the association of family units, with graded responsibilities arising from hereditary status. Can such a democracy endure when economic and educational forces are driving a wedge into every family in Africa? And can the diffusion of authority and the general participation in public affairs, which are natural to an equalitarian and scattered agricultural population, be prolonged in face of the deep economic changes taking place as a result of European influence? Can the co-operative character of African society be transformed into co-operation in the technical sense, or adopted whole into the new corporative systems which in all the variety they display in Europe to-day show a common tendency to destroy the old liberal individualism? And will the potential energy and initiative of Africans be drawn out to their fullest if they are assisted to skip, or to cut short, the individualist phase under which we have been goaded into such immense productivity? These are not questions to be answered academically, and in debating them we must not fall into the error of treating institutions as if they were organic. They were developed by Africans to meet certain needs, and no alien ruler can prolong their existence when those needs have changed without changing their character. But if from long employment of such institutions Africans have developed certain characteristics which we recognize as socially valuable, we can at least help them to frame new institutions so as to give play to these characteristics. And, still more, we can avoid imposing, in the interests of our conception of efficiency, if not, indeed, of mere administrative convenience, institutions which run exactly counter to their genius.

So far in this argument we have been dealing in turn with critics who have taken their stand upon opposite sides. We may now enter, as it were, the administrative head-quarters of the system itself and make a practical survey of the situation it has been designed to meet.

What is the situation before us? The contact of two cultures. Each of the two groups of critics seems to be concentrating too much upon one or other of the cultures and too little upon their actual point of contact. It is upon the realities of this contact that indirect rule must be, and to a great extent has been, based. It should not be diverted from them by theories, scientific or political, as to the desirability of preserving or replacing African culture, and it should recognize that / culture not in isolation, not as it was, nor as it might be, but as at a given moment of contact, it is. Indirect administration must, perhaps, especially guard itself against the temptation to try to revive or preserve what was. It should be as ready to accept the realities of assimilation as it is ready to accept those of conservatism; to invest an advanced urban population with suitable municipal institutions, as to confirm the unquestioned authority of a secluded rain-making clan-head. It is possible that the prolonged anthropological investigations carried out by the administrations of Tanganyika and Nigeria have given a wrong impression: their object was to allow the people, in so far as they themselves desired it, to make a fresh start from familiar ground. Few tribal councils, after years of bewildering disintegration, are able to rationalize about the exact administrative forms with which they will compromise between the past and the present, nor can the political officer make an arbitrary decision for them. Once the familiar forms have been restored, the people are free, and, in the two territories to which I have just referred, are encouraged, to develop and adjust them. In this dynamic relationship the practical administrator is made aware of two apparently contradictory tendencies operating in African society, the one adaptable and the other conservative. When he endeavours, often unconsciously, no doubt, to combine these tendencies into harmonious motion, he must contrive some form of indirect administration.

If, as I have suggested, we have not yet enough experience or expert observation of the process of adaptation to European contact under indirect systems to be certain how and how quickly and successfully it will take place, there is at least encouraging evidence of the racial capacity of most African peoples for adaptation. We can reconstruct something of such adaptation to pre-European contacts. Disparate clans were bound swiftly into strong federations by some dominant personality. Tribes conquered by strangers from the Hamitic north submitted to an effective compromise between the new political centraliza-tion and the old clan-system. Pastoral people moved into tsetse-ridden country and made what must have been a deep and painful social adjustment. Groups fringing a dominant fighting tribe made a rapid and deliberate adoption of their customs: others, incorporated by conquest, were quickly indistinguishable from their masters. Although we should not / generalize too soon about the Afri-cans' reaction to the intrusion of Europe, their vigorous receptivity does at least promise an ethno-logically healthier relationship than has been possible with the Amerindian, the Australian, and Polynesian peoples.

If the preservationist should be asked to take comfort from the adaptability of the African, the assimilator should be invited to consider his conservatism. The places most readily accessible to travellers, among whom these critics are sometimes numbered, are naturally those most open to European influence. Much has rightly been made of the revolution in African transport and its sig-nificance, yet there are still vast areas untraversed by any main road or railway where the old Africa remains more evident than the new, and where a single political officer with a couple of missionaries, a few native teachers, and perhaps an Indian or Syrian trader represents civilization to fifty or a hundred thousand Africans. What alternative to indirect administration is there here except a bar-rier between rulers and ruled crossed only by those anonymous native agents, police, interpreters, and the rest, who almost inevitably abuse the irresistible for-eign authority upon which they draw?

But African social organization can also show its tenacity when exposed to prolonged European influences. This might be expected of a Kano[6] or a Buganda,[7] where the imposing political structures commanded our respect and recognition from the first. It is far more surprising to find that the multitudinous kinship-groups of South-Eastern Nigeria have retained their vitality for thirty or forty years in spite of the strongest social and economic influences, and of all our attempts to group them into manageable units under more convenient adminis-trative forms. I should have found it hard to credit if I had not myself observed the enthusiasm with which they responded to the invitation to revive their old councils and groupings. Another sign of conservatism is surely the fidelity with which Africans seem to cling to their chiefs, even where the position of these has undoubtedly been changed by their association with the foreign power. Many examples could be given from tropical Africa of this fidelity and its very practical results under indirect rule. Even in Southern Africa where chieftainship has been deliberately allowed to crumble into disuse and poverty, the people continue to proffer their barren allegiance. Zulus still fight / over a question of succes-sion. The Transkei Bunga (Council) and the South African Native Conference[8] both contain a large proportion of educated Africans, yet both have recently passed unanimous resolutions in favour of preserving the chieftainship. An African clergyman said that 'some of the natives were of opinion that the continued existence of a tribe depended on the existence of a chief.' In the Bunga requests were made for higher fees for chiefs in order that they might keep up the state and fulfil the obligations still expected of them by their people. Criminal jurisdiction was asked for them and comparisons made in favour of the policy of the Imperial Government in this respect. 'Amongst us natives', said one member, 'the word chief is far-reaching. How we pick our chiefs cannot be understood by other nations. They cannot understand the respect we give the chief. It can only be understood by us.' In Lagos, in spite of all the influences that have been brought to bear upon this large port for fifty years, the townspeople appear to take a far greater interest in the position of the titular head of the submerged kingdom, and the dynastic feuds of his house, than in the affairs of the Municipal and Legislative Councils for all their local African membership. The first impulses of African nationalism roused by the pressure of the dominant civilization seem likely in some parts to take the form of intenser loyalty towards chiefs: the Kikuyu have even asked for the innovation of a paramount chief. Yet it might have been anticipated that chieftainship, deprived of what seem to have been its most essential functions and privileges, would be one of the first institutions to atrophy. We might venture to expect that under indirect rule chiefs—and the majority of Africans under our tutelage recognize chiefs—will remain as centres round which the councils and administrations of their people will develop, themselves becoming increasingly 'constitutional.'

Yet, perhaps, it is dangerous to venture upon even so much anticipation. The great task of indirect rule is to hold the ring, to preserve a fair field within which Africans can strike their own balance between conservatism and adaptation. There is no formula for finding the mean between the two equally mistaken policies of too much and too little intervention: it remains a test of our political judgement.

These then, are some of the characteristics of African society with which the administrator has to reckon. But in this contact there are two / cultures, not one, to be considered. The point is well illustrated by the Indian story in which the Brahmans protested against the prohibition of suttee[9] because it was a sacred custom of the Hindus which should be respected. 'Be it so', replied Sir Charles Napier.[10] 'The burning of widows is your custom. Prepare the funeral pile. But my nation has also a custom. When men burn women alive, we hang them and confiscate all their property. My carpenters shall therefore erect gibbets on which to hang all concerned when the widow is consumed. Let us all act according to national customs.'

There are obvious African parallels. Thus, although we have moved a long way from the righteous indignation with which Sir Harry Smith[11] forbade 'the sin of buying wives' among the defeated Xosa,[12] there are limits beyond which, even in the face of the most convincing scientific plea for a policy of gradualness, we should be unable to extend our tolerance. But the story symbolizes far more than this. It reminds us that the general form taken by the contact is at least as much determined by the nature of our culture as of theirs. Although we may discuss these questions academically as if there were a complete freedom of choice in the selection of a policy we must recognize, without being too fatalistic, that actually certain limits are set by our national character and political traditions. Our view of the contact tends to lose perspective when we excuse ourselves from the necessity of studying our own side of it.

Indirect rule is the characteristically British reaction to the political problem of Africa. It derives partly from our conservatism, with its sense of historical continuity and its aristocratic tradition. Our experience has not taught us to believe in fresh constitutional starts, or in the existence of political principles of universal applicability, though, as the Victorian humanitarians showed, we wavered a little under the influence of the French Revolution. This conservatism may degenerate into an exclusiveness that would deny all possibility of Africans ever being able to reach civilization by way of our natural expression of it. But indirect rule derives equally from our liberalism with its respect for the freedom of others and its conscious reaction from the old selfish type of imperialism. It is another expression of the tradition which allowed, and even encouraged, colonies to develop into dominions and which guaranteed the cultural freedom of French Canadians or / South African Boers. Its danger is to decline into a merely negative attitude, a refusal to undertake distasteful responsibilities. It is because of these qualities that even where British officials have not been working under a definite system of indirect rule like that initiated by Lord Lugard, they have shown a persistent preference for indirect methods and a distaste for forcing their own ideas upon Africans. The great strength of local government in England, and our increasing belief in the principle of voluntarism made us ready to find graded constitutional settings for small African societies. The 'D' court of the small chief with his elders is no anomaly to those accustomed to the amateur justice of petty sessions. The native treasuries express our principle that executive responsibility should always be associated with financial. The critics of indirect rule have not, as far as I know, constructed an alternative system, but when they do, they should remember that, unless it is congenial to our national temperament, however authoritatively it might be promulgated from above, it would assuredly become something different in the hands of the district officer.

This raises an important and final consideration. Administration in Africa must be related to the probable destiny of the territory concerned. Since the loss of America the tradition of the Empire has fostered the development of its dependent communities, and not only those of our own race and colour, towards that form of association in independence which is called dominion status. There is no reason to think that Britain would, or could, prevent her African territories from developing in the same direction. Sir Donald Cameron,[13] who extended indirect rule to Tanganyika and has revitalized it in Nigeria, has stated that he regards it as the best way to fulfil our task, the training of the people in the art of administration so that they may ultimately stand by themselves. It may be that indirect rule is not suited to such conditions as those of South Africa where the hope of the Africans must be to take their place one day in the colonial state, or to those of French Africa which is expected to remain an integral part of a centralized empire. It may be less essential here to preserve continuity and to maintain the pride and unity of tribal societies. Where the future is uncertain as with those native territories which contain small white communities and where British policy is perplexed by two / divergent calls upon its liberalism, it is more difficult to prescribe the best form of native administration. I believe, myself, that in all circumstances indirect rule is more effective than direct as a political training for tribal Africans. The political achievements of Africans under indirect rule already stand comparison with those of their fellows who, as in South Africa, Liberia, and the colony of Sierra Leone, have been obliged to construct institutions from the foundations upwards upon foreign models. Yet indirect rule is only a transitional method. The immediate test of its success will be the frequency with which it receives and requires revision in response to progress: the ultimate test will be the ability with which the African territories take their place in the world as self-governing nations.

MARGERY PERHAM.

Oxford Summer School on Colonial Administration, Second Session (printed privately for the members of the School) (Oxford: Oxford University Press, 1938).

OPENING SPEECH
The Rt. Hon. Malcolm MacDonald,[1] *M. P.,*
Secretary of State for the Colonies

In the course of his tenure of office–brief or long, as the case may be–the Secretary of State for the Colonies has to do and decide many and various things. Not a few of them are dull. Many of them, if far from dull, have a touch of oppressiveness by reason of their weight and complexity, to say nothing of the difficulty of estimating their political repercussions–one of the most popular of which might be the downfall of the Minister himself. But in his life there are some high light; some moments of pure delight. And this moment of opening the Oxford Summer School on Colonial Administration is one of them. Although it is an occasion which is attended by no ministerial anxiety, it is of peculiar importance. Indeed, I can hardly imagine a project more fruitful than this which brings together Civil Servants from every corner of the Colonial Empire, and also from the Sudan[2] and Burma,[3] for the purpose of discussing their common, allied, and separate problems and of listening to various relevant pronouncements by authorities of unquestioned eminence. Great and powerful as may be the Secretary of State, this is a thing that he could not do. Not all the resources at my disposal would enable me to create either a forum or surroundings even remotely comparable with those in which you are going to spend the next ten days. In Whitehall we have buildings of massive dignity; but they can scarcely call forth that inspiration which is one of the magic powers of the steeples and domes and towers of Oxford. Nor, perhaps, can we produce in our echoing halls and corridors that urge to quiet, pure, intellectual effort which haunts, ghost-like, every nook and cranny of this famous, lovely university city. That is why, knowing the limitations of my own office and its environment, I welcome the help which Oxford can give in a sphere in which she is supreme.

I am therefore delighted to have this opportunity of expressing, before everything else, my warm appreciation of the enterprise and foresight of the authorities of the University in organizing this Summer School. The Vice-Chancellor is here to bless you, and the members of the Social Studies Research Committee will watch over your deliberations. But because behind every vital movement you will always find the creative force of a man or a woman, or both, I cannot refrain from singling out Professor Coupland[4] and Miss Margery Perham[5] for special thanks and congratulations. They have both already given much to the Colonial / Empire; but the conception of this School was one of their happiest efforts. Again, I would express gratitude to the authorities of Lady Margaret Hall who have placed this building, with all its delightful amenities, at your disposal. I personally greatly appreciate this opportunity to see the inside of a college, which previously I have only gazed upon from the outside from the punt in the Cherwell in which I did most of my work when I was an undergraduate. Here again one detects the influence of an individual, and no doubt the Principal of Lady Margaret Hall was all the more willing to co-operate in this great enterprise because she is the distinguished sister of a distinguished retired Colonial Governor, Sir Selwyn Grier,[6] whose name, I am glad to see, appears in the list of those who are to lead your discussions.

As you all know, the first School of this kind was held in Oxford last year, and its success was so great and so well deserved that it was decided to repeat it. Thus it has come about that you who are here this year are to have the opportunity of sharing in what my predecessor, Lord Harlech,[7] described as 'a unique and fruitful experience'. Although I understand that it is not the intention that these schools should be held annually–and indeed I think it would be a pity if anything like a routine were to be established in a matter of this kind–we all hope that it will be possible for them to take place at not too infrequent intervals.

I have only very recently returned to the Colonial Office, and you will not expect in the circumstances to hear from me any learned disquisition on colonial administration or any epoch-making pronouncement of policy. How you, who are so closely concerned with practical colonial administration, must tremble whenever a new, green Secretary of State arrives in Downing Street, lest he seeks to assert his authority by hastening into some new, great, ill-considered declaration of policy! For the moment I am following, as closely as possible, the example of that famous character, Brer Rabbit, and lying low and saying nothing. I am picking up many old threads, learning what all of you have been doing since I last had the honour of a brief association with you three years ago, and endeavouring to master the complexities so that I may help you to seize the opportunities of some of the noblest work that the people of this Imperial isle can turn their hands to. Indeed, there is nothing that I should like better than to stay with you during the next ten days, to be a member of this School listening to your discussions. But alas, I am not even allowed to stay here for one leisurely morning. My next urgent engagement is in London shortly after 2.30 this afternoon, and the 30 miles an hour limit prevents the journey from being accomplished with that dispatch which was not only possible but customary in my day at the University.

The curriculum in this Summer School is generous and wise. / It is not strictly confined to what may be termed your professional interests. You are to commence with a series of surveys of those powerful forces outside the British Empire which must profoundly influence the affairs of the Empire itself. Professor Coupland and Sir Alfred Zimmern[8] and Mr. H.D. Henderson[9] will set the Empire in its proper perspective. Then, too, you will have opportunities of comparing the problems which arise in our colonies with those which face administrators in India and the Sudan, as well as in some foreign dependencies. After that Sir Alan Pim,[10] Miss Perham, Mr. Mayhew,[11] and others will talk, with their own peculiar, great authority, our own Colonial 'Shop'. How skilful the organizers have been in their choice of those who should address you! And how wise they have been in providing abundant time not only for lectures but also for discussions! It is in these debates, and perhaps not less in the more informal conversations which will take place out of school, that the exchange of ideas and the hammering out of common principles will result in the breaking down of watertight compartments and in a fuller realization of the general trend of development in the Colonial Empire.

Colonial policy must not be a hotchpotch business, concocted at random each day according to the exigencies and seeming requirements of that particular moment, and perhaps undone the next day when what is expedient seems to have changed. It must have thought and plan and design; it must be constantly inspired by some great, main purpose. Nor must these purposes have application only here and there, in this colony or that; if they are right, they should be the consistent motive force behind policy throughout the whole Colonial Empire. The main policies–whether they are concerned with health, or education, or government, or some other matter–should advance as steadily as may be over the whole front from the Falkland Islands round the world and back to Fiji.

It is sometimes difficult for you when you are busily engaged in day-to-day administration, and for us in the midst of our hectic occupations in the Colonial Office, to 'see the wood for the trees'. But here, in Lady Margaret Hall, you will have leisure to survey, as from some high tower, the whole wood.

What is the main purpose of the British Empire? I think it is the gradual spread of freedom amongst all His Majesty's subjects, in whatever part of the earth they live. We in this country have a passion for liberty; we gained it as a result of long struggles by our forefathers; and we would fight and die for its maintenance again. We feel that it is good for us, and essential for us. And one of our peculiarities is that if we think something is good for us, we think it is good for other people also.

The spread of freedom in British countries overseas is a slow– / sometimes a painful–evolutionary process. The pace varies from place to place, according to local conditions. There may even, sometimes, be inevitable setbacks. But over the generations the evolutionary process goes on. In some countries the process has already reached completion. The Dominions are already completely free, each of them equal in status with Great Britain herself, each of them clothed with all the constitutional rights and powers of fully sovereign nations.

That same spirit guides our administration of the Colonial Empire. Even amongst the most backward races of Africa our main effort is to teach those peoples to stand always a little more securely on their own feet. In spite of the great variety of conditions and of circumstances we can, I think, say with confidence that the trend is towards the ultimate establishment of the various colonial communities as self-supporting and self-reliant members of a great commonwealth of free peoples and nations. The objective will be reached in different places at different times and by many different paths. Before it is reached there may be rearrangements of political divisions; units at present separate may be combined, others may be spilt up into component parts. The important thing is to ensure so far as is possible that whatever changes are necessary should be so effected as to be in harmony with the general aim.

But it will be generations, perhaps even centuries, before that aim is accomplished in some cases. In the meantime *we* are, in greater or lesser degree, responsible for government over a vast space of the earth and over a multitude of peoples. The eyes of the world are set on British Colonial Administration to-day. It behoves us now, more than ever before, to be vigilant and see that the standard of our colonial government is honourable and high.

As I have said, if I have a regret in addressing you to-day, it is that I cannot stay on and go through the School with you. During the next ten days I shall think of you with envy. At the moment I would only return to the point where I began. In declaring the School to be open I express the deep appreciation of all of us to the Vice-Chancellor[12] and to the Social Studies Research Committee as personified in Professor Coupland and Miss Perham for making this gathering possible. This School is the occasion for the setting alight of many torches–destined to be carried to many lands. But while their beams will brighten the paths that lie ahead of us, each torch thus carried forth will always throw back at least one beam of gratitude to the original source of illumination in Oxford. /

INAUGURAL ADDRESS
AFRICA AND WORLD POLITICS
The Rt. Hon. Lord Lugard,[13] *G.C.M.G., C.B., D.S.O.*

I PROPOSE to offer a few comments on the part which the colonies–especially those in Africa–have recently played in world politics on the one hand, and on the other in the evolution of world opinion regarding the relations of the controlling powers to the subject races.

The claims of Germany and Italy for colonial expansion have lately revived the jealousies to which the 'Partition of Africa' gave rise fifty years ago. Italy's attack on Abyssinia[14] caused acute tension in world politics, but has eliminated her from the category of dissatisfied Powers. Germany's claims were at first based on the need for access to sources of raw materials for her industries, and for lands where her surplus population might settle.

Exhaustive statistics compiled by the League,[15] and by an organization of twenty-eight nations for the study of conditions for 'Peaceful Change', together with researches by 'Chatham House', and many other national associations and individual writers* have demonstrated that the denial of sovereignty over colonial territory does not substantiate the German claims–though there are admitted difficulties in regard to currency and foreign exchange. The claim appears therefore to be now based on the prestige accruing from the possession of colonies.

There are probably many who think that it would have been wiser to restore her colonies to Germany under mandate conditions than to have deprived her of them entirely. She has now declared that a mandate would not satisfy her *amour propre,* while her neighbours fear that if restored in full sovereignty she would become a menace to them.

Prompted by the desire for 'appeasement' a 'National Memorial' was presented to the Prime Minister, signed by some 400 persons representative of every section of public life, urging that all African colonies should be placed under direct international control, in which Germany would take her place on terms of complete equality. Such a scheme appears to offer insuperable difficulties. The example of the 'Congo Free State' before it became a Belgian colony has shown that an International State without responsibility to any supervising authority is disastrous.

But an International Council charged with executive functions can obviously be responsible to no other body.

Is it 'practical politics' to assume that a single central Secretariat can administer all Africa, and undertake the day-to-day work which now occupies the time of the various Colonial Ministries of the Powers who exercise sovereignty in that

---

* See Grover Clark, *A Place in the Sun* (1936), 10s. 6d. showing that political control confers no commensurate economic advantage, and that a partial monopoly cannot compensate the cost of administration. /

continent–work which is done at their cost by a very large staff of experts familiar with each territory? Is it possible for a Central Council to formulate policies and record decisions regarding countries of which the majority would be quite ignorant? Who is to decide when members differ on questions of vital importance?

The Governor of each territory, appointed by the Council, would naturally apply the colonial policy of his nation, and we cannot suppose that the highest posts would be given to nationals of the former Colonial Power, for on the principle of 'appeasement' Germany's claims would be insistent. The condition of Tanganyika or Kenya under a German Governor would differ little from transfer. I cannot imagine any system more certain to engender international friction. Finally, is it conceivable that other colonial Powers would be willing (in the words of Sir Daniel Hall) 'to renounce their separate Sovereignties and create a Trust for the administration of all Africa'? For these and many other cogent reasons I judge the proposal to be untenable. It is difficult to understand how its distinguished sponsors could reconcile it with our pledges to the natives.

The 'Next Five Years' Group have also formulated a 'Peace-plan' over the signatures of such men as Lord Cecil,[16] Sir Arthur Salter,[17] Professor Gilbert Murray,[18] Lords Lytton[19] and Allen, and Sir Alfred Zimmern. The Covenant they suggest should be embodied in a new Protocol. Any dissatisfied Power would submit its claims to an investigating committee, and all adherents, including Germany, would be pledged to accept third-party judgement. An aggressor would be the common enemy whom all must coerce by sanctions, or ultimately by war. This proposal only postpones the solution of the colonial problem.

Mr. Amery,[20] who has consistently opposed an Anglo-German deal at the expense of the native population, suggests that colonial Governments which export produce should make an economic agreement with the markets of central Europe for mutual trade with mutual preference. The difficulty of doing so lies in the most-favoured-nation clause, and if adopted we must lose some of our rights under that clause.

For my part I have lost no opportunity of deploring the imposition of quotas in favour of British trade, which deprive the natives of the cheap goods which alone in times of depression they can afford to buy. It has in the past been our proud boast and our justification of our vast Colonial Empire that we sought no / national advantage. The change of policy gives grounds for Germany's claims, and is opposed to the spirit of the declaration by Sir Samuel Hoare[21] at Geneva in 1935. I do not refer to the home market but only to the overseas dependencies, where we are trustees alike for the natives and for the economic requirements of the world.

The interest evoked by the 'Scramble for Africa' died down with the conclusion of treaties vaguely delimiting the territorial spheres of the rival nations. When lately Britain protested against Italy's attack upon Abyssinia, it was argued that during this era of acquisition she had done the same thing herself by the forcible annexation of the Transvaal, the conquest of Ashanti, the protectorate over Uganda, and the overthrow of the Fulani rule in Northern Nigeria. Putting aside the fact that the action was in each case practically forced upon us, we may remind our critics that in every instance without exception the country was restored to its previous rulers. The Dutch-speaking South Africans regained control of the Transvaal and the Orange Free State, and now form a majority of the parliamentary electorate of the whole Union. In the other cases the native rulers were reinstated with powers only restricted in the interests of justice and good government.

It is a relief to turn from the aspect of Africa as a bone of contention between the nations, and to recall how much the Western nations have done for Africa during the past half-century, and their increasing recognition of their responsibilities towards her peoples. In Nyasaland and the Congo, which fifty years ago were in danger of falling under the domination of powerful Moslem slave-traders, tribal warfare, and slave-raids are unknown since the former became a British protectorate and the latter a Belgian colony. Kenya and Tanganyika were then unexplored, and Uganda was the scene of religious wars between Christians and Moslems, and of the bloody rule of pagan despots. In the West small enclaves on the coast and the Niger were held for the import of millions of gallons of noxious spirits.

After the Great War a new spirit seemed to actuate the international outlook, to which the Covenant of the League gave expression. The mandates for the ex-German colonies were primarily concerned with the welfare of the native races, to which the Mandates Commission devoted its attention. Economic advantage seemed no longer to occupy the foreground of the picture. The International Labour Office set up an effective branch to prescribe humane conditions for native labour and several useful conventions have been enacted. A committee—which has since become permanent—investigated not only the question of slavery, but of all analogous restrictions on human liberty, and embodied the results in Conventions on Slavery and Forced Labour. The / Health Section of the League has made invaluable research into the diseases from which the tropical races suffer, and the adequacy of their diet.

Many unofficial organizations came into being—such as the Institut Colonial International and the International Institute of African Languages and Cultures and others for the scientific study of the sociology, languages, and cultural problems of African communities. On all of these, whether official or unofficial, experts of the highest standing were willing to volunteer their services. At a recent meeting of the Executive Council of the African Institute, of which your Chairman is Administrative Director, distinguished representatives of eight different nations took part. The colonies vie with each other in the provision of hospitals, schools, and the training of a native staff.

These are proofs–inconceivable a decade or two ago–of a desire to understand the cultures of the indigenous races and to help them to attain a higher standard of life. We may hope that when in the far future they are able to stand alone, they will look back on their period of tutelage with feelings of goodwill towards their present rulers. The British ideal which you are one and all endeavouring to realize is Co-operation, not Domination, and I most sincerely and cordially wish you all success. /

SUMMARY OF LECTURES AND DISCUSSIONS

This list has been arranged roughly in accordance with the subject-matter and does not exactly correspond with the order in which the lectures and discussions took place.

12. BRITISH NATIVE ADMINISTRATION

[...]

I. PROBLEMS
Miss M. Perham

WE are now passing on from our survey of the background to the study of our main subject, the problems of administration in our colonial dependencies. In considering the general position and ideas of Britain in relation to much that we see in the present world, we may find some reasons for self-satisfaction, but I hope I may be forgiven for introducing the more critical note which is surely necessary when we come to inquire how the yoke of our power fits upon our subject peoples. This is the more requisite since, as compared with officials in the home services, our Colonial Service has inevitably less responsibility towards its own permanent heads, towards Parliament, and, above all, towards the / governed. The continuous criticism–a word which has not the same meaning as depreciation–which is necessary to the health of any bureaucracy is to some extent supplied by members of the Colonial Service themselves, and it has been one of my tasks during my travel and study in Africa to collect and distil this self-criticism.

I propose to consider first our native administration in its more technical meaning and to consider in my second lecture the large economic and political necessities with which it should be brought into harmony.

There can be no doubt as to the main characteristic of our administration today in almost every part of our Colonial Empire, except the West Indies and one or two other territories which are in a more advanced stage of government. The dominant form is that generally described as 'indirect', a transitional method by which indigenous societies are assisted to adapt their institutions for the function of local government. This system succeeds several earlier political phases. In the first days of trade and contact with backward peoples Britain was for long able to evade administrative responsibilities. Later a more assimilative policy was encouraged by our confident equalitarian philosophy and by the modest scope of our first annexations. More extensive acquisitions which followed were treated to the 'protectorate' policy, by which it was hoped that large indigenous societies would continue to function successfully in the new conditions with a minimum of intervention–and expense–upon our part. The shortcomings of both these methods, with a growing appreciation of the vitality and efficacy of native institutions, have led to a wide adoption in recent years of the 'indirect' principles worked out most fully by Lord Lugard in Northern Nigeria.

The dominant note in nearly all the latest reports upon native administration is the attempt to extend or to intensify this principle. This is especially marked in

Sierra Leone; the northern Gold Coast; in Nigeria, where the reforming spirit has been spreading from the south-east to the south-west and the pagan north; in Uganda, especially in the north; in Nyasaland, in Northern Rhodesia, and the Sudan. In Southern Rhodesia the prime Minister[22] has recently introduced legislation to set up courts and council in the reserves, and in commending this to Parliament he quoted largely from the 'Dual Mandate' and declared it the policy of the Government to develop native institutions 'on native lines in so far as such institutions exist'. The three South African protectorates have lately had the advantage of senior officers from Tanganyika, Nigeria, and Uganda and a remodelling from 'protectorate' towards 'indirect' forms has been in process during the last few years.

An interesting point in recent developments by the more experienced / governments has been the movement away from single or few chiefs towards councils and courts of large and fluid membership. There is no doubt that, partly owing to our misconceptions as to the nature of primitive authority, and partly because the individual chief has seemed the most convenient executive agent, we have tended to exaggerate his power where it existed and to invent it where it did not. It will be interesting to watch the experiments now being made in several parts of Africa to correct these tendencies.

These experiments have made us realize more clearly than before the difficulties in the way of carrying out the 'indirect' policy. They are so great that perhaps we sometimes forget that they are not created by that policy but only made more manifest by it. The basic difficulty is one that will appear in its different aspects—education, land-tenure, economic production, law—in all our coming discussions. It is (and here I speak especially of Africa) the great gap between the culture of rulers and ruled. In administration, reduced to its simplest terms, it means that for the most part the people do not understand what we want them to do, or, if they understand, do not want to do it. By some means, day by day, the District Officer has to reach across this gap and induce certain activities. The strongest of these dynamic links is one we least like to admit, that of force. Our initial occupation was seldom completed without some use or show of our superior military weapons and methods, and this superiority is still the ultimate sanction of our government. It is the object of our administration to dilute this force with the greatest possible amount of co-operation based upon a recognition of mutual interests. This is only fully possible by a large general advance in modern education. As administration cannot wait upon this slow advance, we endeavour to instruct the leaders of the people in the objects of our policy, in the hope that they will, by their natural authority, at once diffuse the instruction and exact the necessary obedience. We attempt to bridge the gap further by depressing our standards of efficiency, and also by trying to maintain between the chief and the people, from whom we tend to draw him away, a series of counsellors, sub-chiefs, and headmen who act as further intermediaries.

By all these means we soften the shock of our demands upon native society and lessen the disintegrating results. These palliatives could be carried farther. Administrative and departmental officers might be allowed to relax that pressure for immediate results which tends to isolate the chief and exaggerate and corrupt his power. A greater scope in the exercise of responsibility upon the part of chiefs and others might be secured even at the cost of making those mistakes without which Africans in the sphere of political leadership will not learn to make anything. Greater / efforts could be made, even at the same cost of slowing down the pace of administration, to 'constitutionalize' the exercise of the chief's powers. This would not only retain checks and balances from the past but would prepare the way for more democratic forms in the future. Even so, in the abnormal conditions of Africa, there must be some distortion of the chiefs' power since we have largely changed both its source and functions. It is, indeed, surprising that, in the almost impossible position in which they are placed, there are chiefs whom you and I could name in every African territory who have not allowed their authority to be either emasculated or corrupted. They have held the balance even between their sometimes conflicting duties towards their people on the one hand and their foreign rulers and paymasters upon the other.

A policy of adaptation which is faced by so many difficulties should be tested by frequent investigation of its obscure effects upon native society. Exceptionally qualified officials will be able to carry these investigations a certain distance. They can be carried farther only by those who have the professional training and can obtain the necessary concentration and detachment in their actual fieldwork. That is why anthropologists have been invited to play such a large part in our lectures and discussions during the next few days. They will set their long-range sociological observations beside your practical experience in the ordering of native society. Anthropologists, however, rightly refuse the responsibility of advising directly upon policy. Their task is to offer one of the elements, knowledge of native society as it was and is, that should go to the making of policy. The other elements are to be found in our purposes, political, economic, and moral, in ruling subject peoples. On the last day, therefore, following the anthropologists, we shall attempt, not, indeed, to lay down policy, but to review, in the light of these purposes, the very varied evidence which will have been presented to us by the end of our twelve days.

[...]

24. BRITISH NATIVE ADMINISTRATION

II. PROSPECTS

Miss M. Perham

I SHALL attempt in this address to review our native administration and to consider its immediate prospects in the light of the information and opinions which have been put before us during this School. /

Two main impressions have been formed in my mind. One is that we stand between two periods of administration. The first has been that of occupation, of consolidating our control, of establishing law, order, and a workable structure of government and of initiating economic development. These are straightforward positive tasks. I do not suggest that they are wholly completed. But we are beginning now to see a little more deeply into the complexities, human and physical, of the countries we have taken over. We are being forced to pause and to ask ourselves 'What next? What are we going to do with all these territories—how justify our large dominion, to ourselves, to a questioning world, and to our awakening subjects? How are we going to relate their development to the political and economic world which, as our first five lectures made us realize, has changed so greatly and so unexpectedly in the last ten or fifteen years?'

My second impression is that of the three main agencies through which we have influenced the tropics, political, economic, and educational, the two last have largely escaped the control of the first. While we have been busy elaborating indirect administration, with its Authorities, Courts, and Treasuries, we have done little to relate them to the educational and economic forces which, operating in unofficial hands according to the *laissez-faire* principle, have run upon different, and sometimes contrary, lines.

Upon the economic side our subjects have had a dual life, politically as members of a small tribal administration, economically as citizens of the world. This has been especially true when labour has proved a tribe's most marketable commodity, and we are only just realizing, as Mr. Weaver's address brought out, the serious need to study and regulate conditions of emigrant labour in labour areas and, still more, in relation to tribal life. It may be, as Dr. Leubuscher's address suggested, that trusteeship will require a restriction of capitalist enterprise, whether colonial or metropolitan, among sparse and backward peoples.

These economic maladjustments have been brought home to us in some recent reports, official and unofficial, upon economics and labour, by the riots in the copper belt, and by the West Indian disturbances which Sir Selwyn Grier analysed. The riots in Kilimandjaro and those in S.E. Nigeria a few years ago were largely economic in their causes. The situation in which large groups, as backward labourers or peasant producers, lie outside the boundaries of their local administration and have no means of understanding or of expressing themselves in matters vitally affecting their lives, is not healthy nor even safe. This is illustrated by the main conclusion of the Report upon the Trinidad riots.

In this as in most of our difficulties there is no one rapid easy solution, but only a number of measures which help to lessen it. One, already suggested for the West Indies, is the collective / organization of labourers. Another is the development of local self-government in urban areas and what the Belgians, who have experimented in this matter, call 'extra-customary centres'. We might deliberately attempt to educate chiefs and councils in economic matters. We might also encourage some of those who seek higher education to specialize in accountancy, commerce, or economics, and so enable them in the native press or upon advisory bodies to interpret the unsettling mysteries of economics to their fellow countrymen and also comment upon our imperial economic policy. Another measure, as Mr. Strickland's talk suggested, may be the development of co-operative societies It must be remembered, however, that modern co-operation is not likely to grow immediately out of the primitive tribal variety, since it demands a certain level of enlightened economic individualism and, therefore of education.

On the educational side Mr. Murray's address brought out the degree of incompatibility which still exists between the immediate aims of educational and administrative policy, the one tending to destroy, the other to support, native society. Yet the two have been drawn closer together in the last fifteen years or so by a changed conception on the part of missionary leaders of the values of primitive society; by the new emphasis in educational theory upon training in relation to environment; by the increased control of governments over mission education, and by the entry of government itself into the field. But much more remains to be done before harmony is achieved.

We can now return to the political aspect, having considered its relationship with economics and education. It is very necessary to review our administrative policy since there the anthropologists' contribution seems to have led to certain loss of confidence among members of the School both as to methods and aims. Since the anthropologists have, with design, commented not upon policy but upon its effects, it rests with the administrators to restate their object in the light of the evidence.

If the aim of indirect administration were to preserve native society, this evidence might induce despair. It is, however, something wholly different: to adapt native institutions for the purposes of local government, and that under foreign rulers and in twentieth-century conditions. We need not conclude from the anthropologists that it is hopeless even to attempt this or to make unprofessional efforts to understand native society and the effects of our administration upon it.

Profound modification of native society is inevitable, but the indirect method does preserve some margin for adjustment between what General Smuts[23] calls the steel framework of European government and the vulnerable, minute, and variegated pattern of native society upon which it is imposed. Certain superficial / signs in support of this strike the traveller who studies in action the indirect as against the more direct system–the friendliness of the people; the ease and frankness of their chiefs and counsellors; the maintenance of old customs which have efficacy even in new conditions; the degree of co-operation, as contrasted with mere submission, in such delicate tasks as taxation, sanitation, and forestry measures. For several reasons the results are generally more striking in the larger groups than in the small, and it must be remembered that the anthropologists have taken their examples in the last few days almost entirely from very small, backward areas. Indirect administration demands a more tentative and sympathetic approach towards native peoples, with a readiness to believe, when things go wrong, that the mistakes may be upon our side rather than theirs. Tropical officials may be convicted of suppressing or neglecting native institutions not only on purpose–which may sometimes be necessary–but by mistake. Had the critics, however, made their study in, for example, the Ciskei, Matabeleland, or some foreign territories, an encouraging comparison might have been presented by the northern Gold Coast and the Southern Sudan. The anthropology of the political officer may have limited scientific value, but it has immense administrative benefits. It has further psychological results in that, in a period when Africans are being made to feel a stultifying sense of inferiority, the interest of the foreign official in their history and customs and his recognition of their institutions help to restore individual and social self-respect.

The danger is not so much that we shall abandon our indirect method as that we shall rest too long in a stage which, however interesting and administratively comfortable, should be transitional. Our policy has to be based not only upon research into the past, and sympathy with the present, but also upon purpose for the future of our subjects. That purpose has been first publicly declared by a Secretary of State at the opening of this School–self-government. To that end there can, in the abnormal conditions of our rule, be no natural or gradual development. Our presence precludes natural development. The rapid effects of the uncontrolled, and partly uncontrollable, economic and educational influencies prevent gradual development. The advance will probably be in difficult jerks as regards time and will be uneven as regards population. Far from our native administration being preservative, we probably ought to force the pace if local government is to keep up with the pressure of the educated minority at the centre. I would therefore repeat a proposition I advanced at the last School, and which my travels in the interval have confirmed, that we should consider building up strong provincial governments to act as an intermediary stage / between the kindergarten of indirect rule and the higher education of central representation.

Our ultimate goal also suggests that we should encourage and improve the higher education of Africans. We are, of course, committed to this policy at

Achimota,[24] Makerere,[25] and Yaba,[26] but the question arises as to how we can help African leaders to continue their education after its formal term is past, and communicate to them those social and political traditions which, however powerfully challenged to-day, we still regard as the best not only for us but for those under our tutelage.

How far, as an American writer has recently asked, is our imperialism, economic as well as political, capable of destroying itself? The issue will depend upon this country, upon the knowledge it commands, and the moral energy with which it employs that knowledge. This question takes us on to another plane, and I must leave it to our chairman to attempt an answer in the final lecture of the course.

BOOKS

LUGARD (Lord). *Nigerian Political Memoranda. The Dural Mandate.* 1929. 42s.

CAMERON (Sir Donald). *Principles of Native Administration and their Application.* Lagos, 1934.

BUELL (R.). *The Native Problem in Africa.* 1928. 63s.

MAIR (L.). *Native Policies in Africa.* 1936. 12s. 6d.

PERHAM (M.). *Native Administration in Nigeria.* 1937. 17s. 6d.

Report of the Commission on Higher Education in East Africa. 1937. Colonial No.142.2s. 6d.

EMERSON (R.). *Malaysia* (especially the first and last chapters). New York, 1938. 21s.

MACMILLAN, W.M. *African Emergent.* 1938. 15s.

25. THE PROBLEM OF THE TROPICS

Professor R. Coupland, C.I.E.
The Study of the Tropics.

THE British Empire has been undergoing a process of examination and readjustment since the War. Two sections of the Empire have been dealt with–the Dominions and India. To tackle the third section–the tropical and sub-tropical Dependencies–would in any case be the next task of British imperial statesmanship: and it has been made more urgent by the international factor. It is not a question of German, claims alone. The relationship, political and economic, of the Tropics with more advanced areas is a problem which concerns all the world. Its study and treatment are an essential contribution to a better world-order.

Organized study of the problem is needed to clear the path / for states-manship, and is already afoot. The 'Hailey Survey' of Africa[27] will shortly be published, and its proposals for research will stimulate public interest and will presumably be more or less applicable to the Tropics as a whole. Important work, directly bearing on this problem, is being done at London, Cambridge, and else-where. At Oxford part of the five-years Rockefeller Grant for Social Studies has been allocated to colonial and anthropological research. This Summer School will be repeated, if desired, at intervals; and a course of study, covering one or two terms, on Colonial Administration and allied subjects, is now being organ-ized. The problem of the Tropics should be one of the practical problems for the study of which Nuffield College has just been founded. Other organizations are on an international footing, e.g. the International Institute of African Languages and Cultures, and the Institut International Colonial.

All this study will be 'academic': i.e. it will collect facts, analyse problems, state principles; but of course it will not dictate policy. That is the business of Governments.

Commerce and Colonization.

The basic issue raised by the problem of the Tropics is a moral issue. The great exponents of the British humanitarian tradition, like Wilberforce and Living-stone, thought it our duty not only to abstain from injuring Africa (e.g. by the Slave Trade or other selfish exploitation) but to promote its advancement by a 'positive policy', in which Christianity came first, and then Commerce and Colonization. The first of those factors has been discussed by Professor Murray. How have the other two operated?

Commerce in itself should benefit all parties concerned; and Tropical peo-ples have clearly benefited from the world's demand for their products and their access to the world-market which have enabled them in many areas to raise their standard of living and provide revenue for social services. But economic devel-opment, if not watched and regulated, may be highly injurious to weak and backward peoples, as several black pages of colonial history show. And lesser injury may be done almost unawares. Among many questions which need exam-ination may be mentioned–(1) Export-crops may be encouraged to meet the world's need of raw materials without enough consideration for subsistence in 'slump' periods. (2) Governments may apply a policy of economic nationalism to their colonies to the latters' disadvantage. Ought the 'mandate' principle of equal economic opportunity for all nations to be extended to all the Tropics? (3) The special case of minerals. The world needs them, and their exploitation increases colonial revenues. Its pace can be restricted if native interests require it.

As to Colonization, the growth of 'white' nations like Canada / or even South Africa is impossible in the Tropics, as Livingstone[28] said. The potential advantages of small-scale colonization may be countered by the political difficulties of a 'mixed' society (Hilton-Young Commission).[29] Possibilities of territorial subdivision as advocated by Lord Lugard and others.

The Moral Issue.

In these and all other problems of adjusting the relations of the Western World with the Tropics one is driven back to ultimate questions. Are our professions of 'trusteeship' genuine? On the economic side, granted that we did not go to the Tropics for pure altruism, are we seeking the maximum profit for ourselves or do we put native interests first, content with such profit as remains for us? On the political side, do we regard the natives as subjects or as fellow-subjects, their country as 'belonging' to them and not to us, their peoples as potential 'nations' in a free and equal commonwealth?

The British character, our notions of fair-play and shrewd common sense, and the course of British policy in other sections of the Empire justify the belief that this basic moral issue, once it is closely examined and clearly seen, will be decided rightly. /

Colony of Nigeria, 'Life and Duties of an Administrative Officer in Nigeria' (Draft Pamphlet) (1933). National Archives, Kew, London, CO 583/188/4, ff. 17–21.

Life and Duties of an Administrative Officer in Nigeria.

I.–GENERAL.

Nigeria, which has a larger population than any other dependency of the British Crown, except India, is situated to the north of the Gulf of Guinea on the West Coast of Africa, a place which until recently was considered, and with reason, one of the most unhealthy parts of the world. The advances made in the prevention and control of malaria, together with the improvement in the knowledge of tropical hygiene and sanitation, and the application of this knowledge, have, however, radically altered living conditions on the West Coast, making it, if not a health resort, at least as healthy as many other tropical dependencies.[1] Today an Administrative Officer in Nigeria performs a "tour" of about 18 months; his work contains a greater variety of interest than could be found in any other profession: he can look forward to reasonable living conditions, an initial salary ample for a young bachelor and a reasonable chance of promotion to the higher grades of the service.

The Nigerian climate ranges from a humid even temperature in the coast region to arid semi-desert conditions in the extreme north, where the daily variation between the maximum and minimum shade temperature may be as great as 66°. Along the entire coast line runs a belt, form 10 to 60 miles in width, of mangrove swamp forest intersected by the branches of the Niger Delta and other rivers which are inter-connected by innumerable creeks. The whole constitutes a continuous inland waterway from beyond the western boundary of Nigeria almost to the Cameroons. This region is succeeded by a belt from 50 to 100 miles wide of tropical rain forest and oil palm bush which covers the greater part of the central and eastern provinces of the south. Beyond this the vegetation passes from open woodland to grass savannah interspersed with scrubby fire resisting trees which covers the greater part of the Northern Provinces until semi-desert conditions are reached in the extreme north. Nigeria possesses few mountains except along the Eastern Boundary, though the Bauchi Plateau rises to 4,000 feet above sea level. In addition to the Niger and Benue, which during the rainy season are navigable as far as Jebba and Yola respectively, there are a number of important rivers, of which the Cross River is the largest. Except for Lake Chad in the extreme north-east, there are no large lakes.

Ethnologically Nigeria may be divided, like the rest of the West Coast of Africa, into two main groups; the peoples of the coast and forest region and those of the more open country behind it – the Western Sudan. During the last nine hundred years Muhammadanism has spread gradually over the greater part of the latter area until today it consists mainly of more or less highly organized Muhammadan states (or Emirates). There are, however, scattered throughout the Northern Provinces several small pagan tribes which have managed to survive the attacks of their Muhammadan neighbours owing to the inaccessibility of the country in which they live. The nomadic Fulani herdsmen are to be found wherever there is good grazing for their cattle. In the south one / passes from the progressive and highly organised Yoruba peoples of the west to the tribes of the Niger Delta and the eastern provinces who, protected from aggression by the thick forests and swamps which form their environment, have been able to survive and multiply despite an exceedingly backward and undeveloped organisation. Many of these tribes particularly on the coast have been in contact with European influence from the 16th century and the whole region presents a most unexpected blend of sophistication and primitiveness.

Politically, Nigeria consists of the Colony and a Protectorate. The latter which comprises the major part of the country is divided into a number of provinces, each under the control of a Resident. A province sub-divides into a number of "divisions" each under the control of a District Officer. The provinces are organised into two groups, the Northern and the Southern Provinces. Each group is under the control of a Lieutenant Governor, whose headquarters and secretariat are at Kaduna and Enugu respectively. The Colony consists of Lagos and the country round it, and is under the control of a Commissioner. Lagos, which is the capital, is the residence of the Governor and contains his secretariat and the headquarters of most Government Departments.

DUTIES OF AN ADMINISTRATIVE OFFICER.

The Government of the Protectorate of Nigeria is based upon the principle of trusteeship; the method of administration is that of "Indirect" or "Dependent Rule" through the African Chiefs or councils who are regarded as an integral part of the machinery of government and whose well-defined powers and functions are recognised by Government and in law. The object of this system of administration is to govern the native peoples as far as possible through their own rulers and according to their own customs. Each group of people, the size of which will depend on the number of the tribes who admit a common origin or political organisation in the past, is formed into a Native Administration. The extent to which administrative functions can be exercised by the chiefs naturally varies according to the state of political development attained by each Native Administration. In the Muhammadan Emirates and the Yoruba States the work of the administrative staff is to a large extent advisory and supervisory. Among the clans and villages of such tribes as the Ibo and Ibibio, however, where there are no recognised tribal heads and where the political organisation is not developed beyond the village or clan council stage, the British Administrative Staff take a more direct part in administration.

Each Native Administration had its Native Treasury and Native Courts, and such other institutions (*e.g.,* prison, Public Works staff, etc.) as its standard of development may justify. The Native Treasury receives a percentage (70 per cent in the advanced Native Administrations and 50 per cent in the others) of the revenue collected as direct tax from the people inhabiting the area of the Native Administration. The Native Courts administer the customary local law in so far as it does not conflict with British ideas of justice whether this law be Muhammadan Law or tribal custom.

The aim of the British Administrative Staff is to develop these institutions and by constant advice to purge of abuses and to improve the working of the Native Administration so that it becomes more and more fitted to bear the increasing responsibilities placed upon it. For instance, a District Officer assisted by his subordinate officers is responsible for seeing that tax in a Native Administration area is collected properly, that its incidence is fair and does not press unduly on any section of the people, / that no more than authorized amount is collected by those officials of the Native Administration responsible for its collection, that all of it is paid into the Native Treasury and that the correct percentage is paid over to the Government Treasury. It is his duty to advise the Emir or the Native Administration Council as to the best way in which the revenue can be used and to assist them in spending it to the best advantage by drawing up with the African officials yearly estimates of revenue and expenditure. Once these estimates have been approved he has to see that Native Administration funds are correctly spent on the objects for which they have been allocated, that payments are correctly made and that any work on which these funds are being expended is satisfactorily carried out. In regard to the administration of justice an Administrative Officer, in his capacity as a Commissioner of the Provincial Court is vested with certain wide powers of control over Native Tribunals to facilitate the investigation of complaint with the object of preventing any miscarriage of justice or other abuses. Apart from these two illustrations there are innumerable other matters which call for his assistance, encouragement or supervision and whatever may happen to be the specific object on which he may be engaged for the moment his never-ending occupation is to get to know as much about the people in his district as possible so that they in turn may have confidence in him and be ready to bring their complaints to him and to listen to his advice. More especially is this the case in the more backward districts where the Administrative Officer is faced with the task of trying to assist the people to combine into an organised and united whole, and where it is necessary to make very patient enquiries to discover the original organisation of the people with a view to using it as the foundation on which to develop a Native Administration.

Judicial.–At the moment of writing the revision of the entire judicial system of the Protectorate is under consideration. Under the existing law, however, an Administrative Officer has important judicial functions as a Commissioner of the Provincial Court, with powers that vary according to his rank. The Provincial Court is primarily for the hearing of cases which cannot appropriately be tried in a Native Court, and also as a Court of Appeal from the Native Court, every Commissioner of the Provincial Court having the power subject to certain conditions to transfer any matter from the Native Court to his own. The extent of an officer's judicial duties varies greatly according to the part of the country he is in. Thus in the Southern Provinces in general and in the less developed Native Administrations in particular an officer will find himself called upon to exercise the functions of a Magistrate to a much greater extent than in those places where the Native Courts have reached a high stage of efficiency.

Other Duties.–These are the most important, though by no means the only duties of an Administrative Officer. He may be required to perform the duties of an officer of any department that is not represented in his Division. A junior officer is often placed in charge of the local branch of the Government Treasury and of the local detachment of Government Police. In the Southern Provinces he may find himself functioning as an officer of the Prisons Department and in charge of the divisional prison. He may, in the absence of an officer of the Public Works Department, have to supervise the construction of a road, a building or even a bridge. He must also act as liaison officer between the local chiefs and such departmental officers as visit his division, and ensure that the latter receive from the Native Administration such co-operation and assistance as they may require. In short, an Administrative / Officer must be prepared to undertake any duty that may arise. As the local representative of Government, he is expected on the one hand to deal with any situation that may arise in his district and keep his Resident informed of matters of importance; while, on the other hand, he is responsible for seeing that the general policy and particular instructions of Government are put into effect.

Touring.–An officer will spend much of his time touring the division in which he is stationed. In the Northern Provinces, where distances are greater and the density of population smaller, he will frequently be travelling for a month or more at a time. Except in a very few provinces where tsetse is present (*e.g.,* kabba and parts of the Niger and Benue Provinces), his travelling will be on horseback. In the Southern Provinces, owing to the smaller size of the divisions and the greater density of the population, there is far more office and judicial work and an officer will rarely, unless he is detailed to make a special report on the admin-istrative organisation of a particular tribe or district, be away from the station for any considerable period. Except in a very few divisions, traveling is chiefly on foot, or, in the delta divisions, by canoe or motor launch. An officer will find that most of his touring is away from motor-roads and that his "loads" will have to be taken by carrier transport. Normally, he will not need a tent, because at most of the villages or other centres at which he breaks his journey he will find a rest house maintained either by Government or a Native Administration at which wood and water is supplied at a charge of one shilling a night.

"The primary object of travelling through the province is that the Political Officer may show himself to the people and hear their complaints at first hand, not trusting to the reports which reach him at headquarters. It is only by the advent of a British officer that scoundrels, misrepresenting the Government action, or extorting what they will from the natives in the name of Government, can be caught; for the villagers in their ignorance, supposing them to be genuine, dare not as a rule complain.

It has been abundantly shown by experience that "unrest" resulting in mur-ders and outrages, and eventually necessitating the use of force, inevitably take place among primitive tribes when districts are not regularly and systematically visited. By frequent touring, abuses are redressed before they become formida-ble, the law-abiding people are encouraged to restrain the turbulent and lawless elements and trust and confidence in Government is fostered." ("Instructions to Political Officers," by Lord Lugard).[2]

Examinations.–For the first three years of his service an officer is on proba-tion and is styled a Cadet, or in most cases an Acting Assistant District Officer. At the end of this period he is confirmed in his appointment, subject to his receiving satisfactory reports on his work and conduct, and to his passing the following examinations–(1) Examinations in Law, Colonial Regulations, Gen-eral Orders and Financial Instructions, (2) Language Examinations. Neither of these groups is difficult and most Cadets pass both within their first tour. Newly-appointed officers during their first tours should take every opportunity of studying for them.

In the examinations in the first group the papers are set with a view to test-ing an officer's ability to apply the rules and principles in certain of the more important Ordinances and Regulations, to which he is allowed to refer during the examination.

The language examinations consist of a "progress examination" taken by a newly-appointed officer after six months' residence, which, as its title implies, is intended to serve as a / test to show what progress the officer is making in the study of the native language; and a Lower Standard examination, which can be taken at any time before the date when the officer is due for confirmation. In this examination an officer is expected to show a good working acquaintance with the language and the ability to make himself understood in it and to understand the gist of what is said to him in it.

For his language examination an officer has the choice of several languages, the choice depending to a large extent upon the province to which he is posted. On passing a Lower Standard examination he may receive a refund, up to a maximum of £20, of his expenditure on tuition and books.

LIFE OF AN ADMINISTRATIVE OFFICER.

Before he comes out to Nigeria a newly-appointed officer will be informed whether he is posted to the Northern or Southern Provinces. He will receive instructions as to the actual province and division to which he has been posted either before he sails or in the course of the voyage out, and on his arrival at his port of disembarkation will be met and given instructions as to how to proceed to his destination. An officer is frequently in the course of a tour, transferred from one division to another within a province, or, less frequently from one province to another. He may also for some period of his service be posted to one of the secretariats as an Assistant Secretary, but, save in exceptional cases, will not remain there for more than two tours.

There are a few large stations in the Northern and the Southern Provinces where some of the amenities of civilisation such as good housing a pipe-borne water supply and electric light are to be found, but the junior officer will probably spend most of his time in small stations where none of these amenities exists and where the European population may be limited to a Divisional Officer, one or more Assistant District Officers and a Medical Officer, and possibly an officer from one or other of the Forestry, Agriculture, Police or other Departments. Some of these officers may have their wives with them. This, with periodic visits by the Resident of the province, by officers of the Education and Posts and Telegraphs Departments and by other officers passing through, is all the society he will get.

Wives.–There are very few stations which are unsuitable for a lady and Government does not object to officers who have been confirmed in their appointments bringing out their wives. The permission of Government has to be obtained before a wife may join her husband in Nigeria. Such permission is rarely refused expect in the case of unconfirmed officers.

Health.–The climate and the life in Nigeria is not suited for any but healthy adults and Government does not encourage the bringing out of young children. On the other hand, the country is free from many of the diseases found in other tropical and subtropical countries, and no one who follows the elementary rules of hygiene and who takes quinine regularly need have much fear of his health being seriously affected by prolonged service in West Africa. Free medical and dental treatment is provided by Government in Nigeria, and there are up-to-date hospitals at all the larger centres, while a Government Medical Officer is stationed in almost every divisional headquarters.

Recreation.–Tennis courts and golf courses of sorts exist in almost every provincial headquarters and at some divisional headquarters, and in those parts of the Northern Provinces where there are horses, any station of any size has a polo ground. In large / stations games of cricket, hockey and association football await the energetic. Many of these centres have squash courts and a few have swimming baths. Those who are fond of shooting can always find opportunity to make use of a gun and sometimes of a rifle. Game is not so plentiful as in East Africa, but it exists and the more isolated the station the more chance there is of good sport. It is advisable to arrange for newspapers and books to be sent out from England and to find some interest outside one's work.

Local Leave.–An officer may take three weeks' local leave each tour, free transport for a maximum of six days being provided by Government. This enables him to visit his friends in other parts of the country, or to go on a shooting expedition.

COST OF LIVING

Kit.–Officers should bring out with them camp kit, and their wardrobes should be sufficient to see them through the tour. Those posted to the Northern Provinces are advised to bring a good supply of provisions with them, those in the Southern Provinces need not as they will be able to buy provinces locally from the various trading firms. It is unnecessary to bring out medical stores, kerosene or petrol.

The composition of an officer's outfit depends very much on individual taste, and most of the well-known firms of tropical outfitters have by now sufficient knowledge of the requirements of officers in West Africa for them to give reliable advice on the subject. Officers on first appointment receive a copy of the *Nigeria Handbook*[3] which contains a special chapter devoted to this matter.

Passages.–An officer is granted a free return passage each tour between England and Nigeria. An officer who has received permission for his wife to join him in Nigeria receives a refund of half the net cost of her return passage, provided that she remains in the country for over six months.

Transport.–Free transport in Nigeria is given to an officer and two servants when travelling on Government service or when returning from or proceeding on leave. On the latter two occasions he is given free transport for 96 loads (48 cwt.), on other occasions for loads sufficient for his requirements. Free transport by Government services and in some case by non-Government services is also given for his wife if she accompanies him.

Transport Allowances.–Officers who possess motor vehicles and who use them on Government service may in certain circumstances be given a transport allowance. These may take the form of a monthly allowance or a mileage allowance or both.

Officers stationed in provinces where horses can be kept may also be given horse allowance.

Quarters.–An officer is entitled to free furnished quarters or an allowance in lieu thereof. Government quarters may be roughly classified as permanent, semi-permanent, or temporary. Permanent houses have concrete-block or brick walls with a corrugated-iron or tiled roof and wooden or concrete floors. Semi-permanent houses are built of local mud or pisé blocks with the roof of corrugated iron and most if not all of the floor space concreted. These houses consist of two or more main rooms and the usual offices. The kitchen and servants' quarters are separate. Permanent houses are completely furnished, semi-permanent to a more limited extent. Temporary houses are built of local material with mud walls and a palm-mat, mud or grass roof. They vary greatly in size and style according to the ease with which building / materials and labour can be procured in the district. All except the very best are unfurnished, and an officer living in the unfurnished ones receives an allowance at the rate of £2 a month.

Servants.–An officer will as a rule find it necessary to employ three servants, a "steward" or house boy, a cook, and a "small boy" who assists the steward. Wages vary, but the average wage of a steward is not more than £2 a month, of a cook £2 to £3, and of a small boy 10s. to £1. An officer may find it necessary to have additional servants according to the station he is in or his own pursuits–a groom if he keeps a horse, a garden boy if he is interested in gardening, a water carrier if he lives in a station where water is hard to get and is not supplied by local arrangement.

Cost of Living.–An officer can live on his pay in any station. How much he can save entirely depends on the individual. Naturally, it is more difficult to save in the larger stations.

The actual cost of living varies greatly according to the station. It is possible to live "on the country" but a certain amount of tinned food will be found necessary. Chickens, eggs and corn (in season) are obtainable almost everywhere; other supplies vary according to the locality. In the north, milk and meat can be obtained in most stations, in the south milk cannot be obtained except in a few divisions and meat is harder to come by. Fish can be obtained in stations on the rivers or creeks, and fruit is plentiful in most parts of the Southern Provinces. Vegetables that appeal to a European palate are rare and it is a good plan to bring out English seeds and grow one's own vegetables. Of these beans, cucumbers and lettuce grow best. In large stations and on the railway cold storage supplies and ice can be obtained.

BOOKS OF REFERENCE.

The following books dealing with Nigeria are recommended to those who wish to learn something of the country:–

"A Tropical Dependency" by Flora L. Shaw (Lady Lugard).

"The Dual Mandate" by Lord Lugard.

"The Nigeria Handbook", 10th Edition.

"A History of Nigeria" by A. C. M. Burns.

"Nigerian Days" by A. C. G. Hastings.

"Up Against it in Nigeria" by "Langa Langa".

G. I. JONES,
Assistant Secretary.
Chief Secretary's Office.

L. S. B. Leakey, 'Comparative Methods of Colonial Administration. Record of Third Meeting, December 10th 1930. Colonial Administration in East Africa from the Native Point of View'. Chatham House, London (1930).

Subject: Colonial Administration in East Africa from the
Native Point of View.

Speaker: Mr. L. S. B. Leakey.[1]
Chairman: The Rt. Honble. Lord Lugard,[2] G.C.M.G., etc.

THE CHAIRMAN, LORD LUGARD, in introducing the speaker, said that Mr. Leakey's reputation as an archæologist was not confined to Great Britain, but he would be speaking this evening not as an archæologist, but on Colonial Administration from the point of view of the native Kikuyu. He understood that Mr. Leakey was actually a naturalised Kikuyu, and since he had himself been made a blood brother of the tribe some forty years ago, he supposed he was some connection of the lecturer's.

MR. LEAKEY: At the present day, more than ever before, Colonial Powers are regarding themselves as Trustees for the Natives of the Colonies and Protectorates under their power, and it is therefore of the utmost importance that we should know something of the attitude of the wards towards these Trustees.

At the first meeting of this Group, when the suggestion of a paper from me was mooted, several speakers expressed the hope that I would not confine my remarks on the native point of view to East Africa, but would look at the problem from the wider angle of all Africa. After much consideration, I have decided not to do as they requested.

I feel that the only justification for my attempting to speak of the native point of view is because in almost all ways I am more a Kikuyu than an Englishman. I feel that the value of my paper to this group will lie in the fact that it is absolutely the native point of view and absolutely first-hand information. Because of that I propose to speak almost entirely of Colonial administration from the Kikuyu point of view.

I am well aware that much of what I shall say does not altogether apply to countries such as Nigeria or Tanganyika Territory, but at the same time I feel that very big lessons may be learned, and warnings received, as a result of this study, simply because the Kikuyu tribe is one which has suffered very much from mistakes in Colonial administration.

By far the majority of Government officials in all branches of administration are really trying to do all they can to administer justice fairly, and to do only that which is best for the natives, although it would not be fair or right to try to hide / the fact that there are always to be found a few in every administration who despise the natives as being of an inferior culture, and who do not hesitate to take an unfair advantage of their position of power to abuse them.

But if we put aside such deliberate unfairness, I still have no hesitation whatever in saying that practically every administrative officer I know is continually doing things which are considered by the natives as grossly unjust and unfair, and moreover which usually are in fact unfair and unjust and unwise. The fault is seldom that of the individual officer so much as of the whole administrative system, which renders the administration of real justice almost an impossibility.

The nett [*sic*] result is that we are building up a great body of resentment against the white man, and although I am not an alarmist, I sometimes wonder whether I am not destined to see terrible bloodshed in our colonies as a result of the bad policy unless steps are taken to alter things.

I want you first of all to let me tell you something of the results of the policy of making Kiswahili the official language of East Africa. Kiswahili is the language of the coastal peoples in the region of Mombasa and Zanzibar. It is a brokendown Bantu language with a very large admixture of Arabic, Persian and Portuguese. Unfortunately it has long been believed that this language, which has always been the language of the traders, is fairly universally understood all over East Africa, and it has been made the official language. Every officer of Government has to pass a series of examinations in Kiswahili, and must take the highest of these examinations before his sixth year of service – after that he is required to learn a vernacular language.

In point of actual fact, I suppose that if one said that 5 per cent. of the up-country natives really knew the grammatical coast Kiswahili properly, one would be over-estimating it considerably. It is certainly a high figure for the Kikuyu tribe. About another 40 per cent. can speak what is called "Trader Swahili" fairly fluently, whereas most of them know one or two words. Trader Swahili is totally ungrammatical, and appallingly poor in vocabulary, and usually the infinitive of the verb is made to serve for all tenses. Even good grammatical Kiswahili at the coast, which is a comparatively rich language, is exceptionally poor in words which adequately translate Kikuyu technicalities dealing with land laws, marriage customs, etc.

Now picture an administrative officer armed with his official Kiswahili, and fully determined to administer justice, trying to come to a fair decision upon some intricate point of native law dealing with a dispute over a land claim. Probably neither the defendant nor the plaintiff knows anything but a little Trader Swahili, while most of the witnesses do not even know that. True, he has at his disposal the court interpreter, who is usually a mission-trained native, who of course knows the vernacular, and who has learnt Kiswahili after a fashion from the missionaries.

In point of fact, nearly all cases are heard through an interpreter. Sometimes native assessors are called in to help, but as they too must explain things through / the interpreter, the matter is not an easy one to settle. What is still more important is the fact that the interpreters are always hard put to it to find a way of translating the native words into Kiswahili, since words with an exactly equivalent meaning are lacking; and, since they have got to render an interpretation at once, they are often obliged to give a very inexact interpretation. Nor are court interpreters by any means unbribable, and since it frequently happens that there is no one else present in the court who knows the two languages properly and can act as a check upon the accuracy and honesty of the interpretation rendered, the opportunities for bribery and corruption are immense. Remember, too, that it seldom happens that the administration officer knows his Kiswahili so well that he can think in it, and so in his mind he has to translate the interpreter's Kiswahili version of the evidence given into English.

Is it to be wondered, then, that the native when talking to his friends almost invariably expresses dissatisfaction with the whole system of our administration? Is it to be wondered that the written English account of the evidence taken in cases is but a very distorted version of the truth? Is it to be wondered that when another administration officer at some later date uses this so-called case-law for his guidance he makes still worse blunders in his honest endeavour to follow truth?

Those of you who do not know much about how the administration of a colony is conducted will be asking yourselves why the administration officer has not learnt the vernacular language for himself, thereby doing away with the necessity for an interpreter. Let me explain to you the reasons. It is the rarest thing indeed to find an officer returned to the same station, or even the same province, for two successive tours while he is still a junior officer, and, moreover, during this period he is battling in his spare time with the work necessary for the higher Kiswahili examination, which he must pass before his sixth year.

Vernacular languages, too, are very far from easy to learn properly, and if not properly learnt are almost worse than useless. Remember, too, that a natural aptitude for learning foreign languages is not one of the things which ranks highly in the selection of candidates for the administration, and also that by the time a man gets into the services he is well over twenty. Remember, too, that from the moment he arrives in the Colony he has a great deal of routine work which must be done, so that he can only sit down to learn a vernacular language (should he wish to try to do so) when his brain is already tired. It is the combination of all these factors which forms the reason why practically no administrative officer speaks a vernacular language properly. (There are a few magnificent exceptions.)

Moreover, by the time a man has risen sufficiently high in the service to have a fair chance of being returned to the same province after his leave, he is getting too old to learn a new language at all properly, and also by now he has far too many responsibilities to allow him any time for such pursuits.

It thus happens that, as a result of this policy, despite the fact that an officer is supposed to have passed some sort of an examination in a vernacular language / between his sixth and tenth years of service, this is really an impossibility, and I do not know of an officer who has ever worked in the Kikuyu Province who had more than a superficial knowledge of Kikuyu, although I know several who claim to know Kikuyu, but for whom in practice their little knowledge truly was a dangerous thing.

Since I have attacked this policy so violently, I ought in fairness to mention one or two of the chief arguments with which it is supported (and then I shall criticise these arguments). It is urged that any Colony has a number of healthy as well as of very unhealthy stations, and that therefore a policy of shifting officers continually, especially junior officers, is very desirable, so that all may have their fair share of the good as well as the bad stations, and that the young officers shall as far as possible have "done their whack" on the bad stations before they want to marry.

It is also argued that the available number of men is insufficient for a policy of keeping men to a single province, since each man gets six months' leave every three years, and so, even if there did not exist the question of healthy and unhealthy stations, it would not be possible to keep men throughout their years of service in a single province.

Yet another argument seriously put forward is that it is bad for a station for the same man to be in charge for too long a consecutive period, as, if he gets to know his people too well, and be known by them and liked by them too well, he might become too much like a little local king. It is also speciously argued that since some administrative officers are good and some bad, it would be very hard on a district or province if it had to suffer a bad administrator for too long, and that therefore the policy of changing is a good one.

Now to reply to these arguments. While granting the truth of the statement that some stations, and even some whole provinces, are very unhealthy, and that it would be hard on a man to be condemned to an unhealthy station or province for the whole of his service, I nevertheless contend that it would be perfectly possible to keep a man *within the same language group* and yet give him some time in the unhealthy stations as well as some time in the good ones. I believe that things could be so planned that a man could be kept for all his period of service within a group in which the languages were so similar that a knowledge of one, once fully acquired, would mean that the others could be mastered in a few months, and yet at the same time both the good and bad stations be included in his area.

As to the second point, it may be true that there are insufficient men available for it to be possible to keep a man within a single province all the time, but that is not what I am suggesting, but rather *within one of the main language groups* such as Hamitic, Bantu, etc. And if the staff is not big enough for this to be practicable, then the necessary additional appointments should surely be made. I do not think the other two arguments are sufficiently valid to be worth wasting time over, unless I am asked to do so specifically at the conclusion of this paper. /

I said a few minutes ago that from the native point of view an imperfect knowledge of the vernacular was worse than useless. Perhaps I should modify this, and say that it is not useless, but very dangerous. My reason for saying so is that there is a tendency for natives, if they think a man knows their language at all, to think that he also knows everything about their more common customs (which, of course, does not really logically follow), and so they will neglect to explain them in detail when referring to them, because they think you know all that the custom implies and entails. Very grave injustices tend to result from this sort of thing, as natives in such circumstances believe you have acted unjustly, despite full knowledge of their customs.

This brings me to the whole question of the effects of ignorance of native custom upon administrative problems. In many ways I think that ignorance of custom is even more fraught with dangers than ignorance of vernacular languages, because the discontent and sense of injustice resulting therefrom affect not only individuals, but whole tribes.

I do not, of course, mean that I think every Government official should know all the intricacies of the customs and sociology of the tribe or group of tribes amongst whom his duty lies – this is obviously not practicable – but I want to emphasise the amount of unnecessary ill-feeling and direct injustice which is frequently caused because those responsible for the Government policies do not understand the more fundamental rules governing native life and tribal organisation.

Let us look at a few typical examples. It is by no means an infrequent occurrence for a native district chief to be deposed and another set up in his place, or for the Government to claim the right of selecting the new chief who shall succeed the one who has died. Moreover, there is far too little understanding of the meaning and significance of chieftainship from tribe to tribe. One Government official will hold the firm conviction that all native chiefs are hereditary by native custom, and another that heredity plays no part in chieftainship, and so on. Probably each is right in so far as his views concern one tribe, but the trouble lies in the failure to appreciate that customs vary fundamentally from tribe to tribe.

There is also frequently a failure to understand what are the normal functions of a chief. Among the Kikuyu, for example, the eldest living first-born son of any clan or sub-clan is the normal head or chief of that clan, provided that he has not been deposed by common consent of the male members of that clan. But this man is not at all necessarily the president of the local native councils of justice. Chieftainship in the sense of a man being head of the clan or sub-clan *as well as* the highest authority for native justice in the district, did not exist among the Kikuyu. Under Government control the Kikuyu Reserve is divided up for convenience into a number of districts, which do not necessarily have any direct reference to clan areas, and a Government chief is made responsible for each area. Sometimes the chief was originally chosen from clan heads in the district, sometimes from the senior elders on the native councils of justice. Sometimes neither of / these factors was considered, and some native with no real native authority at all was made chief of the district because of help rendered by him to the Government. Sometimes even a young native, educated at one of the missions and who had served for a longer or shorter period in the District Commissioner's office, would be selected as chief. These Government-selected chiefs are expected to administer justice in their districts by arbitration, they are also expected to exert a good deal of authority and control over the natives in their districts and to keep order. They are supposed to form the nucleus of the Local Native councils, which are courts of native justice, and they are also called in by the Government officers as assessors, and to give advice upon all sorts of native customs in connection with court cases.

The result is that everywhere Government officers may be heard deploring the failure of the chiefs to maintain tribal authority, and everywhere one hears natives complaining of injustice from the native Government chiefs.

By native custom a man could only rise very slowly along the path of eldership towards a position on the councils of justice, and by the time he had become an elder of fourth grade, and was eligible for the post of president of a council or for membership of the inner circle which really decided all cases, he had had a long training in native law and in case law, and was really qualified for the position.

How can a young native who has been appointed chief by the Government, and who is probably only of the first grade of eldership, be expected to know all the unwritten law of the tribe? How can he administer justice fairly? How can he hope to have any real authority over those people in his district of clans other than his own, or even other members of his own clan, when he has no authority over them at all by native custom, and when he is really a nobody and regarded as a usurper? The information, too, which these chiefs supply in connection with queries about native custom is often coloured by the fact that they wish to please the Government officers, without whose backing they would not be chiefs at all; and so it is common to find the administration officers have acquired, and act upon, information which they themselves believe is the truth about native custom, because they have received it from the chiefs, when in point of fact it is nothing of the sort.

A very good example of this came to my notice in connection with my recent work on the committee of enquiry into native land tenure in the Kikuyu Province. A number of memoranda and reports upon the question have been prepared from time to time by Government officers and submitted to the Government. Whereas most of them contained much that was true, they also contained much that was false, or incomplete, and thereby useless. The chief cause of this was that information was obtained mainly from Government-appointed chiefs, and from members of the Government station staffs, such as the interpreters, who seldom were in a position to know the full details of native land system themselves. No one in this country would expect a clerk, or an ordinary man about town either, to know the / intricacies of any of our laws, but they seldom realise that the natives too have legal experts, and that most of the ordinary people do not know all the facts.

This particular question – that of land tenure – is one which should be very carefully studied indeed if it is hoped that Government officers are to administer justice, for it may happen that within a single province, even within a single tribe, the laws of land tenure may vary so significantly that any decision taken in one area based upon information gained in another may be wholly unfair.

Had some real knowledge of native land law been available when the Kikuyu Reserve was demarcated, mistakes could have been avoided which have not only resulted in much injustice, but which are the root of most of the discontent and restlessness among the Kikuyu to-day.

It was commonly believed – and I regret to say there are many Government officials in Kenya who still believe it – that within any tribe all land is communal. Whereas this is to a large extent true of some of the pastoral tribes, it is completely untrue of the agricultural tribes; and the mere fact that Government officials working among any tribe have failed to understand or discover the intricacies of the native land-laws of that tribe, does not mean that such laws do not exist, but merely emphasises the need for study by trained workers with a real knowledge of the language, as well as a freedom from the suspicion which so frequently hangs over the heads of all Government officials when they try to ask questions about native custom.

Among the Kikuyu, all land which was under the occupation of the tribe when the white man arrived was already divided up into innumerable family estates,* each of which was clearly defined and the boundary marks known, not only to the elders of the owning family, but also to the elders of the families immediately neighbouring the estate. The boundaries and boundary marks were mainly geographical features, such as rivers, and also certain trees and special plants. A stranger walking through the country would see no sign of any boundaries, even though he might be standing upon a boundary line, but to the initiated they were as clear as daylight.

Again, no strangers might be shown boundary marks, so that if in the early days a European more enlightened than the rest had asked to be shown boundaries, he would probably not have had them shown to him until he had become a trusted friend of the tribe.

In some – in fact, most – areas, big parts of each estate were virgin bush land or pasture land, and a fair amount of forest area existed, but all definitely divided up. Definite laws existed in four-fifths of the Kikuyu country, prohibiting the sale of any portion of a family estate to another family or clan, or to individuals of another family or clan. On the other hand, temporary "tenants at will" could be given occupation and cultivation rights for an indefinite period, subject always to the right to evict them or their descendants when the family which gave them / these rights should have increased numerically to a point where they required the land for their own use.

In the remaining one-fifth of the area occupied by the Kikuyu a sale was permitted to members of the Kikuyu tribe, but such sales were uncommon and not looked upon as desirable, as no family wished to reduce its area too much, and so give up land which its descendants might need, and so in this area too the system of "tenants at will" was the more common way in which individuals or families could obtain cultivation rights upon another family's estate.

Now much of the land occupied by the Kikuyu was particularly suited to white settlement – especially for the production of coffee – and so large areas of land under Kikuyu occupation were from time to time marked off for white farms, while at the same time those responsible believed they were leaving ample room for all the Kikuyu in that part of their territory which remained unalienated. It seems to have been believed that the evicted Kikuyu families who thus lost all their property could simply go into the uncultivated parts of the remaining Kikuyu country and take up and use as much land as they wanted. No one seems to have dreamed that they could only do so by the kindness of the owning families, and that they then acquired nothing but the temporary right to occupy and cultivate until such a time as the land should be required by the owning families, when the tenants would have to be evicted. At the time, as the Kikuyu population was more or less stationary owing to disease and to raids by

---

*   See Report on Kikuyu System of Land Tenure.

the Masai, there was plenty of room for tenants, and all those whose lands were appropriated for white area moved elsewhere as "tenants at will"; but it must not be forgotten that the sudden change from being landowners to being precarious tenants did not please those whose lands were thus taken from them.

It thus came about that hundreds of families settled down to temporary tenancy in the area which was subsequently gazetted as the Kikuyu Reserve, with no security in native law. Gradually, with the cessation of tribal warfare, the owning families increased numerically, as well as the families of the tenants, and, owing to pressure, the landowners started giving notice to their tenants that they must go. In one or two cases the tenants who were thus being turned out went to the administrative officers demanding help, since everywhere the population pressure was increasing in such a way that it was more and more difficult to get taken in as tenants elsewhere. The results of these cases was that it was announced that all native lands were *Crown lands,* and, as such, only the *Crown* had any right to evict, and the landowning families who wanted to turn out the tenants according to native law were told that they could not do so, even if they wanted the land for their own use. Instead they must go off and try to get land elsewhere in the Kikuyu Reserve. By this the Government meant that since all the Reserve was Crown land, they could go to any part not actually under cultivation – even if it was the area set aside by a large landowning group for a grazing area – and occupy it. But in spite of Government statements that all land in the Reserve is Crown / land, and that tenants could not be evicted when the landowners wanted the land for themselves, the position was not really altered or improved. This was due to the fact that no native will voluntarily remain upon, or will enter upon another's land when he is not wanted, even though he may have Government support for doing so, for no Government support can nullify the anger of the spirits, or avert disasters which it is firmly believed these spirits would bring about.

And so, as congestion increased, vast numbers of natives moved on to European farms as squatters. This suited the farmers well enough, and the Governments issued forms of contract for squatters which are intended to safeguard them; but the squatter system has nevertheless led to much trouble and misery. Time after time I have heard of cases of squatters who have made complaints about their treatment on farms or about their wages – squatter wages are about the lowest in Kenya, the normal figure being twelve shillings per month of thirty working days (Sundays not being counted) – and the replies to their complaints are usually to this effect:

> "You are purely voluntary squatters, and you can terminate your agreement when you like if you give proper notice, and then return to your Reserve."

And because the squatters seldom, if ever, take this step, it is believed that their grievances are really imaginary. The truth, of course, usually is that there is no room for them on their own land (if they chance to belong to landowning families), or else that they belong to families who were rendered homeless by the taking of their land for white farms, and they are no longer able to go back as "tenants at will" because most of the Reserve is becoming far too overcrowded.

Of course anyone who travels casually through the Reserve can find many plots of land which are bush or grass and have no cultivation, but these areas are nevertheless owned, and merely represent either pasture-land for goats and sheep, or areas kept as reserve against the increase in the numbers of the owning family.

Certainly in two of the districts of the Kikuyu province, Meru and Embu, the landowning families have at present plenty of room for other natives to come in as "tenants at will," but what is usually forgotten is that the Kikuyu in the over-congested areas from which most of the squatters come do not know any of the landowning families in the Meru and Embu districts personally, and so cannot go there as tenants. Moreover, when in point of fact it was mooted during the meetings of the Committee on Kikuyu Land Tenure that Kikuyus from the overcrowded Dagoretti district should go as tenants into the less-crowded Embu and Meru districts, the Chief Native Commissioner said that would not be allowed by the Government, as those areas were reserved for the Embu and Meru divisions of the Kikuyu tribe. The population density in the most crowded district of the Kikuyu Reserve is just about five hundred to the square mile, and would be much greater were all the squatters who would like to return to the Reserve able to do so.

In other words, in this part of the country there is about an acre and a quarter per individual for an agricultural people who have to grow their food, their fuel, / their grass for house-thatching, and a crop to supply cash for taxes, and who also want some pasture-land for their live-stock, which consists of cattle, sheep and goats.

I might add here that the white *settler* population of Kenya, inclusive of women and children, number probably not more than 10,000 souls, with 10,472 square miles of land alienated to them, or over 640 acres per individual. And yet there is frequently talk of alienating more land to the white men, whilst when the Kikuyu of the overcrowded districts with less than two acres per individual recently (October 12, 1929) asked whether certain new areas might be added to the Dagoretti and Kyambu districts of the Kikuyu Reserve, the Chief Native Commissioner replied that he could hold out no prospects of land being added to their Reserve.

So far I have only touched upon purely administrative problems. But Colonial administration in its wider sense includes such questions as native agriculture and stock, native education, and native medical services, and we must examine these also from the point of view of the native, and see whether our policy in these matters is really for the benefit of the natives or not.

I must repeat here that I believe that most of what is being done on all these questions is honestly being done with the idea of helping and benefiting the natives, and the question is chiefly one of whether our methods are as wise as our intentions are good.

The idea of improving native agricultural methods and native crops is laudable indeed, nor is there any doubt that some native methods and some native crops are bad, but if I tell you of what has happened and is happening amongst the Kikuyu, you will be able to judge for yourselves whether we have really done much good *from the native point of view*. A number of Kikuyu, as well as of other tribes, are trained by the agricultural department in so-called improved methods of agriculture – that is to say, in European methods – and are sent into the Reserves as agricultural demonstrators. There are also a certain number of young white agricultural officers detailed for work in the Native Reserves, with their headquarters at the larger administrative stations. A great deal of the work is admirable from the European point of view, but by no means all of it is wise from the native viewpoint. For example, the Kikuyu had as their chief seasonal food crops maize, millet (mtama), sweet potatoes and two varieties of bean. They also had as semi-permanent crops bananas, yams and sugar-cane. The maize was principally a small variety of the yellow maize, with a comparatively small yield per acre, and of little or no value for the *export market*. The mtama or millet was not a good variety compared with forms grown in Tanganyika Territory and the Sudan, and also had no export value, and the sweet potato and beans were also of little commercial value. The methods of cultivation were as follows: During the short rains in the autumn months maize, beans called mboco, and sweet potato were all planted together in the same fields, no attempt being made to plant in / rows or in patches, but all three crops being planted closely together over the whole area. By the end of the small rains the beans were ready to be harvested, while the maize was still green and the sweet potatoes had only covered the ground with sweet potato vine, but no tubers had started to form. The beans would be harvested at once, leaving the maize and potatoes. The dry weather following the short rains would ripen the maize, which was harvested next, leaving only the sweet potatoes, which by now were beginning to form tubers. Meanwhile during the dry weather the maize tops as well as the sweet potato vine were used to augment the food supply of the cattle and sheep and goats, and so helped to save the pasturage. During the long rains in the spring the sweet potatoes planted in the autumn would come into full yield, and would continue to yield potatoes throughout the long rains and the next dry season. Meanwhile during the long rains new fields were being planted up, this time with millet, njahi – another kind of bean – and sweet potatoes. Both the millet and the njahi are plants which are slower growing than the maize and mboco bean, and they also need more rain, and are thus particularly suited to the long spring rains, and not to the short autumn rains. Following the end of the long rains, the same sequence of serial harvesting took place – first the bean, then the millet during the dry season, whilst the sweet potato was giving cattle-fodder, although not yet yielding potatoes. (Remember, however, that the potatoes planted in the preceding autumn are now in full yield.) The long-rains potatoes would come into yield when the short rains began, and continue over to the next long rains.

Now the agricultural officers (or the Department), without really knowing or understanding this system (which was both well suited to the local conditions and seasons as well as to the people's needs), decided that some of the crops grown, and all the methods of growing them, were bad, and should be altered. Especially did they dislike the nasty small yellow maize, with its small yield per acre and its uselessness for export purposes, and also the njahi bean, and the millet, neither of which ranked as exportable crops.

So they distributed seed of the white Hickory King maize, with its big yield per acre, and they encouraged the Kikuyu to plant it both in the short and long rains as much as possible, telling him he would get a much bigger yield per acre, and that he could then, from the same acreage, not only have maize for himself, but also a quantity for sale for export, both of which things were true. But they did not take the trouble to find out what was the relative food value of the white Hickory King maize to the old yellow maize.

The Agricultural department also tried to teach the natives to give up planting their crops all mixed up in a single field, and have tried, and are trying, to make them sow their maize and beans European fashion, in lines, and quite separately from the sweet potatoes. Another change – but one which I do not think the Agricultural department are directly responsible for – is the introduction of the European potato, which is rapidly replacing the sweet potato in many areas because / it has a good market value in the towns among Europeans, Indians and also natives.

What are the direct results of this agricultural policy from the point of view of the native? First, the white Hickory King maize, which is in such demand for export, has a much lower food value than the yellow maize, so that although the native is able to sell part of his maize crop for cash, he is not getting such good food value for himself and his family. (But he does not, of course, know this, and is himself quite content on this point.)

Secondly, owing to the encouragement of white-maize growing and the discouragement of mtama growing, white maize is being almost universally grown in the Kikuyu province, both in the long rains as well as the short, and displacing the millet, so that the variety in native diet is being directly reduced, and incidentally reduced by the replacing of one crop by another with a poorer food value, but higher export value.

Thirdly, the insistence upon the importance of planting maize and beans in lines in European fashion and without the sweet potato has not been an entirely unmixed blessing. True, when so planted an acre gives more bags of maize and beans than it would have done by the old method, but you have to set off against that the loss of the sweet-potato crop and the sweet-potato vine for the cattle – unless the sweet-potato crop is planted, say, on another piece of ground. It thus happens that, unless the sweet potato as a crop is to be given up, you are now going to get only about *one and three-fifths* times as much food from *two* acres as you formerly got from *one,* and you have got to cultivate and weed two acres instead of one to get this result, so that it is really a very bad economic proposition, especially in an area already overcrowded.

Moreover, since the Kikuyu country is mostly very hilly, and nearly all the fields are on the slopes of hills, there is another unforeseen disadvantage. Formerly the sweet-potato vine which spread all over the ground protected the soil round the roots of the maize, mtama and beans, so that even after a heavy storm no real damage had resulted from soil being washed away down the hill. Under the new system of lines of maize on a hill-side, a heavy storm tends to wash the unprotected soil from the roots, damaging the plants, and also incidentally gradually denuding the country of its *humus.*

And again the violent discouragement of planting the sweet potato *with* the maize and beans (which means that if sweet potatoes are to be planted at all they must be planted in a separate patch) has resulted in a great decrease in the amount of sweet potato planted at all, and a corresponding increase in the price of what used to be the staple food at most seasons of the year. Instead, the sweet potato is being replaced by the European potato, but the European potato has a very much lower food value, and is also far more prone to diseases. Still worse, its leaf is of no value as cattle fodder, so that its replacing of the sweet potato means that in the dry seasons the cattle and goats are now more and more dependent upon / the dry grass and bush, which are also decreasing in extent as more and more land is cultivated and as the population increases in a limited area in the Native Reserve.

This leads me on to the whole question of native stock, and more especially goats and sheep. I mentioned just now that the combination of two factors – firstly the decrease in the planting of the sweet potato which used to give much useful cattle fodder in the dry seasons, and secondly the increase of the population within a limited space, with the consequent reduction of the area of land left uncultivated and so available for pasturage – has resulted in a greater concentration of cattle and sheep and goats into what pasturage there is left in the Reserves, at all times of the year. The result is that there is a very real danger of denuding the country of grass and bush, especially because the goat and sheep when pushed to it by too little available herbage will pull up even the roots of grass, and utterly destroy it.

To-day, all over East Africa you may hear settlers and Government officials making abusive and ill-informed references to the native goats and sheep, and to a lesser extent to their cattle. It is argued upon the one hand that if only the sheep and goats in the Reserve could be reduced in numbers and strictly limited, the Reserves would be amply big enough for the native population for some time to come. The goat is cursed as *uneconomic* because it yields nothing of any commercial value for export and yet eats up vegetation and destroys pasturage wherever there are too many goats to the acreage available.

If one points out that if the number of sheep allowed, shall we say, on one of the white settlers' farms were to be strictly limited by law, that farm could be split up into a number of smaller farms for European small-holding agriculturists, one is met with the reply that the settler's sheep are of economic value to the country, since they produce wool for export and mutton for local European consumption, whereas the native goats and sheep produce no wool for export, but only meat for local native consumption, and from the skins of which, incidentally, more than 80 per cent. of the women's clothing in the Reserves is made.

It is also argued that sheep and goats ought not to be allowed in the Kikuyu Reserve at all, because it is such magnificent agricultural land (especially suited for coffee, of course), but those who argue thus have nothing to say against the great dairy farms at Limoru, in the middle of some of the best tea and coffee country in Africa.

The fact that the natives kill their goats and sheep but seldom (but not half so seldom as the European likes to believe) is urged against them, and not a few Government officials and others honestly believe that the native only keeps his sheep and goats from sentimental reasons and because of the pride of possession, while others look upon the "lobola" system of *"bride-price"* as the root of all the evil.

The whole of this idea about the native and his so-called idiotic attitude towards his stock is crystallised by the fact that a native, when pressed for money to pay his / taxes or to pay a fine, prefers to borrow it from his employer or to mortgage his next season's crop to an Indian trader rather than sell one of his goats. For goats and sheep are capital, yielding at least 50 per cent. interest per annum.

The outcome of all this is that everywhere there is an attempt to organise a campaign against the native's goat. The native with a little education sees letters to this effect in the local Press, or hears the Government officials discussing it over dinner, such remarks as this not being uncommon: "If I had my way I'd poison every goat in the Kikuyu Reserve to-morrow." The semi-educated natives pass on what they hear and read to the others in the Reserves, so that just before I left the Kikuyu country I heard a number of comments to the effect that since the settlers had been unable to persuade the Government to give up any more of the Kikuyu's land to them, they were now going to try to damage the native by destroying his goats and sheep.

Actually, of course, there is no idea of destroying the native behind these views, most of which are views honestly held and believed to be in the best interest of the natives themselves. But, unfortunately, the holders of these views have not an inkling of the true position of the goat and sheep in native society, or they would not – nay, could not – hold the views they do, and honestly say they had the interests of the natives at heart. For the natives, the goats and sheep and cattle play a number of very important roles in all tribal life and social organisation. They supply meat, and milk and clothing, but these are but minor functions. What is more important is that in them is incorporated for the native the whole of that part of the social system which with us is represented by the banking system and the Stock Exchange. But there is more than that in the goat and sheep problem. Without them no man can marry. Without them most of the ceremonies connected with birth, with the naming of children, with marriage, with death and with mourning are invalid and of no avail. Without them family worship is incomplete. Imagine for a moment that the Russians had come and taken over England as a colony, and that we heard and read that they had plans to overthrow at one fell sweep our banking and currency system, our social organisation and all our religious ceremonies and ceremonial, and you will begin to realise the fear and hatred and distrust that even the most casual talk about limiting native goats and sheep engenders. To replace goats and sheep by a special cattle currency would be useless at present.

Personally I agree that in time the indigenous goat and sheep must be replaced by something else, and that many native customs entailing the use of sheep and goats must be eventually modified, but let us bring this about by slow and gradual education, not by any blind administrative measure, however well intentioned.

Furthermore, why should not better education include the introduction and the breeding of better strains of goats, which might yield rich milk for, say, a new cheese industry, and better breeds of sheep to replace the native wool-less sheep, so that the native could become an exporter of wool like the European, and yet / have his sheep and goats for all his religious and social ceremonies? Or again, ere any plea for action such as the limiting or reduction of live-stock in the Reserves because of congestion, should not the whole question of the need for increasing the size of the Reserves – or at any rate some of them – be examined?

The average population density for the Kikuyu Reserve is already 116 to the square mile, with a density of about 500 in certain areas, whereas, even allowing Government servants and the commercial Europeans who live in the towns to be counted, the average density of population of whites in white areas is still less than two to the square mile. Surely, then, before another single acre is alienated for white settlement, and before any restrictions upon the freedom of the natives to do what they like in the Reserves are contemplated, new subsidiary native

Reserves should be set aside, and organised with facilities for administration, trade and education, etc.

What do we mean by native education and what is the native attitude to education? The British Advisory Committee upon Education in Tropical Countries set out the policy that the education of the native must go hand in hand with religious instruction, and, accordingly, nearly all native education has recently been carried out by various missionary societies with the aid of Government grants.

It thus came about that the native tended to regard the Christian religion as an essential part of knowledge and learning. This position might have continued for a long time but for two things. In the first place, natives very soon came to realise that very many white men who were obviously educated, in that they could read and write and had much knowledge, nevertheless certainly showed by their actions that they had no belief in the Christian religion, and so the necessity of accepting Christianity as preached by the missions in order to get knowledge and learning was questioned. The second thing which brought matters to a head among the Kikuyu was that certain missions, having for many years, in their ignorance of native custom and native words, taught all their natives in diverse ways that so-called female circumcision was good, suddenly turned round and said it was bad, and must be wholly renounced, together with all that it stood for.

Had the question been wisely treated even then, all might have been well, but it was not, with the result that to-day the natives are taxing themselves, and are bringing large sums of money to the Government, demanding schools which shall not be under the direct control of any missionary society. I would like to make one thing clear in this connection if I can, and that is that the new native demand does not mean that they want *no* new religion and *no* new religious ideas, but rather that they do not want the acceptance of certain prohibitions to be the *sine qua non* of education and knowledge.

Above all things they don't want to give up their customs too rapidly because of ignorant but well-meant propaganda. One of the strongest motives behind the immense and widespread desire for education to-day is the desire to be more like the European, and to have more of the advantages which learning has given / him. There are many Europeans, including many Government officials, who hold very strongly that this desire ought not to be gratified too easily, and who would like to see the native's education restricted to the three Rs and to technical instruction for a long time to come. As an ideal this may be desirable, as a practical policy I fear it is impossible. Let me tell you something of what happens when this policy is attempted. So great is the desire for knowledge that natives who are working all day for Europeans are quite willing to spend some of their earnings each month in paying for education. It is no uncommon thing for a group of natives to club together and raise the money necessary to engage a native with some little education to come and teach them every night in a night school.

If this keenness were appreciated, all these night schools might be run upon an organised system, with good qualified teachers, and under proper inspection and control. As it is, knowledge is being passed on by men who are not fully trained, by men who have no idea of accompanying their instruction with any moral or ethical teaching, or any character-training or discipline, and the result is an ever-increasing number of half-educated natives, who, having had no new moral or ethical codes given them, and believing that their new education entitles them to cast away all those parts of their old tribal sanctions and restrictions which were irksome, are a menace to tribal society and to themselves as well as to the Colony as a whole. These semi-educated people are moreover, an easy prey to reactionary propagandists and to Bolshevism.

Unfortunately I have no time to discuss the whole question in detail this evening, but I must say a few words about technical education.

A great deal of attention is being given to-day to the technical instruction of the African, and this is very excellent, but I would have those who organise it pause to consider the foundations of their policy. Is it the intention of these courses to help the native, or to help the white man? Native education is quite rightly paid for out of native taxation, but if this is so, care must be taken to see that the education given is of a nature to help the native.

I have frequently heard it openly expressed by Government officials and by settlers that the aim of native technical education is to train natives for posts upon farms and in the towns – in fact, to train labour for the white man, labour which will be as efficient but cheaper than Indian artisan labour. While knowing that many natives wish to be trained for this work, there are many who do not want to go and work for the white man, but want to use their knowledge in the Reserves. The kind of technical education which these latter want is the kind that will enable them to return to their Reserves and improve their own housing conditions, do better iron work for themselves, develop a native leather industry, etc.

If native taxation is to supply the funds for native technical education, it seems hardly fair that the native should be required to sign a contract that, having completed his training, he will work for so many years for a European, either in / Government service or in private employ. Yet that is what I have heard advocated upon many occasions, because many natives after their five years of training at, say, the N.I.T.D.[3] prefer to go back to their Reserves. It is held by the critics that the knowledge they have gained is thus being wasted, and some of them believe that, having learned a trade, the native goes back to an idle life and makes no use of his knowledge. This is not generally true, but at present he often finds that part at least of what he has been taught at an industrial training centre is of no use to him except in white employment.

Finally, a few words upon medical services for natives. The medical services which a Colonial Government organises for a native people are of vital importance, and the utmost care in organisation is needed if the natives are to get the full benefits from such services. Yet one finds frequently that from the native point of view the medical services are very badly run. I do not want to suggest that the medical officers in East Africa, any more than the officers of any other Government department, are not doing their very best for the natives, but rather that their best efforts are very frequently ruined through their not understanding the native mind or the native language. Government doctors, like administrative officers, are moved from station to station, from district to district, so that it is the rarest thing to find a Government doctor who knows a native vernacular language.

I have yet to hear any native speak of a Government doctor with any feeling of real faith or confidence, except when speaking formally to his Government officer. In any district where there is a Government medical station you will find a small crowd of natives attending for treatment and a number of natives in the wards. But if one knows the district, then one knows that the work being done is but affecting the fringe.

I do not wish to belittle campaigns carried out by medical departments against diseases such as yaws, intestinal parasites, plague, etc. Such work is magnificent, but I am thinking rather of the ordinary medical-practitioner type of work which a Government medical officer should carry out, and could if he knew his district and his people intimately and spoke their language. Despite any figures sometimes quoted to the contrary, I am convinced that the average infant mortality among non-mission Kikuyu is over 50 per cent. between the ages of birth and five years old, and most of this is easily preventable, as is demonstrated in mission stations where elementary hygiene and child welfare are taught.

Unless the Government organises its medical services in such a way that a doctor remains in a district for a long time without being moved, and so is able to get known and trusted by the natives, little can be done to alter this state of affairs. If Government allotted, say, two women maternity workers to each big tribe, allowing them to be stationed permanently in that tribe, they would soon get well known and well trusted, and by moving among the tribe and gradually teaching the native midwives better methods and more hygiene, invaluable work would be done. The present policy of training young unmarried girls as midwives / at one or two centres is not utterly useless, but of comparatively small value, as only the semi-educated natives will allow themselves to be attended by one of these girls, who, according to native custom, are usually not considered qualified to attend a woman in child-birth, even though they may have passed an examination in midwifery and may be really good at this work.

In conclusion, may I say that I have endeavoured to give you a picture of some problems of colonial administration as seen from the angle of the Kikuyu?

I believe that if you had here a man from any tribe in Africa who knew that tribe as I know the Kikuyu, you would be given a very similar picture, varying only in degree and in detail, according to whether the tribe lived in an area and a colony where the contact of black and white was marked, or as yet scarcely noticeable.

I know full well that if you had been given this picture by – shall we say – a man who had travelled among the Kikuyu for a few months, it would have been very different. Even had a picture been drawn for you by one of the senior Government officers now in the Kikuyu province, you would not have had the picture I have shown you. If you were to ask such a man, "Is this picture really true?" you would receive a negative reply, but if you asked another Kikuyu, he would tell you I had not shown the problems half strongly enough.

From the native point of view I believe it is essential that much attention should be given to the whole question of policy with regard to the study of native languages and customs, and of the education given to the Government officers before they are sent out to the Colonies, and I hope that one of the results of this paper of mine will be that this Group gives such questions very serious consideration.

Summary of Discussion

Mr. R. P. Nicholson asked if Mr. Leakey would say more exactly what he thought the effect of bringing education to the natives would be, particularly in respect of the preservation of tribal organisation and customs, which it was often argued should be kept up as far as compatible with progress. Was there not probably some antagonism between Western education and tribal organisation?

Mr. Leakey replied that, whether one liked it or not, whether one aimed at Westernising the natives or at maintaining their own tribal customs, whether education were organised or unorganised, the natives themselves were determined to follow European example. The only way in which the natives could be kept in their tribal ways would be by forcing all Europeans to adopt them also. Since they would inevitably become Westernised, it was essential to see that they got the best ideas, and not the worst, and this could only be done if the whole question of education was investigated and studied by people who understood the native before they started. In Kenya and Tanganyika men were preparing to study the question from that point of view, but they were mostly people who did not possess the necessary basis for making the study.

A Member said the lecturer had given an interesting account concerning the Kikuyu district, but he thought the conditions described were not common to other parts of / Africa. He was familiar with the West Coast, and in his time, some years ago, the officials who went out certainly knew the language of their district – Hausa, Yoruba, Ibo – and a good many of them did take the trouble to get to the bottom of the native mind, though this was perhaps beyond the competence of any European. He heartily agreed that nothing was more disastrous, in India and all the colonies, than the continual changing of officers from one district to another. He would like to know if Mr. Leakey had had any experience of the West Coast.

MR. LEAKEY said he had deliberately limited his address to the Kikuyu point of view, because he had first-hand knowledge of it. The Kikuyu had borne the whole brunt of contact with white people, because they were so near the capital of Kenya, and he felt sure that what had happened there was capable of happening elsewhere in Africa, if administration did not benefit from the knowledge gained. He had discussed the question with a number of West Coast officials, who had agreed that, though they tried to learn the native languages and customs, they had little time to do so. It was not the fault of the officials. The policy was wrong which made them start straight away into work, before they had had time to learn the language.

SIR LAURENCE GUILLEMARD asked if officials did not learn any language before they went out.

MR. LEAKEY replied that they had a year's course at Oxford or Cambridge, during which they were supposed to learn Swahili, as well as anthropology, bookkeeping, and law. But having just finished three or four years of studying for their degree, they were usually tired, and more inclined to have a good time than to study hard. The result of sending them up to study a little of five or six subjects was that they really learnt very little at all of any of them.

THE SECOND SPEAKER asked if Mr. Leakey did not think it was most necessary that the officials in the Colonial Office at home should be obliged to serve in some colony for two or three years before they returned to London, and said what was to be done in the colonies generally.

MR. TOMLINSON said that officials now joined the Colonial Office with a specified liability to serve for one or two years overseas. A number of the men in the Office had visited the Dependencies in recent years. He had been amazed to hear the last speaker say that in former years officials in Nigeria possessed sufficient knowledge of Yoruba and Ibo to enable them to deal with the people. His own experience of twenty years in Nigeria was that in the North the average district officer was able to carry on his work in Hausa, an easy language with no tonic difficulties, without the aid of interpreters, who were rarely allowed, but that until comparatively recently the number of officials who could speak Yoruba and Ibo was very small.

THE SECOND SPEAKER said that possibly there were not many who could speak Ibo, but he had in mind two men who had been on his station who could speak it well enough. /

PROFESSOR H. A. SMITH asked, with reference to the short course at Cambridge, whether Mr. Leakey would prefer a longer course in England, or sending the men out to Africa for training. The question was being considered in the London University.

LORD LUGARD said a third alternative was to go through the present prescribed course in England, and to have a refresher course in England after completing the first tour of service overseas.

MR. LEAKEY said that if possible he would send the men out for two years to the language group in which they intended to serve their whole period and make them learn one of the languages of the group, and let them return for the course in law, economics and other subjects only after they had shown their ability to learn the language. If they could not learn the language it would be no use their going on with the administration service at all from the native point of view.

MISS FREDA WHITE pointed out that a great difficulty was that, if the training was greatly added to, the men were so old before they began to earn anything.

PROFESSOR R. COUPLAND4 said that if the men went out at the end of their ordinary three or four years degree course, they would certainly come back fresher, but there was the difficulty of asking men to commit themselves to two or three years' probationary work, with the possibility of not obtaining a post at the end. After one year, as at present, they are still quite young and can try something else if they fail; but for a longer training there might not be recruits unless they were quite certain of success.

MR. LEAKEY said they would be simply students and would have no responsibility. He thought there would be very few failures as far as learning the language was concerned as under the present system half the failures were due to lack of time for study of the language or to laziness. The first cause of failure would be removed by this suggested period set aside for learning a language, and if the second cause operated when a man knew that his career depended upon it, that man was better out of the service.

SIR HUMPHREY LEGGETT said he would like to ask about a few of the points brought up by the delegates from Kenya, who had shown fairly definitely on what grounds they desired to influence public opinion in England, and, if they were able, the Joint Committee of the two Houses. They seemed to be fundamental points, and he would be glad if Mr. Leakey could answer them from the native point of view.

The first point stressed by the delegates was that white settlement was extremely important as a means of moral and economic uplift, and that a more numerous white settler population, in spite of the consequent abstracting of larger and larger numbers of men from the Reserves to become wage-earners or squatters, would not be deleterious, but advantageous to the natives.

Another point, which Mr. Leakey had, however, answered in advance was that the delegates had strongly affirmed that the land allowed to the Native Reserves under the recent settlement was fully sufficient in area not only for present needs, but also for several / generations to come, and they made this general statement in spite of the overcrowding of the Dagoretti area and the Kikuyu Reserve as a whole.

A very definite statement had also been made by certain of the delegates to the Commonwealth Group of the Labour Party in the House of Commons, to the effect that such ill-feeling as existed in the Kikuyu Reserve was due to quite extraneous people, particularly Indian agitators, and that but for such outside influences no ill-feeling would exist.

He had heard it stated by the Kenya Delegates, both at Chatham House and at other meetings, that the pressure of taxation was not so great as to have any effect upon bringing the natives out to become wage-earners, either for Government departments or for nonofficial employers. In saying that the proportion of people who now left the Reserve for wage labour (32 per cent. for the whole of Kenya, over 50 per cent. for the Kikuyu, and up to 70 per cent. for some other tribes) did not go out of the Reserves for that reason, but many of them as permanent squatters on European farms, surely the argument of the Delegates told rather against, than for, the point they desired to make. Was not the real point simply whether the abstraction of 32 per cent. (or higher figures) was damaging to tribal life?

Another point was in connection with the restrictions upon agriculture. Would the natives like to grow coffee, and would it be a success or a danger if they did? Was there a feeling that the Government adopted these restrictions for reasons influenced by the white settlements?

Lastly, the Secretary of State, in the White Paper of 1927, had laid down as the object to be achieved the greater and closer association of the non-official communities and white settlers in the trusteeship to be exercised by the Government. The white settlers had taken this up as a catchword, though he (the speaker) did not know how the settlers interpreted that it should be done. He would be glad if Mr. Leakey could suggest whether, and if so in what way, this could be done with real advantage to all concerned.

MR. LEAKEY replied that the white settler provided the native with a big market for his produce and opportunities of learning things he could not learn before. A certain number of settlers taught natives handwork, the repairing of cars, and many other things which they could use in their Reserves. He would not have the settler go, but there was the danger of the settler considering himself indispensable. His presence was useful, but things would go on whether he was there or not. If he would realise his responsibility to the native in such things as medical service, education, and so on, he could be very much more useful. As an example, he knew of very many white settlers who had been approached by the natives for permission to have a school on their farms, and about 50 per cent. refused to give their sanction. The result was that schools were being run secretly at night in the villages without any control, and the result was disastrous from the European point of view as well as from the point of view of the natives and tribal organisation. Each European was capable of doing a tremendous amount of medical and educational uplifting, as the least educated among them had more knowledge of these subjects than any of the natives. A great many, of course, were doing something to help the natives on their farms.

With regard to the question of the Reserves, by merely taking the figures for the area and for the population, one got the idea that, except in the Kavirondo and Dagoretti / districts, there was ample room in the Reserves. The Masai Reserve was a large Reserve with a comparatively small population, but the land could not be used for agriculture, because less than two-thirds of the Reserves had a permanent water supply. A pastoral people needed a much larger extent of land than an agricultural people. The same thing applied even more to the other big pastoral reserves on the Northern Frontier. He knew of an area in South Tanganyika, where there was magnificent agricultural land, but a very small population, but if there were any more people to the square mile, they would all die in the dry season. Such Reserves or native areas could be made ample only by enormous water conservancy schemes, for there was plenty of rainfall, though it was not evenly distributed throughout the year.

THE CHAIRMAN asked if there was any vacant land adjacent to the Reserves which could be thrown into them.

MR. LEAKEY said there was no land actually touching the Kikuyu Reserve which could be alienated to them, as they were surrounded by farm areas or forest reserves. Not very far away there was unalienated land to which those Kikuyu who had lost their own land would be only too glad to move. They could have areas marked out as family land, and would start all over again, instead of having to go as squatters, paid only twelve shillings a month for thirty working days.

REV. E. W. SMITH asked if that land could be the same to them if it was so far away from the home associated with their ancestors.

MR. LEAKEY said it would not be the same, but it would be infinitely better than going as squatters, which was the only alternative. He would himself advocate that any farms round the Reserves which were vacated should be bought up by Government and added to the Reserves.

With regard to the unrest in the Kikuyu districts, this dated back before the Indian agitators arrived, it dated to the time when they were suddenly moved from their own land to someone else's. Indian agitators, and also one or two European agitators, took the opportunity of the unrest to crystallise it for their own ends, but if every agitator disappeared, there would still be Kikuyu unrest, for they were so congested that something had to be done. An acre and a half per individual had to supply fuel, food, thatching, and a balance for taxes.

If they had the land, they could easily grow enough for their own needs and to pay for the taxes. It was the lack of land that forced them to go out to work.

The Kavirondo district had 1200 people to the square mile in some areas. The men from that district went out as squatters, usually without their women-folk for periods of from six months to a couple of years. The Kikuyu always took their women-folk with them.

THE CHAIRMAN asked what effect the Land Trust Bill had in allowing leases within the area of the Reserves.

MR. LEAKEY said he believed that one of the reasons for that particular clause in the Bill was to leave a loophole for getting some of the extremely desirable Masai country. / The hope was frequently expressed that the Masai could be turned from a pastoral into an agricultural people, so that they would need less land, and then some of their Reserve could be leased. But the Masai could not spare this land. They had winter and summer grazing, and some land which they did not appear to use had actually been leased, so that two or three times recently the Masai had found their land occupied when they returned at the usual season.

The coffee question could easily be solved. The principle on which restrictions were made was that in small-scale coffee-growing adequate inspection was impossible and disease was liable to spread. The Kikuyu was itching with fury because he had been told that as a Kikuyu he must not grow coffee, but the same difficulties of disease and lack of inspection applied in the case of the Europeans on the borders of Nairobi who grew thirty bushels, or to supply coffee for their own consumption. The solution was to restrict coffee-growing to those who could pay, say, a hundred shillings a year towards the expense of Government inspectors. Most of the Kikuyu did not want to grow coffee, but the few who did would gladly pay the necessary sum, and could make enough profit to repay themselves. Those who did not want to grow coffee on this scale and pay the coffee tax, whether native or European, would not be allowed to grow it.

He felt very strongly on the question of Trusteeship, raised in Sir Humphrey Leggett's last point. There were Europeans in the country who were certainly fit and capable of playing a large part in native Trusteeship. He would have a poor opinion of his own race if he did not think so. The trouble was that the majority of those Europeans who were willing to stand for membership of the Legislative Council were quite unsuited for that particular job. People who had completely failed to make anything of their own farms, and had shown themselves to be hopeless in organising their own affairs, stood for election, and because the better men had no time to give to politics, these others were elected. People who had run through two or three fortunes could become members of the Legislative Council and be appointed to all the finance committees of the Government, simply because they had time for it. If these people who were fit to be on the Legislative Council had the time to spare to do so, it would then be possible to have a larger non-official representation with safety, but not until then.

SIR LAURENCE GUILLEMARD asked how the members of the Council were appointed. He referred to the practice in Malaya, where he had been Governor, and where the system of nomination by the Government had worked perfectly.

MR. LEAKEY said the election to the Legislative Council was in each district by white vote only. It would be hard to go back from the method of election, and if the right people were nominated they would refuse to stand, saying that their farms took up all their time.

REV. E. W. SMITH said the Kenya Delegation had laid great stress on the fact that the settlers were capable of trusteeship because they had done so much in the way of education. They had given him the impression that all farmers among the settlers ran schools for the natives.

MR. LEAKEY said that he would estimate that less than 50 per cent. of the settlers had / schools. Lord Delamere[5] had several schools of a sort, Mr. O'Shea had not, so far as he knew, nor had Mr. Maclellan Wilson, though it was only fair to say that he was quite sure the latter would allow one if it were asked for, but his estate was within a mile of a well-organised mission school with night classes.

MR. WYNDHAM said that one point about the question of Trusteeship was that of developing the responsibility of the settlers. At present they blamed the Colonial Office if things went wrong, instead of having themselves to blame.

MR. LEAKEY said he felt very strongly that those at present representing Europeans on the Legislative Council did not understand what fairness to the native meant. He instanced an example in connection with an electric light company's request for land for a new power-station. There was land twelve miles away that was neither settled nor in the Reserves, but they wanted a bit of land that was in the Kikuyu Reserve. The company represented that the new station would be for the benefit of the whole community, native as well as white, and showed their estimates of the additional number of electric units that would be required within the coming three years. Mr. Leakey had been able to make inquiries, which showed that the estimated increase in the electricity required was due to orders which had been received for power from a few large firms who intended to build new factories. He had put the information in the hands of his father, who was representing the natives' interests on the tribunal set up to report on the matter, but in spite of this the settler members of the tribunal had come to the conclusion that it was definitely for the natives' benefit that their land should be taken from the Kikuyu Reserve for the purpose of the power-station.

PROFESSOR H. A. SMITH said that the main point in Mr. Leakey's paper was that mistakes were made because the officials did not understand the language and customs of the natives. The members of the delegation had contended that the settlers knew the natives better than the officials, having lived among them, learnt their language, and come into closer contact with them. Was this true?

MR. LEAKEY replied that it was absolutely untrue. He knew of one or two settlers who understood Kikuyu better than the Government officials, and one or two who knew Nandi fairly well. Otherwise there were practically none who had the vaguest inkling of native customs. The cases brought by them against natives showed that they did not know anything of the intricacies and special customs of the different native tribes. They had, of course, such elementary knowledge as that some tribes would not touch a dead body and others would, but they had no intimate knowledge of the really important customs and thoughts of the natives.

MR. RENNIE SMITH asked if there was a supply of natives forthcoming able to teach in their own tribes. He would like Mr. Leakey to define the kind of education that should be given. There was a great deal of quarrelling at the present time between the literary and economic or vocational type of education. Also, from the religious point of view, was there not considerable disparity between the teaching of the missionaries and the / deductions made by the natives from the practice of Europeans generally? Could more information be given as to the kind of religious teaching suitable for the native?

MR. LEAKEY said there were a few good schools, organised by the Government, for training native teachers, and there were a number of teachers' training centres run by the missionaries, but not nearly enough. There were any number of natives wanting to train for whom places were not available. Another difficulty was the length of the training course, which meant that men could not afford to train unless some payment could be made while training, as many of them were married and were not exempt from taxes. The native was capable of developing into a good teacher if trained by the right people. The Jeans School, which was doing very good work in that line, could be taken as an example of what could be done. The missionaries were many of them making the mistake of mixing up fundamental religion and ethics with a lot of dogma and moral teaching that had nothing to do with religion, but were really the tribal customs of the English. They were trying to make the native jump from a primitive stage of society to one which most Europeans did not live up to, instead of educating him gradually, and without necessarily aiming at getting him where they were themselves. Some sort of moral and ethical training must be given, as an accompaniment to reading, writing and arithmetic. The natives automatically tended to lose their own social sanctions and control, and unless they were given something else, they would become just as anybody else with nothing to control them. In a primitive state of psychology there must be some unseen Power for the mind to grip on to, as a reason for not killing, lying, stealing and so on. More intellectual people could break away from organised religion, but the vast majority could not do so without breaking away from everything. He would like to see missionary education controlled by an organised body thinking out how Christianity could be grafted on to the old native customs, changing, modifying and altering them, but not sweeping everything away wholesale. He was hoping to write a paper on this subject which he hoped would be published in Africa. The kind of education must vary from tribe to tribe and from individual to individual. He did not favour the policy in Tanganyika of giving the sons of chiefs a very high type of education at Tabora, while the vast mass of the natives were getting very little. The natives would tolerate differences of education and knowledge as between the whites and themselves, but this specialised education was creating a hiatus between a group of natives with Western ideals and education which would not be tolerated. If these sons of chiefs were to govern effectively, the whole level of education must be raised.

PROFESSOR H. A. SMITH asked if Mr. Leakey considered that in opposing polygamy the missionaries were making a mistake and merely trying to enforce English tribal customs.

MR. LEAKEY replied that the only direct reference he knew of in the Bible concerning monogamy was that bishops and deacons should be the husband of one wife. Where there was a definite preponderance of women over men it simply brought about a great deal of prostitution, which was most undesirable. The missions penalised the natives much too severely, though polygamy was not penalised by the law. The Catholics were less severe. Judging from the few Catholic missions he knew, they were merely out for / nominal converts, and after giving the natives six weeks of instruction, they did not mind if they had five wives, but this might not be true elsewhere.

SIR HUMPHREY LEGGETT told a story of a District Commissioner who had been called in to try to put things right in a case where the Mission had been rather severe, and the young official before whom the case came had not been able to understand the dispute, thinking it was something to do with the doctrine of the Holy Trinity. The Commissioner found that the Holy Trinity was the three wives of the man who had been ordered by the Mission to put two of them away. This was a good illustration of the result of insufficient knowledge of the language.

LORD LUGARD asked what the functions of chieftainship were among the Kikuyu, and on what system chiefs were selected, apart from those appointed by the Government.

MR. LEAKEY said the whole trouble was that the system differed from tribe to tribe. The Kikuyu chief was responsible for religious functions and morals, but had nothing whatever to do with the administration of native law and court decisions. The administration of law was in the hands of elders of the first, second, third or fourth grades. In the first grade they attended debates and listened to cases and learnt, but were not allowed to retire, after hearing the witnesses, to discuss the decision, until they had reached the fourth grade. Only elders of the fourth grade could give a decision. The person responsible in the old days as head of the court was elected by the elders from those of the fourth grade by more or less general agreement as the most capable man within the district. Under the existing system of Government chiefs, they might know nothing about native law. One of his best friends was a Government appointed chief, who knew less perhaps about native law than he (Mr. Leakey) did himself. He had been taught a lot, and had been allowed to write it down, but the chief had only reached the first grade of elders, and had been taught nothing, yet he had to be President of all the native courts in the district by Government Ordinance. The Government had, at one time, appointed the late Chief Kinanjui as Paramount Chief of the Kikuyu, although he was not even a clan chief and had not reached the second grade of elders, and if the British had cleared out, the first murder would have been that of this Chief. It was not surprising to him that the Government found that the chiefs had little authority, and frequently could not control their districts in the Reserves.

LORD LUGARD asked what the position of Eiyeki, with whom he had made blood-brotherhood, had been. He had called himself a paramount chief.

MR. LEAKEY said he would probably have been chief of a clan group, but that the Kikuyu had no paramount chief in the Government sense of the word until the Government appointed one. There had been a chief of all the warfare in fighting the Masai, but that was purely an army organisation. There had been a magnificent organisation of police and army combined, which had ensured that all the laws made by the native authorities were carried out, as well as carrying out counter-raids on the Masai, but because they had power of life and death, the first thing the British had done had been to wipe / out the whole of the Njama. To the modern native this wonderful organisation was nothing but a myth. The Government was now trying to build up a tribal police, having deliberately destroyed the basis on which it should have stood. It was pathetic to see the things that had been done from ignorance of native custom. The Kikuyu had suffered more than others, and everything should be done to prevent a repetition of the mistakes with other tribes.

EDITORIAL NOTES

Mercer and Collins, *The Colonial Office List for 1900*

1. *The patronage ... under his directions*: the Liberal Unionist Joseph Chamberlain (1836–1914) was Secretary of State for the Colonies from 29 June 1895 to 16 September 1903.
2. *Wei-hai-wei*: a territory in North-Eastern China and one of the major ports of the Royal Navy in the Far East.
3. *His Highness the Rajah*: the Rajah of Sarawak was Charles Brooke (1829–1917), the second of the three 'White Rajahs' who ruled the kingdom of Sarawak from 1841 to 1946.
4. *school of Musketry at Hythe*: the school of Musketry in Hythe, Kent was established 1853. After 1925, it was also referred to as the Small Arms School.
5. *found on page 16*: Not included.
6. *High Commissioner of the Federated Malay States*: James Alexander Swettenham (1846–1933) was High Commissioner of the Federated Malay States from 8 December 1899 to 18 February 1901.
7. *High Commissioner ... Colonel Commandant of the corps*: Sir Alfred Milner (1854–1925) was High Commissioner for Southern Africa from May 1897 to May 1905.

Harding and Gent, *The Dominions Office and Colonial Office List for 1939*

1. *THE DOMINIONS OFFICE AND COLONIAL LIST, 1939*: The Colonial Office List was renamed the Dominions Office and Colonial Office List in 1926.
2. *By the Director of Recruitment (Colonial Service)*: for more than forty years, Sir Ralph D. Furse (1887–1973) was the leading civil servant judging applicants for the Colonial Service. Furse was educated at Eton and graduated from Oxford in 1909. In 1910, he became Assistant Private Secretary (appointments) to the Secretary of State for the Colonies serving six secretaries of state in the position up to 1930. In 1931, he was appointed Director of Recruitment in the newly established personnel division of the Colonial Office, a position he held until 1948.
3. *By the Crown Agents for the Colonies*: the Crown Agents for the Colonies was a quasi-governmental body attached to the Colonial Office. From offices in London the Crown Agents organized the supply of manufactured goods to Crown Colonies, supervised the expenditure of capital, issued loans and where in charge of recruitment of engineers and technical staff for colonial service.

4. *The Secretary of State ... in 1931*: Lord Passfield (1859–1947) was Secretary of State for the Colonies from 7 June 1929 to 24 August 1931.

5. *C. J. Jeffries*: Sir Charles Joseph Jeffries joined the Colonial Office in 1917. Under the auspices of Ralph D. Furse, he rose in the ranks to become Assistant Secretary and Establishment Officer. In 1930, he was given the job of putting the principle of unification of the Colonial Service into practice. In 1939, he became an Assistant Under-Secretary of State and upon the retirement of Furse in 1948, he became head of the personnel division at the Colonial Office.

6. *M.R.C.V.S.*: Membership of the Royal College of Veterinary Surgeons. The Royal College of Veterinary Surgeons was established by Royal Charter in 1844 and acquired its institutional home in central London in 1853.

7. *Imperial Forestry Institute*: The Imperial Forestry Institute was established in Oxford in 1924 where a School of Forestry was opened in 1905. The purpose of the Imperial Forestry Institute was to provide higher education in forestry to secure the needs of the empire.

8. *Institute of Chemistry*: The Institute of Chemistry of Great Britain was founded in 1877 and received its Royal Charter in 1885 cementing its role as the qualifying body of the chemical professions in Britain.

9. *Ordnance Survey Office, Southampton*: The Ordnance Survey Office was established in 1791 and the mapping agency relocated from London to Southampton in 1841.

10. *Institution of Civil Engineers*: The Institution of Civil Engineers was established in London in 1818 and was the main qualifying body for the civil engineering profession in Britain and the colonies.

11. *A.M.I.C.E.*: Associate Member of the Institution of Civil Engineers examinations were held annually in London. Qualification for the Associate Membership required also that candidates where over twenty-five years of age and had been engaged in civil engineering works for at least five years.

12. *A.M.I.M.E.*: Associate Member of the Institution of Mechanical Engineers. The Institution of Mechanical Engineers was founded in Birmingham in 1847 and relocated its headquarters to London in 1877.

13. *A.M.I.E.E.*: Associate Member of the Institution of Electrical Engineers. The institution was founded in London in 1871 (until 1888 under the name Society of Telegraph Engineers).

14. *A.R.I.B.A.*: Associate of the Royal Institute of British Architects. The Institute was formed in 1834 as the Institute of British Architects in London and received a Royal Charter in 1837.

15. *Lake Steamer Service*: the steamer services for the central African lakes were organized by the Tanganyika and by the Kenya and Uganda Railway and Harbours Departments.

16. *R.N.R.*: Royal Naval Reserve.

17. *Extra Master's or Master's certificate*: Master's certificates gave the holder the right to command specified commercial vessels. The Extra Master's certificates were the highest professional qualification for mariners in the British Merchant Navy.

18. *The Nautical College, Pangbourne*: the HMS *Conway* was naval training school on the Mersey housed aboard ships of that name. The HMS *Worcester* was the name given to the Thames Nautical Training College established in 1862 aboard a ship of that name; the Nautical College, Pangbourne in the county of Berkshire was founded in 1917 to prepare young men for future employment in the Merchant Fleet.

19. *Forest of Dean or Benmore Schools*: the Forestry Schools in Gloucestershire England and Benmore, Scotland.

20. *Royal Sanitary Institute*: The Royal Sanitary Institute was founded in 1876 as the Sanitary Institute. It was the primary qualifying professional sanitary institutions and later renamed as the Royal Society for the Promotion of Health.
21. *Army School of Hygiene*: The Army School of Hygiene at Keogh Barracks, Mytchett in the county of Surrey provided specialized training for sanitation and water supplies in particular in tropical regions.

Regulations for His Majesty's Colonial Service

1. *Secretary of State for the Colonies*: Lewis Vernon Harcourt, first Viscount Harcourt (1863–1922) of the Liberal Party, was Secretary of State for the Colonies from 1910 to 1915.
2. *31 & 32 Vict. c. 72, s. 2.*: the Promissory Oaths Ordinance of 1869.
3. *Appendix 1*: Not included in this volume.

Eiloart, *The Land of Death*

1. *ERNEST EILOART*: Ernest Eiloart was the eldest son in a family of solicitors. At the age of eighteen he became a member of the Honorable Society of the Inner Temple (1872). His mother was the prolific author, Elizabeth Eiloart, and Ernest Eiloart also published on the legal status of women including the short book *The Law relating to Women* (London: Waterlow, 1878).
2. *the Imperial Federation League ... is a reality*: The Imperial Federation League was founded in 1884 to encourage closer constitutional union in the British Empire and it played an importantly role in the initiation of the Indian and Colonial Exhibition in London in 1886.
3. *Ashantee War*: the Ashanti War in 1873–4, after which the Gold Coast was formally declared a British Crown Colony.
4. *the Governor ... his own son*: refers to William Brandford Griffith who served as Acting Governor of the Gold Coast from 1880 to 1881 and as governor from 1885 to 1895. His son, also named William Brandford Griffith, was Chief Justice of the Gold Coast Colony from 1895 to 1914 and a prolific legal writer.
5. *Governor Rowe*: Sir Samuel Rowe (1835–88) served as governor of the Gold Coast from 1881 to 1884. Sir James Marshall (1829–89) was Chief Justice of the Gold Coast from 1880 to 1882 and his successor N. Lessingham Bailey was in office from 1882 to1886.
6. *Mr. Antrobus*: Sir Reginald Laurence Antrobus (1853–1942) was private secretary to three consecutive secretaries of state for the colonies in the period of 1882 to 1886.

'The Medical Services of West African Colonies and Protectorates'

1. *Mr. Chamberlain*: See note 1 to Mercer and Collins, *The Colonial Office List for 1900*, above.
2. *London School of Tropical Medicine*: The London School of Tropical Medicine was founded in 1899. It was renamed the London School of Hygiene and Tropical Medicine and received a Royal Charter in 1924.
3. *Liverpool School of Tropical Medicine*: The Liverpool School of Tropical Medicine was founded in 1898.

'The Organization of the Colonial Medical Service'

1. *THE Colonial Secretary*: See note 1 to Mercer and Collins, *The Colonial Office List for 1900*, above.
2. *Surgeon-General Evatt*: Sir George Evatt (1843–1921) was Surgeon-General from 1899 to 1903.
3. *Sir Joseph Fayrer*: (1824–1907) was a surgeon and physician who had spent forty-five years of his life connected to the Indian Medical Service.
4. *Mr. James Cantlie*: Sir James Cantlie (1851–1926) was a physician and medical administrator who became the first surgeon and lecturer in tropical surgery at the London School of Tropical Medicine.

The West African Pocket Book. A Guide for Newly-Appointed Government Officers

1. *Appendix A*: Appendices are not included.
2. *Forcados*: a small port town on the Forcados River in the Niger Delta.
3. *Sir Patrick Manson*: (1844–1922) was a physician and parasitologist who published a paper suggesting the link between the transmission of malaria and mosquitos in 1894. He also drew up plans in 1897 that led to the establishment of the London School of Tropical Medicine in 1899.
4. *Professor Ronald Ross*: Sir Ronald Ross (1857–1932) was a malariologist who won the Nobel Prize for medicine for his work on malaria.

Lord Elgin, Colonies (General), *Circular Despatch*

1. *questions have been put ... recently administrating*: for example, it had been revealed that in 1902, the Governor of Ceylon, Sir West Ridgeway, had employed experts in marine biology to assess the pearl fishing industry of the territory which had hitherto been operating as an inefficient government monopoly. The experts reported in April 1902, however, no action was taken to implement their recommendations. In November 1903, Sir West Ridgeway retired as governor and in early 1904 he formed Gulf Syndicate, a commercial company, which immediately entered into negotiations with the Colonial Office for a concession of the pearl fisheries in Ceylon. In October of 1905, an agreement was reached whereby Gulf Syndicate, with Sir West Ridgeway as principle managing director, secured the concession without the opportunity for any rival concerns to tender a bid.
2. *ELGIN*: Victor Alexander Bruce, ninth Earl of Elgin (1849–1917) was Secretary of State for the Colonies from 10 December 1905 to 12 April 1908.

Tenth Annual Report of the Executive Committee of the Colonial Nursing Association

1. *The application ... at their worst*: the 1905 Russian Revolution began on 22 January 1905 and reached its height during June and July of that year. It resulted in the Tsar, Nicholas II, signing the October manifesto, which extended the franchise and established the Duma as the principal legislative body. This failed to appease all of the Tsar's subjects and local protests continued until 1907.

2. *Nursing Notes*: a journal for nurses published from 1887 by the Women's Printing Society. The journal was later renamed *Nursing Notes and Midwives' Chronicle*.

Arber, Unpublished Memoir of the Sudan Political Service

1. *H.B. Arber*: Hugh Benjamin Arber (1906–86) joined the Sudan Political Service in 1928 and retired in 1954 as the Governor of the Northern Province.
2. *J.B. Cramer*: J. B. Cramer & Co. was founded in 1824 by the musician, Johann Baptist Cramer. The company produced and sold musical instruments until it was taken over by the piano company, Kemble & Co. in 1964.
3. *Ovingden Hall*: Ovingden Hall was opened as a school for young gentlemen in 1894 and remained on this site until the Second World War when it was relocated to Devon. The site was subsequently reopened as a school for deaf children.
4. *Charterhouse*: Charterhouse School is an English Public School in Surrey founded in 1611.
5. *Wadham College Oxford*: Wadham College is a constituent college of the University of Oxford founded in 1610.
6. *Oxford 1928 crew*: The Boat Race is an annual rowing event held on the Thames between competing eights of Oxford University Boat Club and Cambridge University Boat Club.
7. *Maurice Bowra*: Sir Maurice (Cecil) Bowra (1898–1971), was a classical scholar and Warden of Wadham College from 1938 to 1970.
8. *Harold MacMichael*: Sir Harold MacMichael (1882–1969) was Civil Secretary in the Sudanese Political Service from 1926 to 1934 when he became Governor of Tanganyika.
9. *School of Oriental Studies*: The School of Oriental Studies was founded in 1916 to train administrators for Britain's colonial possessions. Africa was added to the school's name in 1938 and it was thereafter known as the School of Oriental and African Studies.
10. *H. A. R. Gibb*: Sir Hamilton Gibb (1895–1971) a Scottish historian who taught Arabic at the School of Oriental Studies, University of London from 1921 to 1937.
11. *Lawn & Alder*: Lawn and Adler was a specialist shop at 32 Sackville Street, London which claimed to offer Britons moving overseas 'fine quality goods and first class assistance'.
12. *DACS(pers)*: District Assistant Civil Secretary (Personnel).
13. *ADC*: Assistant District Commissioner.
14. *DC*: District Commissioner.
15. *Mamur*: a term used for Egyptian and Sudanese administrative assistants.
16. *prominent Khatmi politician*: Sufi order founded in 1817.
17. *Town Merkaz*: the District Office and headquarter in El Obeid.
18. *angareb*: a rope bed.
19. *SMO*: Senior Medical Officer.
20. *SDF*: Sudan Defence Force.
21. *Mudiria*: the province of a territory of a Mudhir.
22. *DACS (Admin) Civil Secretary's Office*: District Assistant Civil Secretary (Administration).
23. *C. S.'s*: Chief Secretary.
24. *UNP*: Upper Nile Province.
25. *Lord Raglan*: Richard Fitzroy Somerset, fourth Baron Raglan (1885–1964) was a captain in the Grenadier Guards who was seconded to the Egyptian army from 1913 to 1919 where he served in the Sudan.

26. *original Latuka vocabulary*: H. A. Arber, *A Simple Lotuko Grammar and Lotuko Vocabulary* (Juba, 1936).
27. *tukl*: grass hut.

Furse, 'Liaison with Universities in the Self-Governing Dominions'

1. *Private Secretary (Appointments)*: Sir Ralph D. Furse. See note 2 to Harding and Gent, *The Dominions Office and Colonial Office List for 1939*, above.

'Memorandum Showing the Progress and Development in the Colonial Empire and in the Machinery for Dealing with Colonial Questions from November 1924, to November, 1928'

1. *Secretary of State*: Leo Amery (1873–1955) was Colonial Secretary from 6 November 1924 to 4 June 1929.
2. *Permanent Under-Secretary of State*: Sir Samuel Herbert Wilson (1873–1950) was Permanent Under-Secretary of State in the Colonial Office from 1925 to 1933. He had previously been Governor of Trinidad and Tobago from 1921 to 1924 and briefly Governor of Jamaica in 1924 before he had to return to Britain for health reasons.
3. *Dr. A.T. Stanton*: Ambrose T. Stanton was appointed to this position based on experience in Canada and nearly two decades in Malaya.
4. *Sir George Schuster*: (1881–1982) served as Financial Secretary for the Sudan from 1922 to 1927 and Finance Member on the Viceroy's Council in India from 1928 to 1934.
5. *Viscount Milner*: Sir Alfred Milner (1854–1925) was Secretary of State for the Colonies from 10 January 1919 to 13 February 1921.
6. *Lord Lovat*: Simon Joseph Fraser (1871–1933) was fourteenth Lord Lovat and Under Secretary of State for the Dominions from 1927 to 1928.
7. *Imperial College of Tropical Agriculture*: The Imperial College of Tropical Agriculture in Trinidad was founded in 1922 and merged with the University College of the West Indies (Jamaica) to become the Faculty of Agriculture in 1960.
8. *Ordnance Survey*: founded in 1791.
9. *Prince of Wales's College at Achimota*: The Prince of Wales College and School was founded in 1924 in Achimota, near Accra.
10. *St. Helena and Ascension*: The islands of St Helena and Ascension in the South Atlantic Ocean were transferred from the East India Company to the British Crown in 1833.
11. *Mr. Ormsby Gore*: William Ormsby-Gore (1885–1964), was Under-Secretary of State for the Colonies from 1922 to 1929 and Secretary of State for the Colonies from 28 May 1936 to 16 May 1938. In 1929, he became the first chairman of the Colonial Advisory Council on Agriculture and Animal Health (CAC).
12. *Mr. Justice Feetham of South Africa*: Richard Feetham (1874–1965) was a South African lawyer, politician and judge.
13. *Sir Herbert Baker*: (1862–1946) was a leading architect who designed numerous buildings in South Africa, India, the United Kingdom and elsewhere. In Kenya, his most famous work was the Prince of Wales School that opened in 1931 and which in 1965 became the Nairobi School.
14. *Sir Robert Coryndon*: was Governor of Uganda from 1917 to 1922 after which he became the Governor of Kenya from 1922 to 1925.

15. *Professor Sir Rowland Biffen*: (1874–1949) was Professor of Agricultural Botany at Cambridge University from 1908 to 1931.
16. *Makere College for natives in Uganda*: Makerere College was established as a technical school in 1922 in Kampala, Uganda.
17. *Jeanes Training School for Native Teachers in Kenya*: Jeanes Training School for Native Teachers in Kenya was established in 1925.
18. *Appendix III*: Appendices not included.
19. *Mullah*: Sayyīd Muhammad ʿAbd Allāh al-Hasan (1856–1920).

Furse, 'Recruitment and Training of Colonial Civil Servants'

1. *MEMORANDUM BY THE PRIVATE SECRETARY FOR APPOINTMENTS*: Sir Ralph D. Furse. See note 2 to Harding and Gent, *The Dominions Office and Colonial Office List for 1939*, above.
2. *The first covers ... mandatory territories*: The League of Nations designated three classes of mandate: A, B and C. Class A mandates were those territories deemed to have reached a stage of development whereby the wishes of the territory's people must be a principle consideration. There was a single British Class A mandate: Mesopotamia. Class B mandates were deemed to require a greater level of control by the supervising country which had to guarantee freedom of conscious and religion. The mandatory powers were also forbidden from constructing military bases in this class of territory. Britain's Class B mandates were: Tanganyika; British Cameroons; British Togoland. Class C mandates were considered to be best administered as integral portions of the Mandatory's territory. Britain's Class C mandates were administered in conjunction with its regional Dominions and were: the Territory of New Guinea (with Australia); Nauru (with Australia and New Zealand); Western Samoa (with New Zealand) and South-West Africa (with South Africa).
3. *Conference Paper C. O. 10.*: The Lovat Committee was established in 1925 with a mandate to examine the general efficiency of the agricultural administration in the colonies. The committee was named after its Chairman Lord Lovat, then Parliamentary Under-Secretary of State for Dominion Affairs. See also Colonial Agricultural Service, Report of a Committee Appointed by the Secretary of State for the Colonies, this volume, pp. 175–93.
4. *Professor R. S. Troup ... Indian Forest Service*: Robert Scott Troup (1874–1939) was founding director of the Imperial Forestry Institute in Oxford from 1924 to 1935.
5. *Imperial Institute in London*: Tropical African Administrative Service training courses were started at the Imperial Institute in London in 1909.
6. *Professor Coupland*: Sir Reginald Coupland (1884–1952) was Beit Professor of Colonial History at the University of Oxford from 1920 to 1948.
7. *Mr. Ormsby-Gore*: See note 11 to 'Memorandum Showing the Progress and Development in the Colonial Empire', above.
8. *The Gold Coast Government ... administrative officers*: See also Gordon Guggisberg, Confidential Memorandum by the Governor of the Gold Coast, this volume, pp. 159–63.
9. *Commonwealth Fund*: The Commonwealth Fund was founded in 1918 by the Harkness family, who made their fortune through the Standard Oil Company, in the United States of America as a philanthropic organization with the mandate to 'do something good for mankind'. In 1925, it launched Commonwealth Fund Fellowships, which aimed to bring young people from Britain, Australia, New Zealand and other English-speaking countries to study in the United States.

Guggisberg, Confidential Memorandum by the Governor of the Gold Coast

1. *MEMORANDUM BY THE GOVERNOR OF THE GOLD COAST*: Sir (Fredrick) Gordon Guggisberg (1869–1930) was a Royal Engineer, colonial administrator and prolific author. He was Governor of the Gold Coast from 1919 to 1927.
2. *Colonial Hospital, such as that at Accra*: The Gold Coast Hospital (Korle Bu Hospital) opened in 1923 under Guggisberg's governorship.

Colonial Office Conference, Summary of Proceedings, 'Recruitment and Training of Colonial Civil Servants'

1. *Major R. D. Furse*: Sir Ralph D. Furse. See note 2 to Harding and Gent, *The Dominions Office and Colonial Office List for 1939*, above.
2. *Tropical African Services Course to the Universities of Oxford and Cambridge*: The Tropical African Services Courses were instigated at the universities in Oxford and Cambridge as a full year's postgraduate training course for probationers to the Colonial Service in Africa.

Ormsby-Gore, Speech for a Meeting with Vice Chancellors and Headmasters at the Board of Education (draft)

1. *The Rt. Hon. W. Ormsby Gore*: William Ormsby-Gore (1885–1964) was the Under-Secretary of State for the Colonies from 1922 to 1929 and Secretary of State for the Colonies from 28 May 1936 to 16 May 1938. See note 11 to 'Memorandum Showing the Progress and Development in the Colonial Empire', above.
2. *Wye*: The School of Agricultural in Wye Kent was established in 1898.
3. *Kew Gardens*: The Royal Botanic Gardens, Kew was founded in 1759.
4. *Bureaux of Entomology and Mycology*: Established in 1910 as the Entomological Research Committee (Tropical Africa), the administration of the Bureaux of Entomology and Mycology were transferred to the Imperial Agricultural Bureaux.
5. *Imperial Forestry Institute*: Established in 1924 at the University of Oxford and placed under the direction of the Professor of Forestry. Initially, the School of Forestry and the Imperial Institute Forestry were separate entities; however, in 1938 they became a single organization.
6. *Royal College of Veterinary Surgeons*: Established in 1844 when veterinary practice became a profession distinguished by the title 'veterinary surgeon'.
7. *Pasteur*: Louis Pasteur (1822–95) was a French chemist and microbiologist who created the first vaccines for rabies and anthrax and whose experiments supported the germ theory of disease.
8. *Sir Richard Gregory*: (1864–1952) was editor of *Nature* from 1919 to 1939.

Colonial Agricultural Service, Report of a Committee Appointed by the Secretary of State for the Colonies

1. *this Report*: the Colonial Agricultural Service Organization Committee developed from the 'Lovat committee' established in 1925 with a mandate to examine the general efficiency of the agricultural administration in the colonies. The work of the Lovat Committee played an important role in the build-up to the Colonial Conference in 1927. At this conference, the Colonial Agricultural Service Organization Committee was established under the chairmanship of Lovat to draw up a practical plan for the establishment of a unified agricultural service. The committee met from June 1927 to January 1928 and submitted its report thereafter. In addition to the Chairman Lord Lovat, then the Parliamentary Under-Secretary of State for Dominion Affairs, the committee boasted a number of high-profile members. Among them was William Ormsby-Gore, Parliamentary Under-Secretary of State for the Colonies who in 1929 became the first chairman of the Colonial Advisory Council on Agriculture and Animal Health (CAC), which was among tangible outcomes of the work of the Colonial Agricultural Service Organisation Committee. Other committee members included John B. Farmer, Professor of Botany at Imperial College in London; H. C. Sampson, economic botanist at the Royal Botanic Gardens, Kew; Ambrose T. Stanton, Chief Medical Adviser to the Secretary of State for the Colonies; and Ralph D. Furse, Private Secretary (Appointments) to the Secretary of State for the Colonies.
2. *the Central Fund*: this central fund was to be financed by an assessment of one quarter of a per cent on the annual revenues of each of the colonies. The idea never materialized mainly on account of the opposition from a number of colonial administrations unwilling to accept greater centralized control over their financial resources.

Report of a Committee on the System of Appointment in the Colonial Office and the Colonial Services

1. *The Colonial Services*: The Warren Fisher Committee was established in 1929 by Leo Amery, Secretary of State for the Colonies from 1924 to 1929. The committee was charged with inquiring into existing system of appointment in the Colonial Office and to give recommendations for the future development of the Colonial Service. The committee was named after its chairman, Sir Warren Fisher, Head of the Home Civil Service and Secretary to the Treasury from 1919 to 1939. The report of this committee was referred to by Charles Jeffries as the *Magna Carta* of the Colonial Service.
2. *Mandate system*: the League of Nations designated three classes of mandate: A, B and C. Class A mandates were those territories deemed to have reached a stage of development whereby the wishes of the territory's people must be a principle consideration. There was a single British Class A mandate – Mesopotamia. Class B Mandates were deemed to require a greater level of control by the supervising country which had to guarantee freedom of conscious and religion. The mandatory powers were also forbidden from constructing military bases in this class of territory. Britain's Class B mandates were: Tanganyika; British Cameroons; British Togoland. Class C mandates were considered to be best administered as integral portions of the Mandatory's territory. Britain's Class C mandates were administered in conjunction with its regional Dominions and were: the Territory of New Guinea (with Australia); Nauru (with Australia and New Zealand); Western Samoa (with New Zealand) and South-West Africa (with South Africa).

3. *recorded in the published summary of its proceedings (Cmd. 2883)*: for the 1927 conference, see Furse, 'Recruitment and Training of Colonial Civil Servants', this volume, pp. 139–59.

4. *Overseas Nursing Association*: for the Overseas Nursing Association, see *Tenth Annual Report of the Executive Committee of the Colonial Nursing Association*, this volume, pp. 91–105.

5. *if the Board decides ... applicants from elsewhere*: For the Liaison with Universities in the self-governing dominions, see Furse, 'Note by the Private Secretary on Laison with Universities in the Self-Governing Regions', this volume, pp. 113–17.

6. *Major Furse*: Sir Ralph Dolignon Furse (1887–1973) was Assistant Private Secretary (appointments) to the Secretary of State for the Colonies from 1910 to 1930 (during the First World War Furse served with King Edwards Horse). Following the recommendations of the Warren Fisher Committee on Colonial Service Appointments (1929–30), Furse became Director of Recruitment in the personnel division of the Colonial Office from 1931 to 1948. See also note 2 to Harding and Gent, *The Dominions Office and Colonial Office List for 1939*, above.

7. *Wye College*: Wye College in Kent that since 1898 had been a School of Agriculture.

8. *branch of the General Division*: in the internal organization of the Colonial Office, the General Division (or General Department) dealt with matters concerning the empire as a whole as opposed to Geographical Departments, which dealt with individual colonies.

9. *[...]*: In this extract of the source, two sections – dealing with detailed terms and condition of appointment and with the internal organization of the Colonial Office respectively – have been omitted.

10. *Mr. Joseph Chamberlain*: See note 1 to Mercer and Collins, *The Colonial Office List for 1900*, above.

11. *Mr. Ormsby Gore's*: See note 11 to 'Memorandum Showing the Progress and Development in the Colonial Empire', above.

12. *Agricultural Departments of the Colonial Governments*: for the Colonial Agricultural Service Committee, see Colonial Agricultural Service, 'Report of a Committee appointed by the Secretary of State for the Colonies', this volume, pp. 175–93.

13. *Tropical African Services*: a course at Oxford and Cambridge. These courses began at Oxford and Cambridge in 1926.

'Recruitment in Colonial Service'

1. *Sir Warren Fisher*: (1879–1948) was Head of the Home Civil Service and Secretary to the Treasury from 1919 to 1939.

2. *Private Secretary (Appointments)*: Sir Ralph D. Furse. See note 2 to Harding and Gent, *The Dominions Office and Colonial Office List for 1939*, above.

3. *Agricultural and Forestry Research Institutes at Pusa and Dehra Dun*: the Agricultural Research Institute at Pusa (Bihar) was established in 1905 and relocated to New Delhi in 1936. The Imperial Forestry Research Institute at Dehra Dun was established in the Doon Valley in 1906.

4. *India, by Lord Curzon*: Lord Curzon of Kedleston (1859–1925) was Viceroy and Governor-General of India from 1899 to 1905.

Colony and Protectorate of Kenya, *Pensions Committee, Interim Report*

1. *Conference of East African Governors be asked to consider this possibility*: for the Conference of East African Governors, see 'Series "A" Minutes. Conference of Governors of the East African Dependences', Volume 2 of this collection, pp. 119–35.
2. *Appendix 1*: Appendices not included in this excerpt.

Malinowski, 'Memorandum on Colonial Research'

1. *Notes of Conversation with Professor Malinowski*: Professor Bronislaw Malinowski (1884–1942) was a founding figure in the functionalist school of anthropological thought and foundation professor of social anthropology at the London School of Economics in 1927.
2. *Malinowski's article in the Economic Journal, March 1921*: B. Malinowski, 'The Primitive Economics of the Trobriand Islanders', *Economic Journal*, 21 (1921), pp. 1–16.
3. *Rivers and others' Essays on the Population of Melanesia*: Rev. W. J. Rivers, *Essays on the Depopulation of Melanesia* (Cambridge, 1922).
4. *Roberts' Population Problems of the Pacific*: Sir Stephen Henry Roberts, *Population Problems of the Pacific* (London, 1927).
5. *Pitt Rivers' The Clash of Culture and Contact of Races*: G. Henry Lane-Fox Pitt-Rivers, *The Clash of Culture and the Contact of the Races: An Anthropological and Psychological Study of the laws of Racial Adaptability, with Special Reference to the Depopulation of the Pacific and the Government of Subject Races* (London, 1927).
6. *Crime and Custom*: B. Malinowski, *Crime and Custom in Savage Society* (London, 1926).
7. *Of. van Vollenhoven ... 1927*: C. van Vollenhoven, *Het Adatrecht van Nederlandsch-Indië* (1918), vol. 1; and P. Kleintjes, *Het Staatsrecht van Nederlandsch-Indie* (1927).

Perham, 'A Re-Statement of Indirect Rule, Africa'

1. *MARGERY PERHAM*: Dame Margery Perham (1895–1982) was a leading expert on colonial African affairs.
2. *Lord Lugard in Northern Nigeria*: Lord Frederick Lugard (1858–1945) was High Commissioner of Northern Nigeria from 1900 to 1906 and Governor of Nigeria from 1914 to 1919.
3. *Dr. Rattray*: Robert Sutherland Rattray (1881–1938) was a member of the Gold Coast administration who in 1921 became head of the Anthropological Department of Asante.
4. *Mr. Mockerie*: Parmenas Githendu Mockerie (b. 1901) was a Kikuyu teacher, author and chief. His writings include a short autobiography published in M. Perham, *Ten Africans* (London, 1936). The Kikuyu are largest ethnic group in Kenya.
5. *Chief Tshekedi*: Tshekedi Khama (1905–59), from 1926 to 1950, was regent of the Bangwato, the largest of the Twana States in the Bechuanaland Protectorate.
6. *Kano*: the Hausa Kingdom of Kano was founded around the end of the tenth century. After close to 800 years of independence in 1805, it became subject to the Fulani Sokoto Caliphate.
7. *Buganda*: The Kingdom of Buganda was founded in the last quarter of the fourteenth century and retained its independence until it became a protectorate in 1894. On 6 July

1897, the Kabaka, the leader of Buganda, declared war on Britain, but was defeated at the battle of Buddu on 20 July 1897.

8. *South African Native Conference*: was founded in 1912 to promote the rights of the black population in South Africa. It was renamed as the African National Congress in 1923.

9. *suttee*: the practice of newly widowed women immolating themselves on their husband's funeral pyre.

10. *Sir Charles Napier*: (1782–1853) was Governor of the Sindh Province from 1843 to 1847.

11. *Sir Harry Smith*: (1787–1860) was Governor of the South African Province of Queen Adelaide from 10 December 1835 to 13 September 1836.

12. *defeated Xosa*: The Xhosa people were primarily located in the south-eastern part of South Africa.

13. *Sir Donald Cameron*: (1872–1948) was Governor of Tanganyika from March 1925 to January 1931 and Governor of Nigeria from June 1931 to November 1935.

Oxford Summer School on Colonial Administration, Second Session

1. Rt. Hon. Malcolm MacDonald: (1901–81) was Secretary of State for the Colonies from 7 June 1935 to 22 November 1935, and from 16 May 1938 to 12 May 1940.

2. *Sudan*: although Sudan was governed effectively as a British colony, technically the Governor General was appointed by Egypt with British consent.

3. *Burma*: Burma was initially annexed to British rule on 1 January 1886, however, on 1 April 1937 it became a separately administered colony of Britain.

4. *Professor Coupland*: Sir Reginald Coupland (1884–1952) was Beit Professor of Colonial History at the University of Oxford from 1920 to 1948.

5. *Miss Margery Perham*: Dame Margery Perham (1895–1982) was a leading expert on colonial African affairs.

6. *Sir Selwhyn Grier*: Sir Selwyn Macgregor Grier (1878–1946) was Governor of the Windward Islands from 1935 to 1937. He had previously spent time in Nigeria as an Assistant Resident in Zaria Province (1906) and Secretary of Native Affairs from 1921 to 1925.

7. *Lord Harlech*: William Ormsby-Gore (1885–1964). See note 11 to 'Memorandum Showing the Progress and Development in the Colonial Empire', above.

8. *Sir Alfred Zimmern*: (1879–1957) was a British historian and expert in international relations. Zimmern co-founded the Royal Institute of International Affairs in 1919.

9. *Mr. H. D. Henderson*: Hubert Douglas Henderson (1890–1952) was elected to a research fellowship at All Souls College, Oxford in 1934. He also founded the Oxford Economists' Research Group.

10. *Sir Alan Pim*: Alan Pim (1871–1958) was an administrator in India and an adviser to the Colonial Office.

11. *Mr. Mayhew*: Arthur Mayhew (1878–1948) was a former educational administrator in India employed at the Colonial Office with responsibility for colonial educational policy.

12. *Vice-Chancellor*: George Stuart Gordon (1881–1942) was Vice-Chancellor of the University of Oxford from 1938 to 1941.

13. Rt. Hon. Lord Lugard: Lord Frederick Lugard (1858–1945) was Governor of Hong Kong from 1907 to 1912 and Governor of Nigeria from 1914 to 1919.

14. *Italy's attack on Abyssinia*: the Second Italo-Abyssinian war began in October 1935 and finished in May 1936. It resulted in the creation of the colony of Italian East Africa.
15. *League*: the League of Nations.
16. *Lord Cecil*: Robert Cecil, first Viscount Cecil of Chelwood (1864–1958) was heavily involved in developing the League of Nations and won the Nobel Peace Prize in 1938.
17. *Sir Arthur Salter*: (1881–1975) was a former civil servant who was appointed Gladstone Professor of Political Theory at the University of Oxford in 1934.
18. *Professor Gilbert Murray*: George Gilbert Murray (1866–1957) was a classical scholar and public intellectual who was involved with the League of Nations.
19. *Lords Lytton*: Victor Bulwer-Lytton, second Earl of Lytton (1876–1947) was a colonial official and politician who had served as Governor of Bengal from 1922 to 1927 and was briefly Acting Viceroy of India in 1926.
20. *Mr. Amery*: Leo Amery (1873–1955) was Secretary of State for the Colonies from 6 November 1924 to 4 June 1929.
21. *Sir Samuel Hoare*: first Viscount Templewood (1880–1959), Secretary of State for Foreign Affairs from 7 June 1935 to 18 December 1935, when he devised the Hoare–Laval Pact with the French Prime Minister Pierre Laval to end the Second Italo-Abyssinian War.
22. *Minister*: Godfrey Martin Huggins, first Viscount Malvern (1883–1971) was Prime Minister of Southern Rhodesia from 1933 to 1953.
23. *General Smuts*: Jan Christiaan Smuts (1870–1950) was Prime Minister of the Union of South Africa twice, from 3 September 1919 to 30 June 1924, and from 5 September 1939 to 1 June 1948. Smuts was a committed believer in the British Empire and Commonwealth and drafted the preamble to the United Nations Charter.
24. *Achimota*: the Prince of Wales College and School, founded in 1924 in Achimota, near Accra.
25. *Makerere*: Makerere College was established as a technical school in 1922 in Kampala, Uganda.
26. *Yaba*: Yaba Higher College was established in 1932 in Yaba, near to Lagos in Nigeria.
27. *The 'Hailey Survey' of Africa*: W. M. Hailey, *An African Survey: A Study of Problems Arising in Africa South of the Sahara* (London: Oxford University Press, 1938).
28. *Livingstone*: David Livingstone (1813–73) was an explorer and missionary who hoped his Zambezi expedition in 1858 might lead to an English colony in Central Africa.
29. *Hilton-Young Commission*: Hilton Young (1879–1960) chaired a mission to East Africa in 1928, which recommended closer union of the territories.

Colony of Nigeria, 'Life and Duties of an Administrative Officer in Nigeria'

1. *The advances made ... many other tropical dependencies*: Quinine had been introduced into Europe in the seventeenth century; however, it was the discovery of the cause and the mode of transmission of malaria in the late nineteenth century that led to its effective use as a prophylactic.
2. *"Instructions to Political Officers," by Lord Lugard*: Lord Lugard, *Political Memoranda; Revision of Instructions to Political Officers on Subjects Chiefly Political and Administrative: 1913–1918*, 3rd edn, with new introduction by A. H. M. Kirk-Greene (London: Frank Cass & Co., 1970).

3. Nigeria Handbook: A. C. Burns, *The Nigeria Handbook. Containing Statistical and General Information respecting the Colony and Protectorate* (Lagos: Lagos Government Printers, 1917). The handbook went through several editions.

Leakey, 'Colonial Administration in East Africa from the Native Point of View'

1. *Mr. L. S. B. Leakey*: Louis Leakey (1903–72) was an archaeologist and paleoanthropologist whose fossil discoveries and research in East Africa were instrumental in confirming the hypothesis of Africa as the place of human origin. The son of British missionaries in East Africa Leakey was educated in Cambridge and lived most of his life in Kenya.
2. *Lord Lugard*: Lord Frederick Lugard (1858–1945) was Governor of Hong Kong from 1907 to 1912 and Governor of Nigeria from 1914 to 1918.
3. *N.I.T.D.*: Native Industrial Training Depot at Kabete near Nairobi.
4. *PROFESSOR R. COUPLAND*: Sir Reginald Coupland (1884–1952) was Beit Professor of Colonial History at the University of Oxford from 1920 to 1948.
5. *Lord Delamere*: Hugh Cholmondeley (1870–1931), the third Baron Delamere moved to Kenya in 1901 and became the unofficial leader of the colony's settler community.

For Product Safety Concerns and Information please contact our EU
representative GPSR@taylorandfrancis.com Taylor & Francis Verlag GmbH,
Kaufingerstraße 24, 80331 München, Germany

Printed and bound by CPI Group (UK) Ltd, Croydon, CR0 4YY
08/06/2025
01897001-0019